T0087860

A
HISTORY OF CANADA

Volume Two: *From the Royal Régime to the*
Treaty of Utrecht, 1663-1713

BY GUSTAVE LANCTOT
of the Royal Society

TRANSLATED BY MARGARET M. CAMERON

HARVARD UNIVERSITY PRESS
CAMBRIDGE, MASSACHUSETTS
1964

971
L252h
v.2

F
1026
.L263

57400

© 1964
by CLARKE, IRWIN & COMPANY LIMITED

Printed in Canada

A
MARIE
MA CHERE FEMME

8/10/65   pub   6.20

ACKNOWLEDGEMENTS

The author wishes to express his thanks to the Canada Council for the generous help which has enabled him to complete the research for the documentation of his work.

To Mr. Robert La Roque de Roquebrune, who read and made suggestions on the first draft, he owes a special debt of gratitude. At the National Archives, the kindness of the Assistant Deputy Minister, Mr. Pierre Brunet, facilitated considerably the labour of research and copying, and Miss Richard and Miss Bourque made a valuable contribution to the accomplishment of this task. At the Parliamentary Library, Mr. Lusignan and Mrs. Foster co-operated in the examination of printed documents. The personnel of the other archival deposits also gave zealous and unfailing help in the consultation of their collections.

Finally, the author wishes to thank the Social Science Research Council which, with the support of the Canada Council, has contributed to the publication of this volume.

CONTENTS

MAPS

xi

FOREWORD

Under the French régime, the history of Canada can be divided, according to the events which mark them, into three distinct periods: the periods of foundation, of colonization and of expansion. The first volume of this work described the longest of these, the period of foundation, extending from pre-historic origins to the transfer of the colony to royal administration in 1663. It is also the heroic period during which, under the monopoly of the trading companies, indomitable pioneers and missionaries strove stubbornly to establish a new France in Canada in the face of the unceasing and cruel Iroquois wars.

Continuing the chronicle, the present volume studies the period of colonization which begins in 1663 with an officially sponsored emigration of heads of families, *engagés*, soldiers and marriageable girls. These new Canadians adapted themselves to an environment rich in gifts and in promise, and their natural increase in numbers was astonishing. They cleared the Laurentian forest, and they sowed and civilized the land thus cleared on both sides of the river from Tadoussac to Lachine. Jesuit fathers established distant missions and bold *coureurs de bois* extended the beaver trade. They explored an immense territory stretching from the Acadian coast to Louisiana and the mouth of the Mississippi. During this period of a half a century, from 1663 to 1713, in spite of rivalries and Anglo-Iroquois wars, this veritable empire was maintained in its entirety. In 1713 the Treaty of Utrecht confirmed the victory of the anti-French coalition in Europe and made the first breach in the French empire in America by ceding to England Hudson Bay, Newfoundland and Acadia.

It is this period of colonization, during which New France was settled and enlarged that, with the help of contemporary documents, the present volume proposes to recount.

A HISTORY OF CANADA

FROM THE ROYAL RÉGIME
TO THE TREATY OF UTRECHT,
1663-1713

1

LOUIS XIV PLACES CANADA UNDER ROYAL ADMINISTRATION
1663-1713

A new colonial policy. Canada becomes a royal province. Mésy, Governor, and Gaudais-Dupont, Commissioner. Creation of the Sovereign Council: its administrative powers. Political powers of the Bishop: beginning of the theocracy. The councillors. Sale of intoxicating liquor to the Indians. Mayor and syndics. Budget of the colony. Regulation of trade and commerce. Emigration. Creation of courts of justice.

With the year 1663, there opens the second period of the history of Canada, the period of colonization. After a half-century of existence under the régime of the trading companies, New France still had only 2,500 inhabitants. Grouped around three small establishments, Quebec, Three Rivers and Montreal, the colonists lived under constant threat of being driven out of the country by the relentless Iroquois wars.[1]

Louis XIV was deeply distressed by the gravity of the situation, and in March 1663 he issued an edict which withdrew from the Company of One Hundred Associates its ownership of the country and its trade monopoly, and brought the colony under royal administration. This decision was directly related to a new policy for the mother country.

Mazarin had disappeared from the scene in 1661, leaving a France at peace with Europe. In the same year Nicolas Fouquet, the Minister of Finance, who had lived in almost royal magnificence, was charged with malversation and, after a long trial terminating in his conviction, sentenced to end his days in the prison fortress of Pignerol. With the death of Mazarin and the arrest of Fouquet, the way lay open for a new start.

After Mazarin's death, when his ministers asked him to whom

they should address themselves in the future, Louis XIV answered, "To me." This forceful and imperious king chose as his first adviser his Minister of Finance, Jean-Baptiste Colbert, for whom commerce, and especially colonial commerce, represented the "source and principle of wealth." From that meeting between a royal will and a policy of mercantilism, New France was to reap the immediate benefits.

As a beginning in this new "province of Canada," the King decided to establish the customary administration with governor, intendant and Sovereign Council. In 1662 the young king had listened with "extreme kindness" to Mgr. de Laval's complaints about the hot-headed and autocratic Governor d'Avaugour.[2] In order to avoid a recurrence of such dissensions, the King invited the Jesuits to nominate the new governor; but, skilled politicians that they were, they preferred to refer this choice to the Bishop who proposed the Sieur Saffroy de Mésy. A former Calvinist and town-major of Caen, M. de Mésy, after a somewhat prodigal youth, had been converted under the influence of Jean de Bernières, founder of the Hermitage retreat house in Caen. It was there that Mgr. de Laval had known M. de Mésy whose integrity and piety won his esteem. But M. de Mésy declined the Quebec post because of certain debts which he felt he could not, in conscience, evade by such a departure from the country; whereupon the King gave him, as a gift, the means to discharge his obligations. Thus it was made possible for him to accept the royal appointment, and he did so "with the sole aim of procuring thereby the glory of God, the service of the King and the good of the colony."[3]

On May 1, 1663, Louis XIV signed Mésy's commission, which was valid for three years from the date of his arrival in Quebec and which conferred on him "full power" of command over everyone and in all things "necessary for the service and good of the country."[4]

As for the intendant, Louis Robert, Sieur de Fortel, who had been appointed in March 1663, the King cancelled his commission,[5] preferring to entrust the administrative functions to a Sovereign Council. The most important of these functions had been carried on previously by the Quebec Council of 1657. Thus, the King maintained a link with the former régime. However, in order to acquaint himself with the needs of the colony, on May 7 he signed a special commission for the Sieur Louis Gaudais-Dupont, instructing him to go out to Canada and to come back in the autumn. Granted a seat on the Council, Gaudais-Dupont was in this short space of time to gather information on the state of the colony, its natural resources, agriculture, the fur trade and the Iroquois raids. These were the questions on which Louis XIV desired enlightenment before he put into effect his plan to send colonists to populate the country and troops to put an end to the Indian wars.[6]

A few days earlier, an edict dated April 30 (1663) had instituted the Sovereign Council of New France, which was essentially a higher court of justice. The idea of this court of final appeal, the complement of the regional juridical system of the period, had already appeared in the charter of the Company of New France in 1627.[7] It was revived fourteen years later with the official decision to grant royal courts to the colonies, and with the granting of the first such court to Martinique in 1661. The following year the King drew up an edict with the intention of according the same honour to Canada. As a result of the Laval-d'Avaugour quarrel, this document remained in the files, but the provisions which it set out reappear in the order of 1663.[8]

The Sovereign Council of New France had, by the edict creating it, the right of a court of appeal to judge "absolutely and without appeal," save only to the King, all civil and criminal cases, according to the procedure of Paris. Moreover, since the population of Quebec was very small, the councillors, by a special decision, were "commissioned" to act as a court of first instance and to settle cases of minor importance. This clause eliminated the seneschal's court of 1651. The councillors could also report to the Council affairs with which they might be charged by the syndics and the settlers in general. Finally, the Council was vested with the right of "commissioning, in Quebec, Montreal and Three Rivers, and in all other places" judges, clerks of the court, notaries and sergeants of police.[9]

The most extraordinary functions of the Council, however, lay elsewhere. Its possession of exceptional political powers made it unique in the French colonial régime. Louis XIV attributed to it the following prerogatives: ordering the expenditure of public funds, directing the fur trade "and all trade," and even "settling public and private police affairs in the whole country."[10]

In short, excepting only the domain of military affairs and relations with the natives, the King was transmitting to a court of justice the entire administration of the colony. There is an easy explanation for this surprising anomaly. The governors possessed very wide powers of intervention, and in the past they had not always shown discretion in the use of these powers. It had thus become apparent that, since the power of the governor was not tempered by that of an intendant, it was important to entrust the administration of the colony to a responsible body. The creation of such a body was made further indispensable by the disappearance of the Company of New France. Although it was actually the Council of Quebec which administered the country, it did so by virtue of rights delegated to it by the Company of New France, and, when the Company was dissolved, these rights, and indeed the Quebec Council itself, ceased to exist.[11] It must be noted, too, that the powers granted to the Sovereign Council were not absolute. Financially, they were limited to the list of essential expenses established by the previous administration, and could order military expenditures only with the authority of the governor.[12] Finally, the decisions of the Council were always subject to the governor's veto. He represented the person of the King, and in him resided the supreme authority in case of crisis or conflict.[13]

By the terms of the edict, the Sovereign Council was composed of the governor, the bishop (or, in his absence, the senior ecclesiastic), with five councillors, an attorney-general and a secretary. Appointed by the governor and the bishop acting "jointly and in agreement," these members could be changed at the end of a year, or continued in office, as the two heads of the Council considered it "more advantageous."[14]

Previously an order, dated March 21, had required that all lands already granted be brought under cultivation within six months of the publication of the order. If this condition were not met, the grant would be cancelled. In the same order the King had conferred jointly on the governor and the bishop the right to cede to new tenants any land which might thus become vacant.[15]

To the bishop, already supreme in ecclesiastical matters, and a member of the Sovereign Council, were thus granted the same powers as to the governor in the granting of lands as well as in the appointment of councillors. These powers increased enormously the importance of the role of Mgr. de Laval, making him in fact practically the governor's equal.

Since he identified himself with the designs of the Jesuits, his functions helped accentuate the tendency of the time towards ecclesiastical predominance in civil affairs. Moreover, since his

office was permanent, it was from him that the councillors sought
the continuation of their appointments rather than from the
governor, whose period of service was only three years.

M. de Mésy and Mgr. de Laval, with the commissioner, Gau-
dais-Dupont, did not arrive in Canada until September 15, 1663.
They travelled from Tadoussac to Quebec in a small boat.[16]
Three days later, they made haste to set up the Sovereign Council.
They swore in as councillors Rouer de Villeray, Juchereau de La
Ferté, Ruette d'Auteuil, Le Gardeur de Tilly and Mathieu Da-
mours, and then appointed Jean Bourdon as attorney-general.[17]
Since he had no knowledge of local conditions, and also out of
deference towards the prelate to whom he owed his appointment,
M. de Mésy left the designation of all these officers to Mgr. de
Laval, who chose them, to quote Louis XIV, from persons "en-
tirely devoted" to the ecclesiastical interests.[18]

By a ruling of the Governor and the Bishop (January 2,
1664), the councillors were to draw an annual allowance of 300
livres; they would also enjoy the right of precedence in official
ceremonies and meetings. If we can believe Gaudais-Dupont, who
had frequent dealings with them, the councillors chosen by Mgr.
de Laval were "unlettered men, of little experience or knowledge
of public affairs, and almost all incapable of making a sound
judgment in a matter of any consequence."[19] This is the opinion of
a man of law, and is much too sweeping. It could not be applied in
its entirety to Villeray, a reformed adventurer still under suspicion,
but a man of active and subtle intelligence, nor to Bourdon, a man
of useful talents who was at different times a farmer, a surveyor
and a bailiff, and who later became a seigneur. To be sure, none
of them was versed in the law, but they showed themselves to be
shrewd and practical, and although they did not neglect their
own personal interests, they nevertheless administered the colony
efficiently.

The first question of importance to figure in the deliberations
of the Council was that of intoxicating liquors. The sale of liquor
to the Indians had provoked the great quarrel between the former
governor, d'Avaugour, who authorized it, and the Bishop, who
forbade it under pain of excommunication. By an order of September 28 (1663), the Council prohibited the sale of liquor to
the Indians. It also prohibited giving them liquor "under any
pretext whatsoever." The order was voted unanimously with Mgr.
de Laval present, and after the Council had "heard the opinion"

of the Jesuits who had been asked to give evidence. Any infraction incurred a fine of 300 *livres,* to be allotted in thirds to the informer, the Hôtel-Dieu and the Public Treasury. A second offence could be punished by flogging or banishment.[19a]

The order resulted in a sudden decline in the liquor traffic which prudently went underground. But a first violation in November was followed by several others. In the course of the winter "the disorder" spread to such an extent that a number of habitants, especially in Cap Rouge, St. François-Xavier and Sillery, openly engaged in the sale of alcohol. Rather than bring such a large number of delinquents into court, the Council in April pronounced it illegal, under pain of a fine or flogging, to keep liquor in a house "without written permission from the Governor." The Council also renewed its previous prohibition of sale with the added threat, for all persons, of "confiscation of all their property, and of banishment."[20]

In another sphere, the Council decided to make an innovation and to replace the syndic of Quebec, whose office had been abolished by d'Avaugour, with a mayor and two *échevins,* which, to quote Mother Marie de l' Incarnation "sounded impressive."[21] On Sunday, October 7, 1663, "a number of the most important habitants" elected the first Canadian mayor, Jean-Baptiste Le Gardeur de Repentigny, Gentleman, and two *échevins,* Jean Madry, Surgeon, and Claude Charron, Merchant. The creation of these offices, in a village richer in "open spaces" than in "numbers of people," was considered somewhat premature and was greeted with jeers. The Council, therefore, revoked the election and re-established the office of syndic. It was not until August 3 (1664), however, eleven months later, that Claude Charron was elected syndic. Even then the habitants protested that the interests of a merchant were incompatible with those of the common people, and his appointment was annulled. On September 14 he was replaced by Jean Lemire, a carpenter. That same year, Three Rivers in its turn elected a syndic, as Montreal had done without interruption since 1647.[22]

Immediately after its installation, the Council gave its attention to the financial state of the colony. The very modest revenues at its disposal came from only three sources: a tax of twenty-five per cent on beaver skins, one of ten per cent on moose hides, and the receipts from the Tadoussac fur trade. D'Avaugour had leased the rights to this trade to seventeen notables at a price of 50,000 *livres,* this on his own authority and without guarantee. The councillors promptly cancelled the lease, and after abandoning the idea of administering the trade themselves, they granted a new lease to Aubert de La Chesnaye. This lease, dated October 24 (1663), was to run for three years at an annual rent of 46,500 *livres*.[23]

There was also a small special revenue (6,932 *livres* for 1663), which was administered by the Council. This revenue, the proceeds of a tax of ten per cent on goods imported from France, created in 1660, had been earmarked in 1662 to pay off the debt of 170,000 *livres* outstanding against the former Community of Habitants. It was expected that the duty would be abolished once the debt was completely amortized. The tax was maintained by the Sovereign Council, which assumed responsibility for collecting it. At least on one occasion, it also changed the basis of the tax: in June 1664, since the price of beaver had gone down and that of imported goods had gone up, the Council decreed that the duty should be levied only on wine and brandy, thus reducing the revenue considerably. But in the disbursement of the proceeds the role of the Council was purely formal. It acted as an agent, transferring to the creditors a sum which had been collected through the tax.[24]

The real revenue of the colony fluctuated according to the year between 45,000 and 50,000 *livres*. This revenue was obviously very modest, but it was sufficient for the needs of a colony of less than three thousand souls. As for the budget of expenses, it can be presented under three headings: salaries of the governor-general and of the governors in Montreal and Three Rivers, including the pay of sixty soldiers, 30,400 *livres;* administration of justice with the salaries of councillors and royal judges, 3,400 *livres;* and missions, hospital services and aid to education, 7,200 *livres*. The average total amounted to 48,950 *livres* which, even with a few unforeseen expenses, did not normally exceed the receipts of 50,000 *livres*.[25]

After finances, the second domain of the Council was commerce. It comprised two separate and distinct divisions: the fur trade based in the country and trade in merchandise from France. The Council was concerned only in principle with the first. As a result of the colonists' protests, the King, by an order of March 1662, had restored freedom of trade, this to the great satisfaction of the habitants who were now free to sell and barter their beaver at will.[26]

Commerce with the mother country was quite another matter. The Council regulated it as strictly as the former Council of Quebec had done. It was the Council which granted to the

French merchants licences allowing them to sell their cargoes in the colony. It imposed on them the obligation to transport one *engagé,* two barrels of salt, some iron and coal for each ten tons of tonnage, and they were forbidden to trade in furs.[27] On their arrival in harbour, the merchants or their clerks had to present the invoices of the cost price of their goods to the Council, which fixed the rate of profit they could demand. In 1663 the tariff was set at fifty-five per cent, in addition to the ten per cent import tax, which increased the price the Canadian consumer had to pay by sixty-five per cent over the price in France. In the case of liquids, where compensation was made for leakage, the profit could rise to one hundred per cent.[28]

Moreover, for a period of one month, beginning one week after the arrival of the ships, the merchants could sell wholesale only a tenth part of each kind of merchandise, and they had to sell it in Quebec. After this period, they could send no more than a quarter to Montreal and Three Rivers, whose settlers were, however, free to come and buy in Quebec. These restrictions, which put Montreal and Three Rivers at a disadvantage, may be explained by the fact that these towns were not represented in the Council, all of whose members came from Quebec. Any infraction of the regulations was liable to a fine at the discretion of the Council.[28a]

Following the King's decision to make provision for populating the country, which was the urgent necessity of the moment and the only hope for progress, the Sovereign Council assumed a function which the former Council of Quebec had never had. It became responsible for the maintenance and settlement of colonists sent by the King. In 1663, of 279 passengers, men and women, who set out from La Rochelle, sixty died at sea and sixty disembarked at Placentia in Newfoundland. Only 159 went ashore in Quebec, and of these twelve died in hospital after their arrival.[29] Even the recruits who survived were not of the best quality. Most of them were inexperienced young men who arrived "almost completely naked." To these and to the families and unmarried girls, the Council, acting through the Governor and the Bishop, distributed clothing, stockings and shoes. With the exception of three, the thirty-eight marriageable girls were carried off by the bachelors during the first months after their arrival. Some hundred colonists were distributed in the Quebec region, ten were assigned to Three Rivers and only six to Montreal, the rival settlement which was not very popular in the ecclesiastical and merchant circles of the capital.[30]

CANADA UNDER ROYAL ADMINISTRATION   11

The Council made it a point to supervise the quality of the emigrants; it complained of certain emigrants drawn from La Rochelle, who were "lazy workers"; it asked for colonists from Normandy who were "hard-working and industrious" and "much more religious." It demanded moral character as well as physical aptitude, and it did not hesitate to send back to France useless persons incapable of working the land or guilty of "misconduct." Only the honest worker was welcome in New France.[31]

Most of the colonists came to the country, according to the regular system, as *engagés* for three years. When they set out, they received an advance of thirty-five *livres* on their wages, and this advance was paid back to the Council by those who hired them at wages of from sixty to one hundred *livres* a year, according to their trade or experience. When the *engagés'* contract expired, they were free to return to France or to settle in the country as artisans or "voluntary" labourers, or to take up land as "habitants" and acquire the right to hunt, to fish and to engage in the fur trade. This system had the advantage of training newcomers in the tasks of Canadian agriculture, so "different from those of France," so that at the end of three years they had gained the experience necessary to work their own land.[32]

When the council undertook to reorganize the system of justice, its first act was to decree, in September 1663, that "henceforth no costs would be paid" by parties appearing before the royal courts of justice. The following year this order was extended to the lower courts, thus translating into practice the "King's intention" to establish, "for the good of the colony, a system of free and summary justice, requiring neither barristers, nor prosecutors, nor lawyers." This system of justice, administered without any expense to the parties concerned, was maintained to the advantage of the population until the edict of 1677, which fixed a fee for judges and officers of justice, but which made no provision for such a fee for cases brought before the Council.[33]

Continuing its judicial programme, the Council, in October, established two royal courts of justice. The first in Three Rivers replaced the former seneschal's court of the Company of New France; the second in Montreal came into conflict with the seigniorial court which had been established there by the rights fixed in the original concession. In October M. de Mésy also exercised the governor's prerogative as he understood it: he commissioned the Sieur de Maisonneuve as Governor of Montreal, although in fact Maisonneuve had been acting in that capacity for almost twenty years, having been appointed by the Society of Montreal exercising the right conferred on it by the King in 1644.[34] However, on March 9 (1663) the seigniory of Montreal had changed hands. In order to assure the continuity of its work of evangelization, the Society of Montreal, which now counted no more than about ten members, had transmitted its property and its rights by gift to the Seminary of St. Sulpice. The Abbé Souart, Superior of St. Sulpice, and Maisonneuve immediately protested against the Council's act which transgressed the Seminary's seigniorial right to render justice, and against the Governor's act which was an infraction of a royal edict. The Council promptly took refuge in plainly specious and unjustifiable legal formalities. However, in March 1665 the King's Council intervened to confirm the Seminary's sole right to appoint the Governor of Montreal. The following year an order of the Intendant, Talon, restored to it its seigniorial courts and at the same time excluded any royal court of justice. Thus Montreal defended itself victoriously against these two incursions on the part of Quebec into its administrative autonomy.[35]

CHAPTER TWO

ECCLESIASTICAL ORGANIZATION AND POLITICAL CRISIS
1663-1665

Mgr. de Laval and the Quebec Seminary. Centralization of the diocese. Fixing of tithes. Attitude of the Iroquois. Peace parleys. Dissension between the Governor and the Council. Imputations against Mésy. Intrigues of Villeray and Bourdon. Causes of their suspension. Mésy appoints a new Council. Protests of Mgr. de Laval. Death of the Governor. Judgment of Colbert.

While the colony was adapting itself to the royal régime, Mgr. de Laval's indefatigable apostolic zeal was laying the real foundations of the Church in Canada. The system of church organization which he adopted originated in the Council of Trent, but it had ceased to function in Europe. Instead of establishing permanent parishes, Mgr. de Laval created a seminary in Quebec in which he registered all the members of the secular clergy as they applied to him. From this seminary he sent out the priests required for the exercise of "functions, parochial and other," in the country. Any priest so appointed could be "transferred, recalled or dismissed" at the pleasure of the Bishop. All tithes were turned over to the Seminary to be "possessed in common and administered" by the Bishop, and the Seminary was required to provide subsistence "for all ecclesiastics, and to maintain them" in sickness and in health either in their residences or in its community. Only the Sulpicians in Montreal and the Jesuits were not subject to this rule of which the object was complete and absolute centralization, a dictatorship both spiritual and material.[1]

The order establishing the Seminary was signed by Mgr. de Laval on March 26, 1663. In April it received royal sanction in letters patent, which fixed the tithes at a thirteenth part of "the fruit of man's labour" and "the natural product of the land." The

13

decree was registered by the Sovereign Council on October 10; and immediately the settlers of Quebec, who for thirty years had received the services of the Church without charge, protested so vigorously against its application that a month later Mgr. de Laval agreed to allow them to pay the tithes at one twentieth for a period of six years. At Three Rivers people even opposed the posting of the royal order. Faced with this opposition, and in spite of support from M. de Mésy and the Council, the Bishop felt obliged to extend to the whole colony the reduction he had granted to Quebec. This he did in February (1664), but to no avail. On the contrary, the resistance grew when it was rumoured that the term "the fruit of man's labour" in the royal order gave the clergy the right to demand "a tithe of eggs, cabbages, timber, cordwood and generally any kind of goods." In vain the Bishop announced officially in March that tithes would be levied only on grain. The opposition remained adamant, and for four years the parishioners refused to pay any tithes. The difference between the prelate and his flock was not finally resolved until August 23, 1667, when an order signed by Tracy, Courcelles and Talon fixed the tithes at a twenty-sixth part of products of the soil. That ruling was to remain in force until the end of the French régime.[2]

Meanwhile the threat of Indian attacks continued to hang over the colony. Fortunately, the raids were interrupted for the time being by a variety of circumstances. The Five Nations were in the midst of a critical period which forced them to adopt a prudent and diplomatic policy. A severe famine and an epidemic of smallpox had thinned the ranks of the warriors. The Mohawks had also suffered heavy losses at the hands of the Mohicans of the East, while the Senecas were dangerously pressed by the redoubtable Andastes of the South. Finally, their Indian and French captives told them, and the Dutch from Manhattan confirmed the report, that the Great Ononthio of France was preparing a powerful expedition destined to destroy their villages.[3]

At this juncture, one party in the tribal councils urged that they hurl the war hatchet into "the deepest abysses." Those who proposed this policy doubtless did so with the mental reservation that once the storm threat had passed they could take up the struggle again and fight "more fiercely than ever." In August (1663), urged on by Garakontié, a true friend of the French, the Onondagas sent a delegation to Montreal and, in the name of all the tribes except the Oneidas, offered to conclude a general peace. In Maisonneuve's answering speech satisfaction was tempered with mistrust, but he assured the Indians of the peaceful intentions of the colony. This peace overture of their allies did not stop the raids of the irreconcilable Oneidas. That autumn they captured two soldiers in Three Rivers and held them prisoner, although they did not subject them to the bastonnade which was the rule when prisoners were brought back to the villages.[4]

Encouraged by Maisonneuve's reception, Garakontié set out again for Montreal in the spring of 1664. He had with him an important delegation of Onondagas and Senecas and the prisoners from Three Rivers. Unfortunately, a party of Algonquins on the war-path heard of the movements of the Iroquois flotilla. Attacking from an ambush at the Sault St. Louis they killed, captured or scattered the ambassadors and liberated the two Frenchmen. Prospects for peace were very dim and they almost vanished during the summer, when a party of Oneidas killed several colonists in their fields, and kidnapped a girl at Three Rivers and another, just a child, on the Island of Orleans.[5]

In spite of these raids, however, envoys from the Cayugas arrived in Quebec on September 18. In the name of the Five Nations, excepting the Oneidas, they presented, according to the Indian custom, twenty gifts strung out on a rope: ten for the French and ten for the Algonquins. The theocratic tendency of the time is revealed in the *Relation,* which notes that of ten gifts, the six handsomest were given to Mgr. de Laval, the Jesuits, the Ursulines and the Hospital Sisters, and which omits any mention of the Governor's share.

M. de Mésy had no confidence in the sincerity of the delegation, but he answered the ambassadors with a fine speech, and gave them an even greater number of presents than they had brought. The Governor's suspicions were soon confirmed, for even as the parleys were in progress one Montrealer was killed and two others were wounded by Indians in ambush at St. Mary's current. The Iroquois arquebus, it seemed, would not be hung up.[6]

Some months before these events, a serious dissension had broken out in the higher ranks of the administration between the Governor and the Council, and the quarrel assumed the proportions of a political crisis. The traditional account of its origin is based on an unverified memoir of the time and cannot be accepted. This memoir is from the very clever and equally untruthful pen of Councillor Villeray, a man who had been imprisoned for debt, who had entered the former Quebec Trading Council "by illicit ways and means," who would later be dismissed from the

Sovereign Council by Governor Courcelles and Mgr. de Laval, and declared by royal sentence "unfit to hold any public charge in Canada." Villeray was well educated, very intelligent, past master in the art of debate; his flagrant misdeeds had not prevented him from furthering his own interests nor from enlisting the help of powerful protectors. In 1665 the King declared that he, as well as Bourdon, was "completely devoted to the Jesuits," which infers that he supported the Jesuit policy of clerical domination in civil affairs. Greedy for gain as well as for influence, Villeray later on went so far as to establish a butcher shop in his house where his wife took in the customers' money. It is this dubious, crafty and self-interested individual who asserts that the disagreement between the Governor and the Council arose from the Governor's cupidity and the refusal of the councillors to raise his salary.[7]

In fact, the minutes of the Council show these assertions to be completely false. Far from giving evidence of greed, Mésy offered in November 1663 to accept the salary of any one of the last three governors, at the choice of the Council. In December the Council itself fixed the salary which the councillors continued to vote to Mésy, without any complaint on his part, right to the end of his term of office. It is also untrue that he violated precedent by refusing to pay for blankets and utensils supplied to the garrison. As Governor, he dispensed the soldiers' pay, and a sum to cover this expense was included in his salary. In refusing to make any contribution to general maintenance, however, he simply followed the example of his predecessor, the scrupulous d'Avaugour. Villeray himself testified that "the Community was entirely responsible" for the upkeep of the garrison. The allegation that Mésy claimed travelling expenses to which he had no right is false as well. Here again, he followed the example of Governors Lauzon and d'Argenson, in whose favour the King and the Council of Quebec had authorized these expenses. Again there is no warrant for censuring Mésy because he kept some of his predecessor's possessions and certain presents from the Indians, since he did no more than conform to the custom followed by d'Ailleboust and Lauzon. Even the Jesuits, on occasion, retained the Indians' gifts instead of handing them over to the Governor to whom they were specifically destined.[8]

A century later the imaginative Bertrand de La Tour, who carries falsehood to the point of describing the industrious Quebec pioneers as "a mob of rebels, libertines and blasphemers, drawn largely from the dregs of the common people," also slanders Mésy. His unscrupulous imagination invents two reasons for censure. He accuses Mésy of the sale of liquor to the Indians and of opposing the first tithes. These fresh charges are just so many fabrications. The records of the Council show that the Governor supported unreservedly both the imposition of tithes and the prohibition of the sale of alcohol. But La Tour's most preposterous allegation is that on one occasion Mésy ordered his soldiers to fire on Mgr. de Laval. He later withdraws the statement, but such a flagrantly false and odious accusation gives some measure of the lengths to which the partisans of Laval were prepared to go in their efforts to blacken the reputation of Mésy.[9]

This was an age of extreme deference towards the Governor, the King's representative, the man in whose person the authority of the King resided. The real cause of the quarrel between Mésy and the Council lay in the presumptuous usurpation of authority on the part of Villeray, Bourdon and the latter's son-in-law, d'Auteuil. Colbert's irrefutable testimony is that these "creatures" of the Bishop and the Jesuits exploited the inexperience of a military leader in juridical matters and sought "in diverse ways" to insure that the decisions of the Council should reflect "their ideas" and increase clerical influence.[10]

The cabal persisted in its unwarranted interference and soon attributed to itself the "falsely claimed power" to settle appeals. It even went so far as to advise appellants not to address themselves to the head of the Council. Villeray was guilty of actual dishonesty and malfeasance, for he bribed bailiffs in order to get copies of the notices which they served. Justly outraged at this scheme to appropriate authority by fraud, Mésy refused to play the part of King Log. On February 7 (1664) he issued an order stipulating that all matters concerning the interests of the King were to be referred to him, and that all those relating to police and justice were to be referred to the Council. He added that councillors were forbidden, on pain of "interdiction," to consider appeals themselves instead of presenting them to the Council. This order did not deter the trio of conspirators, who persisted in their intrigues. The Governor, therefore, acting on his commission which conferred "full power" to administer justice, suspended Villeray, d'Auteuil and Bourdon. In the order of suspension, dated February 13, the three councillors were declared guilty of insubordination and of illegal practices, and of attempting to make themselves "masters" in the Council instead of acting in the interests of the King and the public. This suspension was to continue until a royal decision on the matter should be made.[11]

The Governor had his order read formally to the Bishop during a session of the Council. At the same time he invited Mgr. de Laval to proceed "on the advice of a public assembly," with the appointment of new councillors. The Bishop sent a written answer to this message, stating that "neither his conscience nor his honour nor the respect and obedience" which he owed the King allowed him to act in the matter before "legal judgment" had been pronounced on the accused councillors.[12]

When they had declared their respective positions, the Governor and the Bishop continued to occupy their seats at the Council without any outward sign of disagreement. The three councillors were reinstated in their charges, d'Auteuil in March, and Villeray and Bourbon in April. Calm appeared to reign once more. A few days later the Council, without any opposition whatever, voted 1,000 *livres* to the Governor for travelling expenses according to the custom established under Lauzon and d'Argenson. It then granted 400 *livres* to Bourdon for special services. The calm, however, was only temporary. In the course of the summer Villeray and Bourdon returned to their old tactics of ignoring the Governor's authority. In August M. de Mésy had to call Villeray to order during a meeting of the Council, and to forbid him to "cabal" with the other members. Shortly afterwards Villeray nad the effrontery to declare publicly that the suspension of the councillors had been out of order.[13]

The quarrel in the Council came to a head during the meeting at which Jean Lemire was to be sworn in as syndic of Quebec. The Governor supported the people's choice while the leaders of the bourgeois and clerical faction in the Council, the Bishop's deputy, the Abbé Charny, his brother-in-law La Ferté and the stubborn d'Auteuil, tried at the meeting of September 19 (1664) to bring in a remonstrance against the swearing-in of Jean Lemire. M. de Mésy, however, silenced them by announcing that, as their office had expired, they were no longer members of the Council, and it was now in order to choose new councillors. He added that he had brought the matter to Mgr. de Laval's attention several times, but that the Bishop had refused to take part in any nomination. It was therefore his duty to declare that the Sieurs de Villeray, de La Ferté, d'Auteuil and Bourdon had now ceased to be members of the Council. Bourdon was the only one of the four to question this decision, but he spoke with such insolence that the

Governor had him ejected from the meeting by force, and ordered him to proceed to France to justify his conduct. As for Villeray, he had already set out for Paris with a fabricated story designed to weaken in advance the very strong case which the Governor would submit.

On September 24, in the absence of Mgr. de Laval, M. de Mésy appointed three new councillors and a new attorney-general. The Bishop had received notice of the meeting, but had sent word that "he could not be present, as he was unwell."[14] After the meeting he protested that these appointments were illegal since they had been made without his participation. He deposited a declaration of opposition with the secretary of the Council, and at the first opportunity, had his stand in the issue announced from the pulpit of the parish church. Meanwhile, the Governor had gone on a pilgrimage to Ste.-Anne-de-Beaupré. On his return (October 5), he countered the Bishop's curious procedure by having the town crier circulate a "poster" explaining his action. In the quarrel the Jesuits sided with the prelate to such a degree that the Governor accused them "everywhere and openly" of refusing him "confession and absolution."[15]

However, with the disappearance of the rebellious councillors, the crisis was at least partially resolved, and the new Council carried out its functions regularly, although Mgr. de Laval refused to attend any of its meetings. On New Year's Day 1665, the Jesuits, as good politicians, came and paid their respects to the Governor, "although he was on bad terms" with them. The Governor, for his part, sent them his "compliments" and he also sent greetings to the Bishop, who did not return the courtesy. This painful situation between the two heads of the country continued for some months, until death put an end to it. In March the Governor fell gravely ill and made his peace with the Church. He received Mgr. de Laval at his bedside, and the two former Hermitage brothers joined hands and prayed together. On May 5 M. de Mésy died. In his will, which was characterized by a deep sense of justice, he made a number of gifts to religious institutions, and at his own request he was buried in the paupers' cemetery.[16]

M. de Mésy was a conscientious soldier, whose obligations towards Mgr. de Laval made it difficult for him to act independently during the early part of his term. When, very soon, he found himself faced with a theocratic cabal, he proved to be impulsive and unfitted for a battle of wits, and he defended himself, as he said, "in cavalier fashion." This in no way diminishes the strength and the right of his cause. His misfortune is that his version of the events has not come down in history. For his "important papers" were "sequestered, torn up and burned" by his adversaries, who "boasted that they would never be seen again." As a result, he was condemned without being heard, on the allegations of his enemies. The opinion of Colbert, who read the dossiers, is worth remembering as the final judgment in the matter. "The Jesuits," he writes, "accused M. de Mésy of avarice and violence, and the Governor accused them of wanting to encroach on the authority entrusted to him by the King so that . . . since the Sovereign Council was entirely made up of their creatures, all decisions were made according to their ideas; and this made it necessary for M. de Mésy, who seems to have a good deal of sense, to send the attorney-general of the said Council here to give an account of his conduct."[17]

Thus, according to Colbert, to the well-established intrigues of Villeray must be added the collusion of the Jesuits. But the most astonishing thing about this cabal is Mgr. de Laval's attitude to it. Although a member of the Council, he did not intervene either to restrain the excesses of M. de Mésy's adversaries or even to insure the respect due to the King's representative, who was, moreover, the man of his choice and his friend. Instead, he took up the defence of the two rebels, who were supported in the Council by his deputy, the Abbé Charny. The Bishop had already tried to divert to himself the authority of Governor d'Avaugour, and one must conclude that the intrigues against Mésy constitute another attempt to establish a clerically oriented government. Proof of this may be found in the instructions given to Talon by Louis XIV himself. "Since the Jesuits have assumed an authority which outreaches their profession," the King enjoins his Intendant to take care that the "spiritual" authority, which is the bishop's, shall remain "inferior" to the "temporal" authority, which belongs to the governor. The King did not forget these intrigues, and he frequently repeated the injunction to repress any inclination towards ecclesiastical autocracy in the colony.[17a]

Mésy's death put an end to the conflict which had divided the population of Quebec into two hostile factions. An interim governor, Le Neuf de la Potherie, had been chosen by M. de Mésy, and he took over the reins of government. The colony, nevertheless, was still harassed by anxiety. The promised help from France had not arrived, and small bands of Iroquois were prowling around the posts and along the shores of the St. Lawrence. In April (1665) they killed three men working in the fields in Montreal, and captured two others. In July they carried off the intrepid and wise interpreter of the fort, Charles Le Moyne. In August they attacked a fleet of canoes manned by four hundred Algonquins on its way down Lake Superior with a rich cargo of furs. Happily, by this time the fate of the country no longer depended on the outcome of skirmishes on the Indian frontier. In June the first troops had disembarked in Quebec, the advance guard of the force which the King was sending to put an end to the constant threat from the Iroquois nations.[18]

CHAPTER THREE

TRACY IMPOSES PEACE ON THE IROQUOIS NATIONS
1665-1667

Tracy's mission. The Carignan regiment. Appointment of an intendant: Talon. Conclusion of the Mésy affair. Maisonneuve forced to leave Montreal. Construction of forts. Courcelles' campaign. Peace parleys. The English in Manhattan. Campaign against the Mohawks. Peace imposed on the Five Nations. The colony ceded to the West India Company. Fur trade and commerce.

At last, after two long years, Louis XIV was going to keep his promise to come to the aid of New France. The Comte d'Estrades had been appointed Viceroy of America, but he was now engaged on a diplomatic mission in Holland, and to replace him the King commissioned on November 19, 1663, the Sieur Prouville de Tracy as Lieutenant-General of North and South America. M. de Tracy's otherwise distinguised career as officer and administrator had been interrupted during the Fronde when, as a result of anti-Mazarin activities, he found himself a state prisoner. He had been drawn into the factious party in the wake of his patron, the Duc de Longueville, and his misadventure had taught him the folly of being bound by loyalty to the wrong people. So when, after his release, he was able to resume his career, he resolved to avoid any such error in future.

At sixty-four years of age, M. de Tracy was still very active, with something of the musketeer's love of military pomp and public ceremony. His commission, dated November 19, 1663, ordered him first to recapture Cayenne from the Dutch and to settle certain administrative difficulties in Martinique and Guadeloupe, then to proceed to Canada to free that country from the dangerous Iroquois threat. He set out from La Rochelle in February 1664 with a fleet equipped for war, and sailed straight to the West Indies. When he had planted the fleur-de-lis once more in Cayenne, and re-established order in the West Indies, he set sail on

22

April 20, 1665, for Canada, but unfavourable winds in the Gulf delayed his arrival in Quebec until June 30. Meanwhile, the first
companies of the Carignan regiment had arrived on June 19,
amidst great rejoicing.[1]

M. de Tracy was welcomed with the greatest enthusiasm by
the population of the little capital. Men, women and children
gathered at the port, and greeted him with acclamations. The
Lieutenant-General stepped ashore, preceded by twenty guards
and four pages in the royal colours, and the crowd escorted this
procession to the church, while the bells rang out in full peal. The
secular clergy and the Jesuits were grouped at the door of the
church, where the King's representative received holy water from
the hands of the Bishop. He was then led to his place in the choir
where he refused a proffered prie-Dieu and knelt on the stone
floor. As they sang the triumphant *Te Deum* that followed, the
voices of choir and clergy were vibrant with the joy of a whole
people, who for thirty years had yearned for peace without ever
daring to disarm, and who at last were assured that peace was
near.

During the next few days the Hurons hastened to Quebec to
greet the new Ononthio. They expressed joy at his coming with
so many soldiers "to make the land strong and to give new life to
the French and the Indians." On July 6 the Lieutenant-General
convoked the Council appointed by M. de Mésy, thereby recognizing its validity, and presented his commission, which was duly
registered.[2]

Almost a year before the arrival of M. de Tracy, the scene of
the Laval-Mésy affair had shifted to France. In the autumn of
1664, when confronted with the Governor's members of the cate-
gorical accusations against the cabal, and the false protestations of
innocence of Villeray and Bourdon, Colbert was shrewd enough to
realize that the malcontents were plotting to bring the Council
under ecclesiastical domination. Once informed of the facts, the
King went back to his first plan which was to send to Canada an
intendant charged with the administration of justice, law and order, and finance, and on March 23 (1665) he appointed Canada's
first intendant, the Sieur Jean Talon. On the same day he appointed a new governor, Daniel de Rémy, Sieur de Courcelles, to
replace M. de Mésy. These two newly appointed dignitaries
reached Quebec on September 12 after an exhausting crossing of
117 days, and on September 23 M. de Tracy installed a new
Council. The term of office of the councillors appointed by M. de

Mésy had expired, and their successors were chosen by M. de
Tracy and the Bishop. In fact, in his anxiety to be on good terms
with the episcopal power and "not to quarrel with the missionaries," M. de Tracy re-established the original Council with its
bias in favour of the Jesuits. However, once the Council had registered the commissions of Courcelles and Talon, M. de Tracy
did not call it together again for a year and during the interval its
administrative functions passed into the hands of the Intendant.[3]

There still remained to be settled the matter of Mésy's "violent action" against some councillors. In March 1665 the King had
ordered that an inquiry be carried out by M. de Tracy, acting with
two other newly appointed officials, the Governor and the Intendant, with the right, if justified by results, to send Mésy to France
for a final decision. Louis XIV rejected Villeray's testimony as Colbert had done, but he did not exonerate the Governor. His chief
reason was the allegation of the two agitators that Mésy had ordered them to go to France "on his own authority" and on "twenty-
four hours' " notice. On examination, this charge proves to be completely false, at least in the case of Villeray, since he had left of his
own free will in August. The death of M. de Mésy had changed the
situation completely. The dossier was examined, but it was not
considered "appropriate" to proceed with the inquiry, especially
since Mgr. de Laval and the other individuals concerned did not
bring any charges. Only the Jesuits took action, a full year after
the death of M. de Mésy. In May 1666 they requested an investigation into certain derogatory assertions which the late governor was
alleged without proof to have made about them, and which had
not been revealed before that time. However, they listened to the
advice of their friend and partisan, M. de Tracy, and decided it
was more politic not to press their charges. The Intendant wrote
to the Court that it seemed wise to "bury" the affair along with the
memory of the impulsive Governor. Courcelles and Tracy were
in agreement with him on the matter, and Louis XIV and Colbert
promptly expressed approval of their opinion.[4]

Before the echoes of the Laval-Mésy quarrel had died down,
Mgr. de Laval had become engaged in a second feud at the other
end of the colony. The target of the Bishop's powerful opposition
was Maisonneuve, the founder and governor of Montreal, and this
disastrous quarrel was to lead to his departure from Canada. Mgr.
de Laval was ex officio head of the religious communities in the
colony, and in this capacity he had learned of the transaction carried out in 1653, when Maisonneuve needed funds in order to
raise a fresh levy of emigrants for the colony. At that time Jeanne

Mance had handed over to Maisonneuve a sum of 20,000 *livres* which had been given by Madame de Bullion to endow the Hôtel-Dieu. In exchange the Hôtel-Dieu had received one hundred *arpents* of land. Now, suddenly, twelve years after the exchange had taken place, the Bishop claimed that, as Maisonneuve could not produce written evidence of the donor's approval, he must repay the money to the hospital. Maisonneuve explained that Madame de Bullion had wished to remain anonymous and for that reason had given her approval verbally, but that confirmation of her approval could be found in a further gift of 20,000 *livres* which she had made for the same purpose on the same occasion. He added that the money had made it possible to reinforce powerfully the colony in a moment of dire stress. But his plea fell on deaf ears; Mgr. de Laval persisted in his demand that the money be repaid. Ever since his quarrel with the Abbé Queylus, the Bishop had viewed with disfavour any plans for the development of Montreal, and under the influence of the Bishop, M. de Tracy soon revealed the same lack of enthusiasm. When the controversy was reported to him, he intervened with all the force of his supreme command. In October (1665) he issued an order (in the guise of permission) to the Governor of Montreal to go to France in order to settle "some private business." In other words, Maisonneuve was being sent to Paris to defend his conduct in the Hôtel-Dieu affair. Maisonneuve had established the missionary outpost of Montreal right on the Iroquois frontier, and for twenty-three years his courage had been the chief bulwark of the settlement. Now, under the double pressure of Laval and Tracy, this lay apostle was being forced to leave the country to which he had dedicated his labour and his life. In Paris, the Seminary of St. Sulpice supported him, but in order to obviate a difficult situation, they decided it was wiser not to send him back to his post. They maintained his title of Governor until 1668 when they accepted his resignation. The most remarkable figure, after Champlain, in the early history of New France died in Paris in 1676, and he died still protesting the unjustifiable claim of Mgr. de Laval. As a matter of fact, the legality of the exchange between Jeanne Mance and Maisonneuve had been recognized by the King's Council in 1667, but Mgr. de Laval persisted for twenty years in presenting his claim to St. Sulpice. In 1695 Laval's successor, Mgr. de Saint-Vallier, ordered that it be abandoned.[5]

Now that Canada had an army, the thoughts of the whole country from Quebec to Montreal were concentrated on the war against the Five Nations. Beginning in June (1665), every ship that

arrived from France brought troops, and the last contingent landed
on August 20, too late to undertake a campaign before the winter.
Companies of the Orléans, Chambellé, Poitou and Lallier regi-
ments which had come with M. de Tracy were now joined by the
twenty-four companies of the Carignan regiment under their colonel, the Marquis de Salières, so that this colony of three thousand
people now had an imposing army of twelve or thirteen hundred
men. Immediately after his arrival M. de Tracy had begun to pre-
pare for the coming campaign. On July 23 he started the construction of forts along the Richelieu, the invasion route into Iroquois
country. These forts were intended as bases for supplying the
troops and caring for the wounded, but they also had another object. They would "remove any desire on the part of the English"
to establish themselves on a tributary of the St. Lawrence. The
first fort was built at the mouth of the Richelieu and was given
the same name. The second, Fort St. Louis, was built at the Chambly rapids and was linked by road to Montreal, and the third,
Fort Ste. Thérèse, was established three leagues farther upstream.
The chain of forts was completed the following summer by the
erection of Fort Ste. Anne, on an island at the entrance of Lake
Champlain, and of Fort St. Jean, a little farther down the Richelieu. All these forts were of the same simple construction. Each
consisted of a solid palisade flanked by bastions and enclosing
barracks and storehouses. In the following months, Talon made
all haste to supply them with the munitions and stores needed
for the coming campaign.[6]

The arrival of troops and the erection of forts excited lively
apprehension among the Iroquois. On December 2 the faithful
Garakontié appeared in Quebec leading a deputation of Onondagas, who returned the captive interpreter, Le Moyne, and made
proposals for renewing the peace. M. de Tracy in his turn liberated three prisoners belonging to their tribe, and assured the
envoys that the King would protect any nation which buried the
war hatchet.[6a]

Still acting on his policy of strength, Tracy authorized the im-
petuous Courcelles to undertake a campaign against the Mohawks,
although it was mid-winter and the troops were quite unaccustom-
ed to the rigours of the climate. On January 30 (1666) the Governor left Fort Ste. Thérèse without even waiting for his Algonquin
guides. His force consisted of about five hundred men, among
whom were forty-five Canadians. Every man, including Courcelles
himself, carried a thirty-pound pack of arms, provisions and blan-

kets, and they slept in the open on the snow. The detachment lost its way; instead of coming out at the Indian villages they found themselves at the Anglo-Dutch village of Corlaer twenty leagues to the east, and there they were given help. All that was gained by the expedition was that, on February 20, they captured two Indian lodges and killed four scouts at the cost of six of their own men. When they got back to Quebec on March 17, their supplies of food were almost exhausted, and some of their men had died of exposure. In the bitterness of failure, Courcelles placed the blame for the disaster on Father Albanel, whom he accused of delaying the arrival of the Algonquin guides. M. de Tracy tried to smooth down the Governor by congratulating him on the courage with which he had led the campaign, but at the same time he advised him "not to quarrel with the black gowns."[7]

In spite of the failure, the expedition of Courcelles served to show the Iroquois that distance was no protection against French attacks. That did not prevent the implacable Mohawks from killing two men near Montreal. On the other hand, ten ambassadors from the Senecas soon appeared on a peace-seeking mission. On May 22 they signed a treaty recognizing that the members of their nation were subjects of the King of France, and asking for "black gowns" to preach the gospel to them. Two months later a deputation of Oneidas arrived. In the name of the Mohawks, as well as in their own, they implored the favours of peace and evangelization, and on July 12 a treaty with the Oneidas was ratified.[8]

The Dutch had warned M. de Tracy to be on his guard with the Mohawks, and he thought he should get further information before concluding any agreement with them. Accordingly, he dispatched messengers to Manhattan. Just a few days after they had left, however, news arrived that a band of Mohawks had killed three men from Fort Ste. Anne and captured four others. Among the dead was M. de Tracy's own nephew, M. de Chazy. Such arrant treachery could not go unpunished. The men on their way to Manhattan were immediately recalled, and four days later, M. de Sorel set out with a punitive force of two hundred soldiers and eighty Indians. However, they met a party of Mohawks on their way to Quebec, and they decided to return with them. The Mohawks had with them the four prisoners, and they offered to compensate, according to Indian custom, for the murders which they had committed. On August 28 the Mohawks and Oneidas already in Quebec were joined by delegations of Senecas and Cayugas, and by a few Onondagas. Three days later, in the Jesuits' "park," M. de

Tracy presided over an assembly at which, for the first time, representatives of all five Iroquois tribes were present. The Senecas and the Cayugas presented a gift of fifty-two bead belts and reaffirmed their decision to maintain the peace, but the Mohawks and Oneidas confined themselves to non-committal expressions of peaceful intentions.[9]

These last two tribes were probably counting on help from the English, who had recently become their neighbours. Charles II, in violation of international law, had granted to his brother, the Duke of York, all the territory between the Connecticut and Delaware rivers including New Holland. In August 1664, although England and Holland were at peace, the Duke's deputy, Colonel Nicolls, had seized the little capital of Manhattan and rechristened it New York. Soon after, war broke out between England and Holland, and in January 1666 France also declared war against England. Alarmed at the possibility of a French offensive, Nicolls tried to persuade the English colonies to allow him to lead them in an invasion of the Richelieu valley, but Massachusetts feared reprisals from the Abenaki allies of the French, and rejected the proposal. So, to protect himself from any hostility on the part of New France, Nicolls wrote to M. de Tracy, making great protestations of friendship, and citing as evidence of goodwill the help that M. de Courcelles had received at Corlaer. In return for this kindness, he asked just one small favour, that France should respect British territory. M. de Tracy assured him, in reply, that his peaceful intentions were unchanged even though the English had had the bad taste to capture the ship that was bringing him his winter's supply of brandy.[10] Meanwhile the Mohawks and the Oneidas refused to commit themselves, and the leaders of New France had to make the choice between peace and war. Because the Jesuits' chief concern was evangelizing, and since they were already choosing missionaries for the Cayugas, they were anxious to preserve the peace, but Talon urged that an offensive be launched immediately. That seemed to him the only way to stop the raids of the Mohawks, who had been harassing the country for twenty years. His argument was decisive; on September 6 (1666) M. de Tracy decided to launch a campaign,[11] and twelve days later the expedition set out.

The force was made up of six hundred regular soldiers, and six hundred Canadians, the men from Quebec under Repentigny and the Montrealers, the famous "bluecoats," under Le Moyne. With a hundred Huron and Algonquin scouts they embarked in a fleet of three hundred boats and canoes and paddled up the Riche-

lieu to Lake Champlain, which they entered on October 5. At the
southern end of Lake George they had to disembark and continue
their journey on foot. Laden with heavy packs of provisions, arms
and baggage, they advanced slowly through thick bush broken only
by narrow, winding trails. On October 16 they reached the Iroquois country and advanced to attack the first village, which they
found deserted. The inhabitants had fled, leaving behind great
stores of corn and provisions. Pausing only long enough to take
"necessary refreshments," the troops marched against a second, a
third, and a fourth village. They found them all deserted, and with
their harvests gathered in. Just as the sun was setting an Algonquin woman, who had once been a prisoner of the Mohawks and
knew the country, took M. de Courcelles by the hand and led him
to the last village, Andaraqué. It was the largest of the villages,
and was defended by a palisade twenty feet high, flanked by four
bastions. The Mohawks had meant to make a stand here, but
when they heard the trumpets and drums and saw the French
troops advancing, bristling with rifles and with colours flying,
they fled to the nearby forest, from which shelter they shouted
defiance and fired a few random shots in the direction of the invaders. On entering the village the soldiers were astonished to discover that it contained about a hundred bark houses, each with
room for eight or nine families, and all equipped with provisions,
utensils and tools. That night, after a day of forced marches and
triumph, the men ate their fill and slept on dry beds in the huts
of Andaraqué.[12]

The following day, the troops were drawn up in line of battle
in the presence of Tracy and Courcelles, and, in the name of the
King of France, Captain Du Bois took possession of all Mohawk
lands. At the conclusion of this ceremony mass was celebrated and
a *Te Deum* was chanted by the Abbé Dubois, the chaplain of the Carignan regiment. The soldiers erected a cross and a post bearing
the arms of France, and the rest of the day was spent in burning
the five villages with their standing crops.

Since there had been no military engagement, the Mohawks
survived the destruction of their villages and were able to take
refuge with their sister nations, but the signal punishment dealt
out to them taught them that it was no longer safe to defy the
power of New France. The campaign left them without resources
in a devastated country, and famine eventually wiped out some
four hundred of their number.[13]

Tracy had committed his first error in launching his campaign too late in the season. He made a greater error when he did not follow up his success by attacking the Oneidas. He thought it was too late to take further action, and accordingly, he withdrew from the Iroquois country, and reached Quebec on November 5. On his return Tracy gave an open-air feast to his Iroquois hostages. When during the meal one of the number, Chief Agariata, boasted that he had cut down M. de Chazy with his own hand, the outraged Lieutenant-General ordered that the murderer be seized and hanged forthwith. Three days later, Tracy sent the captive Mohawk, le Bâtard Flamand, and two Oneidas with messages to their people, commanding them to come to Quebec within four moons in order to conclude a treaty of peace.

In the colony the news of the expedition's success brought great joy to the colony and a deep sense of relief to all its families. Mgr. de Laval ordered a *Te Deum* to be sung in the cathedral church on November 14, and on the same day the mass was followed by a solemn procession of thanksgiving.[14]

On April 20, 1667, le Bâtard Flamand and the two Oneidas reappeared in Quebec, but without the designated hostages and prisoners. Tracy sent them back once more to warn their respective nations that, if within two moons they did not agree to bury the hatchet, the army would invade and ravage their country. The threat had the desired effect; on July 5 delegates from the Mohawks and Oneidas presented themselves and accepted the conditions which had been laid down. As a guarantee of good faith, they offered whole families as hostages, and they even asked that "black gowns" be sent to their people. The Jesuits rejoiced to see a new field opened up to their missionary zeal, and the whole colony reaped the reward of its long heroic struggle. The Onondagas had renewed their treaty of friendship some months earlier, and when the Oneidas and the Mohawks finally agreed to bury the hatchet, New France was at peace with all the Iroquois nations. That peace, which was signed on July 10, 1667, was to last for eighteen years.[15]

In France, Colbert, a foremost promoter of trade, was bent on an expansionist programme of colonial and economic development. Scarcely a year after the dissolution of the Company of One Hundred Associates, he again placed Canada in the hands of a trading company, only this time the company's domain was spread over several continents. In May 1664 Louis XIV signed a charter which granted to the West India Company a veritable commercial empire: the West India Islands, the mainland of South America from the Orinoco to the Amazon, the coast of Africa from Cape Verde to the Cape of Good Hope, as well as Canada, Newfoundland, Acadia and the mainland as far south as Florida.[16]

In its territory the Company enjoyed judicial and property rights and seigniorial rights as they were already established. It could appoint, under royal commission, governors and members of sovereign councils, as well as judges, who were to be guided by the Custom of Paris. It could dispose of its lands by sale or feudal lease, and it was even empowered to sign treaties of alliance with neighbouring peoples. Most important of all, in order to make it possible for the Company to provide for "the maintenance of the colonies," the King granted it a monopoly "of all the commerce and navigation" of the countries named in the charter. The monopoly was to last for forty years, and during that period the Company was to pay no import or export tax on its goods. As under the Company of New France, the French inhabitants and the natives converted to Christianity enjoyed the rights pertaining to the status of "native-born French subjects." Finally, the Company was to have the privilege of appointing priests to their charges and it undertook to build churches, as well as to transport members of the clergy to the colony, and to support them there.[16a]

As the charter was not registered in Paris until July 31, too late to send cargoes to Canada, the Company did not take possession of the country until the following year. On July 6, 1665, its agent-general presented the King's edict to the Sovereign Council for registration, and New France became the property of the West India Company.[17]

Talon very soon realized that Canada was not likely to prosper under this new régime. The country needed settlers, and it also needed to extend and develop its chief source of wealth, the fur trade. However, the Company's charter, which granted very comprehensive rights, imposed no obligation to colonize, and the Company, which had been organized for intercontinental trade, had no interest in building and strengthening a colony. Probably because it preferred not to become too deeply involved in Canada's domestic affairs, it did not exercise its prerogative of appointing a governor and councillors. These appointments were made by the King, and the Company was represented in the Council only by its agent-general.[18]

The situation with regard to the fur trade was somewhat more complicated. As soon as its ships arrived in Quebec, its agent, the Sieur Le Barroys, claimed for the Company the right to

exercise its monopoly, and M. de Tracy transferred to it the Tadoussac fur-trading post and the taxes on beaver pelts and moose
hides. These were the sources from which the former Community
of Habitants had drawn the revenue required to meet the ordinary
expenses of the country, and since the colonists were still taxed to
meet these expenses, they asked to be allowed to retain their right
to trade with the Indians. This request was granted to them, but
on condition that all pelts be delivered to the Company's stores
where they would be bought for resale in France.[19]

In the general area of trade with France, the Company's
clerks insisted upon the full rights of its monopoly, and refused
to allow the slightest privilege either to those French merchants
who were in the habit of exporting to Canada, or to the inhabitants of Canada themselves. It even disputed the right of the latter to send directly to France for articles which they needed for
their own use and to trade with the Indians. Talon immediately
protested to Colbert: such a policy, he wrote, could not fail to discourage emigration. It was at variance with the King's directive
to encourage his subjects to engage in commerce. The settlers
were "disheartened" by this unreasonable prohibition which restricted them to one means of livelihood, the tilling of the soil.
Convinced by these arguments, Colbert decided to intervene, and
he succeeded in persuading the Company to make a concession.
The habitants were to be allowed to import goods for barter, and
to export their pelts to France, but only for one year. The situation was clarified and the Company's rights and responsibilities
defined in the terms of a royal order dated April 8, 1666: the domain of the West India Company included the Tadoussac trading
post as well as the taxes of twenty-five per cent on beaver pelts,
and ten per cent on moose hides, and the Company undertook to
give a fixed sum annually, as the Community had formerly done,
to meet the ordinary expenses of the colony.[20] Talon estimated
these charges at 46,500 livres, but Colbert fixed the figure in 1666
at 36,000.[21]

To sum up, the charter of the West India Company did not
dispel the confusion which had characterized the administration
of the colony since Richelieu's time, and New France was still
subject to a double authority. The effective government was in
the hands of the King who appointed the governor, the intendant, and the members of the Sovereign Council. Civil and military administration were directed by the King, who also laid down
policies for colonization and economic development. Although

nominally owner of New France, the Company's only sources of revenue were the taxes on furs and hides, and the Tadoussac fur trade. It continued to maintain its seigniorial rights and its title to all lands, but it left the granting of concessions in the hands of the intendant. This dual régime persisted until 1674 when the charter of the Company was revoked.

CHAPTER FOUR

COLONIZATION AND DEVELOPMENT
1665-1668

Jean Talon, the first Intendant. His functions and instructions. His vision for Canada. Method of colonization: emigrants, "King's daughters" and soldiers. Increase in the number and size of families. Assimilation of the Indians. Aid to colonists. Importation of farm animals. Agriculture. Industry. Commerce. Search for an ocean port. The beaver trade. The coureurs de bois. The Indians and the liquor traffic. Departure of Talon. His successor, Bouteroue. Courcelles and the militia.

While M. de Tracy was taking steps to insure the safety of the colony, the Intendant devoted himself entirely to the development of the country. Talon, who was chosen by Colbert to be Canada's first intendant, came from a family of magistrates, all believers in the Gallican doctrine of the right of kings. He had served as commissioner to the armies and later in the important post of Intendant of the province of Hainaut. The product of a sound classical education, he could carry on a discussion in Latin or write pleasant occasional verses. Colbert knew him as a man of courtly manners in whom intelligence and imagination were combined with an inexhaustible capacity for hard work. His career in New France was to reveal in him a mind of broad vision, capable of building for the present and planning for the future.[1]

This first intendant arrived bearing a commission which entrusted to him the entire civil administration of the colony. Only the army was excluded from his jurisdiction. As Intendant of Justice he could hear cases of any category, take proceedings against persons accused of any crime, give judgment in civil actions, and order all things as he deemed necessary and proper. As Intendant of Finance he administered the public funds, and audited the military expenses of the Governor; and as Intendant of

Police, he was empowered to "do and order" anything that served the public good.[2]

Talon brought with him, as a complement to his commission, another equally important document, a statement of precise instructions from the King. Colbert had composed the memorandum, and a glance at its main items allows one to gauge the spirit of the directives imposed on the Intendant by the Court. In the first place he was informed that, although the piety and zeal of the Jesuits had made a very important contribution to the progress of the colony, they had nevertheless been guilty of assuming an "authority exceeding that of their profession." Louis XIV therefore enjoined his Intendant to take care that the "spiritual" authority of the bishop and the Jesuits should remain inferior to the "temporal" authority of the King. Remembering the excesses of Villeray and Bourdon, the King instructed Talon to observe the behaviour of the councillors, and to change them or continue them in office as circumstances might dictate. In the sphere of economics, he recommended that new farms be grouped in close proximity to one another; that farmers be urged to grow hemp and raise cattle; that arts and manufactures be encouraged; that a shipbuilding industry be established. Louis XIV indicated his intention of settling the soldiers of the Carignan regiment in Canada, and he reminded Talon that the children of the colony were to be given a proper education and brought up as pious Christians and dutiful subjects of the King.[3]

Colbert's instructions constitute a remarkably broad and realistic programme of development for Canada. The religious directives reflect the spirit of an age when the tendency of the State was to reaffirm its Gallican liberties, while the aim of Mgr. de Laval and the Jesuits was to make of Canada a missionary country dominated by theocratic influence. This divergence of views reflects in no way on the sincere Catholicism of the King and his officers; it merely reveals two interpretations of the doctrine of Church supremacy. The powers conferred upon the Intendant were practically discretionary, and in Talon Colbert was to find a collaborator equal to the mission entrusted to him.

From his first sight of the mighty St. Lawrence and the rich lands that lined its shores, Talon was fired with enthusiasm for New France. A few weeks after his arrival, he described in glowing terms the natural advantages and resources of the country: "unlimited territory, a healthful climate, immense forests, a fertile soil, abundant furs, potential mineral wealth." "This country," he wrote to Colbert, "has never had the attention it deserves." It could be built into a great realm "and we could establish a monarchy here, or at least a very important State."[4] Alas, Louis XIV and Colbert were engaged in a war with Great Britain, and neither of them could see Talon's vision of an empire beyond the Atlantic. Moreover, the political education of both King and Minister imprisoned them in the concept of a continental France, so they answered that, "even if the King were not occupied with other affairs," it would not be "prudent to depopulate his kingdom" in order to colonize a country which could not sustain an increased population. France had a population of twenty million souls, and the real reason for the King's lack of enthusiasm was that he was already haunted by dreams of conquest, and he could not, as Colbert said, maintain at the same time "big armies and big colonies."[5]

Although his grand plan received no encouragement, Talon threw himself heart and soul into the task of carrying out the programme laid out by the Court. Fortunately, the policy decision to send out emigrants, at the expense of the Royal Treasury, had already been made. The West India Company undertook to recruit and transport colonists at the rate of one hundred *livres* per person: ten *livres* for enlisting a candidate, thirty for clothes and sixty for passage. In this way 429 immigrants landed in Quebec in 1665. The following year the Company brought out thirty-five *engagés,* at its own expense, to work for the habitants. Two hundred and eighty-six were brought over in 1667 at the King's expense and 228 more in 1668.[6] Almost all these colonists came from the northern provinces, from Picardy to Aunis. As Dieppe was the principal port of embarkation, the greatest number came from Normandy and Ile-de-France. The next largest contingent came from Poitou and Aunis, by way of the port of La Rochelle.[7]

It was not difficult to recruit emigrants; the prospect of owning land free of taxes, with the privilege of hunting and fishing, was a most attractive one for the poverty-stricken French peasant, especially since he could also count on help from the King until he harvested his first crop. Talon set severe standards for the selection of emigrants, and when he complained that there were among them old men and mere lads, Colbert promised that all care would be taken to respect the Intendant's wishes, and to send only men "over sixteen years of age, and under forty" and "fit for work."[8]

The authorities in Quebec were even more exacting in their

choice of girls destined for marriage with the bachelors of the colony. Some of the girls came from religious orphanages; these were chosen with the help of parish priests in Normandy, or of the Seminary of St. Sulpice in Paris. Elsewhere candidates had to present a certificate of good conduct before they embarked. The Intendant insisted that the girls must not be too delicate; Canada needed strong, healthy young women "at the child-bearing age." Talon even added the recommendation that there should not be "anything unattractive in their appearance." During the crossing the prospective brides were under the supervision of nuns or of distinguished ladies such as Madame Bourdon, Jeanne Mance or Marguerite Bourgeoys. These "King's daughters," as they were called, were very carefully chosen for their moral and physical qualities. They were very superior immigrants, the best of that period. It is not surprising that the young men of the colony found these fresh, healthy girls very attractive, and they were married, thirty at a time, almost as soon as they landed. Authors of fictitious travel tales, such as La Hontan and Beauchesne, have scattered their books with slanderous stories about the "King's daughters," but there is not one single authoritative document which might lead one to suppose that any prostitutes were sent to Canada. The rumour which crops up from time to time can always be traced to ill-informed persons who confused the Laurentian colony with the West Indies to which women of ill fame were sometimes sent. Female immigrants to Canada were above reproach.[9]

This subsidized emigration did not bring in enough colonists for the needs of the country, so the Court put into effect its original idea of demobilizing in Canada the four companies of the Carignan regiment which constituted the garrison. In 1666 six captains and ten subalterns, attracted by the free life of the country, decided to accept the advantages which the Intendant offered them, and to take up land grants. The next year seven officers committed themselves still further by marrying Canadian girls, and soon the King began to encourage such marriages by means of bonuses. Soldiers' pay was continued while they were getting settled on the land, and they "applied in crowds for wives and farms."

The Carignan regiment gave the country 412 settlers in 1668, and about 100 in 1669.[10] Some soldiers from other companies also decided to remain in Canada, and the Intendant gave each of them a gift of money, as well as tools and provisions.

Talon's programme of immigration and soldier settlement was complemented by practical measures to increase the population. In 1668 the first royal grants were made to fathers of large families. Denis, the father of fifteen children, and Tilly, the father of ten, received respectively 1,500 and 800 *livres*. Talon also provided funds to hasten the marriage of dowerless "ladies" born in the colony. To each prospective bride from France he gave a wedding present of 50 *livres* in kind to help the young couple set up housekeeping. The King suggested suitable ages for marriage, eighteen years for boys and fourteen for girls.[11]

One of Colbert's ideas for expanding the population was that they should go back to Champlain's noble dream of teaching the Indians French ways and incorporating them into the colony. In 1667, when Talon proposed to organize stable communities of Hurons and Algonquins, Colbert recommended that the Indians should be encouraged to live near the French settlers and to mingle with them so that "henceforth they should all be one people and one race." He suggested that native children be gathered together in schools and taught the Christian faith and French customs, and that Indian families be incorporated into the colony to facilitate intermarriage. The King even offered a wedding present of 150 *livres* to any Indian girl who married a French husband. Mgr. de Laval, the Jesuits, the Ursulines and the Sulpicians were under constant pressure from Talon to carry out the task of integration, and they worked hard at it. Once again, however, the effort to assimilate the natives proved fruitless. The Indian, and more particularly the Indian woman, could be converted and more or less depaganized, but they would not adopt the French way of life. As Mother Marie de l'Incarnation said, "a Frenchman goes native more easily than an Indian becomes French."[12]

Before the arrival of colonists, Talon was faced with the problem of providing them with homesteads in the seigniories. He cleared as much land as he could with the small labour force at his disposal. This land was broken and sown in two-*arpent* plots, so that the immigrant could be settled immediately on his own farm. All he needed was a few bushels of flour, and this was advanced to him. In return, he was asked to clear two *arpents* of forest land which would be ready for newly arrived colonists three or four years later. Within its limits, this system brought excellent results. The Intendant, of course, was restricted in his choice of location for new farms. These had to have frontage on a river, for in that country of virgin forest the rivers were the only roads, and fish was a very important item in the food supply. Talon tried to place the new arrivals near "old-timers" so that they might have the benefit of their experience and advice.

In the year 1666 alone, more than 250 new farms were established. Gradually, during this period of systematic immigration, the banks of the St. Lawrence were dotted with settlements from Cap Tourmente, ten leagues below Quebec, to Lachine, three leagues above Montreal, although there still remained stretches of four or five leagues without any farm on either side of the river. New houses were built on the south side of the Island of Montreal, and the fields around the forts of the Richelieu "were covered with beautiful wheat."[13]

Talon would have liked to follow the recommendations of the Court and to group the new farms in villages. He could see several advantages in such an arrangement: rapid defence against Iroquois raids, convenience for religious organization and for mutual help. To provide a model, he founded three villages: Bourg-Talon, Bourg-la-Reine and Bourg-Royal, on the left bank of the St. Charles River opposite Quebec. The land for these villages was procured by somewhat high-handed means. Without even obtaining compensation from Colbert for the seigneur, Talon simply expropriated it from the Jesuits' seigniory of Notre-Dame-des-Anges. The farms were triangular, and their boundaries radiated from a centre like the spokes of a wheel. They were much sought after and very quickly occupied, but the experiment was possible only because the villages were in the immediate vicinity of Quebec. Elsewhere the farms had to have frontage on a river.[14]

Talon's plans were not limited to the human population. He realized that the colony needed farm animals, and they too were imported at the King's expense. The colonists already had oxen and cows, more than 2,000 in 1665, which they used for ploughing. Imports brought the number up to 6,900 in 1671. But there were no horses; only one horse had been brought into the colony, and that was in 1645. Between 1665 and 1672, about eighty stallions and mares were landed in Quebec. They were distributed to different habitants on the understanding that within three years each farmer was to give a foal in payment, and these foals were distributed on the same conditions. This scheme increased the number of horses though somewhat slowly. Breeding of sheep and pigs brought more rapid results. Eighty sheep were imported between 1665 and 1668, and ten years later their descendants numbered 719, while the pigs multiplied so rapidly that in 1671 their numbers were sufficient to supply the needs of the colony.[15]

Crops were quite as important as livestock, and Talon did not forget them. Newly arrived immigrants were provided with wheat, barley and oat seed, and as they replaced the seed after their first harvest, a certain variety of crops was maintained. Flax and hemp were introduced, and by 1669 the women were spinning the fibres and weaving linen cloth. Two years later the colonists harvested enough flax to supply all the linen they needed, and soon they were manufacturing cordage for their vessels. From their wool they made cloth of several different weaves and textures, and they even spun hemp from thistle fibre. The Intendant thought tobacco would be a good crop for Canada, but the Court rejected this suggestion since it did not want to create competition with the West Indies.[16]

While he was implementing plans for agricultural expansion, Talon was also carrying out his ideas for starting small industries and manufactures. Since cowhide was plentiful, he established a tannery, and soon afterwards the country was supplying almost a third of its own shoes. There were six hatters in the colony, so he set them to work making hats. In order to stimulate the sale of grain and to reduce the large sums spent on wine and brandy, which amounted to more than 100,000 *livres* a year, he had a brewery built at his own expense. The King encouraged his project by giving him two beer vats, and the brewery produced two thousand kegs of beer a year for local consumption and two thousand for the West Indies. Talon also asked for "workmen and tools" to man and equip the "workshops" which he set up in the hope of establishing other manufactures in the colony. Many of these small industries prospered, and soon the Intendant could boast that Canada produced everything necessary "to clothe him from head to foot."[17]

With the approval of Colbert, plans were set on foot to exploit the inexhaustible wealth of the Canadian forests. Barrel staves and flooring boards were exported to the West Indies, and masts were sent to La Rochelle. Yet Talon had even bolder projects in mind. In November 1666 he set up a shipyard and had a keel laid down for a vessel of 120 tons. The next year a similar vessel was built to fill an order, and in 1669 three other ships made of "native wood" had been built and launched.[18]

Still another preoccupation of the tireless Intendant was the search for minerals, but the lead mine in Gaspé was disappointing, as were Quebec's coal mine and the deposits of iron pyrites. The copper of the Lake Superior country was so far away that its possibilities could not even be explored, so there remained only the iron mine at Three Rivers, and although it produced a good quality of iron, it could not be worked economically.[19]

Talon was more successful in his efforts to expand the fishing industry. In 1666 the Sieur Lespinay began to hunt seals and to extract seal oil. Fishermen were urged to take more cod from the St. Lawrence. In 1667 Talon bought the catch from nine boats, and, after using some of the fish to feed the troops, he exported the rest to the West Indies. He had plans for establishing fish-drying stations, and he also encouraged the exportation of salmon and eels.[20]

Talon could well congratulate himself on the success of so many ventures, but he realized that production was not in itself the key to prosperity. The country needed markets. France could only take masts, and perhaps hemp, but the Antilles offered a better outlet. One cargo was sent there in 1666, and in 1669 three ships were employed in the West Indian trade. From Canada they took salmon and eels, green and dried cod, peas, fish oil, lumber and even beer. They exchanged these products for sugar and tobacco, which they took to France, and they came back to Quebec laden with cargoes of linen and woollen cloth, wine and general merchandise for the everyday needs of the colonists.[21] The St. Lawrence route was long, however, and closed by ice for five months of the year, and to meet the need for a winter port Talon proposed a bold and far-sighted plan. He suggested that at the end of the war, which Holland and France were waging against England, France should stipulate as one of the terms of peace that Manhattan be restored to Holland, who would then cede the territory to her French allies. Canada would thus obtain a second outlet to the ocean and "would keep New England confined within its borders." Later Talon returned to the attack, and proposed that Manhattan be conquered by force of arms, since acquiring it was the best means of protecting the colony against the Indians as well as against the English.[22]

When, in 1668, the Treaty of Aix-la-Chapelle put an end to his dreams, the Intendant set to work to establish inland communication between Canada and an ocean port in Acadia by way of the Chaudière River and the St. John or the Penobscot. In 1671 he ordered Saint-Lusson to explore the possibilities of these routes, and when he had heard the explorer's report, he was hopeful that with relays it would be possible to go from Quebec to the Atlantic in a week, and to maintain communication with the mother country throughout the year.[23]

The small size of the population limited the development of Talon's new industries, and the fur trade continued to be the country's chief source of wealth. A year after restrictions were removed in 1666, 550,000 pounds of furs were delivered to the Company and resold in France. Talon, who was less concerned with the Company's profits than with the interests of the habitants, suggested that the trade should be put into the hands of "a company made up of inhabitants of the country," including himself. Colbert, however, rejected this proposal for two reasons: the limited financial resources of the colonists, and the steady decline in the price of furs over the last six years. It was difficult to answer this latter argument when the Company complained to the Sovereign Council that it was buying beaver pelts at ten *livres* a pound, and selling them at eight. In October 1668 the Council reduced the buying price to nine *livres*, but at the same time it besought the King most earnestly to grant the colony complete freedom of trade with the mother country. Thanks to the intervention of Talon, who had returned to France, this request was granted. The order, which was signed on April 13, 1669, was a major concession to the habitants, who were already free to trade with the Indians, and who could now send their furs directly to France and receive in return the articles and goods which they required. Consequently, all that remained of the Company's monopoly was its ownership of the land and the proceeds from taxes on beaver pelts and moose hides. In 1670 their profit from these sources was 70,000 *livres*.[24]

For some time now, perhaps since 1665, a change had been taking place in the fur trade. At first, the *coureurs de bois* had been nothing more than scouts, whose business it was to induce the Indians to bring their furs down to the French markets in Montreal and Three Rivers, but now they began trading either for themselves or for third parties. Disregarding completely civil and religious bans, they used liquor as an article of barter, and in the winter of 1667-1668 the abuse had become so flagrant that, even in the settlements, "drunk and disorderly" Indians were a common sight. The next step was taken when the *coureurs de bois* went farther into the forests and cut off the supply of furs near its source. In exchange for furs they offered brandy or very cheap wares, with the result that the Indian got very little for his bale of pelts, and the honest habitant was unable to get back the advance he had made to the trapper. In order to solve this problem the Sovereign Council renewed its injunction against the sale of liquor. At the same time (February 29, 1668) it placed certain restrictions on hunters; they were required to report to the senior official of the community each time they went into the forest, they could take with them no articles suitable for barter, and their supply of liquor was limited to one jar for each week's absence.[25]

When these new orders proved to be as ineffectual as the earlier ones, the authorities suddenly reversed the policy which had been in effect since 1663, and on November 10 (1668) the Sovereign Council made a fundamental change in the laws governing the liquor traffic. Talon was about to relinquish his post, but he was present at this important meeting together with his successor, Claude de Bouteroue, the Bishop and the Governor. While deploring the disorders caused by the sale of brandy, and condemning the "idle, disreputable libertines" who went into the forests and harvested most of the furs, the edict allowed the sale of liquor to the Indians within the limits of the settlements. The permission was represented as a means of bringing the natives into social and commercial relations with the most respectable people of the colony. It was provisional and subject to the King's pleasure. The law warned the Indians that they must not abuse the privilege granted to them. The penalty for drunkenness would be the pillory and a fine of two beaver skins, and any disorderly conduct would be punished with the full rigour of the law.[26]

Although it repudiated the existing civil and religious laws prohibiting the sale of alcohol, this decision was supported by almost all the councillors, and notably by Villeray, the great partisan of the Bishop and the Jesuits, who was also a churchwarden. Only the Bishop and the Sieur de Tilly refused to sign it. Moreover, the Bishop maintained his excommunication against traffickers in alcohol. The measure, with its futile appeal for moderation addressed to Indians who were incapable of moderate drinking, was undoubtedly the work of Talon, and it is hard to understand what a man who had three times approved the ban on selling alcohol hoped to gain by it. The law prohibiting the traffic had proved ineffective, and he may have thought that the worst excesses would be avoided if the sale of liquor was regulated. Or perhaps he thought that if they could buy alcohol at the settlements, more Indians would refuse the cheap prices of the *coureurs de bois* and would bring their furs down to the regular markets.

Whatever may have been the reasons for the Council's decision, its results were very soon apparent. Soldiers, workers and even habitants invaded the forests with liquor and goods for barter. To stem the flood the Council issued a new edict in June 1669 forbidding travel in the forests without an official licence. The following year Courcelles added an order intended to restrain the vendors of alcohol who were plying their trade well outside the limits of the settlements, all the way up to Calumet Island on the Ottawa. On his return from France in 1672, Talon himself issued an order forbidding unlicensed trading in the forests. He denounced such desertion from the colony as detrimental to the progress of agriculture and the establishment of families. This order of 1672 is the first document in which the activities of the *coureurs de bois* are condemned on economic and social grounds.[27]

At the end of Talon's first term of office, Louis XIV had good reason to express satisfaction with the manner in which his servant had carried out the mission entrusted to him. With the scanty means at his disposal, he had accomplished the magnificent task of peopling an empty colony and infusing it with economic life. However, in 1668 he asked the King's permission to return to France, pleading that he was worn out after three years of very hard work in a harsh climate. He also had other reasons for asking to be recalled. The relation between the Governor and the Intendant was a somewhat uneasy one. While in theory the Governor took precedence over the the Intendant he was now merely the commanding officer of a few companies of soldiers, while the powers of the King and his Minister were exercised through the Intendant. Courcelles chafed at being thus relegated to a secondary position, and his bitterness and jealousy made life difficult for his colleague. Talon's relations with the ecclesiastical powers were equally unhappy. A convinced Gallican, he had been charged by the King to temper the clerical domination in the colony. Having observed for himself that the direction exercised by the Jesuits tended "to extend beyond its natural limits," he did not maintain them on the level of authority which they had previously enjoyed. It is then not surprising to find him reporting that he was opposed by the Bishop and the Jesuits more often than he was approved.[28]

To continue the work begun by Talon, the King chose Claude de Bouteroue, a "learned, polite and gracious" gentleman, with Gallican inclinations. He was able to make himself loved and feared at the same time, and he had many other "good and admirable qualities." He proved, however, to be unequal to the active role which Canada demanded of its Intendant, and he preferred above all to administer the Sovereign Council in its juridical functions.[29]

Judging by his bitter complaints, one might have expected that M. de Courcelles would seize the opportunity to take an active part in the development of the colony, but he did not do so. However, in his own military domain, he made one essential contribution by creating the Canadian militia. The proposal for the establishment of such a force is contained in a letter from the King, so that we may accept the date of the letter (April 3, 1669) as that of the founding of the militia. Acting on the King's suggestion, the Governor formed the settlers into companies, with captains and non-commissioned officers. He instructed them to provide themselves with rifles, powder and shot, and to practise certain exercises so that they would be ready when called upon. Courcelles was essentially a soldier, and his qualities were those of the disciplined officer quick to make decisions in moments of crisis and firm in carrying them out. During the winter of 1669, three French settlers killed six Oneidas, seized their furs and escaped. In the spring, three soldiers, inspired by the same motive, killed a great Seneca chief. The Iroquois who were naturally angered by these murders, became restive, and the peace was seriously threatened. The Governor acted promptly, and went up to Montreal, where a large number of Indians, including some Senecas, had come to trade. The three soldier-murderers had been arrested, and on July 6 they were executed by a firing squad. The Indian witnesses of the execution were very much surprised since their custom was to give presents as compensation for murder, but such prompt and pitiless justice impressed them and dispelled any inclination they might have felt towards reprisals. Courcelles also performed at least one noteworthy act of civil administration when he excluded the intriguer, Villeray, from a new Council which he appointed. He disliked cabals, and Villeray was, he declared, far too prone to favour the proposals of the Jesuit missionaries.[30]

CHAPTER FIVE

ECONOMIC INNOVATIONS AND ORGANIZATION OF THE COLONY
1669 - 1672

Talon's second administration. Aids to settlement. The Indian situation. Garakontié and Courcelles. The Récollets return to Canada. Economics: agriculture, tar, potash, tanning. Exploration: La Salle and the Sulpicians. The French in the West. Hudson Bay. Des Groseilliers, Radisson and the Hudson's Bay Company. Land grants: the seigniorial régime. Talon's departure. Results of his work. Evangelization. Administrative organization.

After a very brief respite, Talon was to resume his labours. Convinced that no other man could replace him in the work he had begun, Louis XIV appointed him Intendant for a second term. He set out from La Rochelle on July 15, but his ship was forced by a storm to put in at Lisbon. A second departure was followed by shipwreck a few miles from shore, and this time Talon returned to Paris. He re-embarked in May 1670, and after a voyage of three months reached Quebec, where the Superior of the Jesuits reported that his safe arrival brought great joy to all.[1]

During his stay in France, Talon had been mindful that Canada's great need was for an increased population. The year before he had sent out 150 girls to be married and 239 other settlers. In the summer of 1670 the number of inhabitants was swelled by the addition of five companies of fifty soldiers each from the Carignan regiment and by 164 immigrants. In the following year there were 165 immigrants, and in 1672, 150. After that date the flow of emigrants from France was interrupted. France was at war with Holland, and since the King needed big armies, he decided that he could not also have big colonies. Hence, no assistance would be given to emigrants. But a remarkable achievement had already been realized. From 1665 to 1672 there settled in the country 2,608 immigrants, of whom 1,846 were settlers from France, and 762 were soldiers who took up land. There were also about 700 births a year.[2]

Talon also sought means to increase the number and the size of families. He obtained a royal order granting an allowance of 300 *livres* a year to fathers of ten children and 400 to fathers of twelve. Other provisions of the order were designed to encourage early marriage and child-bearing. Men who married before the age of twenty and girls who married before sixteen would receive a "King's gift" of twenty *livres* on their wedding day. When honours were being awarded or positions filled, preference was to be given to fathers of large families. It was even recommended that a fine be imposed on parents who did not arrange marriages for their sons and daughters when they reached the ages of twenty and sixteen respectively. The Sovereign Council passed a motion requiring bachelors who had worked out their contract as *engagés* to marry within a fortnight of the arrival of the ships bringing brides. Failure to comply entailed loss of the privileges of hunting, fishing and fur-trading.[3]

On his return to Canada, Talon had found the Indians in a restless and warlike mood. A band of Seneca hunters had attacked a Mascoutin village, killing some of its inhabitants and capturing others. The attackers in turn had been cut to pieces by Algonquin allies of the Mascoutins. War appeared imminent, but the Onondaga chief, Garakontié, intervened and succeeded in preventing further hostilities. He then persuaded several of the Iroquois tribes to send envoys with him to Quebec where, in July, they would find large numbers of Algonquins assembled for trade, and could hear a message from the French Ononthio. At the meetings which were held in Quebec nine Algonquin and Iroquois nations were represented, and the Governor gave solemn warning that any attack on France's Indian allies would be severely punished. At the same time the large gathering of Indians offered a unique opportunity for the authorities to show the esteem in which they held their friends, for it was during this visit that Garakontié was baptized. The cathedral was crowded with Indians for the impressive ceremony. With the Governor acting as godfather, Garakontié received baptism at the hands of the Bishop.[4] After the ceremony, the new convert was honoured by a salute of the fort's guns and was received by the Governor who also gave a great feast to all the Indians assembled.

Neither the Governor's blunt warning, nor his show of friendship succeeded in tempering the warlike spirit of the Senecas. Since their lands on the shores of Lake Ontario were protected from Montreal by the dangerous rapids of the St. Lawrence, they felt they could raid, without fear of reprisals, the beaver grounds of their neighbours who had declared themselves subjects of France. Talon offered to build two posts at his own expense, one on the north and the other on the south side of Lake Ontario, with a boat to maintain communication between them. These posts would remind the Iroquois of the force of French arms and would protect the Ottawa hunters who helped to supply the fur markets of Canada. The King, however, replied that Talon should consult with the Governor and the idea went no further. Then Courcelles decided to carry out his own plan to lead a scouting party up the St. Lawrence to Lake Ontario and to show the Senecas that their territory was no safer from invasion than the Mohawks'. On June 2 (1671) he left Montreal with fifty-six soldiers and volunteers, and the interpreter, Charles Le Moyne. At the Eel Fishery, he announced to the Iroquois that he had learned of their warlike intentions, and that, while this time he had come on a friendly mission, he could also come into their country to make war. Duly impressed by the seriousness of this threat, the Senecas abandoned their hostile designs, and Courcelles returned to Quebec well satisfied with the result of his expedition.[5]

Talon's second term of administration brought changes in the religious picture. In 1665 the King had recommended to the Intendant that he should maintain the superiority of the royal authority over that of the Church. In France the Intendant had reported to the Court that the Jesuits' direction sometimes troubled the consciences of their penitents, and about the same time, a memorandum from the Carignan regimental chaplain complained that the confessional was being used as a means of intervention in private affairs. Fénelon expressed very succinctly the King's own idea when he said that in his kingdom "the King, rather than the Pope, is head of the Church." So Louis XIV decided to offset the authority of the "principal ecclesiastics" in the country and to give the people a choice of confessors. The Récollets had been New France's first apostles and their Superior, Father Allard, gladly accepted the King's invitation to go to Quebec with four members of his community. The Bishop could not forget that Talon was responsible for removing the ban on the sale of alcohol.

As for the Jesuits, they were still bitter about the expropriation of Notre-Dame-des-Anges, a measure which had been imposed upon them by the Intendant. For these reasons the proposed return of the Récollets had "not been desired by the Bishop and the Jesuits," but they accepted it as gracefully as they could. There is doubtless a grain of irony in Talon's report that "the Récollets established a community in Quebec to the delight of clergy and laymen alike," but the Jesuit *Relation* for 1670 also notes that the arrival of the Récollet fathers in August brought "added joy and consolation" to the colony.[6]

As soon as he stepped ashore, Talon resumed his task of developing the country. His first target was the expansion of agriculture, and he urged the colonists unceasingly to increase and vary their crops. He set an example himself in his seigniory, Les Islets, on the St. Charles River, where he even planted hops. In recognition of his achievement, the King granted him the three villages Bourg-Royal, Bourg-la-Reine and Bourg-Talon, and conferred on him the title of Baron des Islets. Following the Intendant's example, the seigneurs applied themselves seriously to the cultivation of their land. In 1672 Captain de Laubia's seigniory on Lake St. Peter, and M. de Berthelot's on Ile Jésus both had harvests of three hundred pecks of fine wheat, and the colony exported ten thousand pecks of peas to the West Indies.[7]

The three ships engaged in the West Indian trade had been built in Canada, and in order to give further stimulus to shipbuilding Talon obtained from the King a bounty of four *livres* per ton. In 1672 the keel was laid down for a warship of four hundred tons capable of carrying thirty-eight guns.[7a] Tar was essential for shipbuilding, and Talon was responsible for experiments in the manufacture of tar and potash, both products of the forest and both useful as articles of export. Alix's tar works in Baie St. Paul, which opened in 1671, produced a small quantity of very good, but very expensive, tar. The earthquake of 1673 damaged the furnaces, and three years later the works ceased production. Follin's potash plant in Quebec, which was subsidized by the Intendant, produced an excellent quality of potash, but its production slowed down almost to a halt after the departure of its founder in 1674. However, another of Talon's enterprises met with complete success. Starting in 1671 with a grant of 3,000 *livres*, François Bissot developed a thriving tannery at Pointe-Lévis. He tanned deer, elk and cow hides, and he also cured seal and porpoise skins which were used for making muffs, jackets and waterproof shoes.[8]

The King and Colbert had been blind to the vision of a "great Kingdom" of Canada, but Talon was not alone in seeing it, and other enterprising private citizens realized as he did the importance of combining exploration with trading. In 1667, at the age of twenty-four years, Robert Cavelier de La Salle put aside his Jesuit's gown, and left Rouen to go and join his brother, a Sulpician priest, in Montreal. The Seminary made him a grant of land to the west of the town, just below the rapids, but he soon became interested in the great question of the day, the exploration of new territories and the extension of trade. He conceived the ambitious idea of discovering a way across the continent to the South Sea (The Pacific), and he became so preoccupied with the possibility of discovering the westerly route to China that his domain near Montreal came to be known as Lachine. His first voyage was made in company with the Sulpicians Dollier de Casson and Bréhan de Galinée who intended to extend their missions towards the west. On July 6, 1669, the Sulpicians with seven men and La Salle with fourteen left Montreal, and the groups travelled together as far as the western end of Lake Ontario where they separated. La Salle turned east again, and we next hear of him hunting on the Ottawa the spring of 1670. The Sulpicians spent the winter north of Lake Erie, and on March 23, 1670, they took possession of this territory in the name of the King of France. They then continued their journey by Lake St. Clair and Lake Huron as far as the Jesuit mission at Sault Ste. Marie, and from there returned to Montreal in June 1670.[8a]

La Salle's second journey was undertaken at the request of Talon and the Governor, to seek a river flowing into the Gulf of Mexico. The journey lasted two years, during which time the members of the expedition maintained themselves by hunting and trading. It is difficult to know with any certainty the regions through which La Salle travelled, but it seems certain that he did not reach the Ohio, and that he made no new discoveries.[9]

Daumont de Saint-Lusson was commissioned about the same time to carry out another expedition and it achieved more concrete results. Saint-Lusson's orders were to press on as far as possible towards the west in search of some river flowing in the direction of the South Sea, the highway to China. On the way he was to try to locate the copper mine which was reported to exist north of Lake Superior. He spent the winter near Lake Huron and reached Sault Ste. Marie the following May. With the help of four Jesuit fathers and the interpreter, Nicolas Perrot, who had great in-

fluence among the tribes west of Lake Superior, he assembled delegates from fourteen nations of the up-country. On June 14 (1671)
a cross and a post bearing the arms of France were erected outside
the Saulteux village, and in the name of the King Saint-Lusson
took possession of "all lands as far as the South Sea." A *Te Deum*
was sung, and the ceremony concluded in the evening with a bon-
fire.[10]

While he was thus encouraging exploration of the lands to
the south and west, Talon's thoughts were also turned to the
north. He shared the ambition of many Canadians to find an overland route to Hudson Bay. The need for French explorers to
reach that rich fur country was all the more urgent since the
Indians reported having seen ships in the Bay. In August 1671
Talon commissioned the young Canadian Saint-Simon and Father
Albanel to establish communication with Hudson Bay in order to
carry on trade in that region with the Indians. The explorers set
out from Quebec on October 25, 1671, and travelled up the Saguenay and through Lake St. John and Lake Mistassini. From there
they made their way by 800 leagues of waterways, constantly interrupted by falls and rapids, to the Rupert River and the shores of
James Bay which they reached on June 28, 1672. There they saw
English boats and English posts with "great piles of beaver pelts."
They established friendly relations with several nations to whom
the missionary preached the first elements of the Christian faith,
and they planted the arms of France in several places. Then, with
their mission accomplished, they set out on the return journey
and reached Tadoussac on August 1.

When he heard the story of this exploration, Talon considered
the possibility of establishing trade by way of Hudson Bay.[11] The
French, however, had arrived too late; the English were in possession and, by an ironic turn of fate, they owed this good fortune to the enterprise and intelligence of two *coureurs de bois,*
the brothers-in-law Des Groseilliers and Radisson from Three
Rivers. Des Groseilliers had come from France, and had worked
for years in the service of the Jesuits in the Huron country where
he had learned Indian languages and adapted himself to Indian
ways. Radisson was born in Three Rivers. He was ten years
younger than Des Groseilliers, and even captivity and torture at
the hands of the Iroquois had not quenched his thirst for adventure nor subdued his restless spirit.

The epic adventures of the two men had begun in 1659 when
they set out with a canoe laden with arms and other goods to

trade with the Indians to the west of Lake Superior. In the course of their dealings with the different tribes, they heard of rivers leading to Hudson Bay. In the summer of 1660 they brought down to Montreal a fleet of sixty canoes laden with 200,000 pounds of furs, a real godsend for the economy of the whole country. To their great indignation, the Trade Council levied the twenty-five per cent tax on their own pelts, and it was probably in order to avoid the payment of such tax in Quebec that they conceived the idea of transporting their furs from the West to Europe by the shorter Hudson Bay route. With this idea in mind, Des Groseilliers embarked for France where he first presented a plea for recovery of the tax which he had paid. When this petition was refused, he made a contract with a ship owner from La Rochelle to carry on trade by way of the Hudson Bay route. The partners were to meet at Percé in the spring of 1662, but the ship from La Rochelle did not appear.[12]

Disappointed in his attempt to find a backer for his scheme in France, Des Groseilliers went with Radisson to New England, and in Boston he found some merchants who were interested in the project, but in two successive years attempts to organize an expedition ended in failure. In 1665 the two adventurers accepted an offer from Colonel George Cartwright to sail to England.[13] There at last, they found substantial sponsors, but it was only in June 1668 that an expedition of two ships sailed for Hudson Bay. Only one of them, Des Groseillier's *Nonsuch,* under Captain Gillam, reached James Bay; Fort Charles was then erected on the Rupert River. The following year the *Nonsuch* returned to London with a cargo which brought in enormous profits. In the first glow of this success the Hudson's Bay Company was formed with the King's cousin, Prince Rupert, at its head, and on May 2, 1670 Charles II signed a charter granting the newly formed company a trade monopoly and ownership of the country. The two brothers-in-law were made partners, and they set out that same month to take over direction of the Fort Charles trade. From this vantage point, it was very easy to persuade the Indians to trade on the spot instead of taking their furs, as they had done until that time, to the French traders on Lake Superior.[14]

However, Des Groseilliers and Radisson did not maintain their harmonious relations with their English associates, and after quarrelling with them over a reduction in their salaries, they went to France in 1675. Colbert forgave them their desertion, but he gave no support to their schemes. Des Groseilliers returned to

Canada, while Radisson enlisted in the French Navy where he comported himself with distinction. In 1681 he returned to Canada, but his next venture into Hudson Bay did not take place until 1682. This time he and Des Groseilliers entered the service of the *Compagnie du Nord* which had just been established in Quebec under Aubert de La Chesnaye. The brothers-in-law took two ships into the Bay, and founded a post on the Nelson (Bourbon) River. In the course of the season, they carried on their normal trade and also captured two English ships with their cargoes of furs. When they arrived back in Quebec Governor La Barre restored one of the captured ships to its Boston captain and in December 1683 the partners went to France to seek support for their enterprise and compensation for the prize that had been confiscated. They were disappointed on both counts: Louis XIV, recognizing that England had a grievance, reprimanded Radisson instead of compensating him, and he ruled that the twenty-five per cent tax must be paid to Quebec for furs taken from Hudson Bay. That meant the loss of a quarter of their profits. Bitterly resentful, Radisson again allowed himself to be tempted by attractive offers from London. In May 1684 he left France secretly for England where he was appointed "superintendent and director" of the fur trade at a salary of 100 pounds sterling a year. Back once more on Hudson Bay, he surprised and kidnapped the French at Fort Bourbon, and carried them off, with their furs, to England. He remained in the service of the English Bay Company until his death in 1710.[15] With Des Groseilliers, he revealed the possibilities of the Hudson Bay route, and his initiative inspired the creation of the Hudson's Bay Company.

The defection of Radisson effectively ended Talon's dream of French operations in Hudson Bay, and the idea was not revived until years later. Talon would also have liked to send a French expedition to discover the Northwest Passage. He suggested the man to lead such an expedition, Captain Poulet of Dieppe, and the project was seriously considered in 1670 and again in 1671, but it was not carried out. However, one of Talon's plans for exploration was realized, though after his departure from Canada. It was at his suggestion that Frontenac was to send Louis Jolliet on an expedition to explore the Mississippi.[16]

As Talon's policy of agricultural expansion was being put into effect, it became apparent that certain changes in the system of land tenure were needed. Accordingly, the Intendant was called upon to execute a royal order designed to bring a greater proportion of the land under cultivation. The Company of New France had committed the error of ceding vast seigniories to favoured proprietors who often failed either to settle their holdings or to bring any large part of them under cultivation. As a result it sometimes happened that several leagues of territory were left without a single habitant. In March 1663 the King had empowered Mésy and Mgr. de Laval to revoke these grants, but since no cadastral survey existed, it was difficult to take action. Compilation of the necessary record indicating the limits of each holding and of the land under cultivation was begun under Talon's orders in 1667, but it was not completed until 1669. In 1672 Louis XIV issued a new order reducing by half domains which had been granted before 1662, and assigning the land thus recovered to new proprietors. Any land which, at the end of four years, remained unbroken, would be forfeit to the Crown. Talon first asked holders of 400 *arpents* to present a statement containing the names of their tenants, as well as the limits and extent of all cleared land. He then proceeded to carve new feudal grants out of the vast domain which had been repossessed by the Crown. In the name of the West India Company he granted in one month (October-November 1672) sixty seigniories along the St. Lawrence from l'Islet-du-Portage to Ile Perrot. These seigniories were limited to a reasonable size, generally one league square. A few were larger, but none exceeded two leagues square. A certain number of them which had been promised or assigned previously to officers or notable persons were already leased or in process of improvement by their owners.[17]

Terms of tenure, which had been somewhat vague, were now precisely defined. The following obligations were generally stipulated in the seigneur's title deed: to swear faith and homage to the Crown, to maintain a dwelling on his property, to preserve oak trees for naval construction, to report mines or minerals discovered, to reserve land for roads, and to obtain royal confirmation of the grant which carried with it judicial powers, high, middle or low, as the case might be.[18]

Tenants holding grants from seigneurs were obliged by contract to maintain a dwelling, and to preserve oak wood and reserve land for roads. Their rents were generally a *cens* of one *sou* for each *arpent* with frontage, and a *rente* of one *sou* for each *arpent* of the holding. It was also customary to add a fat capon, or twenty *sous*, or a half peck of wheat for each acre of frontage. Tenants were obliged to have their flour ground at the seigneur's mill, and to remit a fourteenth part of the flour in payment. They were required to work for the seigneur for three days a year at seeding and harvest time, or to pay a cash supplement. A tenant could sell his leasehold, but if he did so he paid his seigneur *lods et vente*, amounting to one twelfth of the sale price. Conditions of tenure varied slightly, but the seigneur could not alter the contract and the intendant, who was arbiter in any disputed case, was always inclined to favour the tenant. The tenant was certainly not exploited; for a holding of 120 *arpents*, free of all further charges, he paid about 173 *sous* a year.[18a]

In Quebec and Three Rivers lots for houses and other establishments were allotted successively by the Company of New France, the West India Company, and the King. Under Montmagny, the *cens et rentes* ranged from one *denier* (a twelfth of a *sou*) to half a *sou* a year. After 1665, under the intendants, rents increased, and were sometimes as high as five and half *sous*. In Montreal the Seminary of St. Sulpice, as seigneur, assigned lots at rents which made them accessible to all applicants.[19]

The seigniorial system in Canada was the natural descendant of the feudal régime as it existed in France in the seventeenth century. By that time it had lost its arbitrary features and been liberalized by the action of kings and of custom. Montmorency, as Viceroy, introduced seigniorial tenure in 1632 by his grant to Louis Hébert, the Company of New France continued it, and Talon systematized it in 1672. Under this system the Canadian colonist enjoyed much better social and economic conditions than the French peasant. His lease was a contract freely accepted, and if his rights were infringed upon he could count on the protection of the law, and probably the sympathy of the intendant. The régime did not in any way favour the seigneur who was required to lease his lands at very small rentals and to maintain roads and a community mill. On the other hand, it made a considerable contribution to the wellbeing of the tenant, to his independence, and even to his social advancement. It hastened land clearing, stimulated immigration, and helped the colony to expand. In each seigniory a church was built near the manor house and the mill. From the seigniory was born the parish which became the moral and economic foundation-stone of New France.

The two-year period which had been set for Talon's second administration was drawing to a close. Ill health had dogged him for six months of the year 1671. His relations with the Jesuits and the Governor continued to be strained. The Jesuits could not forget that it was the Intendant's report with its reference to their

monopoly of religious authority which had led Louis XIV to send
their rivals, the Récollets, to Quebec, and to support their rivals,
the Sulpicians, in Montreal. Courcelles, still resentful of the positive achievements of his colleague, kept putting obstacles in his way,
at the same time treating him "as a subordinate and almost as a
servant." This failure to work in harmony with the Intendant was
one of the reasons for the Governor's recall. Talon and Courcelles
embarked on the same ship in November 1672. The new Governor,
M. de Frontenac, had been installed in September, and had expressed his appreciation of the work accomplished by the departing
Intendant. Talon left behind him a country which he had guided
in its first steps towards the realization of his prophetic vision. The
regrets of the people went with him. Many of them had seen him
when "like a common father" he visited "from door to door" almost all the houses and cabins between Quebec and Montreal.
Even his adversaries, the Jesuits, were generous enough to admit
that they were losing in him Canada's most precious possession,
and to wish that he might come back to finish the work "which he
had begun for the great good of the country."[20]

Only one element in the community expressed no regret at his
departure: the merchants, who considered that he took too active a
part in business. Talon had been brought up in a society which did
not consider it improper for a public servant to engage in private
business, and in 1665 he made a profit of 10,000 *livres* on goods on
which he paid no duty. It was doubtless these transactions which
prompted Colbert's warning of the following year: "His Majesty is
quite persuaded that you did not go to Canada to exploit in your
own interest opportunities offered by your position." The Intendant answered that he had built a ship with his profits, and Colbert
congratulated him both on his shipbuilding achievement and on
the establishment of trade with the West Indies. With this encouragement from the Minister, Talon had a second and a third ship
built, the last in partnership with Courcelles. La Chesnaye probably spoke for all the merchants when he complained that the Intendant imported goods free of transportation, insurance and duty,
and then formed a company which snatched all the business. A further complaint was that Talon made a fine show of promoting
exploration and searching for copper mines when, in reality, he
was engaged in trading, and that these so-called explorers were sub-
servient to him since he granted all the trading licences. Talon
himself admitted that he had warehouses in Canada, and that Saint-
Lusson took presents from him to the Indians, and brought back

beaver pelts which defrayed the cost of the expedition.[21] It would seem that Talon's commercial activities were almost indispensable in a new colony with few resources and with very little capital. Certainly they helped to bring about a remarkably rapid economic expansion. They also received Colbert's seal of approval, and history's judgment should be no more severe than that made by a contemporary who was also a wise colony-builder.

In 1672, at the end of Talon's administration, the domain of New France stretched from Labrador to Lake Superior and the valley of the Ohio. The inhabited portion of that vast territory lay along the two shores of the St. Lawrence from Cap Tourmente to Ile Perrot. The population, swelled by subsidized immigration and soldier settlement, had reached about 6,500.[22]

Quebec, the little capital, counted with its suburbs about a thousand inhabitants, and was very proud of its buildings: the Château St. Louis, the residence of the Governor, the Bishop's palace and the seminary. About fifteen priests were attached to the seminary from which they were sent out to charges in parishes or seigniories. Six Récollets occupied their original house on the St. Charles River. In the Jesuit college twenty fathers and brothers taught about a hundred children, and in the *petit séminaire,* which was founded in 1668, young French boys and a few young Hurons received instruction from the Jesuits. Eighteen Ursuline nuns devoted themselves to the education, both practical and intellectual, of French girls and three or four Indians, while about twenty Hospital Sisters took care of the sick and poor. Mgr. de Laval had established a school at Cap Tourmente, about fifteen miles from Quebec, where boys were trained in agriculture and in trades. Three Rivers had perhaps 150 inhabitants, and its stockade protected a church, the local governor's residence and about forty houses. It was still an important fur market, and it had become the centre of a wheat-growing district. Montreal, which had a population of about five hundred, had become the principal fur market of the colony. Eight or ten Sulpician priests ministered to the religious needs of the inhabitants of Montreal and the neighbouring country. The boys went to the Abbé Souart's school, and the girls were taught by Sisters of the Congregation of Notre-Dame.[23]

Missionary work had been intensified and extended. The Jesuits had missions in the settlements, at Tadoussac, Sillery, Sainte-Foy, Cap-de-la-Madeleine and La Prairie. Since the conclusion of peace with the Iroquois, they had built a chapel for each of the Five Nations, and they also had missions far in the west, at Sault

Ste. Marie, Michilimackinac and Green Bay. The Sulpicians, too, had been engaged in the work of evangelization, and in 1663 had won over to the Christian faith a village of Cayugas at Quinte (Kingston). Christianity made only slow progress, however, since the Indians refused to abandon their superstitions or to adopt the Christian rule of marriage. Baptism was conferred in most cases on children and on the sick. "Meagre results," comments Father de Rochemonteix, "for superhuman efforts." Yet the missionaries continued to sow the seed in the hope of a future harvest.[24]

The administration of the colony was simple, in accordance with its needs. In Quebec there were a governor, an intendant, a Sovereign Council, a senechal's court and a provost's court; in Three Rivers and Montreal, local governors and courts of justice. The colony also maintained four companies of soldiers. The budget was increased in the course of these years by the intendant's salary, a raise in the governor's salary, gifts to Mgr. de Laval for church needs, to the Récollets and to various individuals, but the receipts of the Public Treasury remained at 36,000 *livres,* paid by the West India Company. This sum represented a part of the receipts from the Tadoussac fur trade and from the taxes on moose and beaver skins. It had been fixed in 1666 at a figure considerably below the total profits from these traditional sources of public funds, and below the amount required to meet expenses. It remained unchanged even when the budget increased, and the deficit was made up by the Royal Treasury. The average annual cost of administration was between 60,000 and 70,000 *livres,* of which the King paid 25,000 or 30,000 *livres.*[25]

There was a supplementary tax of ten per cent on imports of "dry" goods which, in October 1670, was replaced by levies of ten *livres* a cask on wine, twenty-five *livres* a keg on brandy and five *sous* a pound on tobacco. Since this revenue, which continued to be called "the ten per cent," was reserved to pay off the debt of the former Community of Habitants, it could not appear in the table of annual receipts.[25a]

Beside the ordinary budget, it is important to note some of the extraordinary expenditures for the defence and colonization of the country. Expenses for twenty-four companies of soldiers engaged in the Iroquois war were 234,000 *livres.* The construction of forts on the Richelieu cost 15,000 *livres,* to which must be added 15,900 for the campaigns of Tracy and Courcelles. Costs of transport for colonists and animals were 55,810 *livres* in 1665, 41,700 in 1667 and 36,000 in 1668. Statistics are not available for the whole period, but these figures show that in the space of four years, from 1665 to 1668, the King's expenditures for the benefit of his colony amounted to at least 398,410 *livres*.[26]

It was Canada's misfortune that in 1672 Louis XIV, obsessed by the vision of himself as "Sun King," left Colbert's plans only half realized. Talon found himself deprived of the resources upon which his work depended, and this sudden failure of royal subsidies must have influenced his decision to return to France. He had not finished his task, but the work which he had accomplished remained solid, fruitful, and remarkably broad in its scope. He had found New France a struggling colony whose only resources were the beaver trade and a few fields of wheat. He left a new France. The country had doubled its population; it could supply all its own needs in food and clothing; it was beginning to develop industries and shipbuilding, and it had established a triangular trade with the West Indies and the mother country. Talon had established a free and prompt system of justice, and he had reformed the seigniorial system for the benefit of the people. Louis XIV had been blind to his vision of a "kingdom" in Canada, but it was thanks to Talon himself that his dream of a great country would one day be realized. His departure was deeply regretted even by his enemies.

When he arrived in France, Talon was honoured by a long audience with the King, during which they discussed the Canadian situation. The following year he was appointed to the honorary post of "first valet of the royal wardrobe," and two years later he became secretary to the King's cabinet. At the same time he was made Comte d'Orsainville. He was frequently consulted by Colbert on Canadian affairs, and in 1681 he thought of founding a general hospital in Quebec. Since the suggestion evoked no enthusiasm among the Bishop's following who feared that Talon might be sent out as governor, it was allowed to drop. Jean Talon died in 1694; he has remained in history as the Great Intendant, the founder, after Champlain, of New France.[27]

CHAPTER SIX

FRONTENAC IN QUEBEC. JOLLIET ON THE MISSISSIPPI POLITICAL REORGANIZATION
1672-1675

Frontenac governs without an intendant. Convocation of the different orders. The Governor makes police regulations, creates échevins, observes the conduct of the Jesuits. Fur trade and English competition. Erection of Fort Frontenac. Repression of illicit hunting. Frontenac-Fénelon-Perrot quarrel. Jolliet explores the Mississippi. The West India Company abolished. Re-establishment of the office of intendant. Reorganization of the Sovereign Council. Mgr. de Laval, titular Bishop of Quebec. Penalties imposed on coureurs de bois.

Louis de Buade Frontenac, Knight and Count of Palluau, who was chosen to succeed Courcelles, was a godson of Louis XIII and the protégé of Gaston d'Orléans, the uncle of Louis XIV. He was related through his mother to the influential Phélypeaux family, and he had married one of the "divinities" of the age, Anne de la Grange-Trianon. Madame de Frontenac did not accompany her husband to Canada, but, as a member of the Court circle she was in a position to advance her husband's interests and to defend him when the need arose. Frontenac had served with distinction in several campaigns, and had been wounded at the battle of Orbitello. According to Saint-Simon, "he was very intelligent, very much the fashionable gentleman, and completely penniless." It was partly to escape the pressing demands of his creditors that he asked, through the offices of friends, to be appointed to an obscure post in a distant colony. Energetic and imperious to the point of violence, infatuated with his position, unhampered by scruples, very much given to ostentation and endowed with a gift for the written and spoken word, such, at fifty years of age, was the man whom the Sovereign Council installed on September 12, 1672, as

Governor and Lieutenant-General of Canada, Acadia, Newfoundland and other countries in North America.[1]

Frontenac, like Talon, fell in love at first sight with the country, which was "much less wild" than he had anticipated, and with the "magnificent" situation of Quebec. Again like Talon, he came armed with royal instructions: to maintain the progress of the colony, not to allow the Jesuits "to carry ecclesiastical authority beyond its proper limits" and "to counterbalance their influence" by supporting the Sulpicians and the Récollets. He was to use these directives as guides in his future conduct.[2]

Strong in the authority conferred upon him by his commission, the new governor lost no time in demonstrating his dignity and his power. On October 23 he convoked the "three orders" of the colony in the new Jesuit church in Quebec. He actually recognized four orders: the clergy; judges; the nobility, composed of four gentlemen and four officers; and the third estate, represented by a group of bourgeois and notable persons of the town led by the syndic. Speaking before almost a thousand persons, the Governor delivered an exhortation on the duty of obedience which they owed the King, after which he made each order swear a special oath of fidelity. The meeting was simply an occasion for ceremonial pageantry with no political significance whatever, and yet it evoked a warning from Colbert who, in a letter dated June 13, 1673, advised that the Governor should "only rarely, and still better, never" call the whole body of the country together in this way. He later added the suggestion that the office of syndic be abolished, for "the syndic . . . presents requests in the name of all the inhabitants, whereas it is desirable that each man speak for himself, and that no one person speak for all."[3]

The King did not appoint a successor to Talon, thinking perhaps that he could be reappointed if his health improved after a stay in France.[3a] In this situation Frontenac considered himself to be sole head of the administration, both civil and military. He forgot that in the absence of an intendant the Sovereign Council recovered its political powers. He forgot, too, that his instructions were simply to preside at meetings, although he had the right to remonstrate and to prevent any deviation of the Council from its functions. Interpreting this right as giving him complete direction of the Council and filled with the idea of his supreme power, Frontenac promulgated a series of orders for the administration of the town of Quebec. These very elaborate and practical regula-

tions were published on March 23, 1673. They dealt with public
markets, taverns, cleanliness in streets and houses, fire prevention
and the suppression of disorder. They also provided for the election of three *échevins,* one of whom would be an administrative
judge who, every six months, was to hold a meeting open to all the
inhabitants. The purpose of these meetings was to consider means
of expanding agriculture and commerce, and to fix prices of merchandise. This second innovation, like the first, met with royal
disapproval; Colbert wrote to remind the Governor that internal
administration was not his office, and that police cases were the
business, not of the *échevins,* but of the local judge. He pointed
out that, in issuing these orders, Frontenac had exceeded his powers, and he enjoined him to respect the royal will in future. However, as the King did not wish to subject the Governor to the
humiliation of overt reproof, he did not revoke the order. As a
result of Colbert's advice the syndic's function was discontinued.
The last syndic held office in Montreal in 1674, although *échevins*
are mentioned in Quebec in 1677 and 1678.[4]

In other directions, Frontenac was seriously hampered by lack
of funds. In 1672 Louis XIV was at war with Holland, and since
he had a fleet of one hundred ships to maintain, as well as an army
of more than two hundred thousand men, he decided not to spend
any money for Canada, and he did not even send the *engagés*
that Frontenac had asked for. He did, however, send out sixty
young women emigrants, among them five "ladies." They arrived
on September 3, and all except two were married before November 13.[5] The following year Frontenac proposed a change in
the membership of the Council to ensure greater expedition in
affairs of justice. Acting with the West India Company, he petitioned the King to increase the number of councillors. The request
was granted, and two new members were appointed, the first to receive royal commissions.[6] Frontenac also endeavoured to stimulate
small industries: a new process for extracting potash gave excellent
results; shipbuilding and the West Indies trade continued to
prosper. For his own benefit, Frontenac exported flour, peas and
lumber to the Islands and he even considered buying a ship for the
trade. Courcelles had begun to organize the militia, and this work
was carried on by the establishment of commands in parishes
where none existed.[7]

Natural arrogance and a sense of the importance of his position convinced Frontenac that no sphere of activity lay outside his
jurisdiction. The King's instructions to safeguard the independ-

ence of the civil administration and to foster the assimilation of the natives supplied a pretext for close supervision of the clergy, and especially the Jesuits. Scarcely two months after taking office, he expressed astonishment that the Indians of Notre-Dame-de-Foy, only one league from Quebec, were not learning French and were still leading their errant life. Speaking of men who went out cheerfully to face the possibility of martyrdom in the mission fields, he had the temerity to revive the old slander that the missionaries were "more interested in converting beaver than souls." He also accused the Jesuits of making the confessional a means of meddling in intimate family affairs, and he protested when, in a sermon dealing with the refusal of absolution to vendors of alcohol, a Jesuit declared that "it was beyond the powers of the temporal arm to change what was ordered by the spiritual authority." Frontenac even required that missionaries obtain travel permits directly from him. When he even opened letters which were on their way from the Jesuit fathers to France, the King signified clearly that he had gone too far. In a letter of April 1675, Louis XIV cautioned Frontenac to "use restraint and tact in his dealings with members of the clergy." Specifically, he was to leave them free to come and go anywhere in Canada without a passport; their correspondence was not to be censored; and they were to be summoned before the Governor only for essential reasons. The letter was a private one, but once again it constituted a sharp reproof of the autocratic methods of the Governor.[8]

From the moment of his arrival, Frontenac had been concerned with the protection of the fur market. For the most part the furs were brought down by the Hurons and Ottawas acting as middlemen for the Indians on Lake Superior and Lake Michigan: the Sioux, Folles-Avoines, Miamis and Illinois. But this region was also the source from which the Iroquois from the Lake Ontario country obtained the furs which they traded to the English in New York and Albany. These English buyers urged the Iroquois to establish a meeting place with the Ottawas on the north shore of Lake Ontario, so that all the trade would be diverted to New York and Albany. As a result the Iroquois responded by sending frequent missions to convert the Ottawas to this idea, and some Iroquois chiefs probably listened sympathetically to English hints that they should break their treaty with the French.[9]

To obviate this very real danger, Courcelles and Talon had considered establishing a post at the entrance to Lake Ontario. Frontenac, for his part, had very soon discovered from the example of the Governor of Montreal, François Marie Perrot, that the fur trade was an excellent source of private revenue. Perrot had married a niece of Talon, and had used this relationship to maintain a very profitable trading post. His agent, Brucy, stationed on Perrot's island above Montreal, intercepted the furs as they came down from the West. Frontenac considered that a post at the eastern end of Lake Ontario would allow him to forestall the English traders, and at the same time it would protect the Sulpician mission at Quinte. He particularly wanted to cut off furs on their way to Albany, and he may perhaps have thought that obliging middlemen would make it possible for him to derive some personal profit from the post.[10]

There was probably something of all these motives behind the plan which Frontenac carried out in the summer of 1673, without waiting for Colbert's approval. On July 12, with a fleet of canoes and flat boats carrying four hundred men recruited by conscription, he arrived at the mouth of the Cataraqui River on the north shore of Lake Ontario where Kingston now stands. On the next day the men set to work. La Salle, whom Frontenac had adopted as his adviser, had gone ahead to invite the Five Nations to come to Cataraqui, and they had accepted the invitation. Accordingly, while his men were busy erecting the fort, the Governor appeared with forty guards in uniform and granted an audience to sixty representatives of the Iroquois tribes. He explained to them that his object in building the fort was to safeguard the peace, and to establish a post in their country to which they could bring furs for barter. During Frontenac's stay, Indians from north and south of the lake met and fraternized. He gave them many presents, but he won them over still more by his manner of easy familiarity. He even invited the chiefs to his own table, and the result of this tactful wooing was that they all assured him of their loyalty and desire for peace.

When the Governor returned to Montreal, he left behind at Cataraqui a fort consisting of a warehouse and two other buildings protected by a palisade. Soon, land was broken and sown, and the post was stocked with cows, pigs and chickens, and the following spring articles were laid in for trade.The greater part of the expense was met, in cash or credit, by Frontenac. Moreover, he applied to Colbert for permission to form a company to exploit the trading-post. He had already chosen his partners, the merchant Le Ber and the West India Company's agent, Charles Bazire, and presumably his share of the profits would help to repair his damaged fortunes.[11]

Frontenac had inherited from his predecessors the problem of the *coureurs de bois,* and a letter from the King on this subject, dated June 5, 1672, had reached him very soon after his arrival. Louis XIV pointed out that this great "abuse" was retarding "the progress of the colony and the cultivation of its lands." The illicit fur trade had a great attraction for certain workers freed from their contracts and anxious to escape from the hard work of tilling the soil, and indeed from any sort of discipline. They were attracted to the life of the woods by quick profits, the lure of adventure, and freedom from moral restraint. The King, particularly anxious to stop this drain on the strength of the colony, directed Frontenac to forbid all trading except by licence signed by the hand of the Governor, and to require all workers, except those under contract, to marry and settle down. Frontenac responded promptly to this directive, and just two weeks after his arrival he issued an edict prohibiting unlicensed hunting and trading. Outfitting *coureurs de bois* was also declared an offence. The penalty for outfitting was a fine and confiscation, those for illicit trading were flogging for the first offense and the galleys for the second. *Coureurs* already in the woods were required to return to the colony, and those failing to comply would be punished by flogging and branding. This order was followed a year later (June 5, 1673) by a still more rigorous measure of repression, when it was forbidden on pain of death, to remain more than twenty-four hours in the forest without express permission from the Governor.[12]

Coureurs de bois, however, continued to defy orders and threats of ever-increasing severity, and to live outside the settlements. When they were forced by the necessities of their trade to return to civilization, they were protected "openly and secretly" by the connivance of people of all classes who benefited from the contraband trade. Towards the end of 1672 the Governor admitted that their number was increasing, and that the boldest among them had begun to take their beaver to the English. Montreal was their supply centre, and Governor Perrot employed them so openly for his own profit that in 1673 Frontenac had to remind him of his duty to carry out the King's orders.[13]

Late in the autumn of 1673, Judge d'Ailleboust of Montreal sent a police sergeant to arrest two *coureurs de bois,* but their host, M. de Carion, allowed them to escape. Irritated at such insubordination, Frontenac despatched Lieutenant Bizard to arrest Carion. Bizard carried out the arrest, but without first informing Governor Perrot, as the rule required in such cases. It was only after the arrest had been made that Bizard delivered Frontenac's letter to the Governor of Montreal. Infuriated by this violation of discipline, Perrot threw the letter in Bizard's face and had him arrested, but released him the next day. Frontenac in his turn was outraged when he heard what had happened, and he summoned Perrot to Quebec to give an account of his conduct. At the same time he wrote to the Abbé Fénelon of the Montreal Seminary to say that he hoped to settle the matter quietly. Perrot went to Quebec in answer to the Governor's summons, and the Abbé Fénelon accompanied him, but when, on January 29, Perrot presented himself at the Château St. Louis, Bizard arrested him, and held him prisoner. The following day the affair was brought before the Sovereign Council, where it remained bogged down for months in legal formalities arising from the contestations and objections of Perrot, who was completely exasperated by his continued detention.[14]

The Frontenac-Fénelon quarrel was an offshoot of this controversy. Embittered by the failure of his mediation in favour of Perrot, the Abbé Fénelon had gone back to Montreal, and on Easter Sunday he preached a sermon full of thinly-veiled allusions to the Governor's conduct in general, and in this specific case. He held up as an example of the good administrator the one who reconciles adversaries, who does not make his subordinates feel the weight of his authority and who does not dabble in trade. La Salle heard the sermon, and gave a summary of it to the Governor, who, infuriated at this public attack, summoned Fénelon to appear before the Sovereign Council. Fénelon came to the meeting of August 21, but refused to accept the Council's jurisdiction and declared that he recognized only the authority of the Church. The Vicar-General then intervened, and several Sulpicians were questioned but the Council was obviously biased against them. Frontenac too addressed the Sulpicians in incredibly violent language. He even went so far as to drive the Abbé d'Urfé out of his presence, brandishing his stick at him as he did so.[15]

Finally, on September 6, 1674, the Council ordered that the cases of Perrot and the Abbé Fénelon should be referred to the King, and in accordance with an order from Frontenac, Perrot and Fénelon embarked for France at the end of November. The whole affair was wound up the following year by a letter from the King which issued reproof and penalties without giving satisfaction to anyone concerned in the quarrel. The Sieur Perrot, who had been guilty of violating royal authority in the person of the Governor, had already been condemned to three weeks imprisonment in the Bastille. However, his ten-month detention in the Château St. Louis was pronounced to be "somewhat too rigorous a punishment" for his misdemeanour, and it was declared that he would be reinstated in his post after apologizing to Frontenac. The King expressed disapproval of the Abbé Fénelon's conduct and forbade his return to Canada. Finally, it was brought to Frontenac's attention that he must not have orders carried out in the jurisdiction of local governors without notifying them, and that, in the case of the Abbé Fénelon, he should either have referred the matter to the ecclesiastical authorities, or sent him to France.[16]

The eventful year of 1674 saw the return to Quebec of Louis Jolliet, the first Canadian-born explorer. Jolliet had studied at the Jesuit College, and had been engaged for some years in the fur trade. At the age of twenty-eight he was very familiar with the region around the Great Lakes, and he could speak some of the Indian languages. Commissioned by Talon and Frontenac to discover the Pacific Ocean by way of the Mississippi, he reached the mission of St. Ignace at Michilimackinac, north of Lake Michigan, on December 8, 1672. There Father Marquette, a missionary from the station, joined the group as an interpreter. On May 17, 1673, the party of five men in two canoes followed the shores of Lake Michigan and Green Bay, and went up the Fox River. Two Miami guides led them across a portage, and they continued their voyage down the Wisconsin. On June 17 they entered a broad river flowing towards the south; Jolliet knew that he had discovered the Mississippi. He proceeded cautiously down the mighty river, marvelling at the beauty of the country spread out on either side. Great forests alternated with vast plains where herds of buffalo pastured, while overhead flew Canada geese and wild turkeys. Sixty leagues down the river from the mouth of the Wisconsin, Jolliet landed with his party at an Illinois village whose inhabitants gave them a friendly welcome. He then continued on past the south of the Missouri to an Arkansas village at 33° north latitude, and here the Indians told him that he was only a few days journey from the sea. Jolliet knew this sea could be none other than the Gulf of Mexico, but, as he had achieved his object and did not wish to risk a possibly dangerous encounter with the Spaniards, he turned northwards again on July 27. He spent the winter at Sault Ste. Marie and did not arrive in Quebec until July 1674. He had almost completed his return journey when misfortune overtook him. His canoe was swamped in the Lachine rapids, and he lost his maps and his diary. However, Frontenac was delighted to hear the story of his travels, and wrote to Colbert that Jolliet had dis-

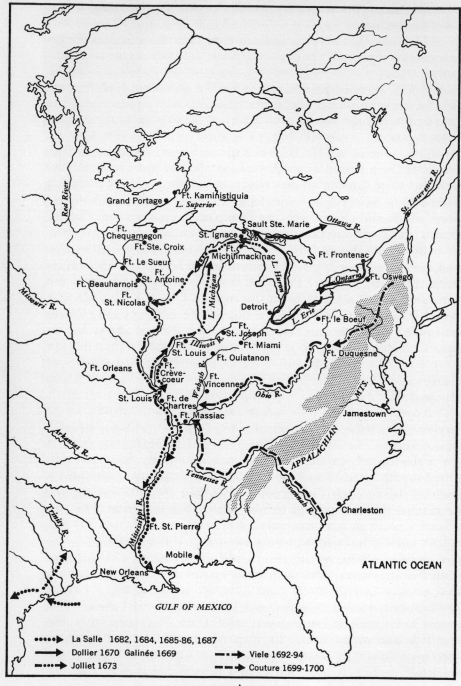

EXPLORERS' ROUTES

covered "marvellous country which opened up the route to the Gulf of Mexico."[17]

The year 1674 also brought another radical change in the political organization of Canada. The West India Company was staggering under a debt of 3,000,000 *livres,* and in December 1674, Louis XIV revoked its charter. Thus, "Canada or New France, Acadia, Newfoundland and other islands" once more reverted to the Crown. For the second time Canada, ceasing to be the property of a trading company, became a royal province. On May 24, 1675, the King leased all the rights of the former company to Jean Oudiette for a period of seven years at 350,000 *livres* a year. This lease included Canada on the condition that Oudiette should pay a fixed sum to meet public expenses as the West India Company had done. He would also inherit the Company's rights to the Tadoussac fur trade and the taxes on moose and beaver skins. Moreover, he would have the exclusive right to sell beaver pelts in France, and since the debt of the Community of Habitants had finally been amortized, Louis XIV ruled that the proceeds from the ten per cent tax on alcohol and tobacco would also belong to him. Three days later, Oudiette's lease was transferred to Quebec's great financier, Aubert de La Chesnaye, for 119,000 *livres* a year and an annual present of twelve beaver hats. These agreements left the people of the country free to trade on condition that they deliver their skins to La Chesnaye who bought them at four *livres,* ten *sous* a pound.[18]

Another change in the administration may be attributed directly to Frontenac's imperious temper. Colbert had been especially shocked by the Frontenac-Fénelon episode, the more so since the Abbé d'Urfé, who had suffered such rough treatment, was now allied to him by marriage. He concluded that the powers and functions of the autocratic governor would have to be restricted, and he carried out this reform in two simultaneous moves. The first was to appoint an intendant to take over the regular duties of that office: justice, internal administration and finance. This left the Governor in charge of the army and Indian affairs, with supreme power in case of crisis or major emergency. Louis XIV filled the new post of intendant on June 5, 1675, by appointing Jacques Duchesneau, a royal commissioner in the district of Tours, whose career so far had not been remarkable. As an administrator he was legalistic and methodical, rather than imaginative, and he had a secret ambition to attain a position of authority, honour and wealth.[19]

Colbert's second move took the form of a royal declaration, also dated June 5, which reaffirmed the political powers of the Sovereign Council, and thus limited those of the governor, and in which Louis XIV defined, once and for all, the membership of the Council. It was to be composed of the governor, the bishop (or, in his absence, the vicar-general), the intendant, seven councillors, an attorney-general and registrar. Previously, the councillors had been appointed by the governor and the bishop; henceforth the King would make these appointments himself. Although he occupied third place, after the governor and the bishop, the intendant would preside at Council meetings, invite the expression of opinions, take votes and pronounce decisions. A royal order had abolished the provost's court in Quebec in 1674, and the Council now became a court of first instance, as it had been before 1664. This arrangement lasted until 1667 when the provost's court was re-established and the office of police provost was created to facilitate speedy punishment of crimes.[20]

Mgr. de Laval, who had spent four years in France, arrived at Quebec in September with the new intendant. Until this time Mgr. de Laval, whose position had been that of Vicar-General with the title of Bishop of Petrea, had fought obstinately to have a see created in Quebec, for he felt that as Vicar Apostolic he could not sufficiently support the "ecclesiastical power" in its struggle with the political arm. He also had to resist the Court's intention, which was to keep the Church in Canada an integral part of the Church in France, by making the prelate of Quebec a suffragan of the Archbishop of Rouen. Clement X refused to allow this, and the King finally gave way. A papal bull of October 1, 1674, created the first French see in America under the direct jurisdiction of Rome. Clad in a new dignity, Mgr. de Laval returned to his diocese more determined than ever to uphold the rights of the Church and to hasten the evangelization of the natives.[21]

Meanwhile, Frontenac was keeping up the fight against the illicit beaver trade in which Perrot was the chief offender. In Montreal the interim governor, La Naudière, arrested Carion and Perrot's agent, Brucy, who were both fined in court. Previously, a *coureur de bois,* Jean Thomas, had been hanged in Quebec in June, and a second one, Guillaume Yvelin, was banished from Montreal for two years.[22] This merciless application of the royal order of 1673 finally brought results, and more than thirty forest outlaws came in to civilization and gave themselves up to the authorities. Frontenac offered every incentive to them, and to all the young men of the colony, to settle down on the land. An order of the Sovereign Council, dated April 22, 1675, decreed that no one could engage in the fur trade who did not possess a farm on which he maintained a dwelling. Thus Frontenac tried to ensure that unattached single men who might be tempted by the free life of the forest should first know the counter-attractions of hearth and home.[23]

CHAPTER SEVEN

FUR TRADE AND AGRICULTURE
LA SALLE ON THE MISSISSIPPI
1676-1682

Assembly to consider sale of liquor to the Indians. Royal amnesty for illicit traders. Number of licences fixed at twenty-five. Frontenac-Duchesneau quarrel on chairmanship of Council. Hostilities among Indian tribes. Seigniories granted. Seigneurs' difficulties. Success of farmers. Economic stagnation. Recall of Frontenac and Duchesneau. La Salle explores the Mississippi. Attempt to reach the Mississippi by sea. Failure and death of the explorer.

The severe decrees had resulted in a lull in the illicit fur traffic, but it was of short duration. Even as he issued prohibitions, Frontenac made his need for maintaining contact with the western tribes a pretext for issuing trade permits, and in Montreal Perrot violated the law by giving licences to his own henchmen. The result was a renewed rush of *engagés* and *coureurs de bois* into the interior. When these abuses were reported to him in April 1676, the King addressed a special order forbidding governors-general and local governors (in this instance Frontenac and Perrot) to deliver any trading permits. Colbert specifically instructed Frontenac to abstain from participation in the trade either in his own name, or through his servants or other persons. Expert at shuffling royal orders, Frontenac issued no trading licences, but he continued to grant hunting permits until this, too, was expressly forbidden in 1678.[1]

One constant ingredient in the unrest caused by contraband trading was the liquor question, and it flared up once more at this time. During the absence of Mgr. de Laval, the Jesuits had maintained his order of excommunication against vendors of alcohol. However, when the habitants protested that the sale had been

authorized by a Council decision of 1668, Frontenac supported their
stand and republished the order in question.[2] On his return, the
Bishop was deeply distressed at the legal revival of a practice so
harmful to the work of evangelization. The following year, when it
became apparent that the Governor was inflexible, the Bishop sent
the Abbé Dudouyt to Paris to plead that the King abolish the traffic.
Colbert granted an audience to the Abbé Dudouyt, but after consulting Talon and Bouteroue, he concluded that the allegations
were greatly exaggerated. Interpreting the royal will, he declared
that the episcopal authority should refrain from taking any action
"outside the Church, in a matter concerning police administration." On the other hand, the theologians of the Sorbonne ruled
that in the Canadian situation the Bishop possessed the right to
declare selling of alcohol a "reserved case" in which he alone was
competent to grant absolution. The dispute became more general
and more heated. Duchesneau supported the clergy; Colbert replied that the Intendant had produced no evidence to justify his
allegations against the Governor; Frontenac denounced the Jesuits,
wrongly, as the instigators of the extreme measures taken by the
Bishop. Finally, in order that he might be exactly informed as to
the extent of the problem, Louis XIV ordered that a meeting of
twenty of the most important inhabitants of the colony be held to
discuss and to report to him on the matter.[3]

A joint meeting of this committee of twenty and the Sovereign Council was held at the Château St. Louis on October 26,
1678, with all members of the Council present except Mgr. de Laval. The committee had been chosen to represent the different elements in the colony: officers, seigneurs, merchants and farmers. It
recommended, by a vote of fifteen to five, the maintenance of the
right to sell liquor and the repeal of the ruling on the "reserved
case." The majority affirmed that the reports of disorders were
exaggerated, and that the sale of brandy was a necessary evil since
it was the only means of preventing the natives from bartering their
furs for English rum. The minority believed that prohibition would
result in a higher moral standard among the Indians, and would
benefit agriculture by reducing the number of *coureurs de bois*.
There was doubtless some special pleading on both sides, but it
seems clear that the repeal of prohibition in 1668 was an error on
the part of Talon, and that in this matter practical wisdom should
have made common cause with Christian morality and its spokesman, Mgr. de Laval.[4]

After reading the report of the meeting, Louis XIV submitted the case to the Archbishop of Paris and to his own confessor, Father La Chaise. The two clerics consulted Mgr. de Laval, who had gone to France to present the arguments of the minority. They then proposed that the King forbid the sale of liquor in Indian territory, and that Mgr. de Laval limit his "reserved case" to the infraction of this new prohibition. In accordance with this recommendation, a royal edict of May 24, 1679, forbade holders of hunting licences (which the Governor could now issue) to take brandy into Indian territory. The decision was a half-victory for Mgr. de Laval, since it prevented the scandal of liquor sales in mission areas, but it confirmed the legality of sales in the settlements. Nothing more was heard of the "reserved case," and in 1682 Mgr. de Laval wrote that the disorders caused by the sale of brandy had practically disappeared.[5]

The illicit traffic in furs, however, went on unabated. Deterrents and penalties counted for nothing in comparison with the attractions: big profits, adventure, freedom from moral restraint. There was hardly a family which was not involved in the trade in one way or another. A whole network of beneficiaries and backers, at every level of the social scale, supplied and protected the *coureurs de bois*. Not only did the merchants' provost not arrest them, he was in collusion with them. In October 1679 Duchesneau wrote that "most of the members of the Sovereign Council and men occupying other judicial offices . . . took part in the trade." Some lawbreakers simply took their furs directly to Albany, where they received twice the Canadian price for them. Others had storehouses at La Prairie and employed the Indians from the mission as middlemen. The volume of illicit trade by way of Chambly and the Richelieu had reached such proportions that Frontenac had to establish a station on the route to check the movements of travellers.[6]

Another result of these paradoxical conditions, and a very serious one, was that they aggravated the friction between the imperious Governor and the ambitious Intendant. In November 1679 Duchesneau accused Frontenac of protecting *coureurs de bois,* and named one such protégé, Pierre Moreau, alias La Taupine. He added that Du Lhut, who traded with the Ottawas and the Sioux, worked under the Governor's orders and shared his profits with him. He neglected to say that that very year Du Lhut had negotiated a peace between these two warring tribes and had taken possession of their country in the name of the King of France. In reply to these accusations, Frontenac declared that he would have got rid of the *coureurs de bois* very quickly if they had not been favoured by

Duchesneau. It was the business of the Intendant to bring law-breakers to justice, but he either dismissed the charges against them or limited their penalties to nominal fines, while he himself was engaged in the fur trade in partnership with Provost Comporté, two merchants, Le Ber and Le Moyne, and the great financier Aubert de La Chesnaye. All these charges and counter-charges were transmitted to Colbert who replied, speaking for the King, that Frontenac had not established the basis of his allegations against the Intendant, whereas the evidence that the Governor favoured the *coureurs de bois* appeared very strong.[7]

In the summer of 1680, still in connection with violations of the fur-trading laws, two Council members, La Martinière and d'Auteuil, were commissioned to investigate a case in Montreal. Their report brought to light a number of violations and led to the discovery of stocks of furs in the seigniories of Champlain and d'Autray. Some *coureurs de bois* were arrested, and in April 1681, about ten Montreal burghers were summoned before the Sovereign Council, but the Council, in league with the Intendant, was careful not to penalize the more influential offenders. A few obscure law-breakers were fined, and in July the Council sent a report on the important cases to France and asked to be instructed as to "His Majesty's will."[8]

However, it proved that no answer to this specific request was necessary. In August 1681 three royal decisions, suggested by Duchesneau, arrived in Quebec. They had been prompted by the request of several notable persons desirous of making peace with the law. Thus letters patent declared a complete amnesty for all those who had been guilty of illicit trading. At the same time a royal edict renewed the order against unlicensed trading in Indian country, and specified the penalties for infraction: flogging and branding for the first offence, the galleys for life for the second. A further order stipulated that licences for trading in the far parts of the country were to be granted each year by the governor and countersigned by the intendant. In any one year, licences could be issued for twenty-five canoes, each manned by three men.[9]

These twenty-five permits, or *congés,* were regarded as a means of helping individuals or religious foundations that were in need, and were distributed by the Governor to noblemen, retired officers, officers' widows, public servants or religious institutions. Normally the permits were not used by their original holders, but were sold at prices ranging from 700 to 1,800 *livres.* Each *congé* covered one canoe with three men and trading goods, and on its return journey each canoe could bring sixty bales of beaver pelts worth 150 *livres* apiece. Under Governor La Barre, who took it upon himself to double the number of permits, buyers sometimes sent out two or three canoes for one *congé*. His successor, Denonville, re-established the limit of one canoe but later the number was increased to two. According to La Hontan, money invested in a *congé* brought in 700 per cent interest, while the canoemen received about 1,800 *livres* for an engagement of one or two years.[10]

The two objectives of this new system were to legalize and regulate the fur trade among the numerous tribes, to bring the Indians into the settlements to trade, and to reduce the number of *coureurs de bois*. The number of these outlaws never reached Duchesneau's figure of eight hundred, nor Patoulet's five hundred. Even the lesser of these figures would have represented half the male population between the ages of twenty and fifty. Taking as a basis of calculation Frontenac's estimate of about forty in 1674, one may arrive at a total of two or three hundred. Even three hundred would represent a quarter of the same adult male group, a serious drain on the population, equally harmful to the economic and agricultural expansion of the colony. Although the royal amnesty brought a large number of *coureurs de bois* back into the settlements, it could not wipe them out altogether because the profits of the trade were too high, and the attractions of the life too strong. Between 1681 and 1684, the authorities had again to forbid illegal trade with the Indians and the English. Under La Barre the number of infractions diminished considerably, but only because he issued a very large number of *congés,* and under Denonville the Iroquois war made trading impossible. Many *coureurs de bois* entered the service of licence-holders, and about 1690 those whose occupation was thus regularized came to be known by the more respectable name of *voyageurs*. However, the number of impenitent contrabanders was still large enough to worry the authorities, and on May 23, 1696, a royal order again fixed the galleys as the statutory penalty for violation of the law.[11]

The illicit fur trade was not the only cause of friction between Duchesneau and the Governor. Frontenac's proud temper chafed at the very existence of an officer who exercised an independent authority in a domain more extensive than his own. To make matters worse, Duchesneau had the support, not only of the Council, but of the Bishop and the Jesuits, to whom Frontenac's Gallican ideas were antipathetic. The Governor had at first assumed his customary autocratic attitude in his relations with his colleague, but the Court had promptly reminded him that in civil matters his duty was simply to second the efforts of the Intendant. As for Duchesneau, confident in the strength of his supporters, he also overstepped his authority, and he in turn was called sharply to order by Colbert. Frontenac had behaved indiscreetly, wrote the Minister, but the Intendant's indiscretions had been still more flagrant, and it was sheer madness on his part to set himself up as the Governor's equal.[12]

The great quarrel between the Governor and the Intendant exploded over a question of protocol, for this was an age when questions of protocol were of enormous importance, whether they concerned stools in the Louvre or churchwardens' benches in Quebec. This time the point at issue was the heading of the Council minutes for February 20, 1679. Frontenac insisted that he should be designated "Head and President of the Council," while Duchesneau would appear as "also fulfilling the function of President." However, in the edict of 1675, which confirmed the Council in its functions, Frontenac was given the title "Governor and Lieutenant-General," while the Intendant was designated "President of the said Council." Frontenac, however, refused to concede the point, and for six months he fought Duchesneau and the Council. He became so angry, when opposed by Villeray, Tilly and the Prosecutor d'Auteuil, that he banished these three men to the country, where they were to await an order to leave for France. That episode took place during the meeting of July 4 (1679), and on October 16 Frontenac and Duchesneau accepted the Council's proposal that in future no names should appear in the heading of the minutes. The King dealt with the matter in a letter dated April 29, 1680. Frontenac was reprimanded sharply for claiming the title of Head and President, and also for expelling the three councillors; such presumptuous conduct would have provoked his recall, if friends had not intervened and vouched for his good conduct in the future. Louis XIV added that several letters had brought the Governor's misuse of authority to his attention; these complaints came from private individuals, the Jesuit fathers and members of the Council. The King, however, refrained from humiliating the Governor for the benefit of the Intendant, and he stipulated that the latter was not to take the title of President of the Council either, but simply to exercise the functions of chairman.[13]

While this battle of protocol was in progress, Quebec had more serious cause for worry in the movements of the Five Nations, who seemed ready to make trouble in the West as well as in the East. Early in 1679, as one step in his plan of discovery, La Salle had erected a trading-post at Niagara in a region which the Iroquois claimed as their hunting-ground. The following spring Governor Andros of New York urged the Indians to resist this violation of their territory and to break off relations with Quebec. In the autumn of 1680, in spite of the courageous intervention of La Salle's lieutenant Tonty, the Iroquois of the upper lakes burned an Illinois village, and in September 1681 a Seneca chief, Ammenhat, was killed by a Kiskakon in Illinois country. As the Illinois were allies of the French, Frontenac called upon the good offices of the missionaries, who intervened in an effort to halt the progress of the vendetta, but the Senecas refused to parley. Early in the summer of 1682 some Iroquois youths raided a French storehouse near Fort Frontenac.[14]

In August, when the Miamis, Hurons and Kiskakons gathered in Montreal for the fur fair, the situation looked very threatening. However, the Kiskakons had already sent belts to the Senecas to compensate for the murder of Ammenhat, and Frontenac persuaded them not to make war outside their own territory. At the same time he took precautions in case any trouble should arise in the colony. Militia units were inspected, provisions were stored, and sites for redoubts were marked out in the vicinity of Montreal. This firm attitude made a deep impression on the Senecas who sent a delegation, under Teganisorens, to Montreal. Their envoys were received with great ceremony, and loaded with presents, after which they promised to refrain from attacking the Kiskakons. Although the Iroquois promised not to take up the war hatchet against New France, the situation remained very unstable. There was good reason to suppose that they were merely temporizing, and that, with a fur monopoly with the English as their ultimate objective, they wanted to destroy the Indian allies of the French before attacking the colony itself.[15]

In contrast with the fur trade and exploration, colonization and economic development made very little progress, for the King had maintained his refusal of 1672 to "give any help to Canada." In spite of Frontenac's plea the following year for "labourers and workers of every sort," immigration ceased almost completely. The only additions to the population from outside the country were a few *engagés*, whom the ships were obliged to bring from France, and a few discharged soldiers. For any real growth in population, the colony had to rely on its high birth rate. Fortunately, early marriages were the general rule, and they frequently resulted in families of eight, ten or twelve children. In the healthful climate of Canada, with the number of births consistently higher than the number of deaths, the population increased from 6,705 in 1673 to 10,251 in 1683.[16]

Frontenac encouraged this expansion in population by generous gifts of land. To officers and other persons of substance who applied to him he granted seigniories where young married couples and *engagés,* who had worked out their contract, could find suitable farms. From May to September 1674 he gave title to seventeen seigniories, and from October 1676 to September 1679, acting with the Intendant, he granted twenty-six. The land was for the most part virgin forest, and not every seigneur became rich and successful. Those who were ill-adapted to a life of hard work just struggled along. Some, like Tilly and his sons, and even his daughters, put their own hands to the plough. Some felt the need of supplementary means of earning a livelihood. Hertel and Varennes engaged in the fur trade themselves, or sent their sons out to trade; others applied for commissions in the army or posts in the public service. Nonetheless, seigniories whose proprietors had some experience in business or agriculture made most encouraging progress. Montreal, under the Seminary of St. Sulpice, and the Island of Orleans under François Berthelot, doubled their population and their profits. Beauport and Beaupré, which had the advantage of a situation near Quebec were equally prosperous and the wise Pierre Boucher's seignory at Boucherville was well settled and productive.[17]

On the whole, clearing was going ahead well, partly because the sons of settled colonists had to establish themselves on new holdings. They succeeded because they already had the necessary experience. It was an arduous life, demanding hard, constant labour, for the trees had to be cut down before the little house could be built and the first seeds sown among the stumps; but hard work brought rapid rewards from the land. Soon the farmers "were living very decently, and were incomparably better off than what we call good peasants in France." Even the less prosperous tenant harvested enough wheat to feed his family, and had a few cows and some poultry, as well as quantites of vegetables. The farmers paid no *taille,* no salt tax and very modest tithes, if any; they were free to hunt and fish, and game and fish were plentiful. In a word, they were "rich" according to the standard of the time. In 1681 about 7,000 farmers, with 24,000 *arpents* under crops, owned 94 horses,

291 cows, 572 sheep, and 6,657 oxen which they used for ploughing and as draught animals. In ten years the land under cultivation and the livestock had more than doubled.[18]

The most essential trades had their supply of skilled and semi-
skilled workers: 56 carpenters, 30 masons, 24 cabinet-makers, 26
shoemakers, 17 tool-makers, and even 34 tailors. All these artisans
did a flourishing business, but, on the other hand, Talon's small
industries, shipbuilding, tar-making, rope-making, had practically
disappeared for want of royal encouragement, workmen and markets. Canada's potash was of poor quality and soon lost its market.
Only Bissot's tannery in Pointe Lévis continued to flourish.
A very small export trade just managed to keep alive; two or three
times a year modest cargoes left Quebec for the West Indies. Fortunately, the fur trade, still the colony's principal economic re-
source, made some progress, increasing from 61,000 pounds of
skins in 1675, to 90,000 pounds in 1685.[19]

The Court, which was directly responsible for this unhappy
situation, vented its displeasure on Frontenac and Duchesneau
who, although frequently admonished to work in harmony, quarrelled incessantly. Once again reproof was administered from Versailles. Frontenac was reproached for being presumptuous, exces-
sively autocratic, too ready to seek pretexts for evading the execution of royal orders, prone to double-dealing in matters concerning the fur trade. Duchesneau was reprimanded with equal severity: he had tried to make himself the Governor's equal, had exceeded his powers, and in several matters had abetted the Bishop's
resistance to royal directives. Both were warned that they would be
replaced if they did not mend their ways, and as these warnings
proved ineffectual, the King finally made good his threat. Both
Frontenac and Duchesneau, recalled by an order of May 7, 1682,[20]
embarked for France in the autumn of the same year.[21]

Louis XIV had every reason to take disciplinary measures
against his servants. Frontenac had gone beyond all permissible
limits in his arrogance, his lack of respect for the truth, and his
devotion to his own interests. Duchesneau had been blindly partisan and foolishly pretentious, and he had also evaded his judicial
duty. However, after observing the situation on the spot, the new
governor, La Barre, concluded that there was also a third culprit,
and he wrote to the King that Church and State must share the responsibility for the quarrels between the Governor and the Intendant.

At the end of Frontenac's term of duty, one important item

must be entered on the credit side of his account: his very effective support of La Salle's projects of exploration. The two men had understood one another at once, and Frontenac's imagination had caught fire at La Salle's glowing recital of the benefits to be derived from an exploration of the Ohio and the Mississippi, to wit, extension of the fur trade, expansion of the colony and discovery of the Gulf of Mexico. The Governor recommended the project to Colbert, and presented its author as a very intelligent man, with all the qualities required for the leader of any such exploration. La Salle also took the precaution of offering a generous gift to the Director of Trade, Bellinzani. This double move proved effective and an order of May 13, 1675, granted La Salle a patent of nobility and ownership of Fort Frontenac with the right to make grants in his turn, and the duty to induce Indians to settle there. La Salle received financial backing for this trading enterprise from members of his family, and from other partners, including Frontenac. He was, therefore, able to transform the original outpost into a real fort, flanked by bastions, and to build and stock a trading-post. For most of the associates in the venture, Cataraqui was a trading station; for Frontenac it was also a political outpost guarding the western traffic against inroads from the Iroquois and the English; for La Salle it was a base for exploration. Stubborn, taciturn, unwearying in his efforts, the explorer never for a moment lost sight of his goal, the discovery of a river leading to the sea. An Iroquois village had grown up at Cataraqui, and by 1677 La Salle had gathered there a group of forty-eight French soldiers, artisans, and farmers, with two Récollet priests. The fur trade and agriculture were to supply him with food and funds, and he was ready to establish relays on his route of exploration.[22]

The Prince de Conti and Frontenac continued to press his case in Paris, and in May 1678 letters patent authorized La Salle to pursue "the discovery of the western part of New France." In February of the following year, still trading to keep himself solvent, and with the help of his faithful lieutenant Tonty, he built Fort Conti at the entrance to the Niagara River. Above the falls he built a sixty-ton vessel, and equipped it with sails. The *Griffon*, the first sailing ship on the Great Lakes, set out on August 7, 1679, with twenty-seven men on a maiden voyage which took it through Lakes Erie and Huron and into Lake Michigan. From there La Salle sent the *Griffon* back with a cargo of furs to Niagara, expecting that it would return with fresh supplies. In September he built the little fort of St. Joseph on the Miami River, and, in January 1680 Fort CrèveCœur (Peoria) on the Illinois River. In February, since the *Griffon* had not returned, La Salle set out to walk to Niagara on snowshoes, a distance of about five hundred leagues. He reached Niagara on April 21, only to learn that the *Griffon* had been wrecked near Manitoulin Island, and that a ship bringing him men and merchandise from France had been lost near Percé. Refusing to admit defeat, he set out again from Fort Frontenac in August with a new crew. In December he reached Crèveœur, but he found that Tonty had run out of supplies and evacuated the fort. The expedition continued on as far as the Mississippi, which some of the men suggested they should follow down to the sea, but La Salle was unwilling to abandon his faithful lieutenant, and they returned to Michilimackinac in May 1681. There they found Tonty. Both Tonty and La Salle then returned to Niagara whence La Salle repaired to Montreal to recruit men and to replenish his funds.[23]

Early in the autumn of 1681 the determined explorer set out again and on December 12 the expedition left Fort St. Joseph. Under their leadership, La Salle and Tonty had a party composed of twenty-three Frenchmen, eighteen Abenakis and Mohicans, with ten squaws and three children. As the rivers were frozen, the travellers pulled their boats and provisions on sledges. At Crèveœur they were able to put their boats into the water, and thus, on February 6, they reached the Mississippi. In the Arkansas country they stopped to hunt and to build Fort Prud'homme. The Arkansas and Taensa Indians greeted them in friendly fashion, and they continued down the river to the delta, and on to the sea. After three years, during which La Salle had met every difficulty with indomitable courage, he now tasted the joy of complete success. The riddle was solved: the Mississippi emptied into the Gulf of Mexico. La Salle erected a post bearing the arms of France, and under a cross he buried a lead plate on which the following words were engraved: "In the name of Louis XIV, King of France and of Navarre, April 9, 1682." The little group sang the *Te Deum*, and three rifle shots were fired. With this simple ceremony La Salle took possession of the valley of the Mississippi, and celebrated the birth of Louisiana.[24]

As the explorers set out on their homeward journey, their provisions had run so low that they were reduced to a daily ration of one handful of corn, but they obtained fresh supplies on the way north from the Coroas and the Taensas. La Salle spent the following months trading in order to meet the expenses of the expedi-

tion, and in December he built Fort St. Louis, at the confluence
of the Illinois and the Teatiki rivers, to protect the Illinois and the
Miamis against Iroquois aggression. Meanwhile, in Canada, his
creditors had become alarmed at his long absence and had seized
his furs and other possessions. Governor La Barre, prejudiced by
reports from his rivals, had ordered the seizure of Fort Frontenac
and Fort St. Louis, and when La Salle finally returned to Quebec
his pleas for their restitution fell on deaf ears. Rebuffed in Canada,
La Salle embarked in November 1683 for France, where he received a much kinder reception. The King took him under his
"special protection," and in April 1684 instructed La Barre to
restore his property to him.[25]

Completely won over by the explorer's enthusiasm, and by the
vision of a new colony named in his honour, Louis XIV gave his
approval to a plan for an expedition by sea to the mouth of the Mississippi. In July 1684 a fleet was ready, and in January 1685, La
Salle disembarked with three hundred companions, many of them
adventurers, at Matagorda (St. Bernard's Bay), unfortunately three
hundred leagues west of the mouth of the Mississippi. There followed two years of incredible hardship and misfortune, during
which La Salle built two posts and attempted to find his way overland to the Mississippi. Having failed in his attempt to reach the
mouth of the river, he decided to head for the Illinois villages, living by hunting and fishing.

His resources were diminishing, and the country and the natives were inhospitable. The men were becoming more and more
restive as success seemed farther away than ever. The leader's
somewhat arrogant self-confidence had been an essential ingredient
in his earlier achievements, but in the presence of disaffection and
failure his harsh and tyrannical conduct provoked the mortal hatred of some of his companions. In an ambush on March 19, 1687,
La Salle was shot by two of his own men, Duhaut and Liotot. Soon
after, the assassins were themselves murdered by members of the
party who had remained faithful to their leader. After this trag-
edy, the other members of the expedition scattered. Some joined
the Natchez, and others were massacred by the Clemcoets. Five of
La Salle's men, including his brother Cavelier, Father Anastase
Douay, and his lieutenant, Henri Joutel, succeeded in reaching
Quebec where they embarked for France without revealing the
death of their leader.[26]

Thus ended the life of one of Canada's most remarkable explorers. La Salle was, in the words of Tonty, "one of the great men

of the age, a fine mind, capable of undertaking any kind of discovery." A man of inexhaustible energy and unconquerable will, he conceived the idea of a continent-wide state. Unfortunately for him he was also a man of imperious character, uncompromising in his relations with his equals and a tyrant towards his subordinates. Pre-eminent among his peers, he lacked only moderation in judgment and maturity in command.

CHAPTER EIGHT

THE UNHAPPY ADMINISTRATION OF LA BARRE
1682-1684

A great fire in Quebec. Project of war against the Indians. The Governor's interest in the fur trade. French canoes robbed by the Iroquois. Expedition against the Senecas. Irresolution and incompetence of La Barre. Distress at Camp La Famine. A humiliating peace. Indignation of the western tribes. Versailles's displeasure with La Barre. Tithes and cures. La Barre recalled.

A new governor, Joseph-Antoine Lefebvre, Sieur de La Barre, disembarked in Quebec at the end of September 1682, after a voyage of seventy-eight days. He was sixty years of age, and he was the first governor to bring his wife and children to Canada with him. La Barre had served in the *Parlement* of Paris, and occupied several posts as intendant. In every case, according to Colbert's report, he had displayed utter incompetence and had provoked the hatred of the people by his completely unrestrained conduct. In 1663, although quite unfitted "to command other men," he had been commissioned as a naval captain, and when later he was promoted to the rank of lieutenant-general and took part in a few naval engagements, he showed himself to be equally incapable as a sailor and as a fighter. It was this nonentity whom the King commissioned on May 1, 1682, as Governor of New France.[1]

A new intendant arrived soon after the Governor. He was Jacques de Meulles, Grand Bailiff of Orléans, a man with a mind open to new ideas and capable of adapting such ideas to existing conditions. He came bearing a plan of expansion for the colony drawn up by the Court, but he found Quebec stunned by a catastrophe which would delay its realization. A fire in the Lower Town had destroyed fifty-five houses and the principal shops with all their stock. The Intendant's first task then was to repair the damage, a task in which he was helped by generous gifts of money

85

from a large number of the townspeople, including the rich financier, La Chesnaye.[2]

The new Governor also found himself faced with a difficult situation: the colony was in danger of being drawn into war as a result of Iroquois attacks on the Illinois allies of the French. Before taking any action in the matter, La Barre called together twenty prominent citizens, including Mgr. de Laval, three Jesuits, the Sulpician Abbé Dollier, Le Moyne, Boucher and Du Lhut. They brought out the facts that the English, in order to protect their fur trade (worth 600,000 *livres*), were inciting the Five Nations to take up the war hatchet against Quebec, and that the Iroquois were planning first to ensure themselves against any flank attack by breaking the strength of the tribes allied with the French, and then to attack the colony itself. The only course of action open to the Governor was to ask Versailles for reinforcements of troops and settlers, and to organize a preventive expedition.[3] Colbert's son, Seignelay, who had now become Minister of Marine with responsibility for colonial administration, answered Canada's cry of distress with three companies of marines of fifty men each, but they did not reach Quebec until November 7, too late to undertake a campaign that year.[4]

La Barre had sworn that he would not engage in any sort of business transactions, but unfortunately, he allowed himself to be tempted by the profits to be made in the fur trade. After forbidding all trade in the forests and with the English, except with his special permission, he himself formed a partnership with two important merchants, La Chesnaye and Le Ber, and ceded Fort Frontenac to his partners, who then sent beaver skins from the fort to the English. In the spring of 1683, La Barre pronounced against La Salle, and sent his henchman, the Sieur de Baugy, with thirty canoes laden with trading goods to take command of Fort St. Louis on the Illinois. At the same time he sent the shrewd interpreter, Nicolas Perrot, on a trading and peace-making mission to Lake Michigan. Perrot succeeded in re-establishing peace among the tribes, and founded the post of St. Nicolas at the confluence of the Wisconsin and the Mississippi. He thus assured to New France the friendship of the Sioux and the other tribes in that region.[5] In the North, Du Lhut, who was also commissioned and equipped by the Governor, had founded the posts of Kaministiquia (Fort William) and La Tourette (Nipigon). He made it his mission to persuade the Indians to acknowledge French sovereignty, and to bring their furs to the French post at Sault Ste. Marie rather than to the English on Hudson Bay. He did not hesitate to take strong measures in order to impose his authority, and when two French traders were killed and robbed by Saulteux Indians, the murderers were executed, by his order, before an assembly of four hundred natives. Impressed by this bold gesture, the Indians made no move either to retaliate or to disturb the peace.[6]

La Barre's activities, both official and unofficial, lead one to suppose that he was hesitant when faced with the necessity of choosing between peace and war. In answer to the report that five hundred Iroquois warriors were marching against Michilimackinac from the south, he sent reinforcements to the post, but on August 14, 1683, he also received envoys from the Five Nations. He loaded them with gifts, and demanded that they conclude a general peace with the Algonquins, the Ottawas and the Hurons. The Iroquois answered simply that they would send ambassadors in the spring, but this promise kept negotiations open. Meanwhile, "in order to favour his own little group," La Barre signed licences beyond the normal twenty-five, and authorized a group of fourteen associates to send trading parties to the Illinois. This transaction had at least the outer semblance of legality, but more than sixty colonists, working from Forts Frontenac and Chambly, were engaged in specifically illict trade with Orange and Manhattan. The English even came to Montreal to buy furs.

The population, like the Governor, was undecided as to the necessity or advisability of opening hostilities against the Iroquois. The merchants were in favour of peace, as were the Jesuits living among the Iroquois. On the other hand, de Meulles and Fathers Frémin and Dablon in Quebec, and the missionaries of Sault Ste. Marie and the West, thought that war was inevitable.[7] The situation seemed, however, to have reached a somewhat less critical point when suddenly war broke out. It came as the result of a blunder committed by the Governor, who was apparently attempting at the same time to favour his own trading partners and to stamp out contraband trade. It appears that La Barre entrusted to his envoy Le Moyne a most extraordinary message for the Iroquois. They were to be permitted to challenge French canoes, and to attack and rob any which could not produce official licences. A sample licence was sent to them, so they could recognize those which would be presented by the traders. It would be hard to imagine any more dangerous expedient than this one invented by La Barre which entrusted the policing of canoes to illiterate natives, and exposed all traders, whether authorized or not, to the attacks of

Indians always hungry for booty. The inevitable, of course, happened. On March 8, 1684, a band of Senecas robbed seven canoes bound for Fort St. Louis with 16,000 pounds of articles for barter. When the protesting crews showed their licences, the Indians refused to recognize them. "Don't you know," they said, "that M. Le Moyne told us to pillage any Frenchmen we found in this country and, if they resisted, to kill them?" Ironically enough, the trading supplies which had been seized by the Senecas were, according to the Abbé de Belmont, the Governor's own investment. The raiding party then joined an army of two hundred warriors, and on March 31 the combined forces advanced to attack Fort St. Louis. Under the double command of Tonty and Baugy, the fort withstood a siege of six days, at the end of which the attackers withdrew, hotly pursued by bands of Illinois.[8]

Now that the interests of his own company were threatened, the Governor decided to launch a military expedition even in defiance of Court instructions to avoid war. He reached this decision, moreover, without asking advice either of officers or of leading citizens. De Meulles reported to Seignelay that, "to the great surprise of the Bishop, the Jesuits and all the most respected elements in the country," the Governor consulted only one person, his own partner, La Chesnaye. It was at once alleged that war was going to be fought "to save the beaver trade of five or six merchants of the Lower Town" who had two hundred canoes out and who were afraid of being plundered by the Iroquois. At the beginning of May La Barre sent orders to his representatives in the West, Du Lhut, La Durantaye and Nicolas Perrot, to recruit warriors from the tribes in their region, and to bring them to Niagara in preparation for the campaign. The Jesuits in the Iroquois missions, on the other hand, made every effort to prevent hostilities. Father Bruyas wrote that "it was not right to precipitate a war" for the General's pelts, and Father Jacques de Lamberville affirmed that the Five Nations would be willing to accept an agreement if the offer was accompanied by presents "which the Iroquois seldom resist." The Seneca chief, Teganisorens, did come to Quebec in June to negotiate, but the Governor took him prisoner instead of listening to him. To this first diplomatic blunder La Barre added a second when, on June 15, he wrote to Governor Thomas Dongan of New York, informing him that he proposed to attack the Iroquois and asking him not to sell them arms or munitions. This ridiculous mission to neighbours whose greatest desire was to destroy the French fur trade had perhaps one virtue in the eyes of the Governor: the messengers could take beaver pelts to New York and bring back English goods.[9]

The Intendant assembled the necessary canoes, and on July 29 an army of seven hundred French and three hundred Indians started up the St. Lawrence from Montreal. An auxiliary corps of two hundred French and four hundred Indians came from the West to join the main force at Fort Frontenac. On August 19, the Governor established a camp at Famine Creek on Salmon River north of Oswego, very close to the Seneca villages. He remained there inactive, however, incapable of making a decision in spite of the proud words he had written to the King's Minister: "We shall perish or destroy the Iroquois." Supplies ran low, and in the marshy terrain troops lost their vigour or fell really ill. Meanwhile, in the midst of the campaign, La Barre sent a boat and canoes to barter at Niagara. Obviously the merchant in him was stronger than the soldier.[10]

After weeks of inactivity, the Governor finally sent Le Moyne to the Onondagas to propose a resumption of peace negotiations. However, a certain Sieur Arnaud had just planted the English arms in an Onondaga village. The Iroquois, intensely irritated by this gesture, declared that neither the English nor the French were "their masters." However, while in the case of the Senecas Father Lamberville's peace efforts remained abortive, the other tribes sent delegates to Camp Famine on September 3. In the course of the parleys, the Indians' spokesman, Haaskouan (Big Mouth), who had at once observed the weakened state of the French army, presented the Iroquois demands with an assurance bordering on insolence. After negotiating for several days, La Barre was obliged to submit to humiliating terms. He promised to withdraw his soldiers, and he agreed that the French would refrain from sending help to their faithful allies, the Illinois, while the only condition which the Iroquois accepted was that they should give compensation for the goods they had pillaged. Obviously it was with good reason that the Intendant described the Governor as "more dangerous for Canada than the Iroquois."[11]

As soon as this shameful peace had been patched together, La Barre set off in haste for Montreal, leaving his weakened and famished troops and their officers to get back as best they could. He sent word to the commanders at Niagara that peace had been concluded, and that they were to discharge the auxiliary detachment of French and Indians. The western tribes manifested great indignation at this news, and accused the Governor of treachery. La

Durantaye and Perrot had to call upon all their powers of diplomacy in order to calm them. The army officers and habitants were equally critical of the Governor, who had kept the militiamen from their work for weeks, only to stir up fresh hatred between the Iroquois and the friendly tribes. The one dissenting voice in the chorus of disapproval was that of Father Lamberville who thought fit to write a letter of approbation to be used by La Barre when presenting his own defence to the Minister.[12]

The Court was already dissatisfied with the Governor's conduct of affairs, and a letter specified the various reasons for this displeasure. La Barre was ordered to restore Fort Frontenac to La Salle, and rebuked for issuing licences beyond the legal maximum. He was also reproved for calling himself "Head of the Sovereign Council" and holding meetings of the Council in the Château St. Louis, "by the fireside," with his wife and children in the room. Finally he was berated for having gone over to the side of Mgr. de Laval. Earlier, when he was still fresh from France, he had accused Mgr. de Laval of attempting to "maintain in political and civil affairs the same authority that he had in the spiritual sphere," and also "of shifting skilfully about" in the matter of the fixed parishes.[13]

The problem of the parishes had not been resolved. They had originally all been dependencies of the Seminary, which collected all the tithes and also maintained the priests, who could be transferred at the pleasure of the Bishop. The congregations, however, wanted curés with permanent appointments, who would have a more personal interest in their parishes. The Court would also have preferred this arrangement, which would have reduced in some degree the absolute authority of the Bishop. However, the habitants were not at all anxious to guarantee tithes of 600 livres for each parish. This was the sum proposed by Mgr. de Laval for the maintenance of a priest, and it was very modest payment for a laborious and often ungrateful task performed by selfless and dedicated apostles. Most of the priests had to serve several seigniories, which might be widely separated from one another. The Abbé Morel's parish, for instance, extended from Rivière-du-Loup to Berthier, a distance of twenty-seven leagues. The priests had to make long journeys, in summer in bark canoes, and in winter on snowshoes, with a blanket on their backs and nothing more to eat than a piece of meat with dry bread and water. Even Mgr. de Laval had to travel by canoe or on snowshoes when he visited his diocese. Colbert's contribution to the discussion on the cost of maintaining

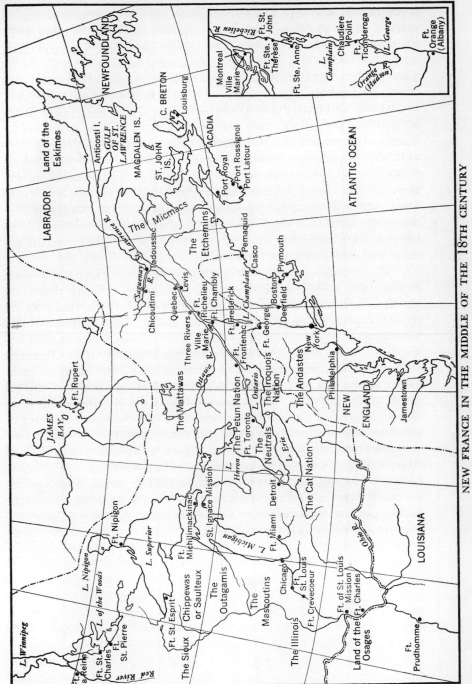

NEW FRANCE IN THE MIDDLE OF THE 18TH CENTURY

a parish was not very helpful, since his figure of 200 *livres* for a priest's salary was based on conditions in France. In October 1678 Frontenac and Duchesneau had reached a more realistic agreement with Mgr. de Laval. Taking into account the higher cost of living in Canada, they had suggested that parish tithes should be fixed at 500 *livres*. The following May, a royal edict ordered the establishment of parishes, and fixed at one twenty-sixth the tithes which were to belong to "the permanent *curé* and not to a transferrable priest." The King's edict remained a dead letter since the parishes did not provide the minimum contribution which had been demanded of them. The King then agreed to make up the deficit from his annual grant to the clergy, and in September 1681 Mgr. de Laval and Duchesneau drew up the boundaries of parishes, of which some fifteen were served by *curés* with permanent appointments. In 1684 the parish contribution was raised by La Barre to 500 *livres* and six more parishes were added to the number of fixed ones.[14]

This decision of the Governor and his support of the Bishop in a dispute with the Récollets were looked upon with disfavour the Court. These minor irritations aggravated a situation created by the Governor's more serious misdemeanours and blunders. The Court could not condone his commerce with the English, still less the fact that he had allowed his own trading activities to lead the colony into war, and the news of the pitiable failure of his expedition was the last straw. When Seignelay learned of the shameful peace, whose only results had been to betray the Illinois and destroy the confidence of the western tribes and to intensify the defiance of the Five Nations, he decided to recall the incompetent Governor. The decision was made in December 1684, and in a letter dated March 10, 1685, the King intimated to the Governor that, in view of his advancing age, it seemed wise to relieve him of his appointment. Quebec looked upon his departure in August with the same satisfaction as Montreal had felt upon the recall of the grasping and arrogant Perrot two years earlier.[15]

CHAPTER NINE

POLITICAL PROBLEMS AND ECONOMIC ACTIVITY
1685-1686

Denonville's mission: to subdue the Iroquois. Weakness of the country's defences. The essential danger: the English. Treaty between Versailles and London promises neutrality in America. Anglo-Iroquois intrigues. Fortification of the colony. Policing of the fur trade. Expedition of the Chevalier de Troyes to Hudson Bay. Canadian exploits. Seignelay's programme. Economic innovations of Intendant de Meulles. Efforts to assimilate the natives. Card money. Recall of de Meulles.

The new Governor, Jacques René de Brisay, Marquis de Denonville, was commissioned on January 1, 1685, and he disembarked in Quebec with his wife on August 1. As colonel of a regiment of dragoons, he had displayed the qualities of a brave soldier and an organizer who, though effective, was more methodical than farsighted. In spite of a certain lack of imagination, he certainly does not deserve the epithet "imbecile" which the acid pen of Saint-Simon attached to his name, and the disinterested integrity which he displayed during his period of administration was in sharp contrast with the mercenary preoccupations of Frontenac and La Barre. His wife, on the other hand, was said to have kept "in the Château St. Louis a room, one might almost say a shop, filled with merchandise." It was also said that she held raffles in order to get rid of her left-over stock. She was at the same time very pious and proper.[1]

Denonville's first mission was to repair the mistakes of La Barre, and to ensure a solid peace by humiliating the pride of the Iroquois and protecting the Illinois and other friendly tribes. He had also to oppose any claims which the English might make on native or French lands. The tour of inspection which the Governor made as a first step in this difficult task revealed a deplorable scarcity of defence works. With the exception of the Château St. Louis, the only fortified places of refuge between Rivière-du-Loup and Montreal were at Three Rivers where there was a high palisade without bastions, and at Montreal itself where only the Mountain mission was protected by a wall. For its defence the colony could count on three hundred soldiers of the Marine, and the militia-men recruited from a population of twelve thousand. After La Barre's fiasco, it would be unwise to rely on support from the western Indians who, in any case, lived four hundred leagues west of Niagara. For the moment, then, Denonville saw no better course open to him than to continue to enlist the services of the Onondagas as peacemakers, and at the same time to build up the country's fortifications in preparation for the war against the Senecas which appeared inevitable.[2]

As Denonville saw the situation, it served no purpose to destroy the vulnerable villages of the Iroquois, since the forest offered them an impregnable refuge. The only salvation for the colony lay in annihilating the Iroquois themselves. The Five Nations could not put more than 2,000 warriors into the field, but the tribes were constantly reinforced by the prisoners (men, women and children), whom they adopted. Their strength came from these additions to their numbers, and also from the arms supplied to them by the English. After observing the situation, the Governor concluded that the enemies "most to be feared" were the English, who, as well as being on good terms with the Iroquois, enjoyed other advantages. Their Atlantic ports were open for navigation throughout the year, and the low prices of their merchandise attracted the furs from the region of the Great Lakes while drawing to Hudson Bay the pelts from the northern country. One way to meet the English threat would be to buy New York, and thus dominate the Iroquois without having to resort to war. Callières, the Governor of Montreal, probably aware of the unrealistic aspects of such a scheme, pointed out to Seignelay that they must at all costs halt the advance of the English who had already planted their arms in Iroquois territory and who were claiming Lake Champlain, and even the St. Lawrence and the Ottawa.[3]

Louis XIV, however, had other ideas. He counted on his influence with his ally and kinsman, James II, to obtain a promise that New York would refrain from helping the Iroquois. In spite of Denonville's warnings about the activities of the Albany traders, the Court remained confident that these difficulties could be dealt with through diplomatic channels. M. Barillon, the French ambassador in London, several times called the attention of James II to the fact that the Governor of New York was ignoring his instructions and sending arms to the Iroquois, but these efforts brought no result. Then, in November 1686 Louis XIV signed an agreement with England stipulating that the colonies in America would remain neutral, even if the mother countries should become engaged as enemies in a European war. Each signatory undertook "to give no aid in men or provisions to Indians" at war with the other. Obviously French diplomats were ill-informed as to the independent spirit of the New York colony and their merchants' impelling desire to appropriate the beaver from the West. In October 1685 Dongan had opened a correspondence with Denonville, but only to reiterate all the English claims. His letters were not conciliatory, and his deeds were even less so. The following spring, he gathered the Iroquois together at Orange, gave them arms and urged them to plunder the French traders. Only the influence of Father Lamberville and presents from Quebec prevented the Senecas from raising the war hatchet. In his letters, Dongan claimed not only the territory of the Five Nations, but also all the western lands as far as the South Sea. The English sent their trading canoes right up to Michilimackinac, where the "cordial" reception given them by the Ottawas and the Hurons was attributable partly to La Barre's disastrous campaign and partly to the fact that the English paid twice as much as the French for their furs. Thus, the treaty of neutrality did not change the situation in America. It remained a dead letter for Dongan, who continued to incite the Senecas to war, and to urge the merchants of Albany to expand their trade in the West.[4]

A survey of the situation convinced Denonville that the only remedy lay in a vigorous offensive based on a solid defensive position, and in 1686 he began to make preparations. He first strengthened the defences of Fort Frontenac, which would be the rallying point for troops; he ordered La Durantaye to build a fort at Michilimackinac, and he instructed Nicolas Perrot and Du Lhut to fortify their posts. Du Lhut was also to build a small fort at Detroit. In September the order to be ready to march against the Iroquois was dispatched to the French in the West and to their Indian allies. In Montreal, Callières made all haste to build a strong wall of logs to protect the settlement. At the same time, in order to conceal his project, Denonville continued to maintain friendly relations with the Senecas, and Father Lamberville took gifts on his behalf to the most important chiefs. To prevent French contra-

bandists from trading with the English the Governor stationed at
Chambly a detachment of eighteen soldiers commanded by a lieutenant. He also made sure that no *coureurs de bois* set out from
Montreal, and with the help of the Onondagas he succeeded in
arresting a few outlaws.[5] Denonville was also aware of the need to
protect Canadian posts on Hudson Bay against English intrusion.
In 1684, in spite of an agreement that each nation would respect
the other's establishments, Radisson, who was once more in the
service of England, had seized the Canadian Company's Fort Bourbon with its eight men and twenty thousand beaver pelts. In reprisal, Denonville equipped an expedition at the expense of the
Company. It was made up of thirty French soldiers and seventy
Canadians, and was commanded by the Chevalier de Troyes, with
Le Moyne de Sainte-Hélène and Le Moyne d'Iberville as lieutenants. The second of the brothers had seized this opportunity to escape from Montreal after a youthful adventure with Geneviève
Picoté de Belestre.[6]

Leaving Montreal on March 20, 1686, the contingent paddled
up the Ottawa, and by river and portage, covered a distance of two
hundred leagues to reach James Bay. "You had to be a Canadian
to endure the hardships of such a journey." On June 20 the force
appeared suddenly before Fort Monsipi (Hayes) on Moose River.
The post was protected by a wall and cannon, but the attackers
forced the door with a battering-ram, and the defenders at once
capitulated. On July 3 Sainte-Hélène and de Troyes, with sixty
men, seized Fort Rupert, forty leagues to the east, while d'Iberville
and thirteen soldiers captured a ship moored to the shore. The
third of the English posts on James Bay, Fort Albany, fell on St.
Anne's day, July 26, and was renamed in honour of the saint. Immediately after the surrender of Fort Albany, de Troyes set out
on his return journey to Quebec.

In the autumn, d'Iberville, left in command, seized an English
ship, on her way to Fort Rupert. A second ship was caught in the
ice near Charlton Island, and two of the four Canadians sent to
reconnoitre were captured and spent the winter imprisoned in the
hold. In the spring of 1687, as the ship was being made ready to
sail, one of the two prisoners was called into service to help the
crew. It so happened that one day he found himself with only
two sailors on deck while the others were busy aloft. Quickly
seizing his opportunity, the Canadian felled the two Englishmen
with an axe and liberated his companion. Then, having armed
themselves, they forced the crew to take the ship with its provisions

and its cargo of furs to Fort Rupert. On the way they met d'Iberville who had set out to rescue them. He must have thought the
exploit a fitting finish to the spectacular success of an expedition
which had made the French complete masters at the bottom of the
Bay. The only post now remaining in English hands was Fort
Bourbon on the Nelson.[7]

La Barre had been interested only in trading, and Denonville's attention was concentrated on preparations for war, so that,
under these two governors, it was left to the far-sighted de Meulles
to take thought for the economy of the country. The moment
seemed propitious for a resurgence of interest in Canada on the
part of the mother country. The war against Holland had been
ended in 1678 by the Treaty of Nymwegen which strengthened
the French frontier, and established France as the dominant power
in Europe. Frontenac and Duchesneau were no longer there to
plague the Minister with their quarrels. Conditions seemed favourable for Seignelay to continue the work of colonial development begun by his father, and he seemed to want to do so. In the
political sphere, he did not mean to allow the Jesuits, or anyone
else, to overstep the limits of their authority, while in the economic
field he was more interested in developing the agricultural settlements than in discovering distant lands. To open up new land for
the younger generation, de Meulles granted about twenty seigniories in 1682 and 1683. As a further assistance to farmers, the regulation prohibiting the seizure of farm animals was prolonged for
a period of six years from 1683. In 1686 the Intendant issued orders for seigneurs to build the mills required by the terms of their
grants,[8] and, in order to stimulate the cultivation of hemp, he
agreed, with Seignelay's consent, to buy the crop at fifteen *livres* a
quintal, two *livres* more than the price of hemp in France.[9]

In 1684, to augment Canada's inadequate labour force,
Seignelay sent out a number of *engagés,* among whom were children of twelve and fifteen years of age. When the Intendant protested, he was offered convicts and salt smugglers, an offer which
was refused. The following year 150 acceptable *engagés* arrived,
but Denonville recruited a certain number of them for the troops,
and the habitants still needed workmen. In order to meet this
need, de Meulles ruled in April 1685 that soldiers could hire
out their services by the month at wages of ten or twelve *livres,* or
by the day for one *livre* three *sous* and board.[10]

Progress could be detected in other sectors of the country's
economy, but it was very slow. Since 1682, the *Compagnie du Nord*

had been extending its trade in the Hudson Bay area, and in May 1685, it was granted a monopoly for twenty years. In March of the same year the King decreed that colonists of noble birth could engage in commerce without loss of rank. In an attempt to expand the very small West India trade, export duties were removed and in 1685 Riverin sent cargoes of peas and lumber to the Antilles. That same year, lumber and wheat from Quebec were sold in La Rochelle.[11] De Meulles encouraged the tannery at Pointe-Lévis and established a tile-yard, and in 1686 he opened a modest cloth mill for which six weavers were sent out from France. Finally, Riverin was backed by the Intendant in his venture of a fish-drying plant on the lower St. Lawrence.[12]

Such modest achievements were all that the small industries of the colony could hope for without more Canadian capital or more generous royal subsidies. Only the fur trade, the basic element in the country's economic structure, was once more moving ahead. Exports of furs had risen from 61,000 pounds in 1675 to 95,000 in 1683. Having been reduced to a quarter of the latter figure as a result of La Barre's disastrous expedition, they were now slowly increasing again.[12a]

Immigration had fallen to one or two hundred *engagés* and a few families a year, although the army continued to swell the number of new settlers. Between 1675 and 1686 about 180 soldiers married and took up land. Versailles again put forward its idea of assimilating the natives, and in order to convert them to a sedentary life, de Meulles undertook to have the women taught to weave, and to give each man, on his marriage, corn and hemp seed, a cow and a pig. To help carry out this programme, France provided six factory girls who proved to be unskilled and incapable of teaching Indian girls anything. In Montreal, the Sisters of the Congregation dedicated themselves to the hopeless task, and in Quebec, the Ursulines displayed commendable goodwill, but de Meulles considered that they were making a grave error when they tried to teach Indian girls to read and pray instead of giving them the practical education of a peasant. No demand was made on the fund of 3,000 *livres* which had been set up to give wedding presents to the Indian brides of French settlers, and the money was used to help newly married French couples. In short, the effort to convert the Indians to French ways ended in total failure.[13]

De Meulles found himself faced with one very serious economic difficulty in the shortage of currency. The malady was chronic, since each year the colony exported a large part of its cash to

pay for goods bought in France. Barter had provided the answer
to this problem during the early pioneer period: furs, tobacco and
wheat had served as currency. Later, in an effort to discourage the
export of cash, the Quebec Council increased the value of money
in the colony by twenty-five per cent. In 1685, however, a real crisis arose when the Intendant was stranded with no funds with which
to pay the colony's five hundred soldiers. He then invented a temporary expedient. He took playing cards, and after inscribing each
with a value, fifteen or forty *sous,* or four *livres,* he signed it and
stamped it with his seal. An order dated June 8, 1685, stated that
in the emergency the cards would serve as legal currency, and
promised that they would be redeemed as soon as the ships arrived
with the royal funds. The "card money," as it was called, was accepted without difficulty, and was duly redeemed in September,
but the King expressed strong disapproval of the experiment because of the ease with which the card money could be counterfeit-
ed. The expedient worked so well, however, that the authorities
had recourse to it several times later on, and finally, card money
was recognized as official currency in the colony.[14]

Between October 1685 and July 1686, de Meulles was in Acadia, where he carried out a census. He also prepared a most remarkable report on that part of the country.[15] In September he was informed that his term of office was ended and that his successor had
already been appointed in April. His recall was the result of campaigns carried on simultaneously by the Jesuits and the Sulpicians.
The Jesuits were anxious to see their partisan, Duchesneau, once
more in Quebec, while the Sulpicians' candidate was M. de Champigny, a kinsman of their Superior, M. Tronson. Denonville was a
friend of Champigny, and he had personal reasons for adding his
voice to those of de Meulles's adversaries: he was irked by the Intendant's zeal for innovations, and he reproached him for being
too anxious "to make money." La Hontan defended de Meulles
against the latter charge by saying that "the Intendant's private
transactions did no one any harm, and on the other hand, helped
many poor people to earn a living." The annalist of the Hôtel-
Dieu said simply of de Meulles: "He did his duty," and this is
high praise when one remembers the difficulties with which he had
to contend: lack of public funds, incompetence in one governor,
La Barre, and personal antagonism on the part of a second, Denonville.[16]

57400

CHAPTER TEN

THE EXPEDITION AGAINST THE IROQUOIS AND THE LACHINE MASSACRE
1686-1689

Resignation of Mgr. de Laval. Morals, manners and mentality of the age. Slow progress in mission work. Intendant Champigny. English encroachments. Denonville's expedition against the Five Nations. Iroquois envoys captured and sent to the galleys. Devastation of the Seneca villages. Iroquois reprisals. Peace parleys. Treason of Kondiaronk. The Augsburg League and the Anglo-French war. Lachine massacre. Recall of Denonville.

Two years before the departure of de Meulles, New France had suffered a severe loss with the resignation of Mgr. de Laval. For twenty-five years Canada's first Bishop had devoted all the resources of his mind and his will to the task of extending and strengthening the church which he had founded. He had sought out and fulfilled every possible moral or religious obligation, and he had fought hard and bitterly to keep the ecclesiastical authority free from encroachment by the temporal power. Buildings his diocese on the rock of Roman discipline and evangelical faith, he had established some twenty-five parishes and missions, and extended the mission fields of the three orders working in Canada from Acadia to Lake Michigan. In 1681 he made a second pastoral tour of his diocese from Cap St. Ignace to Lachine. He travelled two hundred leagues in a birch-bark canoe, and after his return from the journey, which took two and a half months, his life was threatened by a grave illness. His resources of physical strength had already been heavily drawn on by infirmities and unremitting work, as well as by the austere habits and constant mortifications which were the rule of his private life. With characteristic courage he accepted the heart tremors and dizzy spells which followed his illness as a warn-

ing that his work had become too arduous for him. After laying
the last stone of his diocese by creating the Cathedral chapter, he
left Quebec in November 1684, and presented his resignation
which was reluctantly accepted by the Court. When efforts to dis-
suade him from his decision proved unavailing, Louis XIV asked
him to choose his own successor, and he selected the King's chaplain, the Abbé Jean-Baptiste Chevrières de Saint-Vallier. The Abbé
de Saint-Vallier, who was thirty-one years old and the son of a rich
and noble family, was highly recommended by the Jesuits for his
deep piety and his ardent zeal. The choice was approved by the
King, and in 1685 Mgr. de Saint-Vallier took office in Quebec as
Vicar-General. He was consecrated Bishop in Paris in 1688, immediately after the official resignation of Mgr. de Laval.[1]

Social behaviour in Canada had changed considerably with
the passage of time. Of the eight hundred soldiers who settled in
the country, many had been drawn, according to the custom of the
age, from the unruly and undisciplined elements in their communities. After being discharged from the army, some of these
restless individuals married and settled down on the land, but
others became more or less idle adventurers who sowed the seed
of moral laxity and indiscipline in the colony.[2] Their group was
swelled by the addition of a certain number of former *engagés* who,
after completing their three-year contract, declared themselves to
be "volunteers" or independent workers. The legalization of the
sale of alcohol helped to draw this rootless element in the population into the illicit fur trade whose attractions were so much more
powerful than royal edicts or Council decrees. Even though their
sisters might have to work in the fields to replace them, it sometimes happened that sons of needy seigneurs allowed themselves
to be seduced by the lure of profits and the easy morality of life
among the Indians. Young men were not likely to resist temptation when the example to succumb was set by high-ranking officials
of whom some concealed their illegal transactions but others, like
Perrot in Montreal or Valrennes in Three Rivers, carried them on
quite openly. It was not even difficult for the *coureurs de bois* to
carry on the trade; they could always find accomplices who would
provide them with supplies and hide them at need. Moreover,
when they came back to the settlement they did not abandon their
immoral habits; on the contrary, they flaunted their ill-gotten
gains, and paraded their dissipation and disorderly conduct. Many
of them did not return to civilization at all, and these were a total
loss to the economy and the population of the country.

The influence of the *coureurs de bois* resulted in a certain lowering of the standards of rectitude and decency which had been those of the colony in its earlier days. In 1676 Duchesneau expelled a woman from Quebec for immoral conduct, and at the same time he denounced certain evils of the age: the abuse of alcohol, debauchery, luxurious living. The dissipation accompanying Montreal's fur fair provoked a general denunciation of Canada's young people by the austere Governor. The young men, said M. de Denonville, were undisciplined, and had no other ambition than to trade in the forests, where they gave themselves up to all sorts of disorders, "debauching women and girls, and dressing in Indian clothes, completely naked" [*sic*]. The women fared no better at the hands of the Governor than the young men. Most of them, in his opinion, "just wanted to be ladies and do nothing."[3]

It is interesting to notice that, except in the case of the *coureurs de bois,* the Church was less sweeping in its judgments. In 1682 Mgr. de Laval censured immodest women, but only when they violated the sanctity of the church by appearing with hair "curled in a manner unworthy of a Christian woman" or improperly dressed "in indecent garments displaying under transparent veils, bare arms, shoulders, bosoms." Four years later Mgr. de Saint-Vallier denounced the luxury and vain occupations in which his flock indulged: "feasts, balls and dancing, plays and other forms of public performances." According to La Hontan, the Sulpicians in Montreal kept close watch on the morals of the people, and the Jesuits were said to use the confessional and the offices of pious informers in their effort to direct the conduct of persons under their care. In spite of such criticism, all of which emanates from extremely puritanical sources, the moral quality of the Canadian colonist does not appear to have deteriorated to any considerable extent. To be sure, he sometimes refused to recognize his obligation to pay tithes or to observe the fur-trading and liquor laws, and he was seldom lacking in self-conceit. Every man considered himself a "gentleman" and every woman, a "lady." It was an insult to be called a "peasant."[4]

Questions of precedence and privilege were of the greatest importance in the higher circles. Churchwardens battled with officers for first place in religious processions, and only gave way to judges when commanded to do so by a royal order. So many burghers took to carrying swords and calling themselves "esquire" that the Intendant declared it illegal to carry a sword, and in April 1684 the King specified that only those subjects who held patents of nobility could use the title "esquire"; misuse would be punished be a fine. The members of the Sovereign Council were not permitted to wear the magistrate's gown, but they could carry swords. Pretentiousness in some cases, a taste for luxury in others, and an overall vanity and greed for wealth were apparently the all too human frailties of a population whose morals were, almost without exception, in a very healthy state. It was said that "thanks to the care taken by Mgr. de Laval to give them good priests, Frenchmen in Canada usually led a more regular life than Frenchmen in France," and Mgr. de Saint-Vallier expressed the same opinion in 1688.[5]

Progress in the work of evangelization was slow, and real conversions among the adult native population very rare. Quite a number of Indians accepted baptism, either because they did not want to disappoint the missionaries, or for motives of self-interest, but very few of them gave up their licentious habits. Moreover, the Jesuits and the Sulpicians disagreed on the manner in which conversions could best be brought about. The Jesuits preferred to keep the Indians in their own villages, segregated from the French population. The Sulpicians, on the other hand, advocated integration of the natives into the colony. The civil authorities also thought that the Indians would gain by living among the French since only in that way would they learn to speak French and adapt themselves to the settled life of the farmer attached to his own land. The rivalry between the two orders was very keen, and the Sulpicians had proof that their work was being impeded by the Jesuits, who were favoured by Mgr. de Laval and who wanted to reserve their monopoly as missionaries in "a land which they had watered with their sweat and their blood."[6]

Such was the social atmosphere in New France in July 1688 when the new Intendant, Jean Bochart, Chevalier de Champigny, arrived in Quebec with his wife, a cousin of Mgr. de Laval. Champigny, most anxious to fulfil the responsibilities which his office imposed upon him, at once set about the task of preparing for the expedition planned by the Governor.[7] Denonville's fixed idea was that war with the Senecas could not be avoided. He continued to negotiate with them in order to deceive them about his own plans, but he believed neither in their sincerity nor in the duration of the peace. He was convinced that the peace was for them no more than a screen behind which they would destroy the Indian allies of the French before attacking the colony itself. Nor had he faith that any intervention which the Court might undertake with the

King of England would eliminate anti-French intrigues in New York. He knew that in that year (1686) the merchants and fur buyers of Albany were furnishing arms to the Iroquois, advising them to get rid of the missionaries, and inciting them to war against the French.[8]

In November thirty English traders sent by Dongan to Michilimackinac were captured and plundered by a detachment of two hundred Frenchmen and Indians under the leadership of La Durantaye. The following May a second English contingent led by Major Patrick McGregor met Tonty and his Illinois west of Lake Erie. They were scattered, and their possessions seized. In June the Indian warriors from the West under Nicolas Perrot, and the detachments of La Durantaye and Tonty, which were on their way to join Denonville's army at Frontenac, all met at Detroit. Here, as a precaution against any English encroachment in that region, La Durantaye repeated a ceremony performed earlier by La Salle, and proclaimed the sovereignty of the King of France over all lands surrounding Lakes Erie and Huron.[9]

The influence of Father Lamberville had deterred the Senecas from any hostile act during the summer of 1686, and he invited them to meet the Governor at Fort Frontenac the following spring. Towards the end of the winter (1687), Denonville called up the militia, but the memory of La Barre's ill-fated adventure was still fresh in the minds of the militiamen, and they protested the order. However, after the Governor and the Bishop had made statements explaining the situation, they agreed to march.[10]

In June the force was ready. It was made up of 930 militiamen and 400 Indians from the colony. On the 17th, in accordance with the plan which had been agreed upon with Denonville, Champigny set out from Montreal with fifteen canoes. In order to keep the expedition secret, he seized the Cayugas around Quinte.[11] A large number of Onondagas had already assembled at Fort Frontenac, and as the customary feast was in progress, ninety-five guests were seized by Champigny's orders and chained to stakes. In this position, they burst into the defiant death chant usually sung by prisoners about to be tortured or burned.[12]

The explanation of this act of treachery was that Louis XIV had asked La Barre in July 1684 and Denonville in March 1687 for Iroquois prisoners to man his galleys. The King obviously was thinking of prisoners of war, and not of men traitorously surprised in the time of peace. Denonville also did his part in answering the King's request. As he was proceeding up the St. Lawrence

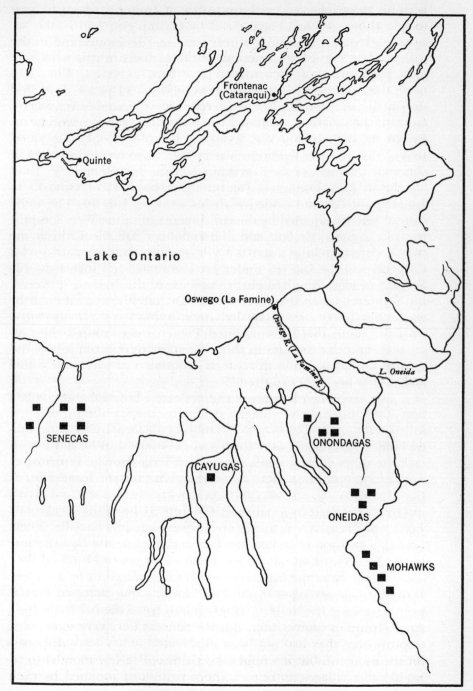

THE FIVE NATIONS OF THE IROQUOIS.
(After a map of 1668 in the Depôt de la Marue.)

with his troops, he captured a number of Iroquois whom he sent
to join those who had been seized by Champigny, and in the autumn thirty-six Iroquois prisoners were sent to France and to the
galleys. The immediate reaction of the Indians to this wholesale
kidnapping was not what might have been expected. They had
more than once killed missionary negotiators in peace time, and
they made no protest when they received comparable treatment.
Instead, three nations proposed the following year to negotiate an
agreement with Denonville. Even in the colony, only one voice,
that of the Abbé de Belmont, was raised in protest against the un-
christian treachery of the Governor and the Intendant.[13]

From Fort Frontenac Denonville crossed Lake Ontario to
Irondequoit Bay and landed with his army on July 10. There the
eastern force was joined by the contingents from the West compris-
ing 180 *coureurs de bois* and 400 Indians.[14] On the 13th, as the
troops were marching towards a village, the advance guard under
Callières and the Indians under La Durantaye fell into a double
ambush of eight hundred enemies. Some of the Indians scattered,
but Callières attacked vigorously and Denonville, even though he
was under heavy fire, succeeded in bringing up the main force,
with the result that the combined French forces routed their as-
sailants. French casualties in this encounter were seven killed and
twenty wounded, while thirty-four Iroquois warriors were killed
and twenty-five were captured.[15]

The army then laid waste the country whose inhabitants had
fled. They burned the villages, destroyed the standing crops and
killed a large number of pigs.[16] On July 19 Denonville proclaimed French sovereignty over the Seneca country, but he did not attack the other Iroquois tribes, and four days later he returned to
Fort Frontenac. From there he went to Niagara, the focal point of
the western trade, and erected a post with store rooms and living
quarters protected by a palisade. On July 31 he again proclaimed
French sovereignty over all the country explored by La Salle. Then,
leaving a garrison to protect the fort and to close the beaver route
to the English, he set out on the return journey to Montreal.[17]

At first sight, the expedition of 1687 appeared to be a success.
It disabled the strongest of the Five Nations and increased French
prestige among the western tribes. It also freed the fur trade from
Anglo-Iroquois competition. But the Senecas were very soon going
to prove that they had not been eliminated. They were dispersed
for the moment, but it would take them only a few months to rebuild their villages, to restock them with corn supplied by their

four sister nations, and to re-equip themselves with English arms and English merchandise. Before long the French were to learn the truth of the Indian Atavia's prophetic saying: "The man who meddles with a wasps' nest and who doesn't kill all the wasps is likely to be stung." One might also wonder whether this preventive expedition was justified at a time when Father Lamberville and the Onondagas were achieving the object of keeping the colony at peace. The great trader, La Chesnaye, and his friend, Champigny, were most anxious to protect the French fur trade; but would they not have achieved this end more surely if they had offered the Indians prices as attractive as those offered by the English?

Denonville himself came to have doubts about the results of his expedition. He was beginning to think that the real solution to the country's economic and military problem lay in the acquisition, by purchase or conquest, of New York. If France held New York, Albany would be eliminated as a commercial or territorial rival.[18] But this was only a distant dream and the Governor had to give his immediate attention to the defence of the colony, for the Iroquois "wasps" very soon began to sting. The late summer and autumn were marked by a number of symptomatic and disturbing incidents. In August some colonists were killed on their way to Fort Frontenac. Along the Richelieu a band of 150 Mohawks burned houses, took prisoners and even besieged Fort Chambly, and some of their raiding parties came up the St. Lawrence and into the Ottawa. Denonville stationed a detachment of 120 *coureurs de bois* under Vaudreuil at the eastern end of the Island of Montreal, but, although a vigilant watch was maintained, some houses were burned and several farmers were killed. Even the Onondagas, who up to this time had maintained the peace, captured three soldiers at Cataraqui along with Mlle d'Allone, who was said to have been engaged to La Salle.[19]

As Montreal was most seriously threatened, Governor Callières ordered that in each seigniory a shelter should be built with a palisade, behind which the inhabitants could take refuge in case of need. Denonville extended this system to the whole colony, and in September he also ordered that all men, and boys above the age of thirteen, should provide themselves with rifles, and carry them loaded when going to work, and even at mass. Signal fires were made ready to warn the people of any enemy approach and to order them to take shelter.[20]

In Europe, a second treaty of neutrality was signed by France and England in 1687. In the autumn of that year Quebec sent back to New York the English traders captured at Michilimackinac and Detroit, and in the following July New York returned Mlle d'Allone and thirteen Frenchmen who had been held by the Iroquois. Otherwise the English colony made no change in its policy. In December (1688) Dongan, who in the spring had offered arms to the Five Nations, demanded the return of the Iroquois sent to the galleys, and the demolition of Forts Frontenac and Niagara. In England an anti-papist revolution had deposed the Catholic James II, and in October 1688 his son-in-law, William of Orange, the declared enemy of France, was proclaimed King. Versailles informed Denonville that, treaties notwithstanding, any agreement between the Courts of England and France must be considered untrustworthy, and that he must be ready for a possible English offensive.[21]

The Canadians became more and more anxious as the Governor was faced with ever more difficult decisions. Knowing that Dongan had promised arms to the Iroquois, Denonville gave up the idea of a second expedition, and decided to rely on negotiations to restore peace. He sent back a few prisoners with a great many gifts, and in answer to this overture, a delegation appeared in Montreal early in June (1688). The envoys who represented the Onondagas, Cayugas and Oneidas, were accompanied by about nine hundred warriors. In an assembly presided over by the Governor, the Onondaga, Big Mouth, vaunted the strength of his tribe which, had it not been moved by friendly feelings for the French, could have burned and destroyed the colony. He then demanded the release of all Iroquois captives held by the French. Denonville agreed to this demand but only on condition that the Mohawks and the Senecas should also send envoys to treaty with the French. Thus no final agreement was reached and the delegates maintained their uncompromising attitude. On July 18 they affixed their totems to a declaration affirming that they were owners of their country and that they recognized neither the French nor the English as masters.[22]

These parleys were followed by a series of sudden sporadic raids. In June the Onondagas attacked the Indian allies of the French, and in July bands of Mohawks, sweeping down the Richelieu, burned houses and killed livestock at Contrecœur, Sorel, St. Ours and St. François. Denonville requested that the Iroquois be sent back from the King's galleys, and he also ordered the evacuation of Niagara. The order was executed on September 15 and, as La Hontan had abandoned his post at Detroit in April, only Fort Frontenac was left to guard the colony's western frontier.[23]

Denonville had asked for eight hundred soldiers, but only three hundred were sent, much too small a force for offensive action, especially since the western forts had been abandoned. So the Governor had perforce to aim at the alternative goal of a peace treaty. The Onondagas had not succeeded in their effort to get representatives from all the Five Nations, but in mid-August they sent an interim delegation to beg the Governor to have patience. The summer passed without serious hostilities, the harvest was safely gathered in, and hopes for peace were high, when suddenly a disastrous event changed the picture completely.[24]

The prime mover in this event was the Huron chief, Kondiaronk, known as "the Rat." He was intelligent and daring, but he proved to be fickle and, like all his people, quick to betray on the impulse of the moment. He had thought at one time of coming to terms with the Iroquois, with the idea that his tribe could serve as middlemen for the western trade. Then, in 1687, he had allowed himself to be won over by Denonville's arguments and presents, but he exacted from the Governor a promise that the French would completely destroy the Five Nations. In 1688, counting on this agreement, Kondiaronk gathered a band of one hundred warriors for a campaign against the Iroquois. Then, when the commander of Fort Frontenac informed him that delegates from the Five Nations were about to sign a treaty with Denonville, Kondiaronk, fearful that his *volte-face* and his projected expedition might cause the Iroquois to attack his people, decided to destroy any possibility of peace between the French and the Five Nations.[25]

He hastened with his warriors to La Famine (Oswego), and when the Iroquois envoys appeared he attacked them, killing some and capturing others. When the chief, Teganisorens, protested that they were ambassadors, "the Rat" answered that he had had orders from Denonville to attack them. To prove his good faith, he set his prisoners free and swore that he would be avenged for the Governor's trickery. He kept one warrior whom he turned over to La Durantaye as a prisoner of war, and who was at once executed by a French firing squad. This was exactly what Kondiaronk had desired, and he sent an Iroquois slave to report to his people that the French had killed one of their ambassadors. After this double betrayal, the Huron chief could well say: "I have killed the peace." The sinister traitor then paraded impudently about Montreal, and Denonville did not dare either to execute him or to send him to the galleys.[26]

In spite of such apparently wilful provocation from the French the Five Nations did not move at once, but spent the winter concerting a plan for a summer offensive. In the West, Nicolas Perrot reaffirmed the rights of the colony and on May 8, 1689, he took possession of the region extending from Lake Michigan to the Mississippi. On Hudson Bay, where he was directing the affairs of the *Compagnie du Nord* and combating the efforts of the Hudson's Bay Company, d'Iberville captured three English corvettes with their cargoes of furs before returning to Quebec in October. Meanwhile, the essential event concerning Canada had taken place in Europe. On May 7, 1689, William III, who had formed the League of Augsburg to reduce the power of Louis XIV, declared war on France. The effects of the disturbances in Europe were felt at once in America; on June 27 delegates from the Five Nations assembled in Albany expressed their satisfaction at the prospect of fighting beside their English "brothers" who supplied them with arms for their coming campaign.[27] As the winter and spring passed without hostilities, Canada allowed itself to be "lulled by a false hope of peace." Although Atavia had warned him of the imminent danger of an Iroquois attack, Denonville had neglected the elementary precaution of regular patrols. Then suddenly the catastrophe struck. In the night of August 4-5, under cover of heavy rain, fifteen hundred Iroquois crossed the river at the foot of Lake St. Louis and entered the sleeping village of Lachine. At daybreak the villagers were awakened by war whoops, and the warriors, brandishing their tomahawks, rushed into the houses where they killed the men and captured the women and children. After the first frenzy of slaughter, the victorious Indians set fire to the houses and committed the most barbarous atrocities, burning prisoners, hacking open the bodies of pregnant women, and burning children whose flesh they ate on the spot. Twenty-four persons were killed during the raid, and of the fifty who were taken prisoner forty-two were put to death with varying degrees of cruelty.[28]

At four o'clock in the morning, news of the attack reached the post at Verdun, and twenty-four men went in pursuit of a band of Iroquois. The messenger then went on to Montreal where he found the Governor-General and his wife. Denonville had seven hundred men in the town, but he was completely stunned by the disaster and so obsessed by the threat to Montreal that he stayed there with most of the troops and set only one hundred men under Vaudreuil to reinforce Fort Rolland at Lachine. Vaudreuil, blindly obedient to the Governor's orders, refused to allow Subercase from the neighbouring post at Verdun to hunt down the Iroquois, although many of them were scattered about the neighbourhood, while others who had raided the brandy stores of the French were sleeping off their drunkenness. The next day, August 6, one hundred volunteers from Verdun attacked a roving band of the enemy. Fifty Frenchmen and thirty Indians under La Roberge also made a sortie from Fort Rémy, but they were repulsed with a loss of half their men, of whom twenty, including the valiant La Roberge, were burned at the stake.[29]

Such, briefly, is the story of the Iroquois raid whose importance has perhaps been exaggerated by the name of the "Lachine massacre." Savage as the attack was, it did not disconcert the Canadians. In the autumn a party of colonists drove off an Iroquois band from Pointe-aux-Trembles, and about the same time a company of one hundred *coureurs de bois,* "the musketeers," was formed to pursue the enemy whenever his presence was reported.[29a]

Denonville seemed completely demoralized by this murderous guerilla warfare, and quite incapable of conceiving any rational plan of defence and reprisal. For five weeks he kept his soldiers busy transporting the wheat from the Sault mission into the town. On September 2, on the assumption that it would be difficult to maintain supplies at Fort Frontenac, he gave Valrennes the disastrous order to evacuate the fort, and in October the garrison withdrew to Montreal after having mined the buildings and walls and thrown the fort's guns into the lake. The route to the West was now open to the Iroquois and the English. This black picture of disaster is relieved by one modest success. A group of twenty-eight young Canadians led by Du Lhut and Manthet attacked a party of twenty-two Iroquois on the Lake of Two Mountains. Their canoes were overturned and eighteen Iroquois were killed on the spot. Three prisoners were burned later by the Indians, to whom the French had handed them over, and only one of the band escaped to carry the story to the tribe.[30]

Denonville was not to remain much longer in office. Reports from Callières made Seignelay realize that the Governor's honesty and sincerity could not compensate for his shortcomings. Audacity and a gift for diplomacy were two qualities without which it was impossible either to make friends with the Indians or to fight them. The Governor himself admitted that he was overwhelmed by the anxieties of his situation. The colony could not forgive him his two major blunders of policy: he had violated a much-needed peace without good reason, and he had committed an act of treachery by seizing Indians and sending them to the galleys. It must, however, be said in his defence that the campaign that

he planned against the Senecas would probably have brought about
a general peace, and that Kondiaronk's treachery was the real
cause of the war which was actually fought. The King recalled the
Governor in May 1689 on the flattering pretext that his services
were needed for the war in Europe, but the post to which he was
appointed was that of assistant tutor to the King's grandson, the
Duke of Burgundy.[31]

CHAPTER ELEVEN

IROQUOIS WAR. EXPEDITIONS INTO ENGLISH TERRITORY. SIEGE OF QUEBEC.
1689-1690

Frontenac appointed Governor for a second term. Project to conquer New York. Evacuation of Fort Frontenac. More Iroquois raids. Expeditions against Corlaer, Salmon Falls and Casco. Iroquois peace parleys. Pacification of the western tribes. Frontenac advocates war. Skirmish with the English at La Prairie. Phipps and the English fleet before Quebec. Siege of Quebec. Failure and retreat of the English. Economic hardship in the colony.

Although Frontenac's clandestine traffic in furs, and still more his autocratic temper, had occasioned his recall in 1682, the King now chose him to replace Denonville. Since his return to France seven years before, the former Governor had lived quietly on the fringes of the Court as the guest of the Marshal of Bellefonds, whose influence had procured for him a pension of 3,500 *livres*. At the age of sixty-seven, Frontenac entered upon his second term of office, and the King indicated the special service which was required of him: "to procure the peace" which was an urgent necessity for the colony. The royal instructions also included the customary warning not to allow ecclesiastical authority to be extended "beyond its proper limits," but other clauses suggested that in this respect, as well as in others, the fiery Governor would be expected to change his ways. He was not to allow any trade to be carried on in his name, and he was to "maintain harmonious relations with the Bishop of Quebec" and the Jesuits.[1]

A few days after the King had signed Frontenac's commission, the situation in Canada was completely changed by England's declaration of war on France. The English were now officially the chief enemy of France in America. Accordingly, new instructions

113

charged Frontenac with a military operation of major importance, an attack against New York. The idea of winning New York for France was not new. In 1667 Talon had suggested that, as a means of protecting Canada from Indian attacks, Louis XIV should obtain possession of "Manhattan and Orange either by conquest or by purchase." Fourteen years later, when Manhattan had passed into the hands of the English, Duchesneau had again proposed that France buy New York with the object of establishing an important French base on the Atlantic and cutting off the western trade from the English.[2]

In January 1689, Callières had drawn up a plan for concerted land and sea operations against the English colony. He would lead 1,400 soldiers and 600 militiamen by Lake Champlain to attack Albany; a town of 150 houses defended by 450 men would fall an easy prey to the superior French force. From Albany the expedition would proceed to New York, where it seemed certain that the land army, supported by two warships, could force the surrender of a garrison of 550 men. The King gave his approval to the undertaking, and on June 7 he issued orders to Frontenac who would command the expedition from Quebec. His instructions also made provision for the situation which would exist after the conquest. Only those colonists who professed the Catholic faith and recognized the sovereignty of the King of France would be allowed to remain. "With respect to all other foreigners, men, women and children," His Majesty considered it "expedient that they be expelled from the colony, and sent to New England and Pennsylvania or elsewhere." Once again, the King's commitments in Europe prevented the execution of this plan for action in America. Since preparations for an invasion of Ireland had first priority, La Caffinière with his two warships, and Frontenac with the merchant fleet did not reach Chedabucto in Acadia until September 15, too late to make their attempt. The following year, Callières again put forward the plan, but the Minister answered that other "important affairs" made it impossible for the King to consider an expedition against New York.[2a]

Frontenac, accompanied by Callières, arrived in Quebec from Chedabucto on October 12. He had brought back seventeen Iroquois from the galleys, among them the Cayuga chief, Ouréouaré, whose confidence he had won during the voyage by his assiduous attentions. The Governor disembarked at eight o'clock in the evening to the accompaniment of salutes from the guns of the fort and volleys of musketry fire. He was met by the members of the

Sovereign Council and a group of townspeople bearing arms, and the whole town was illuminated with lamps, torches and lanterns. The following day, a solemn *Te Deum* was sung in the cathedral, and the ladies of Quebec called at the Château St. Louis. Frontenac's return was greeted with joy by the people who remembered him as the man who had given them "peace, abundance, safety."[3]

The Governor went immediately to join Denonville and Champigny in Montreal where he was instantly aware of the "consternation of the people" and the low morale of the troops after the massacre of Lachine. On learning that the order had been dispatched to abandon Fort Frontenac, he at once expressed his dissent from this decision which had been made by Denonville and Champigny, and from Lachine he sent fifty canoes with a strong relief detachment under d'Ailleboust de Manthet to prevent the evacuation. The convoy, however, was less than ten leagues on its way when, to the acute disappointment of the Governor, Valrennes and the garrison from Frontenac arrived in Montreal.[4]

While he was in Montreal, Frontenac reviewed the troops, and assigned them to the positions where the threat was most serious. The posts were also provided with guns, which could be fired to warn the habitants of the presence of the enemy. After completing these preparations, Frontenac returned to Quebec to write and dispatch his reports to the Minister. On November 13, very soon after his departure from Montreal, 150 Iroquois attacked La Chesnaye, killed 20 of its inhabitants, and carried off 20 prisoners. The raid was carried out under cover of a blizzard, and although Callières sent a party of Indians in pursuit of the raiders, they succeeded in making good their escape. The people were panic-stricken, and Frontenac begged the Minister to dispatch a military force strong enough to put an end to the bold aggression of these "cursed savages," for there were not enough troops in the country to man the existing posts and to carry out an effective campaign against the Indians.[5] Frontenac's request was made in November, and it would take months for the troops to arrive from France. Meanwhile, action had to be taken on the spot, and the Governor's aim, after organizing the farm communities for defence against raids, was to forestall any combined offensive of the English and the Iroquois. With this end in view, he launched three separate attacks against the English colonies. The largest force left Montreal in February 1690. Its leaders were Manthet, Sainte-Hélène and d'Iberville, and it was made up of 114 Frenchmen and 80 Indians from the colony. Marching on snowshoes and sleeping on the snow, they advanced to Corlaer (Schenectady), a settlement of eighty houses, six leagues from Albany. Late in the evening of February 18, the invaders succeeded in getting inside the palisade and infiltrating the sleeping town. At the signal of an Indian war whoop, they attacked the houses and killed their occupants. At daybreak they set fire to all the houses except the one belonging to Mrs. Alexander Glen, who had often helped French prisoners. Sixty old men were spared, as well as the women and children, and thirty Iroquois prisoners were set free so that their people might know that Quebec was not making war against them. During the return journey, the contingent lost sixteen French and three Indians killed by Iroquois who had been sent in pursuit of them.[6]

The second expedition was organized in Three Rivers under François Hertel and three of his sons. Twenty-four French and twenty-five Indians set out on January 28, 1690, to attack the village of Salmon Falls north of Boston. In a surprise attack, they captured the defence towers, killed thirty defenders, took about twenty prisoners, and burned houses and farm buildings. Two hundred English settlers from the neighbouring village of Pescadouet tried to cut off the invaders' retreat, but after a sharp encounter the Frenchmen dispersed the English force, and Hertel went with thirty men to join Portneuf's detachment, which had already set out on its expedition.[7]

Portneuf had left Quebec on January 18 with fifty Frenchmen and sixty Abenakis. They proceeded slowly southward, hunting as they went and, reinforced by Hertel's force, they appeared on May 26 before Casco which was protected by a real fort with eight guns. The garrison attempted a sortie, but in the face of heavy fire, the Franco-Indian force pressed its attack so hard that on May 29 the fort surrendered with its seventy men and its women and children. The fort and the houses were burned and most of the prisoners were handed over to the Abenakis. Captain Davis and a few others were taken to Quebec, where they arrived with the returning force on June 23.[8]

These raids served to keep the English colony in a state of alarm, but Frontenac's real objective was to achieve peace with the Iroquois either by skilful negotiation or by a vigorous offensive. As lack of troops ruled out the latter possibility, he decided to put his faith in the influence he had once had with the natives, and to try the former course. In November he sent Ouréouaré with some other Cayugas to invite their nation to come and celebrate the return of their father, Ononthio. On November 9 (1690) the messengers returned to Montreal with Chief Gagnyoton who, in a speech addressed to Callières, gave no indication of friendly inclinations, but on the contrary recalled the grievances of the Iroquois: the treachery of the French at Fort Frontenac and the destruction of the Seneca villages. In Quebec Frontenac refused to receive these ill-disposed delegates, but Ouréouaré pointed out to them that, by liberating their warriors at Corlaer, Ononthio had shown that he was at war with the English and not the Iroquois. In the spring Frontenac renewed his peace offensive by dispatching a second group of Indians with peace belts and an invitation to parley. The Indians were accompanied by the Chevalier d'Aux and four other Frenchmen, and the Iroquois, after delivering the Chevalier d'Aux to the English, burned two of his companions and kept the others prisoner. Still refusing to be discouraged, Frontenac freed his Indian captives, but the Iroquois refused every peace overture and gave no quarter to their French prisoners.[9] Hostile bands of Indians continued to infest the colony; they were repelled at Pointe-aux-Trembles and Sorel by the patrols which Frontenac maintained in service, but they killed some colonists at Bécancourt.[10]

In the western region, three events had seriously undermined the French influence: La Barre's shameful pact, the peace parleys from which Denonville had excluded the nations of the Great Lakes and the massacre of Lachine. Moreover, the western tribes were naturally tempted to conclude an alliance with the Iroquois and the English and thus to profit by the higher prices paid for beaver in Albany. Alarmed at the negotiations to bring about this alliance which were being carried out by the Ottawas and the Senecas,[11] La Durantaye sent Zacharie Jolliet from Michilimackinac to warn Frontenac who at once organized an expedition and chose La Porte de Louvigny to lead it. Champigny questioned the wisdom of entrusting this particular task to a man who had a warehouse in Quebec and who travelled to his post with trading supplies in his baggage. Frontenac stood firm, however, and charged Louvigny with a three-fold mission: to prevent any Iroquois-Ottawa alliance, to suppress drunkenness among the natives, and to prevent scandalous intercourse between French subjects and squaws.[12] Louvigny set out on May 22 with his force of 143 *voyageurs* and 30 soldiers. After an encounter with an Iroquois war party at Lac des Chats, in which they cut their adversaries to pieces, they arrived at Michilimackinac towards the end of June and learned to their great satisfaction that the envoys had not yet left for the Seneca country.[13] Nicolas Perrot was a member of Louvigny's party, and his influence, reinforced by presents and a message from Frontenac to "his children," persuaded the Ottawas to maintain their alliance with the French and to hang up the war hatchet.[14]

Perrot followed up this diplomatic success by making a tour of the tribes in that region. As a result, 500 Hurons, Nipissings, Cristinaux and Ottawas took 110 canoes to Montreal where on August 19 they delighted the colonists by unloading furs worth 100,000 crowns. Frontenac conferred in solemn assembly with these allies from the West, and at the meeting of August 24, invited them to make war on the Iroquois. To his Court dress he had added an Indian feather headdress and a tomahawk, and as he sang his war song the Indians responded as he had hoped they would to the spectacle of the great Ononthio inviting them to take to the war-path. In turn, the chiefs burst into their war chants, and the meeting concluded with a feast at which two oxen and six dogs were consumed with two casks of wine and several kegs of plums. After the feast tobacco was distributed to the gathering. Later Frontenac completed this demonstration of friendship and goodwill by inviting several chiefs to be guests at his own table.[15] On August 29, while the Indians were still at Montreal, an English force was reported at Chambly and the Indians joined a company of twelve hundred men whom Frontenac assembled at La Prairie. However, as the enemy did not appear, the troops were disbanded, and after one last meeting during which they promised to follow orders from Quebec, the western Indians set out for home laden with ammunition and presents.[16]

On September 4, the band of English militiamen and Indians, which had been reported earlier at Chambly, eluded the scouts and attacked La Prairie. They surprised the workers in the fields and the soldiers outside the fort, and in a brief skirmish killed or captured about twenty persons. They then withdrew before help could arrive from Montreal.[17]

This troop, under Schuyler, was an advance guard of an army of invasion which New England had ready to march against Montreal. The plan had been drawn up in New York in the spring. A land force, to be supported by the Iroquois nations, was to act in conjunction with a naval expedition against Quebec. After the capture of Port Royal in May, militia detachments under the command of Colonel Winthrop began to gather at the meeting place on Lake Champlain where they were joined by bands of Iroquois.

About one thousand English and fifteen hundred Indians were assembled when some recruits arrived "still red" with smallpox. Some of the soldiers and a very large number of the Iroquois contracted the disease. When more than three hundred Indians had died, the others fled from the camp, shouting that a plague had been visited upon them, and after their defection the invasion by land was abandoned.[18]

The sea invasion, however, was quite another story. On October 10, Frontenac, who was in Montreal, was suddenly informed that an English fleet was approaching Tadoussac. He set out at once, leaving an order for Callières to follow him with the troops and militia detachments from the Montreal region, and he reached Quebec on the 14th. Fortunately, he had given orders in the spring for the defences of the town to be strengthened by a wall of pickets reinforced by stone redoubts, and at the first news of the approaching fleet the Sieur Provost, who was in command, had entrenched the approaches and planted batteries at various points in the Upper and Lower Towns. The banner of Notre-Dame was flown from the cathedral spire, and in a pastoral message Mgr. de Saint-Vallier exhorted the whole country to fight "the enemies, not only of the French people, but of our faith and our holy religion."[19]

As the English came up the St. Lawrence, they tried to send boats ashore at Rivière-Ouelle, but they were driven back by the villagers under the leadership of their *curé*, the Abbé Francheville. Such resistance was rare, however, and a number of prisoners were captured from the villages along the shores. On October 16 the ships with the English flag flying at the masthead were moored in the stream before Quebec. The fleet was commanded by Sir William Phipps, a former ship's carpenter, whose knighthood was a reward for the salvaging of a sunken Spanish treasureship. The capture of Port Royal in May had been an easy triumph for him, since the garrison counted only a hundred men, but in the enthusiasm of victory the New Englanders had conceived the much more ambitious project of taking Quebec. In the course of the summer 2,300 men were recruited and an imposing fleet of 34 ships was equipped for the expedition. The colonists' ardour was fanned by resentment caused by the cruel Franco-Indian raids, and by the hope of a rich conquest which would at the same time deliver them from the threat of invasion. The undertaking also had something of the spirit of a double crusade for the New Englanders since they were launching an attack against papists, some of whom had intermarried with pagan savages. Four ministers were attached to the expedition, and religious exercises were held daily.[20]

As soon as the fleet had dropped anchor a messenger bearing a white flag was sent ashore. Major Savage was led blindfold to the Château St. Louis where he was received by Frontenac and his officers in uniforms resplendent with gold braid and lace. The English officer then read a message from Admiral Phipps. It proclaimed that he had come under orders of the colony of Massachusetts and in the name of the Sovereigns of England: the fleet had been sent to avenge the cruelties perpetrated by the French and their Indian allies. In order to avoid bloodshed, Frontenac was called upon to surrender; if he refused, the city would be seized "by force of arms" and "with the help of God." After delivering this ultimatum Savage handed the Governor a watch which showed ten o'clock, and told him that he would be allowed one hour in which to consider his answer. However, Frontenac was, in the words of Bussy-Rabutin, "the last man in France to allow himself to be intimidated," and he had his answer ready: "I shall not keep you waiting. The mouths of my cannon and my rifles will answer your general."[21]

The following day (October 18), Major Walley landed with fourteen hundred men at Beauport and, in the face of rifle fire from the militia of Montreal and Three Rivers, succeeded in establishing himself on the heights. The guns of the larger English ships bombarded the town, and the batteries answered. A ball aimed by Sainte-Hélène brought down the Admiral's flag, which was retrieved from the water by a group of bold, young patriots in a bark canoe.[22] At daybreak on the 19th, the warships opened fire with all their guns, but they suffered severe damages from the French batteries and had to withdraw. The next day, the English force, preceded by an auxiliary force of Indians, advanced from Beauport in battle order with the intention of crossing the St. Charles River. Two hundred volunteers, having come out to meet the enemy under Longueil and Sainte-Hélène, took full advantage of the shelter offered by thickets and brush. Every one of their shots found its mark in the serried ranks of the English, so that at the end of a day of courageous fighting, the invading force was forced to retreat to its camp on the heights of Beauport.[23]

During the night, Phipps landed five pieces of artillery, and at daybreak on the 21st the troops charged towards the St. Charles; but they were harried by fire from men lying in ambush ahead of them, and raked on the right by militiamen from the Island of Orleans, reinforced by forty apprentices from the school at St. Joachim. The English defended themselves valiantly, cursing the "bandits" who attacked from behind bushes, and challenging them to come out and fight in the open, but they did not succeed in forcing the French position. They were withdrawing in good order when suddenly they heard the tocsin ring out from the cathedral, and thought it was the signal for a mass sortie. The orderly retreat became a rout, and during the night the invaders re-embarked leaving their guns behind them.[24]

On October 24 the fleet moved down river as far as l'Arbre-Sec (St. Laurent), near the middle of the Island of Orleans. At the suggestion of Mlle Lalande, one of the prisoners who had been taken on the way up the river, Phipps agreed to an exchange, and sixteen prisoners were handed over by each of the opposing forces. The fleet then continued on its way to the sea and arrived in Boston on November 19. The expedition had been a complete failure. Six hundred men died in battle or from sickness, nine ships were lost during the homeward voyage, and the merchants, who had tried to set up as conquerors, lost 50,000 pounds sterling. French casualties were limited to six dead and twenty wounded. The people of Boston made Walley the scapegoat for the fiasco, and one of the chaplains distilled their bitterness in an epigram: "Of what use is an army of lions if it is led by a rabbit?" Massachusetts found some consolation, however, in the thought that the expedition had probably saved New England from the raids of a thousand "French half-breeds."[25]

In Canada, the expulsion of the enemy brought an upsurge of pride and confidence. On Sunday the English Admiral's captured flag was carried through the town to the sound of drums and deposited in the cathedral. The *Te Deum* chanted by Mgr. de Saint-Vallier was followed by a solemn procession in honour of the Virgin, the patron saint of the colony, and the church in the Lower Town was baptized Notre-Dame-de-la-Victoire. A display of fireworks in the evening ended a day of rejoicing.[26]

In this climate of triumphant confidence, Frontenac again suggested that France undertake to conquer the English colonies, "to hurl a thunderbolt" at the old Boston puritans, and to hunt out the people of Massachusetts "in their lair." He offered to lead an attack against Albany himself, if he were given the necessary troops. However, the Governor's letter reached France after the death of Seignelay, and the new Minister, Pontchartrain, had his hands full with the war in Ireland where, in July, France had suf-

fered defeat at the Battle of the Boyne. Consequently, no attempt
was made to exploit the victory of the colonists. The King closed
the episode by striking a commemorative medal bearing the following inscription in Latin: "To France victorious in the New
World, and to Quebec delivered from the enemy, 1690." He also
sent personal congratulations to Frontenac, and, in recognition of
the valour of the militia, conferred titles of nobility on two of its
officers, Hertel and Juchereau de Saint-Denis.[27]

The Iroquois war and Phipps' expedition had between them
practically exhausted the resources of the colony, which had received little help from the mother country. Of eleven ships from
La Rochelle only three had proceeded as far as Tadoussac. These
had taken refuge in the Saguenay, and had continued their journey
to Montreal after the departure of the English fleet. The help
they brought was quite inadequate, especially since rain and
fog had ruined "the finest wheat crop in the world." The harvest
was very poor and "everything else" was in short supply. To ensure that the soldiers would be fed, Champigny had to quarter
them on the habitants who received the army pay directly. During
the winter everyone had to accept an austere régime of restriction
and privation. Even Frontenac was "reduced to drinking water."
However, having successfully met the challenge of invasion, the
country looked forward to the future with hope and confidence.[27a]

CHAPTER TWELVE

FRONTENAC'S INDIAN POLICY
EXPEDITIONS AGAINST THE IROQUOIS
1691-1696

A hard winter in the colony. Support from the western Indians. Supplies from France. English raid on La Prairie. Iroquois raids. Madeleine de Verchères. Manthet's expedition against the Mohawks. Trade and parleys with the Indians. Re-establishment of Fort Frontenac. D'Iberville's expedition to Hudson Bay. Frontenac's campaign against the Onondagas and Oneidas.

After the defeat of Phipps, the politic Mohawks thought it wise to reach an agreement with Quebec, even though their four sister nations were preparing a great offensive. Accordingly, in March (1691) a band of Mohawk warriors came to inform their Christian compatriots at Sault St. Louis of their desire to end hostilities. Delegates then took the same message to Callières in Montreal, where it was favourably received.[1]

The winter and spring of that year (1691) were a period of great hardship in the colony. War parties had exhausted the stocks of provisions, and the price of wheat doubled. The people lived largely on fish which they caught through holes in the ice, and as soon as the snow disappeared they supplemented this limited diet with herbs and roots from the forest. At the same time although it had successfully withstood an invasion, the colony was still very vulnerable to attack. Stocks of ammunition were so low that under Champigny's orders gutters were melted down to make bullets. The habitants went to their work in the fields armed and in groups, and the Governor gave orders to strengthen the fortifications of the three towns.[2] But even when beset by pressing anxieties in the East, Frontenac did not forget to maintain the friendship and support of the western Indians or to keep the Canadian market supplied with their furs. In May 1691 the Sieur de Courtemanche gathered the chiefs of the western tribes in an assembly at Michilimackinac, and they promised to continue their war against the Iroquois.[3]

In July the Canadians were cheered by the arrival of thirteen French ships laden with munitions, food and merchandise. A little later a group of Ottawas arrived in Montreal, and after leaving their furs at the market, proceeded on to Quebec. There they were feasted by the Governor and they marvelled at the size of the ships in the harbour. Still more impressed by the salvoes of artillery fire with which the colonists celebrated France's victories in Europe, they carried back to their distant tribes the story of the might of France. At the same time, Frontenac sent a convoy of munitions and merchandise to the western posts to be distributed among the tribes in order to ensure the continued friendship of these valuable allies.[4] In the colony itself, however, the situation suddenly became critical. In May, nine hundred Iroquois warriors launched the invasion of which the Mohawks had given warning. The country people took refuge in the fortified posts, but the Indians ravaged the country, killed animals, burned houses and even captured a few isolated colonists at Contrecœur.[5] On the other hand, on June 7, during a surprise attack, a detachment of Canadian and Indian regulars, led by Vaudreuil, entirely wiped out a band of forty Oneidas at Repentigny.[6]

When the Iroquois appealed to their English friends for help, Peter Schuyler was sent with a force of four hundred militiamen and Indians to capture the fort at La Prairie. Warned of their approach, Callières set out from Montreal with eight hundred men and sent M. de Valrennes with a detachment of 120 soldiers to defend Chambly.[7] During the night of August 10 (1691), the invaders made a sudden attack on Callières's outposts, but they encountered Valrennes's party which had been posted behind a shelter of trees. A violent battle ensued, during which the enemy charged three times and fought bravely. On the French side, Valrennes inspired his troops with his own courage, le Ber gave expert leadership to the militia, and Chief Routine spurred on the Ottawas, all to good effect: the Mohawks faltered and led the English in such headlong flight that baggage and colours were left behind on the battlefield. Forty-five French and a hundred English soldiers were killed in the battle, and the number of wounded on both sides was considerable.[8]

The Five Nations had suffered severe losses at Repentigny and La Prairie, and Franco-Indian scouting parties continued to keep a close watch and to harrass any wandering bands, with the re-

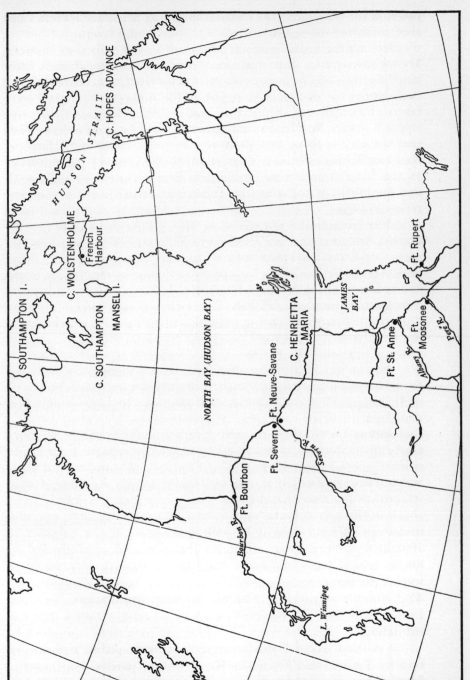

MAP OF HUDSON BAY, WITH ITS FORTS, IN THE 17TH CENTURY.

sult that for the time being the raids stopped, and the farmers were able to gather in a providentially abundant harvest. Frontenac adopted a firm attitude when about this time the Governor of Massachusetts and John Nelson, a shipowner from Boston, proposed an exchange of prisoners and a neutrality pact. He laid down as a condition for opening negotiations the return of prisoners taken at Port Royal. Frontenac also believed that the time was ripe for a French offensive in America, and he recommended to the Minister d'Iberville's plan to conquer the whole island of Newfoundland and make it a base for the cod fishery. However, as all the King's forces were engaged in Europe in the struggle with the Anglo-Dutch coalition, he refused to embark on any adventures overseas.[9]

The Iroquois did not abandon their idea of collaborating with the English to suppress French competition, and they continued their sallies on the trade routes. In February (1692) they were beaten off at Ile Tonihata by a party under the command of Beaumont, but they succeeded in turning back or scattering several convoys of *voyageurs*. In July Chief Chaudière-Noire's warriors captured habitants at Lachine and La Chesnaye and on Ile Jésus, but Vaudreuil and his men pursued them and cut them to pieces at the Long Sault. In the West, true to their promise to Courtemanche, the Indian allies harried the Iroquois villages and inflicted severe losses on the enemy.[10] Again in 1692 the colonists harvested their crops unmolested, but, unfortunately, the crops themselves had been seriously damaged by grasshoppers. However, as if to compensate for this loss, the red squirrels and the eels were more abundant than usual. The vessels from France brought large quantities of goods and munitions, and Frontenac was ordered to abolish the bounties which it was customary to pay in time of war, ten crowns for a scalp and twenty for an English prisoner.

The King had taken very seriously a warning that a second invasion of Canada might be attempted, and in the summer of 1692 he sent out a squadron under the command of M. du Palais, but although the ships spent months in Spanish Bay ready to waylay the invading fleet, they did not sight a single English sail.[11] The rumour of invasion was not without foundation, however. Phipps, who was now Governor of New England, knew how weak the defences of Quebec were, and he would have liked to undertake an expedition. He did not succeed in uniting public opinion in favour of his scheme,[12] and in New York dissension between the English and Dutch groups created a further obstacle to any project of invasion.

Meanwhile, the English continued to incite their Indian allies to aggressive action. In October (1692) four hundred Iroquois attacked the fort at Sault St. Louis, and were driven off after a brief skirmish. Small bands raided the country districts at various points, including Sorel and St. Ours, and killed a few workers in the fields.[13] On October 22 one of these raiding parties tried to surprise the fort of the Verchères seigniory. The seigneur's fourteen-year-old daughter, Madeleine, seeing Indians in the fields, had barely time to run to the fort and bar the door. She had with her two soldiers, a servant, her brothers, aged ten and twelve years, and a few women. After arming herself and all the men including her brothers, she replaced her cap with a man's hat and took command of her little troop. She made them fire shots at intervals from different loopholes, and during the night they kept repeating the watchman's cry: *Bon quart*. In this way she hoped to make it appear that the fort was well manned, and her stratagem was successful. The Indians stayed at a respectful distance until, on the third day, the gallant little party was relieved by a French patrol.[14]

Frontenac knew that the Iroquois always chose the summer to go on the war-path, while the winter, when the bare trees offered no shelter to the warrior, was given up to hunting. In January 1693 he took advantage of this knowledge to launch an expedition against the most implacable of the tribes, the Mohawks.[15] Under the leadership of d'Ailleboust de Manthet a contingent of seven hundred men, including regulars, militiamen and Indians, set out on snowshoes for the Mohawk country, which they reached on February 16. The first two villages had been abandoned, and the whole population made a stand in the third; it was captured after a fight during which thirty Indians were killed, and three hundred including women and children were captured. After burning the three villages, the troops set out for Quebec, and two days later they scored a further victory against an Anglo-Indian force of six hundred men which attempted to intercept them. During the return march to Quebec the troops were on very short rations, but this hardship, and the others which they had endured, had their reward in the salutary fear inspired by the expedition in English and Iroquois alike.[16]

However, this foray was also a challenge to Phipps to carry out his plan for an invasion of Canada, and knowing this, Frontenac again strengthened the fortifications of Quebec, while Callières built a little citadel in Montreal. In July, seven hundred Iroquois came and camped at the St. Louis rapids to await the arrival of their English allies but on hearing that Callières was ad-

vancing with eight hundred men they withdrew. In June the
fleet which the New Englanders had been expecting from England
arrived in Boston. Unfortunately, it had plague on board, and
besides, there was no invasion force ready to embark; so, after a
fruitless wait, Admiral Wheeler set sail again for England.[17]

Spirits rose high in Quebec as the threat of invasion receded,
and the colonists were further cheered by the arrival in July of
ships with food, munitions, merchandise, and, still more important, 426 soldiers. Their satisfaction was complete when, without accident or molestation of any kind, they harvested bounti-
ful crops.[18] Now Frontenac could turn his attention to the beaver
pelts which had been piling up for three years in the western posts
because the traders did not dare to risk exposing their canoes to Iroquois attacks. On the Governor's orders, Louvigny left Michilimackinac in August 1693 with a fleet of canoes manned by 700 men,
including 250 Frenchmen. The canoes carried 1,000,000 pounds of
furs which were unloaded in Montreal. It was a fortune for the
country. After the fair, Frontenac invited the chiefs to his own
table, and on September 6 he exhorted a great gathering of all the
Indians present in Montreal not to falter in their struggle against
the common enemy. The Indians left Montreal loaded with the
customary presents, while Tonty and Nicolas Perrot were again
charged with the duty of keeping the peace among the western
tribes. Tonty's post was Fort St. Louis on the Illinois, while
Perrot's post was at Chouagen (Chicago) at the south end of Lake
Michigan.[19]

During the summer of 1693 the Iroquois, alarmed by Manthet's expedition and harassed by forays from other tribes, offered
to engage in negotiations. Frontenac refused to parley, declaring
that it was for him to make proposals and that if his terms were
rejected he would take measures to impose them.[20] In April 1694
he presented these terms to a delegation led by Teganisorens:
the Iroquois were to conclude a general peace with all the Indian tribes, including those which were allies of the French, and
in token of their good faith they were to surrender all their French
and Indian prisoners. Before the delegates left, he repeated this
declaration at a gathering at which the chiefs of the western tribes
were also present.[21]

Three months later, Governor Fletcher of New York countered Frontenac's move by calling his own meeting of the chiefs of
the Five Nations. He urged them to break off negotiations with
the French, and after a second meeting at Onondaga, he too made

a generous distribution of gifts: rifles, hatchets, clothes, rum and tobacco. The Senecas and Cayugas accepted the gifts, but that did not prevent them from sending envoys to Montreal, nor did it prevent these envoys from refusing to commit themselves to the French.[22] In the West, in spite of the "secret" intrigues of the Iroquois, the commanders Cadillac at Detroit, Tonty at St. Louis, and Courtemanche at Fort Miami, kept the Indians on friendly trading terms with Canada. The Iroquois, finding themselves thwarted on every side, resumed their guerilla tactics in an effort to force Frontenac to conclude a peace. In the spring of 1695 prowling bands were seen from time to time, and during the summer they killed a few colonists near Montreal.[23]

However, the Five Nations were still not agreed on a united policy, and Frontenac thought the opportune moment for action had come. On July (1695) he sent the Italian officer, Crisafy, with six hundred men to rebuild Fort Frontenac as a trading-post and a military base. The day after the party set out, an order to abandon the undertaking arrived from the Minister, but it did not deter Frontenac from carrying out his plan. A new fort was erected, larger and more solidly built than the earlier one.[24] Frontenac explained to the western tribes who came down to Montreal for the annual fur fair, that the strategic position of Fort Frontenac would make it possible for him to impose a general peace on the common enemy, and thus to benefit all the tribes. In the meantime, however, the Franco-Indian alliance came within an ace of being destroyed. A disloyal Huron chief, Le Baron, allowed the Iroquois to circulate their stories of high English prices for furs and free-flowing English rum, and only a stroke of good fortune prevented some of the Hurons and Ottawas from going over to the enemy. Iroquois and Ottawa hunters were returning together from hunting when the Ottawas, in a passion of vengeance against their traditional enemies, killed fifty of the Iroquois, and took twenty-two prisoners. After that there was no further question of a pact between the two tribes, a situation which was eminently satisfactory for the French.[25]

Some time previously, Frontenac had received instructions to give every facility to d'Iberville, who was planning an expedition to Hudson Bay. The *Compagnie du Nord* was anxious to recapture the forts which had been seized by the English, and on July 11, 1694, d'Iberville arrived in Quebec with two ships. He undertook to finance the expedition on condition that all captured ships and booty should be his. In Montreal his brother Sérigny recruited 110 Canadians who, instead of regular pay, were to receive half the prize booty and half the profits from the furs. On September 24 the French force laid siege to Fort Nelson, and three weeks later the garrison of fifty-three men surrendered the post with its guns and flags. D'Iberville spent the winter on the Bay carrying on a profitable trade, and when he returned to La Rochelle in October 1695 he was richer by about 30,000 *livres*. His triumph was short-lived, however. Just a year after his return to France, an English expedition under William Allen recaptured Fort Bourbon, and with it England recovered command of Hudson Bay.[26]

For two years Frontenac had been considering a punitive expedition into Iroquois country, and now, in the summer of 1696, the moment seemed propitious. The English had not succeeded in working out a plan for invasion, and the Iroquois were weakened by the loss of some of their finest warriors. Frontenac, who was now a remarkably vigorous veteran of seventy-four, commanded in person a force of two thousand men, including regular soldiers, militia and Indians. The army was equipped with hand-drawn guns and mortars. As they proceeded up the Oswego by a series of difficult portages, Frontenac was carried in a canoe "on the shoulders of fifty Indians singing and shouting with joy."[27] On August 5 they advanced in two divisions against the main village of Onondaga. It was protected by a palisade forty feet high, but the Indians had fled after burning their lodges. The troops spent the next few days destroying the standing crops, and plundering the caches of grain, tools, arms and furs. In the village they found the mutilated bodies of two Frenchmen who had been killed quite recently. Only one prisoner was taken, an old man who, in spite of Frontenac's protests, was burned by the Indians. He displayed extraordinary fortitude, refusing to give any outward sign of suffering, and shouting defiance at his torturers: "Learn from me how to die, French dogs, and you Indians their allies, the French dogs' dogs!" From Onondaga, Vaudreuil led his division against the Oneida village, nine leagues farther on, where his men captured some thirty persons and freed four French prisoners. Then, after destroying the harvest and burning the huts, they returned to Frontenac's camp.[28]

On August 9, the army started on its homeward journey, and on the 20th it reached Montreal. The campaign had lasted forty-six days. At the cost of four Frenchmen drowned, and three Indians killed by enemy fire, it had reduced two of the Five Nations to flight and famine. It had not diminished the enemy's fighting force nor eliminated the threat of guerilla warfare, but the victors had subjected the proud Iroquois to the supreme humiliation, the destruction of their family "wigwam" and the violation of the land of their fathers. The campaign confirmed France's domination over the upper country from Oswego to Lake Superior, and it won the alliance of the tribes in that region. Louis XIV recognized the importance of this success by granting Frontenac the cross of the Order of Saint Louis.[29]

CHAPTER THIRTEEN

CONQUEST OF HUDSON BAY
AND INTERNAL QUARRELS
1697-1698

Hesitations of the Iroquois. Expedition against Boston. D'Iberville captures Hudson Bay. Disagreement between Frontenac and Champigny. Mgr. de Saint-Vallier. Mgr. de Laval. The Tartuffe *incident. The Saint-Vallier - Callières quarrel and the interdiction of the Récollets. Liquor scandal. Surplus of beaver. Abolition of* congés. *Peace of Ryswick. Iroquois peace proposals. Death of Frontenac.*

After the destruction of their villages, the hungry and humiliated Onondagas and Oneidas sought help from the English. When, in September 1696, the Governor of New York offered their envoys nothing more than blankets and iron pots, they told him that since the English did not choose to fight in their support, they would have to conclude a peace with Ononthio.[1] Accordingly, in February and again in August (1697), several delegations sought to reopen parleys with Frontenac, but he met their overtures with the same firm answer he had given before: he would receive ambassadors only if they had been instructed to accept his conditions. The Iroquois were not quite ready to submit to this ultimatum, but during the summer of 1697 they made only two minor raids, on St. Lambert and La Prairie.[2] This moderation was dictated as much by necessity as by prudence. They had to defend their own villages against Huron and Ottawa incursions, which, in the course of the spring, had cost them two hundred warriors.[3] In the West, however, Iroquois intrigues were stirring up tribal rivalries. The Sioux attacked the Miamis who in turn robbed the French. In 1697 they even captured Nicolas Perrot, who was saved from torture only by the intervention of the Outagamis. In an effort to halt the spread of disaffection Lamothe-Cadillac went down with three hundred Ottawas, Hurons and Potawatomis to Montreal. Where Frontenac made such good use of his talent for native diplomacy that before the delegates left Montreal in September they had promised to maintain the peace in their own country and to continue to harass the Iroquois villages.[4]

In May Frontenac had been informed that both European powers were contemplating offensive action in America, and he had been commanded by the King to raise a corps of fifteen hundred men. The force was to await orders to proceed to Pentagoët where it would join an expedition commanded by M. de Nesmond and directed against Boston. Frontenac and Champigny at once gave orders for mobilizing the manpower of the colony. The rural population supplied one man from each house, but the townspeople could meet their obligation by paying the keep of soldiers who replaced them. By this means the required force was constituted during the early summer months. However, Nesmond had been given a two-fold commission: before proceeding to Boston, he was to make a stop at Placentia and from there to intercept the English squadron on its way to Hudson Bay. The French fleet was delayed by headwinds, and when it reached Placentia on July 24, the English ships were no longer in those waters. In August a council of war also concluded that it was too late in the season to carry out the project of invasion. Accordingly, Nesmond sent word to Frontenac that his forces would not be needed, and the imposing squadron of eleven vessels and four fireships returned to France without accomplishing either part of its mission. The expedition had not been completely fruitless, however, since the presence of a French squadron in American waters had effectively discouraged any English plans for invasion of Canada.[5]

During the winter of 1697, Louis XIV decided to recapture Hudson Bay with its fur market, and in March d'Iberville was given command of a fleet of five ships. The thirty-one Canadians whom he added to his crew were to be paid 30 *livres* a month, and they had permission to trade for their own account, while d'Iberville himself, to the great chagrin of the *Compagnie du Nord,* was granted a monopoly of the fur trade in the Bay until 1699.[6] The fleet was delayed by fog and ice, and when on September 4 d'Iberville's ship, the *Pélican,* dropped anchor in front of Fort Nelson, the other vessels had not arrived. The next day the enemy's ships appeared, the *Hampshire,* the *Dering* and the *Hudson Bay.* Although the first of these carried fifty cannon, and each of the others had thirty-two, while to this combined strength the *Pélican* could oppose only forty-four guns and a hundred and fifty able-bodied fighters, d'Iberville at once went into action. He bore down on the *Hampshire,* and when it sheered off, turned his guns on the *Dering* and the *Hudson Bay.* Meanwhile, the English were concentrating their fire on the mast of the *Pélican* in an effort to disable her. After three hours of sustained fighting, the *Hampshire* drew up to the *Pélican.* Captain Fletcher charged d'Iberville to surrender, and upon his refusal each commander drank the other's health. The enemy then launched its heaviest broadside, but the balls struck above deck, and most of the damage was done to the bulwarks. The *Pélican,* on the other hand, aimed low, and after several balls had gone home in the hull, the *Hampshire* veered about and sank. Stunned by this disaster, the captain of the *Hudson Bay* hauled down his flag while the *Dering* withdrew and made good its escape. D'Iberville had to abandon any idea of pursuit since the hull of the *Pélican* was badly damaged. That astounding victory of September 5, 1697, was won, at the cost of seventeen soldiers wounded, by the sheer audacity and skill in seamanship of the commander, and by the courage of his men.[7]

The following day a storm struck the Bay. The *Hudson Bay* sank as did the badly damaged *Pélican,* but the crew of the latter succeeded in reaching shore, and with the arrival of three other French ships, the *Profond,* the *Palmier* and the *Wasp,* d'Iberville was able to reorganize his force. On September 12 he opened fire on Fort Nelson, but the commander, Henry Bailey, refused to surrender. However, when d'Iberville warned him that no quarter would be given, the garrison of fifty-two men forced their commander to capitulate. Eleven days later d'Iberville set sail for France, and he arrived there in November.[8]

Since peace had been signed at Ryswick on September 20, d'Iberville made plans to exploit his monopoly. In November he also solicited the post of Governor of Newfoundland, with the intention of establishing a base for important cod fisheries. The Court, however, decided to entrust to him the more important task of establishing a colony on the banks of the Mississippi. New France's best sailor and most remarkable soldier was not destined to return to Canada but to become the founder and the first governor of the colony of Louisiana.[9]

The project of linking Louisiana to Canada by the valleys of the Mississippi and the Ohio had a dual purpose: to debar the Carolina English from trading in French territory and to forestall the English scheme for getting a footing at the mouth of the Mississippi. This latter idea had been suggested to them by the book of the Récollet Hennepin who had the effrontery to claim that he had discovered Louisiana before La Salle. In June 1698 the King entrusted to d'Iberville the mission of founding the new colony, and on March 2 of the following year, the great sailor rediscovered the delta of the Mississippi and planted a cross to confirm the French sovereignity already proclaimed by La Salle. In April the French flag was hoisted over the first post, Biloxi, and in 1700 d'Iberville became the first governor of the colony which took shape over the next few years as new posts were established.[10]

In spite of the King's warning to Frontenac, religious and administrative difficulties were a characteristic feature of his second term, as they had been of his first, and it soon became apparent that the Governor and the Intendant were not a well-matched team. Although he had become less violent with age, Frontenac was as intractable and imperious as ever. Especially impatient of any activity which limited his own, he constantly encroached upon the domain of his colleague, while Champigny resented keenly the arrogance of the Governor who treated the "effective administrator of the colony as if he had been a treasury clerk."[11]

Not only were the two men incompatible in temperament, their programmes for the country brought them into conflict at every point. Frontenac pressed for the development of the fur trade. His special friends, Louvigny and Cadillac, were important traders, and he was a partner in their enterprises. Champigny too, had a personal stake in the business world, but his particular sphere of interest was the import trade so he tried to bring down the costs of shipping, and he favoured the development of commerce and agriculture rather than the fur trade. The Governor's patrons in Paris were the Minister of Marine, Pontchartrain, and the Grand Commis de Lagny, while Madame de Frontenac and her friends were in a position to speak for him at court. Champigny for his part could count on support from the farmers-general, who held the trade monopolies, the Seminary of St. Sulpice, and the Jesuits in Paris. The cold war between the Governor and the Intendant could not but be detrimental to the welfare of the colony, and the King, after repeated admonitions on the subject, warned them that he might be obliged to recall them.[12]

Strains and tensions were apparent in the ecclesiastical sphere as well as in civil affairs. The new bishop, Mgr. de Saint-Vallier, was a high-minded and sincerely pious young man, but stubborn self-will and a somewhat indiscreet zeal for reform made of him, as

Father Tremblay said, a firebrand and a trouble-maker. He quarrelled with his canons and in 1689 he shocked and distressed Mgr. de Laval by abolishing the system which made all parishes dependencies of the Seminary of Quebec. The old bishop declared in bitterness that, instead of working to strengthen the Church in Canada, his successor was serving as "the devil's instrument to work its destruction."[13]

A few years later, the Bishop also quarrelled with the Governor. In the early winter of 1693 a group of amateur actors had been organized especialy for the entertainment of the officers and ladies who constituted the Governor's own social circle. They presented Corneille's *Nicomède* and Racine's *Mithridate,* and Frontenac announced that plans were well advanced for a presentation of *Tartuffe.* The title role was to be played by Lieutenant Jacques de Mareuil, and he would be supported by the two pretty daughters of a toolmaker who were being coached for their parts at the Château St. Louis by the Governor himself.[14]

When *Tartuffe* was first presented in public in 1667, the Archbishop of Paris had forbidden his flock "to read, present or witness," it under pain of excommunication. Mgr. de Saint-Vallier, shocked that the Governor would allow, and even encourage, the presentation of such a play, at once took counter measures. In a pastoral letter dated January 17 (1694), he declared it a sin to witness "corrupting and impure plays" such as *Tartuffe.* A second order, charging Mareuil with having made blasphemous statements, denied him access to Communion until such time as he had achieved a state of "salutary penitence." The *Tartuffe* scandal and the rift between the Château St. Louis and the Bishop's palace were the talk of the town. The Governor had given no indication that he meant to abandon his project, and when directly challenged and asked by the Bishop if *Tartuffe* would be presented, he answered: "Why not? You can see it in Paris." Mgr. de Saint-Vallier declared that he would give 100 *pistoles* to prevent such a scandal, and the Governor, amused, took him at his word and accepted the offer. The Bishop paid his 1,000 *livres* to the Governor who distributed the money among the needy people of Quebec. It had been an expensive funeral, but *Tartuffe* was buried.[14a]

The *Tartuffe* case was closed, but the Mareuil file was still open. Mareuil had actually received Communion at Christmas, and he resented the Bishop's sentence, pronounced without warning, and based on an irreverent song which he had written two years earlier, and which he and everyone else had forgotten. He took the first steps to justify himself, but in order to spare the Bishop any embarassment, the Attorney-General, d'Auteuil, obtained an order from the Sovereign Council for the arrest of Mareuil and his detention in the Intendant's palace. He then managed to make the case drag on until November. Frontenac was furious at this travesty of justice, the more so since Mareuil had been his guest. Finally, on November 29, he presented himself before the Council and ordered that Mareuil be liberated, and that the case be submitted to the King for a decision. Mareuil, having recovered his freedom, returned to his lodging in the Château St. Louis.[15]

Still another quarrel broke out in May 1694, the famous case of the prie-Dieu in Montreal. It arose in the Récollets' chapel on the occasion of the reception of a new member into the order. The Bishop was to officiate at the ceremony and the Récollets had reserved a prie-Dieu in the choir for Governor Callières. As Mgr. de Saint-Vallier walked through the church, he ordered the prie-Dieu to be placed outside the chancel rail; but when the Governor arrived, the officers in attendance put it back in the choir. Before the service began, Mgr. de Saint-Vallier came and whispered to Callières that if he persisted in occupying that place, he (the Bishop) would have to leave the chapel. The Governor remained in his place, and the Bishop, making good his threat, left the chapel without carrying out the ceremony.[16]

The next day the prelate ordered Father Denis, the Récollets' Superior, to remove all the prie-Dieu from the choir; but Callières came with his officers and had them put back. The Bishop then decreed that the chapel should be closed, and it remained closed for two months. At the end of that time, the Récollets reopened their church and continued to conduct their services even after being specifically forbidden by the Bishop to preach or to hear confessions. In his final admonition to the rebels, the Bishop insinuated that Callières maintained "relations" with Madame de Ramezay, the sister of the Récollets' superior. Supremely indignant, the Governor answered with a violent attack on Mgr. de Saint-Vallier which was read at his order by the town crier. As a result of this series of feuds, the Bishop was ordered by the King to present himself in Paris and explain his conduct. In Paris the Superior of the Récollets, speaking on behalf of the Récollets in Montreal, expressed their submission to the authority of the Bishop, and obtained for them the removal of the sanctions which had been imposed.[17]

At Versailles, the constant stream of letters and complaints concerning these quarrels had irritated the King, and he referred all these matters to the Council on Complaints to be disposed of once and for all. In a letter dated June 8, 1695, Pontchartrain, writing in the name of the King, censured the violence of Frontenac's actions. He considered also that the episode of the 100 *pistoles* did the Governor no credit. D'Auteuil was ordered to apologize to the Governor in the presence of witnesses. To the Bishop it was made quite clear that he had incurred the royal displeasure. He was forbidden to return to Quebec, and the King asked him for his resignation. The Bishop succeeded in evading this last order, however, and when, in 1697, Bossuet suggested that he should not be kept away any longer from his flock, the King allowed him to return to Canada, but not before giving him a solemn warning: "Return to your diocese, but see to it that you re-establish perfect peace there; for if I hear any further complaints, I shall not hesitate to recall you, and such a recall would be permanent."[18]

While all these quarrels kept Quebec and Montreal in a state of ferment, a chronic malady, the alcohol problem, had again reached a critical point in the West. The beginnings of the trouble went back several years. At the important western centre of Michilimackinac, three villages were grouped around the fort, the French village of about sixty houses, and those of the Hurons and the Ottawas with a total of five or six thousand people. The Superior of the Jesuits' western region had his headquarters there, and from there supervised the missions at Sault Ste. Marie and at St. François-Xavier on Green Bay. There, too, traders and their employees gathered in large numbers. The law of 1679 prohibited the sale of brandy in the Indian villages, but the strictness with which the law was enforced depended in large measure on the personal convictions or interests of the Governor. At first the law was honoured more in the breach than in the observance. Then, under Denonville and the vigilant La Durantaye, it was strictly enforced, but after the return of Frontenac and the appointment of Louvigny as commander at Michilimackinac in 1690, trade in alcohol once more became very active.[19]

The missionaries complained and urged Mgr. de Saint-Vallier to put an end to the situation. The Bishop took up the question with the government and the Court, and the Jesuits in France made representations to the King. In 1692, as a result of these efforts, Louis XIV directed Frontenac and Champigny to see that the law of 1679 was enforced. Accordingly, Champigny issued an order restating the existing law, but Frontenac, as usual, found means to evade the royal command. As commander of the army he ruled that alcohol could be sold "in places where there is a French garrison." He thus opened the door to the liquor traffic, and the opening became wider in 1694 with the arrival of another new commander at Michilimackinac.[20]

Louvigny's successor was Antoine Laumet, the son of a family of lawyers and merchants, who had invented a noble lineage for himself under the name of Cadillac. He was intelligent, well-educated, ambitious; he had a witty tongue and a facile pen, and he had been clever enough to win the protection of Frontenac by flattering the old man's vanity and by abusing the Jesuits at every opportunity. Unscrupulous as to methods and anxious only to make money quickly, he used every means to stimulate the fur trade. Commanders of other posts, following his example, used their soldiers as middlemen, and allowed them to trade on their own account. As one important article of barter was brandy, the Indians were free to indulge their passion for strong drinks, and they did so on every occasion in spite of all the missionaries' remonstrances and objurgations. No serious discipline was maintained among the soldiers, whose chief occupations were fur-trading and gambling, while the easy morality of the Indians encouraged casual sexual relations between their women and men at the posts. In 1695 Father Pinet raised his voice against the "scandalous relations" which went on "at all hours of the day and night," and several years later Father Carheil condemned the wanton morals of the soldiery in still stronger terms. "All our Indian villages," he wrote, "are haunts of drunkenness and vice. We must be delivered from the garrisons and their commanders who . . . are the worst enemy of our missions." The Jesuits felt quite justified in refusing absolution to such impenitent offenders, and Champigny advocated the abolition of all *congés* as a means of cutting off these abuses at the root.[21]

Interests still more powerful than the Jesuits were petitioning the Court of the abolition of the trading licences. The farmers-general who held the monopoly on the sale of beaver in France were embarassed by their accumulating stock of furs. Until 1693 they had received about 90,000 pounds of skins a year, and it had been comparatively easy to dispose of each year's harvest of furs before the next one arrived. As early as 1690 Champigny informed the Minister that Frontenac was using the war and the dispatch of troops to the distant posts as an excuse for granting special permits, and about the same time the quantity of beaver from the West increased considerably. The King ordered Frontenac to prohibit trading by the troops,[22] but the pelts continued to pile up in the posts, and in 1692 the Canadian market was flooded with 200,000 pounds of furs.[23] Frontenac tried to lay the blame for this crisis on his predecessors,[23a] and in order to relieve the situation the King authorized a reduction in the price paid for furs. The order was signed in May 1695, but the Governor and the Intendant managed to delay its application until July 1697.[24]

In 1695, when conditions were apparently improving, 600,000 pounds of pelts were brought down to Quebec. The farmers-general were faced with ruin, and since in this matter their interests coincided with those of the Jesuits, who were striving to wipe out the evil of the licentious *coureurs de bois,* the two groups united to bring pressure on the Court. The King listened sympathetically to their plea and on March 21, 1696, he issued an order cancelling all *congés.* Failure to comply with the order would be punishable by service in the galleys. At the same time the King decreed that all western posts, with the exception of St. Louis on the Illinois, were to be closed.[25] But when Champigny pleaded that such a move would be disastrous for the economy of the country, and Frontenac added that it constituted surrender of the western trade to the English,[26] the order was modified according to the Intendant's suggestions.[27] The posts would remain open but with very small garrisons whose members were absolutely forbidden to trade.[28] When the troops were withdrawn by Frontenac and their duties were carried out by a small guard, it became apparent that the garrisons had served no other purpose than to provide opportunities for their officers to engage in the fur trade.[29] On June 15, 1698, Champigny signed an order forbidding trade in the interior and ordering all *voyageurs* to return to the settlements.[30] In July the Ottawas brought their furs down to the fair in Montreal, to the satisfaction of all concerned. A certain number of *voyageurs* complied with the Intendant's order in the autumn of the same year, and about sixty returned during the next two years, while eighty-four migrated to Louisiana. Some stayed in the west and were joined by others from Montreal, and there were still soldiers on guard duty in the posts whom Frontenac continued to provide with trading supplies. In one way or another, clandestine trading crept back into the colony, where it could always count on the connivance necessary for its survival.[31]

On September 20, 1697, a treaty of peace was signed at Ryswick by France and England. With a view to preparing the accession of his grandson to the throne of Spain, Louis XIV restored most of the European territory which he had acquired since the peace of Nymwegen. In America the treaty re-established the pre-war *status quo*. France regained all the Hudson Bay posts except Fort Albany, but in Newfoundland she retained only Placentia and her fishing rights and while Acadia was restored to her, its frontier was withdrawn from the Kennebec to the St. George River.[32]

News of the peace reached Quebec on January 28, 1698. In June, Colonel Schuyler, representing Governor Bellomont, brought back nineteen French prisoners from New York, and Frontenac recipro-cated by handing over all the English prisoners in Quebec except a few who had been converted to Roman Catholicism and prefer-red to remain in Canada.[33]

The Five Nations also wished to put an end to hostilities, and after hearing of the treaty from the English, they made no further raids. In the course of the winter, however, the western Indians allied with the French killed a hundred Iroquois warriors includ-ing their great chief, Chaudière-Noire,[34] and as a result of these losses, the Oneidas stipulated that the western tribes would be ex-cluded from the treaty which they proposed to sign with the French. Furious at such a suggestion, Frontenac threw the ambas-sador's symbolic belt in his face, but he was less discourteous to-wards the Onondagas' envoy, Blasio, perhaps because he was the only Indian who had ever married a French wife. Blasio was sent to advise his tribe that they should subscribe to the peace if they wanted to be spared a punitive campaign.[35]

In August 1698 Bellomont informed the Iroquois that they must not attack the French nor the Indians living within the French sphere of influence in the East but only the western tribes. Thereupon the Wolf tribe declared that in the event of an Anglo-French war they would remain neutral, and "let the war hatchet fly over their heads." This was the first time such an idea had been expressed by an Indian tribe.[36] Frontenac disregarded Bellomont's intervention, and announced that if envoys of the Five Nations brought back their French prisoners, they could take home with them the Iroquois prisoners being held by the French. The effect of this message was all that could have been hoped for; in Septem-ber an Onondaga chief arrived in Quebec to negotiate for a gen-eral peace.[37]

Frontenac did not live to see the conclusion of the peace which had been the constant objective of his Indian policy. He was sud-denly taken ill in November 1698, and on the 28th of the month he died. He was seventy-six years old. On December 9 the Bishop was present at his funeral service which was held, as he had requested, in the Récollets' church. In his funeral oration the Récollet Father Gohier praised the qualities which Frontenac had displayed as administrator, soldier and servant of the King and the Church.[38]

Frontenac was dynamic, brave, even foolhardy, violently self-willed, imperious, even insulting; he was ridiculously vain, and he was sometimes guilty of ignoring royal instructions which did not serve his own selfish interests. But commanding a military force in which regular soldiers fought shoulder to shoulder with militiamen and Indians, he contained and rolled back the English offensive against Canada, while at the same time he tamed the Iroquois and destroyed their power to threaten the colony. His short-sighted economic policy led him to encourage the fur trade at the expense of agriculture, but his Indian policy was that of a diplomat and psychologist of high order who knew how to combine with rare skill imposing manners, familiarity and flattery, disdain and blackmail. His serious defects of character were balanced by even greater positive qualities, which earned for him the title of "saviour of his country."

CHAPTER FOURTEEN

THE GREAT IROQUOIS PEACE
AND THE CANADA COMPANY
1699-1703

Government of Callières. Conclusion of a general peace between French, Iroquois and Indian allies. Louvigny convicted of illicit trading. Antagonism between Callières and Champigny. Contraband fur and liquor traffic. Lamothe-Cadillac founds Detroit. Abuses of his administration. Failure of the Canada Company. Iroquois neutrality and the War of the Spanish Succession. Departure of Champigny and death of Callières.

On receiving the news of the death of Frontenac, Callières, who was ambitious to succeed him, sent Lieutenant Courtemanche on a secret mission to France by way of New York. Vaudreuil, who was also anxious to be appointed to the post, and who feared he might be the victim of "some Norman trick," sent the Sieur Vincelot to Paris by way of Pentagoët. Champigny was a third candidate. Courtemanche arrived in the capital a few hours before Vincelot, and delivered his letters to Count Callières "who went straight to the King to solicit the appointment for his brother, and the King granted his request." When Pontchartrain, after receiving the official dispatches of the two rivals, went to inform the King of the Governor's death, Louis XIV said that he had already received the news and that he had appointed Callières as Frontenac's successor. It was only just that he should do so. Callières's receptive intelligence, his perfect integrity and his military competence made him the best qualified of the three candidates, and the King recognized these qualities in the commission which he signed on April 20, 1699. Vaudreuil was granted as consolation the post of Governor of Montreal.[1]

The first dispatch which Callières received from Versailles informed him that, as a result of the Treaty of Ryswick, all hostilities against the English and their Iroquois allies must cease. As a matter of fact, a year had gone by without any hostile act on the part of the Five Nations, but they had not yet concluded a formal peace.[2]

The Iroquois, whose pride was wounded and who were being encouraged in their resistance by Bellomont, were reluctant to accept the ultimatum which Frontenac had presented to them. On March 8, 1699, three chiefs came to return a number of prisoners and to assure Callières of their desire for peace, but on September 20 another delegation asked that the French should put a stop to the raids of their western allies against the Iroquois. Callières's answer was that a peace must also include the western nations. The Iroquois, who were at first not willing to accept this condition, had attacked the Miamis. The western tribes had retaliated immediately, the Ottawas at Detroit, the Illinois on the Ohio and the Miamis at Oswego, and they killed fifty-five Iroquois warriors.[3] The news of these losses induced a sudden change of attitude in the delegates. After further parleys with the Governor,[4] and against the advice of Bellomont, the Iroquois finally decided to submit.[5] The adversaries then began the business of rounding up the French prisoners in the cantons of the Five Nations and the Iroquois who were being held by western tribes.[6 and 7]

On July 22, 1701, the opening meeting of a great congress of native nations took place in Montreal. The delegates present represented thirteen western tribes and four Iroquois nations. Kondiaronk, whose earlier betrayal had been forgotten, made an eloquent plea for a general peace. He had been gravely ill when he arrived in Montreal, and when he died after making this last speech, he was given an impressive public funeral.[8]

After separate agreements had been reached with the different delegations, the final general meeting was held on August 4. In a great enclosure of branches, armed soldiers formed a circular cordon. The Governor was seated on a platform decorated with foliage, while grouped around him were Champigny and Vaudreuil, with army officers and the ladies and notables of the town. Thirteen hundred Indians, grouped by tribes, were seated on the ground. After having welcomed each tribe by name, Callières proclaimed a general peace and asked them to live as brothers, and to submit any future quarrel to his arbitration. His words, translated into the languages of all the nations present, were greeted by the Indians with guttural cries of approbation. As a permanent record, each of the thirty-one chiefs received a bead belt. Then each chief expressed his acceptance of the terms proposed and handed over his prisoners to the Governor, at the same time giving him a symbolic belt. Callières then lit the pipe of peace, drew a few puffs himself, and passed it to each of the allied and Iroquois chiefs. A solemn *Te Deum* was sung, and the most impressive international assembly in the history of New France ended with a tremendous feast at which piles of meat were eaten and casks of *bouillon,* the local drink, were drunk. Thirty-eight chiefs affixed totems symbolic of their tribes to the treaty.

A few days after the dispersal of the envoys, delegates arrived from the Mohawks. They had been delayed by the intrigues of the English and their partisans in the tribe. The Mohawk chiefs, in their turn, signed the treaty and even asked that "black gowns" be sent to their villages. The Jesuits, who were only too glad to resume work among the Iroquois, at once established missions in their villages.[9]

For the first time since La Barre's expedition of 1684 had renewed the war against the Five Nations, New France was at peace with all the Indian tribes. That happy situation was the direct result of Frontenac's Indian policy, and only death deprived him of the honour of concluding the peace. The raids by the western tribes which he had fomented, and his punitive expeditions of 1693 and 1696 had so weakened the Iroquois that, in spite of English opposition to such a course, they were forced to submit to a peace dictated by the French.

Callières had successfully continued Frontenac's Indian policy, but a strong sense of duty made it difficult for him to condone the irregular fur-trading of which certain western commanders were guilty. In September 1699 Louvigny had been appointed commander at Frontenac, with the specific instruction to refrain from trading. When Callières was informed by the missionaries that the Iroquois were bringing their furs to the post, the Governor seized the furs and dismissed the commander. He also intended to act in his capacity as military commander and to try Louvigny, but Champigny insisted that the Sovereign Council alone was competent to pronounce judgment in the matter. In October 1700 the case came before the Council. It was referred to the Court, and Louvigny was degraded from his rank as commander. The merchants who were associated with him were also summoned before the Sovereign Council, but thanks to the connivance of two councillors, d'Auteuil and Villeray, they escaped with nominal fines.[10]

Champigny's conduct in this affair aroused the suspicions of

Versailles. A few years earlier, in 1690, he had opposed the appointment of Louvigny to Michilimackinac on the grounds that he had a warehouse in Quebec and took trading goods with him to his post. Now, however, the Intendant was praising this same man's administration at Michilimackinac, and recommending his appointment as town major of Three Rivers. After considering this conflicting evidence, the Minister expressed disapproval of Champigny's intervention on behalf of Louvigny.[11]

The case of Louvigny once again presented a governor and an intendant at loggerheads with one another. Friction between the two officials had its source in Champigny's support for Vaudreuil as Frontenac's successor. Callières did not forgive this slight, and he was positively insolent in his attitude towards his colleague. "From the very beginning," wrote Champigny, "his manner was more arrogant and discourteous than anything I had ever seen." The Intendant retaliated by trying to incriminate the Governor in connection with insignificant trifles: an alleged sale of horses to the English and the dispatch of convoys to the western posts without the Intendant's formal approval. When the situation became unbearable, Champigny made use of this influence and requested a transfer, and in June 1701, the Minister informed him that he had been appointed Intendant in Le Havre, but that he could not leave Quebec until October 1702 when his successor would arrive.[12]

Although in the case of Louvigny, the Intendant had not fully collaborated in his efforts, Callières remained determined to put an end to the illicit traffic in furs. After the royal declaration of 1697, forty-eight *coureurs de bois* had returned to the colony but there were still about a hundred unreported. A second summons from the Governor in 1700 resulted in the return of twenty, while about sixty went and sold their furs to d'Iberville in Louisiana. Callières lodged a complaint in connection with this latter practice, for trade with Louisiana robbed the Canadian merchants of the price of goods which they had supplied.[13]

In spite of this protest, however, the King pardoned these deserters in order that they might be incorporated as immigrants into the infant colony of Louisiana. As might have been expected, his leniency encouraged the outlaws in their illegal transactions and in their licentious habits with the result that he was obliged once more to decree repressive measures. On May 6, 1702, he issued an order fixing the death penalty for illegal sale of furs in the colony or at Albany or in Louisiana, and at the same time he again prohibited the sale of alcohol to the Indians, for this abuse was, of course, the inevitable accompaniment to illegal trading. In 1703 the order dealing with contraband transactions was again repeated by the Intendant (Beauharnois), and the King once more commanded the *coureurs de bois* to return to civilization. This time he set a time limit of two years. All these repeated orders and injunctions simply serve to show that the situation with respect to the *coureurs de bois* and the liquor traffic had not changed. In spite of royal interdictions and more or less strict supervision by the Canadian authorities, traffic went on in the back-country with the complicity of merchants, and the connivance of the people in general, some judges and even a few members of the Sovereign Council.[14]

Callières's attention was also occupied during these years by a more positive royal project. As a result of the edict of 1696 closing the western posts, Lamothe-Cadillac had had to leave Michilimackinac the following year. No conscientious scruples had prevented him from using his position to make considerable profits from a combined trade in alcohol and furs, and as he was always in need of funds, he was very much disconcerted when he found himself deprived of his very lucrative post. With the backing of Frontenac, he presented to Pontchartrain a plan for an establishment at Detroit on the St. Clair River between Lake Erie and Lake Huron. As well as a pleasant climate and fertile soil, the spot he had chosen had other economic and strategic advantages. It lay athwart the trade route from the West, and a post situated there would block this route to English traders while at the same time constituting a link between Canada and the region of the Miamis and the Illinois.[15]

Thanks to the persuasive eloquence of its promoter, the project was authorized by the Minister and approved by Callières, and on June 2, 1701, Cadillac left Montreal with his second-in-command, Alphonse de Tonty, fifty soldiers and fifty colonists. On July 24 they reached the site of the new post, which they named Pontchartrain in honour of the Minister, and began to build houses and a wall of pickets with bastions. In the autumn, the Indians had a new and astonishing experience when they saw Madame de Cadillac and Madame de Tonty, the first white women to penetrate into the region of the Great Lakes. The colonists cleared a plot of ground, and the wheat which they planted on October 7 yielded an excellent crop the following summer. Soon Hurons and Ottawas from Michilimackinac and members of the Wolf tribe from the West, attracted by the advantages of the place, came and built villages in the vicinity.[16]

This migration from Michilimackinac represented a serious loss for the most important mission in the West, and the Jesuits were deeply distressed at the exodus of so many of their converts, especially since they would find in Detroit all the evils arising from the liquor traffic and the licentious conduct of the dealers in contraband. For Cadillac was not interested in planting a colony; his one desire was to barter alcohol for large stocks of beaver. He was a man "who had never spoken a word of truth," and he slandered the Jesuits without scruple. At the same time he exploited the two hundred inhabitants of the post, usurped the monopoly of the newly formed Canada Company, and even declared himself independent of the Governor and the Intendant. In 1705 influential backers at Versailles obtained his confirmation in the post, and he tried to win Vaudreuil to his cause by bribery.[17] In Detroit, where his one aim was to make as much money as possible, he had no friends, and was "hated alike by the troops, the inhabitants of the post and the Indians." In 1702 Callières had had to intervene when Cadillac had fomented trouble for the Jesuits. Then Ponchartrain warned him that his unfriendly treatment of the missionaries, his protection of the *coureurs de bois* and his presumption in administrative affairs might result in his dismissal. Finally, in 1710, after having put up with Cadillac's irregularities for years, Louis XIV lost patience and recalled him. However, it was apparent that this unscrupulous profiteer had powerful influences working on his behalf, for on leaving Detroit he was appointed Governor of Louisiana.[18]

Meanwhile, the crisis on the European fur market, which had arisen during Frontenac's term of office, became still more acute. Since the farmers-general who held the monopoly were obliged to pay a fixed price for beaver, the quantity of pelts increased each year, and the situation was aggravated by the fact that everyone who possibly could participated in the traffic either legally or illegally. The example of irregular participation came from high dignitaries, from governors such as La Barre and Frontenac, intendants such as Duchesneau and de Meulles, and commanders of posts such as Louvigny and Cadillac. As a result cargoes amounting to 500,000 or 600,000 pounds of skins crossed the Atlantic each year. From 1685 to 1697, the surplus over French and European consumption reached the enormous figure of 850,000 pounds of furs. To rescue the trade from bankruptcy the King bought the accumulated stocks for 3,762,000 *livres,* of which he lost three quarters. He then granted a new monopoly to Louis Guigues who asked for a reduction in the price he was to pay for beaver skins. However, the Canadian agents held a meeting in September 1699 and decided to refuse his request, for they meant to try another plan.[19]

Their object was to reorganize and reinvigorate the trade, and they began by getting Guigues to cede his monopoly to them for 70,000 *livres* a year and the responsibility for meeting the expenses of the administration. They then formed the Canada Company whose by-laws were adopted by a public meeting held in Quebec on October 15, 1700. This was the second Canadian company to hold the fur monopoly; the first had been formed in 1645. Anyone could become a member by subscribing 50 *livres,* the price of one share. The formation of the company was greeted with great enthusiasm. "They thought it was going to make the country's fortune." One hundred and ninety-eight persons hastened to buy stock, among them the Intendant, the Governors of Montreal and Three Rivers, the members of the Sovereign Council, officers, business men and farmers. The total amount subscribed was 287,370 *livres,* and subscriptions came in all the more readily since no capital outlay was required until nine years later in 1709.[20]

As it had no working capital, the Company borrowed the necessary funds in Paris, and found agents who undertook not only to sell the year's furs as they arrived, but to dispose of the previously accumulated pelts. The first year, all went well, but after the outbreak of the War of the Spanish Succession, although the tax of twenty-five per cent on beaver skins was abolished, a contracting market could not absorb all the pelts which were received, and the Company had to increase its borrowings. Soon interest on the debt, with commissions and taxes, absorbed the entire profit from sales, and in September 1704 the Company found itself without funds to pay the administrative expenses of the colony. In order to meet current obligations, the Intendant, Beauharnois, had to draw on the Ministry of Marine and also to create card money. In 1705 the Company's debt rose to 1,812,940 *livres,* while the assets were probably less than 500,000 *livres.* On the verge of bankruptcy, the Company ceded its monopoly of sale in Europe to Aubert, Néret and Gayot for a period of ten years from May 10, 1706. The conditions of the lease stipulated that the Company would liquidate its debt, dispose of its stocks of beaver and reduce the volume of its annual purchases of skins. In June 1706 the King sanctioned these arrangements, thus saving the country from economic chaos.[21] The Canada Company carried on its activities on a greatly reduced scale, and waited for the better days which were to come only after a long and painful period of stagnation. It was not until about 1715, when the stocks of pelts had finally been liquidated and the war was over, that there was once more a demand for beaver from Canada.[22]

Meanwhile, the war which Callières had foreseen had reached Canada. At the great meeting in Montreal, one of the Governor's objectives had been to ensure that the Iroquois would remain neutral in case of an Anglo-French conflict. Speaking to an assembly of their chiefs which was held on August 7, 1701, after the conclusion of the general Indian peace, he had pointed out to them that they could remain neutral, since by their own declaration they were not English subjects. This appeal to their spirit of independence elicited the promise of neutrality which Callières so desired.[23]

It was given none too soon: less than a year later, in May 1702, France and England went to war on the issue of the Spanish succession. Charles II of Spain, who had died without issue in 1700, was the brother of Marie-Thérèse of Austria, and in his will he named as his heir the Duke of Anjou, grandson of his sister and Louis XIV. In January 1701 Louis XIV proclaimed his grandson King of Spain under the name Philip V, and the Spanish ambassador made the famous pronouncement: "The Pyrenees no longer exist." William III refused to recognize Philip as the King of Spain, but at first his English subjects were inclined to accept the Bourbon succession as an accomplished fact. However, in September 1701 the official recognition by Louis XIV of the son of James II as King of England immediately provoked a hostile reaction. The English people were now ready to oppose the designs of the French King by force of arms, and William's policy prevailed even though he himself died two months before the declaration of war.

When news of the war reached Canada in mid-summer, Callières's first thought was to protect the colony from the danger of an Iroquois war. Early in August he held parleys with delegates from the Five Nations who renewed the promise of neutrality they had made the year before, and thus delivered the country, and more specifically the rural population, from the haunting nightmare of Indian raids.[24]

Informed that the authorities in Boston were making preparations for an expedition against Canada, the Governor strengthened the defences of Quebec and Montreal, and ordered the people on the lower St. Lawrence to build shelters. A suggestion came from France that Quebec might take the initiative and attack the English colonies, but Callières answered that such an attack was likely to provoke intervention by the Five Nations in favour of their friends in Albany, and that an Iroquois war would be disastrous for the colony.[24a] But he stirred up the western Indians, and urged them to harass the English in Ohio, Virginia and Carolina, and he declared his willingness to participate in any naval expedition which might be undertaken against New York or Boston. D'Iberville had been drawing up plans for such an expedition since 1701, but they got no farther than the files in Versailles.[25]

Thus, when on August 29, 1702, Champigny's successor, François de la Boische, Sieur de Beauharnois, arrived in Quebec, the country presented the appearance of a peaceful agricultural colony. For sixteen years Champigny had carried out his duties intelligently and conscientiously. He had accepted the responsibilities and defended the rights of his office, and he had displayed firmness and even courage in his efforts to curb Frontenac's despotic tendencies and to protect the missions from the evils of the liquor traffic. Like his predecessors, he had a stake in the business world, but there was no conflict between his personal interests and those of his office, and he never forgot that if the colony was to grow, agriculture must have priority over the fur trade.[26]

Callières made no attempt to hide his satisfaction at the prospect of working with a new intendant, especially as Beauharnois seemed energetic and cordial, and ready to defer to the Governor's authority. Their association was not to last long, however, as Callières died in May 1703. He was remembered as an able soldier, who used his military skill for the protection of his people, and an honest administrator, uncompromising in his pursuit of lawbreakers, whatever their rank or station.[27]

CHAPTER FIFTEEN

THE WAR OF THE SPANISH SUCCESSION
1703-1713

Situation under Vaudreuil. Capture of the Seine *and*
Mgr. de Saint-Vallier. Beauharnois. Riots. Franco-Aben-
aki expeditions. Negotiations for neutrality between
Boston and Quebec. Intrigues. Hostilities in the West.
Haverhill. An English invasion plan. Defeat of Manthet
on Hudson Bay. Walker's expedition against Quebec.
Shipwreck. Defeat of the Fox conspiracy. Peace of Ut-
recht.

To succeed Callières Louis XIV appointed Vaudreuil as Governor-
General of New France. He made the appointment with some re-
luctance, since Madame de Vaudreuil, a Canadian, was a member
of a large family which might prove a temptation to nepotism and
favouritism.[1] In the colony, the appointment was greeted with
almost universal satisfaction. Vaudreuil was a brave and skilful
officer, a man of sound judgment and sympathetic understanding.
Moreover, he had already spent sixteen years in the country and
he had married a Canadian, Louise Elisabeth de Joybert.

The new Governor, who was commissioned on August 1, 1703,
took office in very difficult circumstances. In the course of his first
year a smallpox epidemic caused hundreds of deaths; the situation
of the fur trade was more critical than ever; still more serious, the
War of the Spanish Succession held over Acadia and Canada the
threat of invasion from both Boston and New York. Each of these
colonies had its own reasons for hostility towards New France.
Boston was angry at being excluded from fishing in Acadian waters,
and New York at being cut off from the western fur trade. Boston
tried to win over the Abenakis, New York sought to stir up the
Iroquois, and both cherished just resentment for the cruel Franco-
Indian raids.[2]

The first hostile action which directly affected Canada was the

152

capture on July 26, 1704, of the royal merchantman, the *Seine*. In spite of a vigorous defence directed by her commander, the Chevalier de Maupeou, the ship had to surrender to the superior force of four English warships. Its cargo of munitions and merchandise was worth 1,300,000 *livres,* without counting the silver plate and provisions being sent out to the Governor. The *Seine* had on board Mgr. de Saint-Vallier and a number of priests and officers. The crew and passengers were sent to England, where the Bishop of Quebec lived, free but under surveillance, for five years until he was exchanged in 1709. After leaving England, he spent four more years in France as Louis XIV still remembered the earlier troubles of his administration and still hoped to persuade him to resign his charge. The King's efforts in this regard were unsuccessful, and finally, in 1713 Mgr. de Saint-Vallier was allowed to return to his diocese. Fortunately, Mgr. de Laval had returned to Canada in 1688, and he had directed the affairs of the diocese during the absence of the titular Bishop.[2a]

Beauharnois, who was related to the Minister, could count on his support, but did not attempt to exploit this situation in his relations with the Governor. He maintained his independence, but at the same time he worked in harmony with his colleague and devoted his qualities of reason and understanding to the service of the colony. He gave his special attention to its commercial expansion, and he had a personal interest in the sale of some products, among them salt, of which the high fixed price resulted in correspondingly high profits.[2b] The exorbitant price of salt was the cause of two protest riots in the outlying parishes of Montreal. The first of these demonstrations, which took place on November 18, 1704, was broken up by the Abbé Belmont and the Governor of Montreal, and Vaudreuil issued an order prohibiting "such gatherings."[2c] The second occurred a year later, and this time two of the instigators were arrested and condemned by the Sovereign Council to fines of ten crowns.[2d] The authorities in Versailles did not frown upon Beauharnois's private business transactions, but they censured him most severely for issuing card money, and still more for authorizing important loans to the Canada Company, then on the verge of bankruptcy, and thus aggravating the Minister's serious financial difficulties. It was these dangerous commitments which led to Beauharnois's recall in 1705 after only three years' service. To replace him Pontchartrain appointed two men who were related to him by family ties, the Sieurs Raudot, father and son.[2e]

Realizing that the colony's most pressing need was to prevent any resumption of hostilities on the part of the Iroquois, Vaudreuil sent presents in the autumn of 1703 to the Onondagas and the Senecas, and received assurances from a delegation in Quebec that these tribes would continue to live in peace with their French neighbours. He maintained contact with their villages through the Jesuit missionaries and the interpreters Maricourt and Joncaire who had been adopted, in the Indian fashion, one by the Onondagas and the other by the Senecas. The Governor also continued the wise diplomatic policy of abstention from raids against New York, conscious that any such foray might bring out the Mohawks in defence of their English allies who supplied them with arms and merchandise in exchange for furs from the West. This policy also flattered the naïve pretension of the Five Nations to be "peace mediators" between England and France.[3]

Vaudreuil had been convinced for some time that any English offensive would originate in Boston. Since 1702 the Governor of Massachusetts, Joseph Dudley, had been trying to neutralize the Abenakis who were staunch allies of the French. In June 1703, by plying them with presents and trading privileges, he succeeded in extracting a treaty of sorts from their chiefs whom he met at Casco, but it was an Indian compromise, and a missionary, Father Rasle, assured Vaudreuil that the Abenakis were still ready to raise the hatchet against the English. This proved to be the case, and in August a Canadian expedition against New England, including a band of Abenakis under the command of Le Neuf de Beaubassin seized the village of Wells, ravaged the country, captured about three hundred persons and achieved Vaudreuil's main object by making "irreconcilable enemies of the English and the Abenakis."[4]

The former intendant Champigny, who was now in France, considered this raid an injudicious provocation to hostilities,[5] and his opinion was justified when in the autumn the Boston militia launched such a vigorous offensive against the Abenakis that the latter asked Quebec for help. Faithful to his promise, the Governor sent a raiding force into Massachusetts under the leadership of Hertel de Rouville and his four brothers. Two hundred and fifty Frenchmen and Indians from the colony left Montreal in the middle of winter, and fell on the village of Deerfield before daybreak on February 29, 1704. They scaled the palisade, broke into the seventeen houses, killed seven of their occupants and took 150 prisoners, with a loss to themselves of only three Frenchmen and a few Indians.[6]

In retaliation for these savage raids, Massachusetts and New Hampshire launched campaigns against the Abenakis of Pentagoët and the Acadian establishments at Minas and Beaubassin, in the course of which they took 150 prisoners. In December 1704 Governor Dudley sent Captain Livingstone to Quebec to propose an exchange of prisoners, and in May 1705 Vaudreuil sent Courtemanche back with the English envoy to arrange terms for the exchange. The Governor was glad of an excuse to send an alert observer to Boston,[7] but spying out the land was a game at which two could play. The ship on which Courtemanche travelled from Boston to Quebec also carried Dudley's young son and a merchant, Samuel Vetch. It took two months and a half, a suspiciously long time, to reach Montreal, and in the course of the voyage Vetch unloaded merchandise worth 1,000 crowns and took on board a corresponding quantity of beaver pelts. He also made use of the opportunity to take soundings in the river, and to "make himself quite familiar with the region." The Minister was so alarmed at the imprudence which permitted such blatant poaching and espionage that Vaudreuil was severely reprimanded.[8]

The ostensible business of young Dudley and Vetch was to present to the Governor a plan for neutrality between New England and New France modelled on the agreement which had been concluded by the French and English colonies in the West Indies. Vaudreuil responded sympathetically to the suggestion and, taking as authority the King's approval of an earlier project of the same kind, he sketched a draft for a truce. It stipulated that there should be strict neutrality on land and sea between the two colonies, and that each would undertake to keep its Indian allies within their own hunting-grounds, and at the same time dissociate itself from any outbreak of hostilities among the tribes.[9]

In the hope of bringing home to the English the necessity for such a treaty, Vaudreuil had sent out several war parties, but in March 1706 Dudley had still not submitted the terms to the other governors of New England, and he finally informed Quebec that he considered them too "onerous" to advise their acceptance. So the parleys broke off. They did, however, result in some benefits for both parties concerned: they procured a year's truce between the colonies as well as the liberation of fifty-seven French and forty-three English prisoners, and they also provided both sides with opportunities for espionage. Soon after the breakdown in negotiations, hostilities broke out again between New England and the Abenakis. The latter were incited by the missionaries and supplied with arms by the French.[10] Vaudreuil also abolished one of the "inhuman" practices which had caused deep resentment in the New Englanders: he refused to buy English scalps. He continued, however, to offer "ten Spanish crowns for each prisoner."[11]

In the Quebec-New York sector the situation was reversed; here it was the French who wanted to keep the Indians neutral while the English tried to inflame the hostility of the Iroquois towards New France. In order to foil these English schemes, Vaudreuil was careful to refrain from any offensive in New York. He even allowed the Indians from the missions of Sault St. Louis, la Montagne and Sault-au-Récollet to sell their furs in Albany. To justify this violation of the law forbidding trade with the English colonies, he pleaded the scarcity of French goods and especially the necessity of keeping some control over the Indians, who, if they were not allowed some freedom in trading, got completely out of hand. Pontchartrain, however, was adamant; the Governor must not "on any account repeat this error." The Minister had good reason for his misgivings, for Vaudreuil's policy of toleration resulted in such an increase in the volume of illicit trading with Albany that in 1708 and 1709 the King issued new orders and imposed new penalties for violation of the law; confiscation, heavy fines, even corporal punishment. Vaudreuil, however, could justly argue that the cheap prices of the English wares made it "impossible" to eliminate contraband trade.[12]

While sporadic warfare between Acadia and New England continued, since 1703 there had been a sort of "suspension of hostilities" between Quebec and New York which did not reach the stage of declared peace. The commander at Albany, Peter Schuyler, made overtures with the idea of concluding a treaty, but the policy favoured by the Anglo-Dutch merchants was to destroy the pact between the French and the Five Nations and to seize the western trade for themselves. After 1704 the New York authorities kept urging the Iroquois to send their missionaries back to Quebec and to "give free passage to the Indians from the upper country." They sent belts secretly to the Indians in the Quebec missions and tried to persuade them to settle in British territory. They plied the chiefs with rich presents for themselves and their people. In 1708 New York's offering consisted of 50 pieces of cloth, 10 bales of leggings, 300 shirts, 150 rifles, 10 barrels of gun-powder, 20 pigs of lead, 300 hatchets, 300 knives, and last but not least, 160 casks of brandy. In spite of this massive bribery, the influence of the French ambassador on the Onondagas and the Senecas, with that of the missionaries and the mission Indians, was powerful enough to keep the Five Nations neutral, and this Vaudreuil considered the essential condition for preserving the peace and reassuring the population.[13]

While carrying on a guerilla war against New England and maintaining a truce with New York, the Governor had also to protect the French fur trade, and to keep the peace among the unstable and warlike western nations, who occupied all the lake country from the Ottawa to the Mississippi. In that vast region, the Iroquois claimed as their hunting-ground the lands surrounding Lake Ontario and Lake Erie. The Potawatomi country was between Lakes Huron and Michigan, while the Miamis were south, and the Illinois south-west of Lake Michigan. The Mascoutins and the Fox tribe were strung out along the south-western shore of the lake, and the Sioux territory lay between Green Bay and Lake Superior. To the west of Superior lived the Crees and the Assiniboines. The Huron villages were much farther east, north of Sault Ste. Marie, and the domain of the Ottawas was still farther to the east. Facing one another on the strait between Lake Superior and Lake Michigan were the important Jesuit mission of Sault Ste. Marie, and the strategic post of Michilimackinac. It was Vaudreuil's difficult task to keep the peace among all these tribes, torn by ancient enmities and economic and territorial rivalries. He had also to prevent any of them from making common cause with the Iroquois, who were again trying to monopolize the western trade for the benefit of Albany and to the detriment of Canada. The English, by bribing some of the chiefs, tried to provoke a rupture between the French and their allies in the lake country. They even tried to induce the western Indians to take up the hatchet against the Iroquois. Quebec would then be obliged to choose between the Five Nations and the western tribes, and whatever her choice, her trade would be ruined.[14]

In such a climate hostilities were sure to break out sooner or later. In the winter of 1704, a number of Senecas were killed by Miamis on their hunting grounds, but Vaudreuil persuaded the Miamis to make amends for the killing by giving presents to the Senecas and returning some prisoners.[15] In the summer of the same year a band of Ottawas from Michilimackinac seized thirty Senecas near Fort Frontenac, but once more Vaudreuil, with the help of Joncaire and the missionaries, managed to calm down the

Senecas by making the Ottawas restore their prisoners.[16] Two years later Detroit was the scene of a serious incident. A band of Miamis who had killed a few Ottawas refused the customary compensation, and the temporary commander of the post, Ensign Bourgmont, rejected the Ottawas' complaint. Then, at the instigation of their chief, Le Pesant, the Ottawas attacked a Miami village. They killed five of its occupants and pursued the others who took refuge in the fort. Bourgmont and the Miamis then opened fire on the pursuers, and, in the skirmish which followed, two Frenchmen, the Récollet Father Constantin and a sergeant, as well as several Ottawas, were killed outside the fort. The engagement was very brief, but the situation remained critical. The Miamis plotted with the Hurons to attack the Ottawas, and the Iroquois also signified to Vaudreuil their willingness to "destroy" the same tribe. Fortunately, however, by using the good offices of Father Marest and friendly chiefs, Vaudreuil succeeded in persuading the Ottawas to recognize their obligations towards the Miamis. He thus avoided a conflict which would have been not only disastrous for the fur trade, but dangerous for the colony itself.[17]

While Vaudreuil was engaged in fostering an uncertain peace in the West, he received orders from Louis XIV to press hostile action against New England. Accordingly, an expedition was organized under the direction of Hertel de Rouville and Saint-Ours d'Eschaillons. The order had suggested that raids could be carried out "either by the French or by bands of Indians"[18] and as usual the two were combined in the force of one hundred French and Canadians and sixty Indians which was sent to attack Haverhill on the Merrimack, a village of some thirty houses defended by a garrison of thirty men. The assault was launched half an hour before sunrise on August 29, 1708, and although the garrison and the villagers fought valiantly, the raiders succeeded in dislodging them by setting fire to the fort and the houses. As the Franco-Indian force was withdrawing, it fell into an ambush of sixty English about half a league outside the village, but a bayonet charge dispersed this force and the raiding party, which had lost ten men, returned to Quebec with thirty-five prisoners.[19]

The French forays had already caused the New Englanders to consider projects for invading Canada. In the course of his spying mission of 1705, Vetch had discovered how weak the military situation of the country was. He had reported to London that it could easily be conquered, and in the spring of 1709 New England received the promise that an expeditionary fleet would be sent out. Thereupon Colonel Nicholson assembled on Lake George a force of 1,500 regulars and militiamen and 300 warriors from four of the Iroquois nations. Only the Senecas remained faithful to the treaty of 1701.[19a] Meanwhile, Vaudreuil was gathering his forces in Montreal and keeping a close watch on the frontier. In July he sent M. de Ramezay to Lake Champlain with a troop of 1,500 soldiers and Indians. At Scalp Point they dispersed an advance scouting party of English, but on the Indians' refusal to attack the entrenched camp on Lake George, the expedition returned to Montreal.[20] However, the English still had no news of the promised fleet (which had been diverted instead to the aid of Portugal), and when Colonel Nicholson learned that the French were concentrating their forces at Chambly, he burned his camp and retreated with his troops to Corlaer.[21]

All these military activities had little effect on the country's economy. Agriculture, fishing, exports and industries (with the exception of shipbuilding) were surprisingly active. In spite of the failure of the Canada Company, the fur trade was recovering, but even in the midst of war considerable quantities of furs were attracted by higher prices to New York. In 1707, 120 canoes carrying contraband went up the Richelieu and into English territory. Trade was especially active in the rich fur country of Hudson Bay where both French and English were established. The furs from the English posts on James Bay (Rupert, Monsipi and Kichiskouane) were sent out by the sea route through the Hudson Strait. At the northern forts, Bourbon and Neuve-Savane, the French received twice as many furs as the English, but they took them out by canoe, following the rivers and lakes down to the Ottawa.[21a]

A few private individuals in New France conceived of the idea of taking advantage of the war to organize a raid on the beaver stores of the Hudson's Bay Company. In 1709 the Governor, who had himself invested 1,000 crowns in the venture, sent out a detachment of ninety men under d'Ailleboust de Manthet. Their plan was to seize the furs at Fort Albany for the benefit of the promoters of the enterprise, but in the assault on the fort, Manthet and thirteen of his troops were killed. As Vaudreuil had no very satisfactory explanation to offer for having engaged in such an undertaking for his own profit, his conduct in the affair was severely censured by the King and the Minister.[22]

The term of office of Jacques Raudot and his son Antoine-

Denis had begun auspiciously in 1705. The elder Raudot was a learned jurist with cultivated tastes in letters and music. His experience as judge of the *Cour des Aides,* which dealt with questions of taxation, had helped to develop his strong sense of justice, and in Canada he made it his business to protect the tenant against any possible exploitation by his seigneur. He judged a great many cases himself, and endeavoured to set precedents which would systematize municipal and commercial law, as well as justice in general.[22a] At fifty-eight, he was older than any of his predecessors in the office, and this was probably one reason for the appointment of his son as his assistant and deputy. Antoine-Denis, who was twenty-six years old, was a conscientious and intelligent collaborator. He also made his own personal contribution to the administration of New France and prepared remarkable reports on possible establishments on Cape Breton Island.[22b] Unfortunately, after an initial period of harmony, the traditional pattern of friction between governor and intendant reappeared. Raudot accused Vaudreuil of interfering in the intendant's domain, but he was himself a man of irascible temper whose ill-considered words and fiery outbursts finally exhausted the Governor's patience. In order to relieve a very difficult situation, the King transferred the Raudots to duties in France, and they were replaced in March 1710 by another kinsman of Pontchartrain, Michel Bégon.[22c]

In the autumn of 1709 Nicholson and Schuyler convinced the authorities in London that the time was ripe for an attack on New France, and that the first blow should be struck in Acadia. An English fleet was sent out the following summer and was joined by troops from New England before proceeding to the attack on Port Royal. Vaudreuil had sent reinforcements from Canada, but Governor Subercase could not hold out against the powerful English force, and the fort was surrendered on October 13. The capture of Port Royal produced the same effect in the English colonies as that which had followed Phipps's earlier victory. The colonists were fired with enthusiasm and a desire to conquer Quebec. Accordingly, in the following summer, a second expedition was organized. In July (1711) an imposing fleet of fifteen warships and sixty-nine transports was assembled at Nantasket under the command of Sir Hovenden Walker. The military force, commanded by Brigadier John Hill, included five thousand marines and colonial troops, veterans of Marlborough's campaigns. Nicholson's contingent, which was to proceed overland, included two thousand regulars and militiamen, who, when they reached their camp on Lake Champlain, were joined by six hundred Iroquois warriors drawn from all five nations of the confederacy.[23]

The situation was very grave. To oppose 10,000 English, Vaudreuil could put into the field only about 2,300 men, but a great assembly of 700 Indians in Montreal pledged the support of the Hurons and several western tribes, as well as that of Indians settled in the colony. Entrenchments were thrown up around Quebec, and the Governor gave orders for the women, children and old men to take to the woods when the English fleet appeared. On October 1, six hundred members of the Montreal militia marched into Quebec, where they were joined the same evening by the detachment from Three Rivers. The whole colony was braced for the shock, when on October 7 a ship from France, the *Héros,* dropped anchor in the harbour of Quebec and reported that on its way up the river it had not sighted a single English sail. A small sailing ship from Gaspé gave the same report.[24] With this proof that Quebec was not in danger, Vaudreuil concentrated his forces at Chambly, in order to be ready for Nicholson's advance, but about the middle of October he learned that Walker's fleet had met with disaster and that Nicholson, dismayed at the news, had withdrawn his forces to Albany.[24a]

The whole country rejoiced at the failure of the great English invasion. Services of thanksgiving were held and Notre-Dame-de-la-Victoire was rechristened Notre-Dame-des-Victoires. Priests and laymen vied with one another in writing songs and poems to celebrate Quebec's deliverance from peril, although it was some time before they learned the reasons for the English failure to attack.[25]

Walker, who as a navigator was rash rather than competent, had set sail from Nantasket on July 30. Before leaving he had offered 100,000 *livres* to Captain Denys de la Ronde, who was in Boston as an envoy, if he would pilot the English fleet up the St. Lawrence, but the offer had been indignantly rejected. After entering the Gulf, Walker captured a ship and tried to bribe its master, Captain Paradis, to act as pilot, but this offer, too, was refused. Undismayed, the English admiral continued on his way, as confident of victory as ever. He had brought with him posters printed in Boston which he meant to distribute in Quebec. They announced that Great Britain was undertaking the "pious enterprise" of the conquest of Quebec in reprisal for the Franco-Indian raids. After the conquest, Canadian laymen and priests alike would enjoy all the rights of British subjects, but any who took up arms against the English forces would be "treated as enemies and usurpers," and their property would be forfeit.[26]

On August 23 the fleet was advancing up the estuary of the St. Lawrence west of Anticosti, when a thick fog came down reducing the visibility almost to zero and blanketing the north shore which was much nearer than the navigators realized. In the high wind which accompanied the fog, eight transports were driven ashore and broken up on the shoals of Ile-aux-Oeufs. For two days Walker cruised along the coast picking up survivors of whom there were eleven hundred. Seven hundred victims, officers, soldiers, sailors and women, perished in the shipwreck. A council of war resulted in a decision to abandon the attack on Quebec, and the fleet sailed straight back to England without even pausing on the way to capture the modest French establishment at Placentia.[27]

Once Quebec was freed from the threat of invasion by land and sea, Vaudreuil did not appear to have to worry about the attitude of the Five Nations, for the astute Iroquois now wanted to heal the breach of faith between themselves and the French. Accordingly, in the spring of 1712 a delegation, recognizing their violation of the treaty of 1701, presented excuses for their desertion to the English, and sought reconfirmation of the treaty of neutrality. Although the Governor put little faith in their protestations of friendship, he accepted them with alacrity, for he realized that an open break with the Iroquois would be the worst possible calamity for the colony.[28]

Vaudreuil's caution was quite justified, for the Five Nations continued to work hand in glove with Albany in the effort to achieve their goal of appropriating the fur trade and inciting the western Indians to hostility against the French. They were already in league with the Fox Indians, an insolent, war-like tribe a group of whom had established a village at Detroit in 1711. The Foxes were plotting with the Mascoutins and the Kikapoos to seize the fort and hand it over to the English.[29] In the spring of 1712 they were preparing to attack when a Christian Indian revealed their plan to the commander, and Du Buisson, who had only thirty men at the fort, called on the friendly tribes for help. On May 13 the little French band with its Indian allies laid siege to the Fox village whose inhabitants escaped under cover of heavy rain. The allies pursued them and the next day, in an engagement at Presqu'île near Lake St. Clair, they inflicted upon them a loss of hundreds in dead and prisoners.[30]

As the attempt on Detroit had failed, Schuyler tried to incite the Iroquois to attack the western allies of the French, and the Onondaga chief, Teganisorens, assembled an army of one thousand warriors for this purpose. However, the Senecas opposed the idea and when, in August 1712, it was reported that the French and English had suspended hostilities, the expedition was abandoned.[31]

The atmosphere had already become somewhat less tense when news reached Quebec that peace had been signed at Utrecht on April 13, 1713, but celebrations did not take place until a year later when official dispatches arrived from Versailles. Then a *Te Deum* was sung, and the Bishop officiated at a solemn thanksgiving mass at which the Governor, the Intendant and the members of the Sovereign Council were all present in their official capacity. In the evening salvoes were fired by the guns of the fort, members of the town militia lighted great bonfires, and candles burned in the windows of all the houses. The people of New France rejoiced to see the end of twenty-five years of war, and prayed for a long era of peace. Events proved that their prayer was to be answered, for the peace they were celebrating lasted for thirty years.[32]

CHAPTER SIXTEEN

ACADIA AND THE ENGLISH COLONIES
1670-1689

*Reoccupation of Acadia. English colonies. The Aben-
akis. Grandfontaine's difficulties. Chambly taken prisoner. A Canadian Governor, La Vallière. Anglo-Indian
hostilities. The leader of the Abenakis, Baron de Saint-
Castin. Encroachment on Acadian territory, trade and
fisheries. The Acadia Fisheries Company. Governor Perrot and his contraband trade. English depredations and
Abenaki reprisals.*

Acadia had been in British hands from 1658 to 1667, and, although
it was officially restored to France by the Treaty of Breda, it was
not until 1670 that the colony was actually handed over to French
administrators. The first of these was Governor Hubert d'Andigny,
Chevalier de Grandfontaine who had commanded a company in
the Carignan regiment. With eight *engagés* and a guard of twenty-
five soldiers he established his residence a few leagues from the
frontier at Pentagoët. This seemed to him a more strategic position than that of Port Royal for resisting any encroachments on the
part of the English colonies. The whole of Acadia, from the Kennebec River frontier to Cape Breton had only 441 inhabitants, and
of these 363 were concentrated in the region of Porty Royal. This
was a surprisingly small population in view of the country's great
natural advantages: rich furs north of the Bay of Fundy, good har-
bours on the Atlantic, abundant fisheries on the banks thirty miles
to the south, good agricultural and pasture lands, timber for building, and excellent coal in Cape Breton. In short, Acadia possessed,
as de Meulles reported later, everything that was needed to make
it the finest colony in the world. She could become, wrote another
unidentified admirer, "mistress of all America."[1]

The one dark spot in this otherwise perfect picture was the
presence on Acadia's doorstep of Massachusetts, which, with her

sister colonies, New Hampshire, Connecticut and Rhode Island, formed the federation of New England. This federation, under the effective leadership of Boston, was growing at an astonishing rate. A constant flow of immigrants assured regular development of agricultural resources, and the Kennebec country was occupied by a succession of fine farms. Following the lead of Massachusetts the colonies carried on very profitable cod fisheries in the Acadian coastal waters. A fleet of merchant ships took the cod to Spain or the West Indies, while smaller vessels traded with the English and French fishermen in Newfoundland, exchanging provisions for merchandise which they then smuggled into New England. All this activity was the outward sign of growing prosperity. There were merchants in Boston worth anywhere from 300,000 to 600,000 *livres,* and in the legislative building in Boston hung a peculiarly significant symbol, a gilded codfish.[2] This prosperity was also reflected in a proportionate growth in population. In 1675 New England counted almost 75,000 inhabitants, in comparison with Acadia's 500 and Canada's 8,000.

Acadia had to reckon not only with an aggressive and expanding colonial neighbour, but also with the loose confederation of native tribes which occupied the country between the Kennebec and St. John rivers. The most important of these tribes, included under the generic name of Abenakis, were the Canibas, the Pentagoëts and the Narantsouaks. The Malecites occupied country which lay farther to the east along both shores of the St. John River. The Abenakis were an intelligent race characterized by all the good qualities of the Indian: stubborn courage, patience, skill in hunting. They had fraternized with the French ever since the days of de Monts and the Jesuit missionaries, and they hated the English for the arrogant and brutal attitude which they displayed and which might be summed up in the saying, coined much later, that the only good Indian is a dead Indian. The Indians' hostility was aggravated by the war of extermination, carried on by Massachusetts against the Pequots, an episode of the so-called King Philip's War.[3]

Colbert realized the economic and strategic importance of Acadia. He recognized the utility of linking this Atlantic outlet to Canada by an inland route which would be open in all seasons, and with his encouragement Talon sent Saint-Lusson to explore the possibilities of communication by way of the Chaudière and the St. John. Colbert, however, was still more conscious of Acadia's need of people. In 1671 he sent out thirty young men and thirty girls, and instructed the Governor to encourage the establishment of new farms. At the same time he urged him to allow unrestricted fishing. He recommended further that friendly relations be maintained with Boston, and, surprisingly, that English colonists should be allowed to fish on the same conditions as they themselves imposed on the French, namely, that they pay a tax of twenty-five crowns for each boat.[4]

Although Colbert recognized the value of Acadia, all his resources were required for his Canadian programme, and he left Grandfontaine without funds to carry out the orders he had given. Acadia was in such a state of penury that Talon had to send provisions from Quebec and to ask the mother country to provide hoes and axes, muskets and rifles, powder and lead, and even a flag. The extreme poverty of his colony was only one of the Governor's difficulties. He quarreled with his lieutenant, Joybert de Marson, who reported his grievances to Talon. Acting on royal orders, the Governor allowed the New Englanders to fish off the coast, and he provided for the maintenance of the garrison by exchanging furs for provisions from Boston. The result was that he was accused of favouring the English, and of allowing the population to "die of hunger" while he gathered pelts. The truth was, of course, that he had neither orders to feed the people, nor the means to do so. Finally, realizing that the post offered no future, Grandfontaine asked to be relieved. In 1673 he resumed his rank as captain in the navy, and he later distinguished himself at Cayenne and Tobago.[5]

Captain Jacques Chambly, who was appointed to replace Grandfontaine, had had a brilliant career in Europe before going to Canada with Carignan's regiment. He had directed the construction of Fort St. Louis on the Richelieu which was later to bear his name. He was appointed in 1673 as Commander in Acadia, but in 1676 his competence and zeal in office were rewarded with a commission as Governor.[6] Acadia came under the general jurisdiction of Quebec, and Chambly was following a directive from Frontenac when he restricted foreign trading and fishing in Acadia.[7] Irked at having to submit to French regulations, the New Englanders resorted to armed piracy. Pentagoët was attacked on August 10, 1674, by the buccaneer Juranien Aernauts with a frigate manned by 110 men and piloted by John Rhoades who knew the Acadian coast. The commander of the post and his thirty poorly armed men put up a brave front, but when Chambly was wounded Ensign Saint-Castin and the garrison surrendered unconditionally. After pillaging the fort and removing the guns,

Aernauts sent a detachment to attack the post of Jemsec up the St. John River. There Commander Marson was captured and his ransom was fixed at one thousand beaver. The freebooter then returned to Boston where he left his prisoners, thus proving if any proof were needed, that the English authorities had connived at the attack. Frontenac at once protested, and accused Boston of "harbouring pirates."[8]

After Frontenac had paid the prisoners' ransoms, Chambly returned to Acadia, but he abandoned Pentagoët which had proved too vulnerable to attack, and re-established the capital at Port Royal. Even Port Royal was at this time just a village with wooden houses protected by a poorly-built fort and a garrison of thirty men. Chambly remained there only a short time, as he was promoted in September 1677 to the post of Governor of Grenada, and Lieutenant Marson, who assumed temporary command, died the following year. By this time Colbert seemed to have forgotten the existence of Acadia; not only did he fail to dispatch merchandise for the essential needs of the colonists, he even let five years pass without filling the post of Governor. After the death of Marson it was Frontenac who commissioned as Commander Michel de la Vallière, a member of the Le Neuf family. La Vallière, who was born in Three Rivers, was the first Canadian to be educated in France. In 1676 he was granted the seigniory of Beaubassin at the head of the Bay of Fundy where he leased holdings to about twenty Canadian and Acadian tenants. He was appointed interim Commander in 1678, but it was not until five years later that, on August 5, 1683, he received a commission which made him the first Canadian-born to become a governor in New France.[9]

The English, who could see that Acadia was neglected by the mother country and that Canada had not the means to protect it, lost no opportunity to extend their operations along the frontier and encroach on French and Indian territory. Between 1658 and 1670, during the English occupation of Port Royal, the Abenakis had received merchandise and munitions from Boston in exchange for their furs, and they had had to resign themselves to the harsh terms imposed upon them. On the other hand, when, with the colony in French hands, they could hope to be supplied by friends, their hostility towards the English increased perceptibly. Angered by the New Englanders' custom of selling their Indian prisoners as slaves, the Abenakis rose in August 1676 and destroyed the settlements of Casco and Sagadahock. Hostilities continued with equal barbarity on both sides until the spring of 1678 when, by the

Treaty of Casco, Massachusetts recognized the right of the Abenakis to the region east of the Kennebec and the obligation of each settler to pay a peck of corn a year as rent for land which he cultivated in Indian territory.[10]

During these years another influence helped to strengthen the bonds of Franco-Indian understanding already forged by the French settlers and the missionaries. It was created by the sojourn among the Indians of Chambly's ensign, Jean-Vincent d'Abadie, Baron de Saint-Castin. He had gone to Quebec in 1674 with an escort of Abenakis to inform Frontenac of the capture of Pentagoët, and it appears that he was charged by the Governor with a mission to persuade the Abenakis to "espouse the interests of the King of France."[11]

Saint-Castin settled among these Indians in 1675, and in his youth he succumbed to a natural weakness for women; he contracted an Indian marriage with one, or, according to another version, two, of Chief Madokawando's daughters by whom he had several children.[12] He established himself, perhaps as early as 1676, in a small fort which had survived among the ruins of Pentagoët, and with the co-operation of his Indian friends, he made a considerable fortune by trading with the English. His authority among the Abenakis was uncontested; he was "absolute master of the Indians and their trading operations." He gave proof of such outstanding capacity that Denonville considered he would be the "right man" and the best possible governor for Acadia. Saint-Castin found at least one apologist for his unconventional morals in the Abbé Petit, the *curé* of Port Royal, who had served in the army before taking orders, and whose experience among soldiers may have made him less puritanical than the average parish priest. He considered that, living among the Indians, Saint-Castin "was in a position where he was, as it were, forced to adapt himself to their manner of life." He further declared him to be "fundamentally good, a generous almsgiver" who attended mass on each of his infrequent visits to Port Royal. Recognizing his duty as an honest and honourable gentleman of good family, and on the assurance of the King that his past errors would be forgotten, Saint-Castin eventually responded to the urging of the Bishop and Denonville, and married his Indian wife according to the rites of the Church.[13]

Notwithstanding the peace which they had signed with the Abenakis at Casco, the English continued with greater assurance than ever to extend their line of farms along the Acadian coast. Although the Treaty of Breda (1667) restored Pentagoët to France, and fixed the frontier thirty leagues west of the post, on the Kennebec, the English soon crossed that river. In 1671 they had farms as far east as the St. George River, nine leagues from the Kennebec, and in 1678 they built Fort Pemaquid, also to the east of the Kennebec. Then, as their gradual encroachment provoked no French reaction, they claimed the Sainte-Croix as their frontier, and Governor Dongan called on the French to evacuate all the land to the west of that river. The people of New England worked on the principle that their interests were never limited by the rights of others. As an English commissioner confessed, "the limit to their claims is fixed by their convenience or interest, and they never fail to claim a right to any region which suits them."[14]

While these settlers were staking out homesteads for themselves in French territory, their merchants were bartering munitions, blankets, shirts, tobacco and wine for furs. And their trade was not limited to the Abenakis. They even had stores in Port Royal where they sold cloth and farm tools to the Acadians, from whom they bought cattle. After visiting the colony, de Meulles reported that the Acadians, and particularly the people of Port Royal, "did all their business with Boston."[15]

Even more attractive to the Anglo-Americans than the Abenaki lands or trade with the French colonists were the Acadian fishing grounds which yielded better cod than the Newfoundland waters. The Acadian banks were a real "Peru," but all their wealth went to enrich New Englanders who were allowed to monopolize the fishing. These foreigners supplied themselves with water and wood from the French shore, where they also dried their fish. Only a very few of the fishing boats' masters bothered to pay the fee of fifty *livres* for a fishing permit, and none of them paid[16] Nicholas Denys the modest tax of twenty *sous* a ton for the boatloads of coal which they took back from Cape Breton.

When this foreign exploitation of the colony was brought to its attention, the Court decided to come to the rescue. But instead of acting directly, as he had done in Canada in 1663, the King authorized the establishment of a new trading company in the hope of stimulating the colony's economy. The Acadia Company was created by letters patent of February 28, 1682, with the financial backing of the Marquis de Chevry and under the direction of a Huguenot, Clerbaud Bergier. It was granted a strip of shore land between Canso and Cap Rouge, twelve leagues long and six leagues deep, on which to establish a fishing and fish-drying station. As well as hunting and fishing rights, it enjoyed trading rights with the French islands and colonies in America, with exemption from import and export duties.[17] The first year habitations and a fort were built at Chedabucto, where twenty-eight men took up residence. They fished, and the next year they planted flax, hemp, peas, beans, fruit trees and grape vines, all of which grew well. Bergier encouraged the habitants of the colony, and especially those of Port Royal, to add fishing to their other occupations.[18]

The new enterprise was just getting firmly established when it encountered serious opposition from the English. When they realized that under the new régime they were not to be allowed even a share of the fishing, the New Englanders resorted to piracy. Their buccaneers, among them Carter and Salem, captured six ships from Port Royal and threatened the post at Chedabucto, while the Boston smacks continued to fish in violation of French laws. As a result of Bergier's protests, Louis XIV issued an order in March 1684 which barred foreigners from trading in Acadia and from fishing in Acadian waters. A copy of the order was dispatched forthwith to the New England authorities with the warning that any ship attempting to violate it would be confiscated.[19]

At this critical moment a conflict of personalities intervened to bring misfortune to Acadia. Bergier made unreasonable claims on La Vallière, and when they were rejected, he complained to the Minister that the Governor was selling fishing licences to the English "in order to have something to live on."[20] It was the worst possible moment for a complaint against the Governor to arrive in Paris, and particularly a governor who had originally been appointed by Frontenac; for Frontenac's credit was very low, and the influential Talon was looking for a post for his nephew, François Perrot, whose insubordinate conduct and illegal trading had caused him to be dismissed from his post as Governor of Montreal. Thus, it happened that on April 10, 1684, Perrot became Governor of Acadia. The letter of appointment included a statement which, in view of his past conduct, one would hardly expect to find, even in an official document. In choosing Perrot, so read the commission, the Court was giving suitable recognition to "his experience as Governor of Montreal, and the loyalty which he had displayed in that post."[21]

The result of this appointment was what might have been expected. Very soon after his arrival in 1685 the new Governor, declaring that the colony "could not yet get along without the English," granted fishing permits in violation of the edict of 1684. Then, as if wishing to be "the only merchant in Acadia," he set up business on his own account, sending linen and wine direct to Boston, and even measuring out "in his own house, under the eyes of the foreigners, his pints and half-pints of brandy."[22] The Governor's abuses reduced the little colony's economy to such a pitiable state that in March 1687 he was dismissed from his post, but, quite undaunted, the shameless profiteer settled in the colony and continued his lucrative traffic with Boston.[23]

Anxious to repair past neglect, the Court finally gave serious consideration to the needs of Acadia. On April 5, 1687, Louis XIV appointed as Governor the Chevalier Alexandre des Friches de Menneval, an officer who had been "loved and esteemed by Turenne," and a "brave, wise and experienced man . . . above any mean consideration of personal interest." He was given a directive which specified that the Kennebec was the frontier of the colony and that he must grant no fishing or trading permits to foreigners. Thirty additional soldiers were sent out at the same time, but even with this addition to the garrison, the Governor had only ninety men to defend the whole of Acadia from Cape Breton to the Kennebec.[24]

Another very important decision sent a frigate to inaugurate a coastal police service and to drive off English fishing boats. Defensive works were built at Port Royal under the direction of an engineer, Pasquine, and in order to reduce the number of appeals to the Quebec Sovereign Council, the Sieur des Gouttins was appointed to act as King's Clerk and Judge.[25] The Chevry-Bergier Company, for its part, brought merchandise to Port Royal, but this did not altogether please the inhabitants, probably because the goods imported from France were less abundant and more expensive than those they had grown accustomed to getting from Boston. Meanwhile, since 1672 several Acadian seigniories had been granted by authority of the Governor and the Intendant of New France. There was excellent farming and stock-raising country in the St. John valley and on the peninsula, in some parts of which the fertility of the soil was still further increased by means of a system of dykes or *aboiteaux*. Conditions for colonization appeared to be ideal, but there were very few immigrants. The farmers who were attached to the new seigniories came for the most part from the older settlement of Port Royal, and in 1686 Acadia still had only 885 inhabitants.[26]

Now that foreigners were forbidden by law to exploit her fishing and trade, Acadia began to show signs of recovery and stability, but New England did not readily accept the new laws which her citizens defied even to the point of armed resistance. In April 1687, after having tried unsuccessfully to capture Saint-Castin, Governor Andros pillaged his fort at Pentagoët, and in July a pirate ship seized the post at Chedabucto. Meanwhile, the New Englanders continued to fish and trade along the Acadian coasts.[27]

France tried to fight the battle of Acadia on the diplomatic level by lodging a formal protest in London against these piratical raids. The Abenakis, on the other hand, who claimed the region in which Pentagoët was situated, answered force with force.[28] In the summer of 1688 they burned houses and killed settlers at Casco. The English built defence towers in the country districts, but the raids continued; in June 1689 Saint-Castin's warriors captured the village of Dover; two months later they laid seige to Pemaquid, and this solid fort capitulated on August 15. Here, as in Quebec, it was difficult to organize an effective defence against guerilla bands. The English sent troops from Boston and Plymouth, but as soon as they were sighted, the Abenaki warriors disappeared into the fastnesses of the neighbouring forest. It could be said that these, "the bravest of all the Indians," saved Acadia for France.[29]

CHAPTER SEVENTEEN

NEW ENGLAND INVADES ACADIA
1689-1697

Phipps captures Port Royal. Villebon reoccupies the colony. The Abenakis sole defenders of the country. Errors and inefficiency of Villebon. Indian raids in New England. D'Iberville captures Pemaquid. Church destroys Beaubassin. Peace of Ryswick. Anglo-Abenaki treaty. Brouillan rebuilds Port Royal. Economic stagnation.

While hostilities between the English and the Abenakis continued, and even increased in violence, the situation in New France became still more critical with the outbreak of the War of the Augsburg League in 1689. Hostilities in America began with Frontenac's destructive raids on Salmon Falls and Casco. Exasperated by these attacks and by the restrictions on its fishing and trading activities in Acadia, New England saw in the war a golden opportunity to get rid of its troublesome French and Indian neighbours by invading and conquering Acadia. An expedition was organized under William Phipps who set himself up as admiral of a fleet which he helped to equip with funds from his own pocket.[1]

The squadron of three frigates with sixty-six guns and four transports carrying six hundred men set sail from Boston on May 8, 1690, and after capturing Pentagoët on the way, it moored before Port Royal on the morning of the 20th. The fort, which had no retrenchments and was in a bad state of repair, was defended by seventy-two soldiers and a few habitants. The Commander, Menneval, was paralyzed with gout, and he had no responsible officer to whom he could delegate the defence of the post. In these circumstances he had no alternative but to surrender when called upon to do so. However, he laid down certain conditions: the garrison would receive the honours of war and would be sent to Quebec, the women would be respected, the inhabitants would not be robbed or molested, their religious convictions would not

173

be violated and the church would be left intact. These conditions were confirmed the next day when Menneval went on board the admiral's ship to conclude the formalities. When Phipps went ashore and saw the inadequacy of the garrison and the fortifications, he broke the terms agreed upon on the pretext that goods had been removed from Perrot's stores by private individuals. Menneval was confined to his house, and the soldiers locked up in the church. Phipps seized Menneval's money and clothes and allowed his soldiers to pillage houses and to steal the sacred vessels from the church which was then burned.[2]

At the beginning of June the vainglorious admiral returned to Boston with his prisoners, Menneval, Fathers Petit and Trouvé, and the garrison. The Governor was treated abominably; he was not allowed to return to Paris until months later, and even then he owed his repatriation to Governor Dongan of New York, an Irish Catholic and partisan of the Stuarts who was anxious to win friends in France. At Port Royal Phipps hoisted the English flag and placed the French sergeant Chevalier in command of the inhabitants who, in order to preserve their property, had to recognize King William.[3]

On June 14, a few days after the departure of the English fleet, Captain Robineau de Villebon arrived from France with forty-five soldiers, as well as munitions and merchandise. Finding Port Royal in ruins, he decided to establish himself on the St. John River, but soon after he arrived there, his ship was seized by two English freebooters. Villebon, who was absent from the camp at the time, managed to reach Quebec, and to return to France in search of help.[4] In April 1691, from his camp outside Mons, Louis XIV sent an answer to Villebon's plea: "The state of affairs in Europe" made it impossible for him to re-establish Port Royal. However, Villebon was sent back as interim commander and provided with merchandise, munitions and presents for the Abenakis. With a detachment of forty soldiers provided by Frontenac he took possession of Port Royal, but in the summer of 1691 he established himself at Nashwaak on the St. John River where he built a fort. On his way from Port Royal he had captured an English boat with its passengers, the Boston merchant John Nelson and Colonel Edward Tyng, who had been appointed Governor of Port Royal. These prisoners were sent to Quebec where Nelson, taking full advantage of the freedom which Frontenac imprudently allowed him, won the sympathy of two soldiers and sent them to warn Boston of an attack being planned against Pemaquid. In Boston Phipps bribed them to kidnap or assassinate Saint-Castin, and they set out to do so, but their Acadian guides delivered them into the hands of the French who promptly dispatched them. Nelson himself was sent as a prisoner to France.[5]

Most of Villebon's forty men returned to Quebec, so that in 1692 he had only a handful of soldiers, and once more the Abenakis were the only obstacle in the path of the English invaders. The Indians did not break off negotiations, and they continued to receive English goods either in barter or as gifts, but they refused to give up their alliance with the French and they continued their forays into New England. In June they were driven away from Wells by the vigorous defence of the inhabitants, but they spent the following months ravaging the neighbouring country. In January (1692) 150 warriors under Madokawando attacked the village of York where they killed fifty colonists and took about one hundred prisoners. An expedition of Canadians under Portneuf and Indians led by Saint-Castin was defeated at Cocheco. It was also repulsed in an assault on Wells where, under the command of Convers, the women of the village loaded rifles for the men, and even took part in firing the guns.[6]

Warned by Nelson's message of the French plan to attack Pemaquid, Phipps, who was now Governor of Massachusetts, began the construction of a new fort destined to seal off the frontier. On being informed in his turn of this move, Frontenac sent d'Iberville and Bonaventure with their ships to join forces with the Abenakis and lay siege to the fort. It was now October, an imposing fort had been built and its defenders warned of the enemy's approach, and to the great surprise of his officers and the bitter disappointment of the Indians, d'Iberville refused to attack. The reason for this uncharacteristic conduct was apparently that he did not want to expose to danger "some women and a Sister whom he had on board."[7]

In August 1693 Phipps met the Abenaki chiefs at Pemaquid. Won over by presents and by Phipps's promise to restore their tribal brothers whom he held as prisoners, the chiefs agreed to "throw their hatchets into the sea."[8] There were various reasons for this change of policy. Only by making peace with the English could the Abenakis deliver their brothers from captivity in Boston; but they were also disappointed in their French allies whose presents had not come up to their expectations and who had failed them by not attacking Pemaquid.[9] Much of the responsibility for this disaffection must be laid at the door of Villebon, who was reproved by

Pontchartrain for his lack of care in the distibution of the gifts provided in 1691, and even for selling some of them. Complaints of
Villebon's conduct in this matter, and in various others, had
reached Champigny from Indians, as well as from his compatriots.
Seigneurs and colonists alleged that he abused his authority. He
was accused of trading with Boston, and also of monopolizing the
fur trade for himself and his two brothers, one of whom had taken
an Indian mistress. Precise statements on these matters were supplied to Champigny by French men and Indians alike.[10]

Fortunately, Pontchartrain realized that, whatever might be
his attitude towards the personal weaknesses of Villebon, he could
not remain indifferent to the risk of losing the support of the Abenakis, Acadia's only rampart against English aggression. He dispatched presents and arms, powder, lead and rifles for the warriors, hats and shirts for the chiefs.[11] His timely help bolstered the
self-confidence of the Indians, and still more important, renewed
their faith in France. This confidence was still further strengthened by the exploits of French corsairs on the Acadian coast. A
Bordeaux privateer captured eleven ships in 1692, and Pierre
Maisonnat, the famous "Captain Baptiste," captured several prizes
in 1693 and ten the following year.[12]

In 1694 Versailles decided to launch an offensive against New
England. On July 27 a group of 215 Abenakis under Lieutenant
Villieu attacked Oyster River north of Portsmouth. They captured
two forts and pillaged and burned sixty houses, killing 104 of their
occupants and taking twenty-seven prisoners. Chief Taxous followed up this success with the capture of Groton, and Saint-Castin
attacked Deerfield.[13] Phipps tried to put an end to these raids by
making peace with the Abenakis. Parleys were initiated at Wells
in May 1695 but, thanks to the intervention of Saint-Castin and
Father Thury, they broke down, and after receiving gifts and ammunition from France, the Indians again went on the warpath
against the English.[14]

Hostilities were not, however, to be limited to Indian raids,
and plans were laid in Versailles for the capture of Pemaquid.
This fort, in French hands, would guarantee the loyalty of the Abenakis to the French cause, while at the same time it would protect Acadia and eventually Canada.

D'Iberville was chosen to command the expedition.[15] On July
14 his ships, the *Envieux* and the *Profond*, were in the Bay of
Fundy. It was foggy, but the fog lifted and revealed two English
frigates of which d'Iberville captured one and put the other to

flight. Two hundred and forty-seven Abenakis under Saint-Castin and twenty French soldiers under Villieu were already encamped in the vicinity when, on August 14, d'Iberville dropped anchor before the imposing fort of Pemaquid with its twelve-foot wall and its sixteen guns. D'Iberville called on Chubb to surrender, but the commander answered that even if the sea were covered with French ships and the woods full of savages he would surrender only to force. The following day the French batteries opened fire, and Saint-Castin warned Chubb that if the fort was taken, his ninety-five men would fall into the hands of ungovernable savages. Daunted by this prospect, the garrison insisted that Chubb capitulate; the resistance had lasted only one day. D'Iberville carried out the terms of surrender by sending the captured garrison to Boston. Then, after razing the fort, he sailed for Placentia where he arrived on September 12.[15a]

The English, for their part, did not intend to remain on the defensive. Phipps's successor, Governor Stoughton, organized an invasion force of four hundred New Englanders and fifty Indians under the command of Major Benjamin Church. This troop landed at Beaubassin a month after the capture of Pemaquid, and when Germain Bourgeois displayed a document guaranteeing the protection of King William for the population, the invaders refused to honour it. Instead they pillaged and destroyed the houses and the church. Only the most precious articles were saved by the inhabitants, who escaped to the woods. In October Church's contingent was joined at Passamaquoddy by a frigate and a transport, and thus reinforced, the army laid seige to Fort Nashwaak on the St. John River. After an exchange of artillery fire which lasted two days and in which the French casualties were one dead and one wounded, the English withdrew, taking with them eight dead and seventeen wounded.[15b]

The series of inconclusive attacks and counter-attacks was brought to a close with the signing of the Treaty of Ryswick, which restored to each of the powers the territories it had held before the outbreak of hostilities.[16] The news reached Port Royal in March 1698 in a letter from Stoughton to Villebon. The Governor subsequently received orders from Pontchartrain to maintain the Acadian frontier at the Kennebec, and to refuse the English fishing and trading privileges within the borders of the colony. But the peace had hardly been concluded when the English were back carrying on their trade in Acadian territory and fishing in Acadian waters. In 1698 Villebon made representations to Stoughton on the subject of these violations of the law, and France sent a frigate to patrol the coast. But the next year, following a curious reversal of policy, the Minister authorized the sale of permits to English fishermen with the provision that each boat must take on board a French sailor, who would thus learn English fishing methods.[17]

With the return of peace came a fresh wave of disaffection among the Abenakis, for the French policy-makers seemed to have forgotten the services rendered by their native allies. In 1698 Versailles reduced considerably her scale of gifts, and the following year France sent only ceremonial presents, plumed hats, lace-frilled shirts and fine arms for twelve chiefs. Still more serious, the French had not stipulated in their peace terms that Abenaki prisoners should be repatriated with their French comrades, so that when these prisoners were later released, credit for their liberation went to the English, who also won friends among the Indians by selling them goods at prices much lower than the French ones. In 1699 the Abenakis, with the approval of Governor Callières, signed a peace treaty with the English.[18] One condition was that settlers should be debarred from Abenaki territory. The result was that, since ships from France did not call at Pentagoët, Saint-Castin and his Indians kept up regular trade with Boston, which supplied all their needs and bought all their furs.[19]

On July 5, 1700, Villebon died in the new fort at the mouth of the St. John River to which he had moved from Nashwaak. His lieutenant, Villieu, assumed temporary command but, perhaps because of his record of commercial involvement and quarrels with his superior officer, he did not succeed to the vacant post. Instead the King appointed the active and hot-tempered governor of Placentia, François de Brouillan, who arrived at Port Royal in June 1701. On orders from the Court, Brouillan demolished Villebon's post at St. John and used the materials to build a new fort at Port Royal.[20] In the autumn of the same year Saint-Castin was called back to France to defend his family fortune against the claims of an unscrupulous brother-in-law. His departure removed from the Acadian scene the man whose influence over the Abenakis had kept them hostile to the English and thus saved Acadia, for the time being, from English occupation. Family affairs kept Saint-Castin in France, where he died in 1707.[21]

During the period from 1680 to 1701, which included nine years of war, Acadia made little or no progress. English attacks had prevented the expansion of Nashwaak on the St. John River, rav-

aged Beaubassin and Minas, and ruined the fishing station at
Chedabucto. Emigrants were not sent to Acadia as they were to
Canada, and the increase in the population from about nine hundred souls (in 1686) to thirteen hundred was entirely due to a remarkably high birth-rate. Agriculture and stock-raising increased
by at least one third, but in 1701 Port Royal was still a straggling
village of mean houses dotted along the river bank.[22]

CHAPTER EIGHTEEN

CAPTURE OF PORT ROYAL BY THE ENGLISH AND CONQUEST OF NEWFOUNDLAND BY THE FRENCH
1689-1713

Franco-Abenaki hostilities. Minas ravaged by Church. His defeat at Port Royal. Destruction of Narantsouak. Domestic difficulties and quarrels. Siege and capture of Port Royal. English and French in Newfoundland. D'Iberville's victories. English attempts against Placentia. Expeditions of Subercase and Saint-Ovide. Treaty of Utrecht.

Brouillan had arrived full of new plans for Acadia, but their execution was prevented by the outbreak of the War of the Spanish Succession in May 1702. The Governor immediately proposed a neutrality pact with New England, but his offer was rejected and both the French and the English colonies were faced with possibility of invasion. Brouillan had only sixty regulars and about three hundred militiamen to defend Port Royal, but he hastened the completion of the defences, and sent envoys with presents to the Indians.[1] The English in their turn rebuilt the fort at Pemaquid which had been destroyed by d'Iberville, and the Governor of Massachusetts signed an agreement with the Abenakis. Such agreements were, however, never completely binding on the Indians, and neither they nor the French were deterred from hostile action by prudent fear of reprisals. The Abenakis allowed themselves to be won over again by the Abbé Rasles and in August 1703 they joined Beaubassin's successful expedition against Wells. The English, however, recovering quickly, drove back Beaubassin and his Indians from Saco and destroyed the habitation at Pentagoët. The following year, determined to rid their settlements of the Indian threat, the authorities sent detachments in pursuit of the Abenaki raiders and offered a bounty of forty pounds sterling for a scalp, but the bands continued to elude their pursuers by dispersing and disappearing into the forest.[1a]

The Franco-Indian forays, which aroused the anger of the New England colonists against the Abenakis, also hardened their determination to conquer the stubborn resistance of Acadia, and in the summer of 1704 an expedition set sail from Boston under the orders of Church. The fleet of three warships, fourteen transports and thirty-six fishing smacks carried a fighting force of 550 soldiers. On July 1 the men from some of the small boats landed at Minas, where, after burning fifty houses and the church, they captured forty-five prisoners. The other inhabitants of the village fled to the woods. The fleet then moored before Port Royal where entrenchments had been thrown up by the garrison and the assembled inhabitants. After a summons to surrender the fort, the enemy succeeded in landing and launched a few feeble attacks, but they were repulsed by rifle and cannon fire for about fifteen days. On the 16th two hundred men were detached and sent to Beaubassin where they burned twenty houses. Two days later, as the resistance of Port Royal showed no signs of weakening, the invaders abandoned their attempt and set sail for Boston.[1b]

A winter raid (1705) against the village of Naransouak met with greater success. Colonel Hilton, with a band of militiamen on snowshoes, surprised the Indians, who fled into the woods leaving their huts to be burnt by the invaders. This disaster, which left them without shelter in mid-winter, was a serious threat to the morale of the Abenakis; they began to complain that the French were letting them bear the brunt of the war. The missionaries, acting on instructions from Vaudreuil, urged them to continue to resist the English, and at the same time Port Royal renewed their supplies of lead and powder so they would be in a position to do so.[1c]

Even if there had been no English invaders, the situation in Acadia would not have been encouraging. Brouillan was a brave and energetic soldier, but in Port Royal, as in Placentia, he proved to be overbearing, irritable and mistrustful. He quarrelled with his officers, especially the engineer, La Bat, and the King's Clerk, Des Gouttins. His soldiers were ill-treated and his labourers ill-paid, and he accused the missionaries of encroaching on the domain of temporal power. On the other hand, he was himself harassed by lack of funds, and, when forced to issue card money, he was severely reproved by Versailles. Simultaneously, the local gossips circulated exaggerated stories of his attentions to the charming Madame Barat. The people complained about everyone and everything, from the Governor and the clergy to the price of merchandise. When Brouillan had to go to France to consult a doctor, the Acadians delegated the Sieur Lopinot to suggest to the Minister that the Governor be recalled and succeeded by the more popular Bonaventure. They later requested that the "autocratic Récollets" be replaced by secular priests. Obviously all this bickering and chicanery constituted a serious obstacle to progress. Still more serious was the mother country's neglect of its colony. Versailles left the country "starved for everything," from essential farming tools to household goods. The Acadian had to subsist on the products of the land, which was especially rich around Minas Basin, and on the fish which he could catch just off his own beach. As a sideline, any colonists who could do so carried on a modest trade in furs. The settlers on the St. John River bartered for the most part with the neighbouring colony, exchanging furs for English goods.[2]

Brouillan died at sea on his way back to Acadia, and Bonaventure, the candidate suggested by the colonists, seemed well qualified to succeed him. However, the King, who had forgotten his own youthful errors, rejected him because of an alleged liaison with Madame de Freneuse, and appointed instead Daniel Auger de Subercase who had been until that time Governor of Newfoundland. In October 1706 the new Governor took command of a colony torn by war and internal strife, and at once brought his qualities of integrity and wisdom to bear on the multiple tasks which confronted him: restoration of domestic harmony, preparations for defence, procuring essential help from the mother country, repression of excessive clerical activity in the temporal sphere.[2a]

Just seven months after his arrival, his capital with its inadequate fort and its handful of soldiers was subjected to another English attack. A fleet from Boston anchored in sight of the fort on June 6 (1707). The convoy, which included two warships with twenty-three transports and a number of smaller boats, carried an army of about one thousand militiamen under Colonel March. The Acadians had been reinforced by sixty Canadians recruited by a privateer, and the defenders were organized into small detachments to repel the enemy's landing parties. Subercase directed the movements of his little force in person, and, in the course of the fighting, his horse was shot from under him. The English succeeded in burning a number of houses, but they were driven back by a band of Abenakis under the command of Saint-Castin's son. On the 16th an English battery opened fire, and the French guns answered with a vigorous cannonade. Rumours of French reinforcements together with an unexpectedly vigorous defence from the fort combined to weaken the fighting spirit of the invaders who re-embarked on the 17th, leaving behind some fifty dead. French casualties were limited to one dead and two wounded.[3]

The relief was, however, short-lived. The New England fleet, which had reassembled in Casco Bay, was strengthened by about a hundred recruits, and ordered by Governor Dudley to repeat its attack on Port Royal. On August 20 the squadron, now under the command of Colonel Wainwright, was again moored before the fort, and the following day a considerable force succeeded in establishing a fortified camp after being twice dislodged by artillery fire. On the 31st the enemy advanced in force against Port Royal, but their advance was halted after a vigorous skirmish with Saint-Castin's men who had been lying in wait for them. With reinforcements from the fort the little French troop then took the offensive, and engaged the enemy. Both forces withdrew after a violent skirmish, but the following day the English fleet sailed out of the harbour. Acadia had survived one more attack.[4]

The failure to conquer Acadia brought angry outcries in New England, especially from the fishermen and merchants who were dismayed by the inroads of the French privateers, and from the people in the Kennebec valley who were the chief sufferers from Indian raids. Having discovered that they were not strong enough to deal with the situation themselves, the colonists appealed to London, and in 1708 Samuel Vetch obtained the Queen's promise that a strong fleet would be sent out in the following spring. However, although the fleet was actually assembled, it was sent to the relief of Portugal and never reached America. Meanwhile, Subercase, informed of England's plans for attack, feared the worst, for the colony, which was much too weak to defend itself against a determined enemy, appeared to be abandoned by the mother country. Unfortunately for Acadia, however, France was herself in a critical pass: her armies had suffered defeat at Ramillies in 1706 and at Malplaquet in 1709, and during the dreadful winter of 1709 her famine-stricken peasants were reduced to making bread from ferns.[5]

Meanwhile, the English colonies continued to press for action, and in 1710 a fleet of six warships and six transports was sent out to Boston, where it was joined by fourteen transports from New England. The combined force, under the command of Nicholson, counted, with the ships' crews, 3,400 men.[6] On October 5 the fleet moored before Port Royal, and the next day a landing was effected. Subercase had only 108 soldiers and 100 militiamen, but he opened fire with his guns and killed more than fifty of the enemy. The English had landed their heavy artillery, and on the 10th, after the fort had been subjected to continuous bombardment for four days, fifty habitants and seven soldiers deserted. The following day the garrison presented a request that in consideration of the desperate condition of their defences, the Commander should propose an honourable surrender. An informal council of war having concluded that no other course was open to the defenders, Subercase submitted conditions which were signed by Nicholson on October 13, 1710.[7]

By the terms of surrender the garrison was granted the honours of war and was guaranteed passage to La Rochelle. Colonists living within a three-mile radius of Port Royal were allowed to retain their lands, cattle and grain and were free to leave the country at any time within two years. Those who chose to remain would be required to take an oath of allegiance. On October 16 the garrison marched out from the fort. Its 156 soldiers, who were "practically naked," had to be supplied with food by Nicholson, and in order to meet the debts contracted by the administration, Subercase had to sell to the English the guns from the fort as well as his own silver and furniture.[8]

On October 28 the English fleet sailed for Boston where it was received in triumph. Vetch remained behind with a garrison of 450 men as Governor of Port Royal, now rechristened Annapolis Royal in honour of Queen Anne. It was not long before the inhabitants wrote to ask Vaudreuil's help so that they might leave a country where "they were treated like blacks by the English Governor." Three months later Vetch lent colour to accusations of oppression by ordering Father Justinien and five members of his congregation to be arrested during the celebration of a mass.[9]

Although Quebec and Versailles must have been aware of Acadia's weakness, both capitals were surprised by the fall of Port Royal and critical of its Governor. Vaudreuil considered that Subercase should have retained the force which had been sent to his aid.[10] When he returned to France, the Governor was summoned before a court martial at La Rochelle. Here, however, the verdict was presumably in his favour, since the King appointed him the following year (1711) to a post in Canada and later increased his salary. The Court had consistently neglected Acadia, but with the loss of the Acadian fisheries, it suddenly became sensible of their value. Having done nothing to prevent this outpost of New France from falling into the hands of the enemy, it now proposed to reconquer it.[11]

In 1711 Vaudreuil appointed the young Saint-Castin as lieutenant in command of the Indians and Acadians in the territory which had not been included in the capitulation. His orders were to work in concert with Father La Chasse and the other missionaries to incite the Abenakis to raid Port Royal and the New England villages.[12] As a result, a detachment of sixty English was surprised by a band of Indians at Bloody Creek above Port Royal, where twenty men were killed and forty captured. In July a force of Acadians and Abenakis even invested Port Royal, but without reinforcements they could not maintain a siege. The inhabitants of the region did, however, continue to declare themselves "very loyal" to France, even though in order to be able to bring in their crops they agreed to keep the peace.[13] Thus, the climate in Acadia was one of mutual hostility when in 1712 England and France signed the truce which preceded the Treaty of Utrecht.[14]

Off the Atlantic coast, and within the same political sphere of influence as Acadia, the great island of Newfoundland had its two small rival colonies, St. John's and Placentia. The English colony of St. John's included twenty-eight settlements dotted along the eastern coast north of Cape Race. In 1667 the largest of these posts, St. John's, had only eighty-seven inhabitants, and the entire colony had no more than 523 permanent settlers, who had small gardens and a few animals, but who were essentially fishermen. There were also about thirteen hundred seasonal fishermen who came in the spring from the English ports to which they returned in the autumn. Such was the state of affairs when in 1689 war broke out and the English built small forts at St. John's which were garrisoned by about twenty soldiers.[15]

The French colony on the south shore had eight tiny stations in 1674. Its capital, Placentia, had only seventy-three inhabitants with a Governor, La Poëpe, a dilapidated fort and eight soldiers. In 1687 annual additions of fishermen and *engagés* had increased the population of Placentia to 250, and that of the colony to 663. The colonists had a few cultivated fields and some animals, but they all lived by their fishing. The shipowners of France showed little interest in this excellent station, whose fishermen traded their cod for food and manufactured wares from New England.[16]

When war was declared in 1689, Versailles dispatched twenty-five soldiers to Placentia, but the following February the settlement was surprised and sacked by the freebooter Herman Williamson. Two years later, on September 16, 1692, Commodore Williams made an attack in force with five warships. But the new Governor, the Sieur de Brouillan, had made a great effort to improve the defences of this little capital, and, although his force consisted of only fifty soldiers and sixty Basque fishermen led by the Baron de La Hontan, he succeeded in repulsing the attack. The following year Admiral Francis Wheeler with a still stronger fleet of twenty-four ships bombarded Placentia, but again Brouillan opened fire on the invaders and drove them off.[17]

Such raids constituted a serious threat to the French fisheries, and in order to remove this threat, Louis XIV decided to destroy the English posts and to ruin their fishing industry. Accordingly, on March 31, 1696, Versailles commissioned d'Iberville to carry out this task. The commander's orders stipulated that he would finance the expedition, and that he would receive one third of the prizes, of which the remainder would be divided equally between the King and the shipowners in St. Malo.[18]

D'Iberville the soldier and sailor was also the son of a merchant, and he saw the Newfoundland expedition not only as a mission to destroy an English outpost against New France, but as a chance to create a great cod-fishing monopoly. He had already discussed the project with the merchants of La Rochelle who would undertake to sell the fish on the Mediterranean markets. Brouillan had also a plan of his own, and when d'Iberville arrived in Placentia after the capture of Pemaquid, the Governor had already set out for St. John's with eight Malouin fishing-boats. He had hoped to be able to seize the valuable post by surprise, but when he found the harbour occupied by a fleet of English ships,[19] he turned back and satisfied himself with the capture of a few small posts and thirty fishing-boats. At Placentia Brouillan found d'Iberville with three ships, thirty Canadians hired at his own expense, and fifty of Frontenac's soldiers, and the two leaders united their forces for an attack against St. John's. On November 28 they dislodged a detachment of eighty-eight English soldiers from their position between Petty Harbour and St. John's, and pursued them right into the town. There, the only resistance was offered by the main fort which sheltered 160 men as well as women and children. D'Iberville threatened to bombard the fort, and the commander,

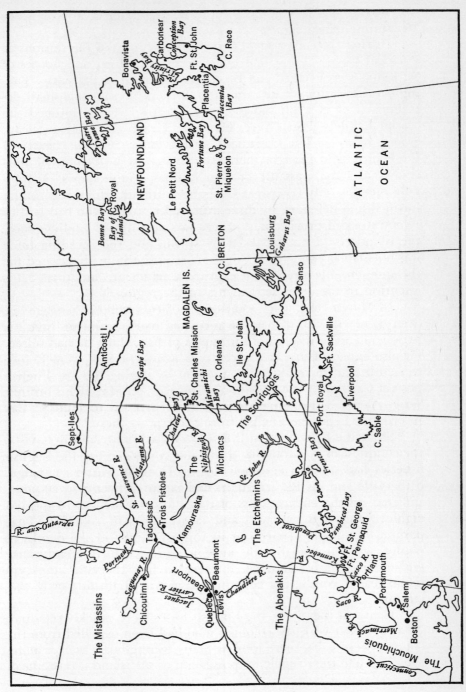

ACADIA AND NEWFOUNDLAND IN THE 18TH CENTURY

who had no regular soldiers to hold it, surrendered on November 30 without firing a shot.[20]

During December small detachments captured the stations at Portugal Cove, Torbay and Quidi Vidi. The forts and houses of St. John's were burned and Brouillan returned to Placentia. Taking over direction of the campaign, d'Iberville sent out small detachments of men on snowshoes who captured and ravaged the coastal hamlets, Port Grave, Harbour Grace and Old Perlican, among others. "The Canadians struck panic into the hearts of the enemy who thought their attackers must be demons if they could march to the assault across such impenetrable snows." D'Iberville met his only reverse at Carbonear Island, which was solidly fortified and defended by three hundred refugees who had laid in a good stock of provisions. As there was no suitable landing-place, the island could not be taken by storm, and the invading force was not strong enough to besiege it. So d'Iberville abandoned for the moment his attempt to capture Carbonear, and turned his attention to the other settlements in the region.[21]

In March 1697, while some of his officers were still engaged in destroying villages, d'Iberville returned to Placentia to leave his prisoners and to dispose of the stocks of fish which he had seized. He also expected that reinforcements would be sent from France to enable him to complete his mission by seizing the last English posts at Carbonear and Bonavista. However, on May 18 his brother Sérigny arrived, bringing him orders to proceed to Hudson Bay in order to expel the English from their posts there.[22]

Since the British flag still flew over Carbonear and Bonavista, the conquest of Newfoundland was not complete, but the English fisheries had suffered enormous losses. In their winter campaign, d'Iberville and his 124 irregulars had captured twenty-seven posts, inflicted on the enemy a loss of two hundred men and captured eighteen hundred prisoners and large stocks of codfish.[23] That dashing campaign, carried out in forest country in the depths of winter, was, on a small scale, an epic of inexhaustible endurance and unconquerable courage. It revealed in d'Iberville an exceptional leader combining bold initiative with lightning-swift execution.

Heavy as they were, the English losses were quickly repaired. The very next year, the colonists who had been expelled from the country were back, there were as many fishing-boats as ever along the coast, and the struggle for possession of the island was resumed.

In 1697 M. de Nesmond was instructed to recapture Newfoundland before proceeding to the attack on Boston, but when, on
August 18, his fleet came in sight of St. John's, the harbour was occupied by an English fleet under the command of Sir John Norris,
and neither admiral took offensive action. In September 1697 the
Treaty of Ryswick restored to each belligerent the territories
which it had held before the war.[24]

After less than five years of peace, Newfoundland again became
the scene of conflict. In 1702 Admiral John Leake ravaged the fish-
ing stations on the French coast, and in April 1703 Vice-Admiral
Graydon sailed into Placentia harbour. When he saw that the
post was ready to defend itself, he withdrew.[25] The following summer, the Sieur de la Grange landed at Bonavista with a hundred
Canadians. There they seized a frigate and burned two buildings.
A few months later a larger force of 450 Canadian soldiers and
Micmacs, led by Governor Subercase, captured Beboule and Petty
Harbour. They were repulsed at St. John's where the defence was
directed by Colonel Moody and Lieutenant Latham, but a French
detachment under Montigny pillaged the settlement at Trinity,
and captured the important post of Bonavista.[26]

In spite of these repeated French attacks, the English made no
attempt to capture Placentia. When in 1707 they took offensive
action, Major Lloyd led a naval expedition against the Malouins'
fishing stations of the Petit-Nord between Cape Freels and Belle-
Isle. In December 1708 the Sieur de Saint-Ovide, following the
example set by d'Iberville, undertook to finance a new expedition.
With a force of 170 French, Canadians and Indians, he captured
St. John's on January 1, 1709, and after demolishing the defences
of the fort, he set its ransom at 7,000 *livres*. In 1710 English privateers marked points for their side by capturing five French ships
and plundering the fishermen's settlement, and in 1711 and 1712
English squadrons twice blockaded Placentia, which was successfully defended by Governor Costebelle. Finally, in 1713 the
Treaty of Utrecht put an end to this exchange of petty hostilities.
By the terms of the treaty Newfoundland was ceded to England,
and this cession proved to be permanent.[27]

CHAPTER NINETEEN

REVIEW: PLACENTIA AND ACADIA
1670-1713

Terms of the Treaty of Utrecht. Placentia: a languishing colony. Increase in the population of Acadia. Agriculture. Way of life. Economic activity. Administration. Port Royal. Lack of roads. Quarrels and recriminations. Virtues of the Acadian. Weakness of the colony: its neglect by France.

After twelve years of war, the Treaty of Utrecht restored peace in Europe. Marshal Villars had won a great victory at Denain in 1712, but France's treasury was empty, and "with sorrow written on his face," Louis XIV was obliged to accept the hard conditions dictated by his enemies' coalition. His grandson, who had become the King of Spain, renounced his claim to the throne of France, the Spanish Netherlands passed into the hands of Austria, and the fortifications of Dunkirk were to be destroyed.[1]

In America, the treaty cut deeply into the fabric of the colonial empire. France ceded to England the island of St. Kitts, the Hudson Bay basin and all its forts and the Bay itself. In Newfoundland she retained only the right to fish and to dry fish on its shores north of Bonavista on the east coast and north of Pointe Riche on the west coast. She suffered an even more grievous loss in the cession of "all Nova Scotia or Acadia as defined by its original boundaries." The French plenipotentiaries had received explicit instructions to agree to this surrender only "in the last extremity," but they were helpless. Under vigorous pressure from New England which was determined to conquer Acadia and thus to lay, once and for all, the spectre of Franco-Indian raids, London refused categorically to restore the colony to France. Of all its Acadian possessions, France retained only the islands of St. Jean (Prince Edward Island) and Cape Breton, and their worth was very considerably reduced since England was in possession of both Nova Scotia and Newfoundland.[1a]

The period of colonization came to an end with the War of the Spanish Succession; 1713 is, therefore, a suitable date from which to glance back at the development of the three colonies of Placentia, Acadia and Canada during their half-century of existence under the royal administration. The smallest of the three, Placentia consisted of nine little settlements spread out along the south coast of Newfoundland. In 1687 the population had reached its maximum of 663 settlers, of whom 488 were *engagés*. The colonist-fishermen owned some 500 fishing-boats, and in the vicinity of Placentia there were about a hundred cattle and a few scattered gardens. In 1705 the capital itself had no more than three hundred inhabitants. In short, the colony of Newfoundland scarcely went beyond the tiny post of Placentia, whose function was to provide protection for the French fisheries and a port of refuge for warships and privateers as well as trading vessels and fishing smacks. In the course of the year 1712, its harbour gave shelter to twenty-four ships from France and fourteen from Quebec as well as five corsairs from the West Indies. The loss of Newfoundland to England apparently caused few regrets. Even those most concerned, the fishermen, were not dismayed, since France had retained the right on which their livelihood depended—to fish on the banks and to dry fish on the two coasts of the Petit-Nord.

The shoreline of France's oldest colony, Acadia, extended officially from Cap Gaspé to the Kennebec River.[2] In contrast to the barren shores of Placentia, Acadia offered the mother country a colonial domain rich with promise. But since the time of Champlain, dreams of a western route to China and the development of a rich fur trade in Canada and the West had occupied the minds of colonial policy-makers, who consistently underestimated and neglected the potential value of Acadia. In 1670 the colony had a population of 441 inhabitants, almost all concentrated around the little capital of Port Royal. Other very small groups were scattered from Pentagoët to St. Peter's on Cape Breton Island. By an unhappy turn of fate, Acadia was restored to royal administration too late to benefit by Colbert's emigration policy. It received only sixty emigrants, among whom there were five marriageable girls, and when the latter arrived in 1672, they found twenty-two bachelors waiting for brides. The establishment of Chedabucto in 1682 increased the population by about a hundred fishermen and settlers, but in the course of the years the colony received from outside its borders only a very feeble trickle of *engagés* and soldiers who could "marry and become habitants."[3]

In short, Acadia's increase in population was due almost entirely to the natural fertility of its people. Some families counted as many as eighteen or even twenty-two children, although, unfortunately, this remarkably high birth-rate was partly counterbalanced by losses from English incursions.[4] The Acadians, who came for the most part from the more westerly provinces, Normandy, Brittany, Aunis and Touraine, were a vigorous and stubborn race. They became firmly attached to their land and their seacoast, and by the successive steps of fur-trading, fishing and farming, they made slow and obstinate progress. The population, which had doubled in fifteen years, stood at 885 in 1686, and although there is no single census for 1713, a compilation of several records would give a total for that year of 2,528.[5]

The inhabitants of Port Royal included artisans, *engagés*, soldiers and public servants, but elsewhere the population was composed entirely of farmers. These latter exploited holdings on which they paid only nominal charges and which they held either as grants from one of the twenty Acadian seigneurs or directly from the Crown. The seigniories themselves were granted in the King's name by the governor and the intendant of Canada, and were subject to the conditions which applied in that province. There was good agricultural land at Port Royal and Chedabucto, but the finest farming country was to be found around Minas Basin and at Beaubassin on the isthmus of Chignecto, where the soil, fertilized by alluvial deposits from the sea, produced rich crops of wheat, rye and barley, as well as hemp and flax. By 1698 the Acadians owned 1,334 cattle, 1,314 sheep and 746 pigs. They had brought 1,573 *arpents* under cultivation and planted 1,600 fruit trees. For 1713 all these figures could be doubled, and some could be tripled. Fruit trees from France were easily propagated, and even grape vines grew without difficulty, while in the competent hands of the women the gardens produced an abundance of vegetables.[6]

The Acadian farmer was also a fisherman whose nets and weirs provided a variety of excellent fish: sturgeon, smelts, eels, salmon, shad and bass. A favourite dish was made with sturgeon and fricasseed chicken. For dessert the Acadians had fruit and maple sugar, and they made quite a pleasant beer with spruce tips, yeast and molasses. In the autumn they shot rabbits, partridges and ducks, and in winter they hunted fur-bearing animals and the seals which provided them with oil and shoe-leather. The neighbouring forest furnished the wood from which they built houses, mills and churches, and from which they fashioned furniture and ploughs. They also became shipbuilders and launched privateer frigates from their own shipyards. The women, no less skilful than the men, made up for the scarcity of manufactured cloth by learning to weave rough linen and woollen fabrics. The authorities in France frowned on this industry, which encouraged competition with the mother country's trade, but local custom still required that every bride should be able to weave a pair of sheets, and every groom to fashion a pair of wheels.[7]

Acadia carried on an intermittent trade with France, exporting masts, elm and ash timber, as well as limestome from Canso (which sold at thirty *sous* a ton), and coal from Cape Breton (which brought twenty *sous* a ton). However, the soft coal was not popular in France, and while there might have been a market for it in New England, the New Englanders saw no reason to buy it when they could steal small quantities and take it back in their fishing-boats.[8] Although there were rich fishing grounds just off their coasts, the Acadians lacked the resources and the experience which might have made them deep-sea fishermen. Six small schooners which they sent out in 1683 were seized by pirates from Salem, and after this first disaster, projects for large-scale fishing ventures, although they were considered in 1698 and again in 1702, were never begun.[9]

Naturally beaver was the best article of exchange, and the Acadians, like the Canadians, hunted beaver and bought skins from the Indians. At the end of the seventeenth century, beaver had become rare in the peninsula, but it was still abundant in Cape Breton, and still more so in the St. John valley, where the fur harvest brought in as much as 30,000 *livres* a year. Everyone who could do so participated in the trade: governors, such as La Vallière, Perrot and Villebon, officers, like Villieu, seigneurs, like the d'Amours, habitants, and even priests and missionaries when a favourable occasion presented itself. For all these people the beaver trade was "the only means by which they could get the French wares they needed." The Acadian enjoyed one advantage over the Canadian in that he did not pay the tax of twenty-five per cent on the price of his skins. He sometimes sold them to the Acadia Fisheries Company which quite arbitrarily assumed a buying monopoly, but he preferred to exchange them at a higher value for English goods which were peddled from door to door "in all the French settle-ments" from Pentagoët to Cape Breton. Protests from France about this illicit traffic naturally remained ineffective, since the mother country did nothing herself to supply the needs of the people.[10]

After moving from Pentagoët to Nashwaak and then to St. John, the skeleton administration of the little colony finally lodged in Port Royal where, in 1698, some five hundred inhabit-ants occupied about a hundred mean wooden houses grouped around a sheltering fort. There the governor commanded a gar-rison which varied, according to the date, between 80 and 150 sol-diers. Under the governor, the King's Lieutenant directed the mil-itary services, and the King's Clerk was charged with the civil, ec-onomic and financial administration. The law was applied by the lieutenant-general, assisted by a crown attorney and a clerk, and judgments could be appealed to the Sovereign Council in Que-bec.[11]

The colonists' one political privilege was the annual election of a syndic who defended the interests of the community, and made representation to the authorities in the form of petitions. The capital had a small church with no residence, a hospital with eight beds, and a dame-school which was opened in 1701. For its defence, the colony could muster the garrison and a militia of 350 men, of whom only 100 had rifles.[12]

There were no roads in any part of the colony, and to get from one settlement to another the colonists had to follow rough trails through field and forest. As their farms and villages were planted on the seashore or on the banks of rivers, the Acadians travelled by boat in summer and on snowshoes in winter. Having no roads, they raised few horses. They preferred oxen which cost less to keep, were equally useful as work animals, and had the added ad-vantage of providing meat for the larder as well as leather for shoes and harness.[12a]

Acadia suffered from the same chronic malady as Canada: quarrels among its high officials. Friction between Grandfontaine and Marson was followed by disputes between La Vallière and Bergier, and between Perrot and Saint-Castin. Villebon was at log-gerheads with Villieu, Brouillan with La Bat, and Subercase with des Gouttins.[13] Heads of the civil administration were on un-friendly terms with the ecclesiastical leaders. Villebon and Suber-case accused the missionaries of meddling in civil affairs and en-gaging in trade, while on the other hand the priests complained of Villebon's tolerant attitude towards his brothers' "debauches."

Pontchartrain claimed that in Minas the clergy exacted "very large tithes although these were not due," and the habitants complained that the priests administered their parishes without consulting either churchwardens or parishioners.[14] It must be added, however, that on different occasions, the Minister, governors, and merchants expressed satisfaction at the virtues and the zeal displayed by regular and secular priests. At least one of the complaints against a member of the clergy now appears somewhat frivolous; Father Justinien was denounced for having overridden the veto of Bonaventure and married Captain Du Vivier and Marie Mius d'Entremont. The priest's excuse was that since their child was being baptized on that day, it seemed proper that the parents' union should also receive the blessing of the Church.[15]

All these quarrels had little effect on the essential life of the colony whose strength lay in its rural population. The Acadians were a vigorous and sturdy race. Conservative and hard-working, they were guided by a strict sense of honesty and deep moral principles, although their spirit of independence sometimes verged on insubordination and their tenacity on stubbornness. The typical Acadian's ambitions were to be a good farmer, a good father and a good Catholic, and in the practice of these virtues they were, in the opinion of Subercase, the happiest people in the world. Mgr. de Saint-Vallier also considered them to be "gentle, and naturally inclined to piety." He would have found them "irreproachable" if they had refrained from selling brandy to the Indians.[16]

Denonville's is the only dissenting voice in this chorus of approval. He speaks only from hearsay when, in words of which almost every one contains a mis-statement, he inveighs against the "miserable Acadian libertines whose heads have been turned by the beaver trade and who have done nothing at all for the land."[17] Doubtless there were farmers who hunted beaver during the winter and who allowed themselves to be seduced by a life of adventure, but they were only following an example set by their leaders. They hunted for the benefit of governors like Villebon and Perrot, or in partnership with d'Amours or Portneuf or Neuvillette. It was natural, too, that, with the example of Saint-Castin before them, a certain number of Acadians should marry Indian women, as Hénault did in Nipisiquit or as Desloriers did in Pentagoët, but the records show only five cases of such mixed marriages before 1685. There were a few traders who, like Portneuf, took squaws as mistresses, but the majority of the Abenakis and Micmacs were Christian, and the presence of missionaries among them kept such exceptional disorders to a minimum. Where the accusations appear well-founded, one may infer that at least some of the culprits were Canadian, since a royal order of 1678 prohibited Canadian *coureurs de bois* from trading in Acadia.[17a]

Contemporaries agree in recognizing the physical and moral vigour of the Acadian people. When the misfortunes of war forced France to abandon them, they formed a united group of 2,500 farmers firmly attached to the land, their country and their religion, a group whose loyalty to its faith and its racial origins was to remain unshakeable.

The question remains, why Acadia did not develop at the same rate as Canada. One answer is that it came under royal administration too late. In 1670 Louis XIV had already embarked on his career of European domination, and he declared in 1672 that he could "incur no expense for his overseas domains."[18] A second reason was lack of interest on the part of commercial companies or individuals who might have helped to develop the colony; the shipowners were not tempted by such a small volume of trade, and the fishermen preferred the Newfoundland banks. Moreover, when enterprising and aggressive New Englanders thought it worth while to encroach on Acadian markets and fishing grounds, France merely issued injunctions which were not backed up by force. Finally, during a period of twenty years of almost constant war, Versailles not only depended on the Abenakis to repulse invaders, but skimped on the arms and supplies which were sent to the colony's Indian defenders. Acadians and natives alike were obliged to turn to New England to supply their most urgent needs. In 1698 Villebon had to import wheat from Boston to feed his garrison, and in 1707 and 1710, even though the two colonies were at war, Subercase had to obtain from the same source food for his people and shoes and stockings for his troops.[19] With such a policy Acadia was doomed in advance. It took the fall of Port Royal to bring home to Versailles the importance of the colony, but it was then too late to save it. In short, Acadia's failure to grow and its final loss can be attributed to three major causes, her small population, France's neglect of her colony, and English colonial encroachments and armed invasion.

CHAPTER TWENTY

REVIEW: CANADA'S POPULATION—CANADIAN SOCIETY
1663-1713

Versailles' colonial policy. Growth of the colony's population. The three orders. Clergy: bishops, resources, virtues, influence. Nobility, seigneurs, officers and public servants. Political importance and military functions. Third estate: judges, syndics and notables. Accession to seigniories. Prosperity and independence of the freeholder. Education. Hospitals and hospices. Troops and militia. Failure of the attempt to assimilate the natives. Formation of a social élite. Evolution towards an egalitarian and distinctively Canadian society.

In the course of this period (1663-1713), while Placentia and Acadia just managed to exist, Canada acquired inhabitants and developed on every front. From a simple trading factory, it grew into an agricultural and commercial colony. This growth resulted from Colbert's policy of expansion through strong colonies, but one principle of this policy was that colonial establishments must never be allowed to develop at the expense of the mother country's trade or industry. In fact, according to the official doctrine, the only reason for the existence of such colonies was to supply the mother country with the raw materials which it required and to provide a market for its products. These two axioms determined all decisions throughout the period of royal administration in New France.[1]

In this period the essential fact is the growth in the colony's population. In 1663 New France had only 2,500 inhabitants, but the census of 1713 showed a population of 18,179. It had increased sevenfold in fifty years.[2] Between 1663 and 1673, the population was swelled by three categories of immigrants: settlers, two thousand; soldiers, one thousand; unmarried girls, one thousand; a total of four thousand. More than half of these four thousand recruits came from the five provinces of Normandy, Poitou, the Ile-de-France, Aunis and Saintonge. These provinces contributed the

basic elements of the population, and thus helped to create the
Canadian mentality and Canadian manners.[2a] After 1673 the only
immigrants were a few *engagés* and workmen who came out in
trading vessels.[3] A good many discharged soldiers took up land,
and about a hundred English prisoners also stayed in Canada.[4]
But the high birth-rate remained the most important factor in
population growth. The King's recommendations and marriage
grants continued to encourage early marriages. Girls were expected to marry at sixteen, and men at twenty, and families of ten or
twelve children were common.[5] The growth in population would
have been still more impressive if it had not been for the inroads
caused by war and natural calamities. The Iroquois war lasted
seventeen years, and cost many lives. Smallpox carried off a thousand victims in 1701 and two thousand in 1703. The colony also
lost a certain number of emigrants and *engagés* who returned to
France, and a considerable number of *coureurs de bois* migrated
to Louisiana.[6]

Four fifths of this population of eighteen thousand lived on
the farms which occupied a strip of land extending along both sides
of the St. Lawrence between Ile-Verte and Chateauguay. The remaining one fifth was divided among the three small towns. Vessels
from France stopped at Quebec, which was proud of its buildings,
the Château St. Louis, the official residence of the Governor, the
Intendant's palace, and the cathedral. The population of the capital was, however, only 547 in 1668, and 1,819 in 1713. The population of Montreal, the great fur market and the colony's bulwark
against the Iroquois, increased from 300 in 1665 to 724 in 1685,
and 1,200 in 1713. Three Rivers counted 180 inhabitants in 1665,
and 299 in 1713. It was a port of call between the two larger towns
and a refuge in time of need for the rural population of the district.[6a]

The social categories (nobility, clergy and third estate) which
existed in the mother country were repeated in the colony, as
were the quarrels on points of precedence associated with them.
Moreover, Frontenac had recognized a fourth category when, in
1672, he convoked judges and members of the Sovereign Council
as a separate group, although in France they belonged to the third
estate.[7]

The secular clergy counted only nine priests and a few junior
clerics in 1667, but over a period of forty years their number rose to
seventy-seven, including twelve Sulpicians. There were also forty-
five Jesuits and thirty-two Récollets. Under Mésy, Mgr. de Laval

and the Jesuits were the dominant influence in both religious and social matters, but their role was gradually reduced, as Talon put into effect instructions from Louis XIV and Colbert. They came into violent conflict with Frontenac, but under La Barre and, more especially, Denonville, they recovered all the ground they had lost. The clerical influence was again reduced under Callières, and Vaudreuil limited it strictly to the spiritual domain. In 1704 Louis XIV rejected a petition for an increase in tithes.[8]

Mgr. de Laval was himself a deeply religious man, who was guided in the direction of his diocese by a strict ideal of Christian belief and virtue, but Louis XIV accused him of invading the temporal domain. The King also reproved him for his opposition to the Récollets and the Sulpicians, and feared that his character was "not entirely suitable" for the bishop of a pioneer see. Mgr. de Saint-Vallier, who was also a sincerely zealous Christian, alienated his clergy by instituting changes in the régime which he had inherited from his predecessor. However, the religious quarrels which mar this period in no way detract from the merit of these two bishops, of whom the first created the Canadian Church and the second established its liturgy, while both held before their flock an ideal of the highest Christian morality.[9]

In regard to property, the various religious orders and institutions were among the most important land-holders in the colony. The seminaries of St. Sulpice and Quebec, the Hospital Sisters, the Ursulines and, above all, the Society of Jesus owned about one third of the seigniories. Moreover, theirs were the most prosperous ones, and to the great regret of at least one intendant, they paid no tithes. The paltry resources of the rural priests who, in 1700, numbered about sixty, were in sharp contrast, with the comparative wealth of the Jesuits. Few of these priests knew the security of a fixed parish. Their lives were hard and their fare meagre. Since they could barely live on their tithes of one twenty-sixth, supplemented by small and infrequent casual fees, the King gave them an annual subsidy which was distributed by the Bishop. This subsidy, which increased from 4,000 *livres* in 1682 to 8,000 in 1686, did not include the royal grants to hospitals and teaching communities. Under Mgr. de Saint-Vallier church revenues amounted to 120,000 *livres* a year, and, according to Champigny, the money could not have been in better hands, for "the members of the clergy led lives of exemplary regularity, and observed the duties of their calling much more strictly than did their brothers in France."[10]

The priests were zealous in the performance o ftheir tasks, although their zeal had something of the excessive quality characteristic of the age. Thus, the Bishop issued pastoral orders regulating the dress which women should wear even in their own homes. The Intendant and the *curés* worked together to keep close watch on the conduct of the colonists and to check any offense against morals. Priests even went so far as to have women arrested *manu militari* for notoriously immoral conduct.[11]

It was said that some of the Jesuits used the confessional and the Congregation of the Holy Family as instruments for meddling in the most private concerns of individuals and families.[12] In a different sphere, they tried, in various secret ways, to exclude from mission work Récollets, Sulpicians and priests from the Quebec Seminary, and to maintain a monopoly in this field.[13] However, such jealousy is perhaps excusable if one remembers that the Jesuits had been in the Canadian mission field since 1632, and that they had served ever since that time with unwearying zeal and dauntless courage. They also founded and maintained the colony's only institution of higher education apart from the seminaries, the college of Quebec. They defended the colony against the tyranny of Frontenac, opposed the demoralizing influence of La Motte-Cadillac in Detroit, and tried to reform the conduct of the *coureurs de bois* and to suppress the evils of the alcohol trade in the far posts. Last but not least, their precious diplomatic activity among the Indian tribes helped to outwit the scheming Iroquois and to preserve for Quebec the friendship of the western tribes. It was with good reason that Vaudreuil wrote of the Jesuits that they "had done and were doing a great deal of good in this country."[14]

Thanks to the "good priests" who, by spiritual direction and example, maintained the true doctrine in Canada, the people there "generally led a more strictly ordered life than the people of France. They attended divine service whenever possible, communicated often and cultivated pious habits." Canadians already had their own national shrine at Ste.-Anne-de-Beaupré. Among those who made the pilgrimage to Ste. Anne we find the names of Mésy and Tracy, and the church choir still contains the votive offering dedicated to the saint by d'Iberville.[15]

The modest nobility, which ranked after the clergy, included in 1667 only four bearers of hereditary titles, four recently created noblemen and a few officers of noble birth serving in the colony. Their numbers were later swelled by the grant of new patents of nobility, and by the establishment of officers from the Carignan regiment, as well as by births. Several officers from the Marine troops, who arrived in 1683, married Canadians, and thus contributed to the continuance of a Canadian aristocracy. It was to the members of this gentry that the King granted seigniories, which, however, did not necessarily bring wealth or even comfort to their proprietors. Their vast domains were for the most part in virgin forest, and even after granting farms to a few settlers, the seigneur received only very small returns from his land. A certain number of seigneurs saved themselves from lives of real poverty by serving as councillors, lieutenants-general or crown attorneys. Those who held commissions continued to serve in the army, and a few sold their land and returned to France. Fortunately, a good number, especially those who had been born in Canada, were able to make their seigniories pay, and to live in comfortable and even easy circumstances.[16]

In 1713 about half of the eighty seigniories in the country belonged to this Canadian aristocracy, but the seigneurs had neither the influence nor the authority of French noblemen. Virtual owners of their land, Canadian tenants, like true brothers of the refractory *coureurs de bois,* did not recognize "the subordination of the vassal to his lord," while militia officers considered themselves independent of both seigneurs and *curés.*[17] However, the seigniorial aristocracy continued to enjoy a certain social prestige and to play its part in the administration of the country. It was from this group that the authorities chose the greatest number of representatives when it was a question of sounding out the opinion of the colony. From this group, too, came the best officers of the period: Bonaventure, the Hertels, the d'Aillebousts, and the Le Moynes.[18]

The third estate, ranked after the clergy and the nobility, included the rest of the population. Its most influential members, and those who represented it on occasion, were "the ordinary judges and the syndics, with the principal merchants and burghers." Within their order the magistrates and crown attorneys occupied the places of honour in public and religious ceremonies. Since their salaries were very modest many of them supplemented their revenues by engaging in business or, more or less legally, in the fur trade. After the men of law, the merchants constituted the most important group, but their importance was only relative even in a country which had no moneyed class. Their condition improved slowly; in 1710 nine of them owned seigniories, but their resources were generally very limited. Raudot notes that only about a dozen of them appeared to "have wealth in their coffers or land," and the only one who amassed great wealth, Aubert de La Chesnaye, lost his fortune before he died.[19]

The rural population made up the great mass of the third estate. The few thousand original settlers had continued to increase rapidly.[20] Year by year they had brought more land under cultivation[21] and planted more wheat until the yield had increased fivefold.[22] With easy access to hunting and fishing, with their own wheat, vegetables, cows and chickens, they were "better off than even good peasants in France," and they lived better than some seigneurs.[23]

In the course of the year, Canadians, city and country dwellers spirit of independence which astonished observers.[24] However, their natural antipathy to discipline and their refusal of authority did not often reach the point of public expression, although they did protest two or three times against the price of merchandise. Pontchartrain and Denonville alleged that they drank too much and worked too little, but it is hard to reconcile such accusations with what is known of the lives of these pioneers, who had to cut their fields out of virgin forest and to fight to protect their crops and lives from Iroquois raids, and who in fifty years quintupled the numbers of their cattle and the area of land under cultivation. It would take captious critics such as Pontchartrain or Denonville to deny them the right to a little relaxation during their forced winter period of rest, to drink a little around a good table with their neighbours, and to sing and dance to the music of their violins.[25]

Education was, according to the custom of the time, left to the spirit of initiative and the devotion of the clergy. The Jesuit college in Quebec was the important institution of secondary education. In 1688 Mgr. de Laval founded his "junior seminary" whose pupils were eventually destined to the priesthood, while the Jesuits alike, living "very comfortably" and free from tax, developed a and the Seminary had primary schools for boys. In 1639 the Ursulines opened a school in Quebec for the daughters of the well-to-do, and in 1697 they established a second school in Three Rivers, The Sulpician Father Souart had a school for boys in Montreal, and after 1692 Brother Charron established several boys' schools in the Montreal region. Mother Marguerite Bourgeoys founded the Congregation of Notre-Dame which established schools for girls, first in Montreal, and later at Sault-au-Récollet, Lachine, Pointe-aux-Trembles, Boucherville, Château-Richer and at Sainte-Famille on the Island of Orleans. The Congregation finally opened a school in Quebec for girls of the poorer classes. The zeal of the Ursulines and the Sisters of the Congregation explains the fact that in these early years the women of Canada were better educated than the men.[26] Mgr. de Laval had founded a trade school at Cap Tourmente which trained carpenters, masons, tailors, locksmiths and shoemakers. Most of the artisans, however, were apprenticed to master craftsmen to whom they were bound for a period of three years and from whom they received board, lodging and clothing.[27]

During the period under review social services were considerably extended. The Hôtels-Dieu in Quebec and Montreal continued to care for the sick, and in 1702 the Ursulines opened a hospital in Three Rivers. In 1692 Jean-François Charron and the Hospital Brothers founded a home for the aged and infirm in Montreal, and in the following year Quebec's Hôpital Général instituted a similar service.[28] In 1688 the Sovereign Council established poor-relief offices in the three towns. These agencies, supported by voluntary donations, distributed alms to the poor and found work for the unemployed. They were also empowered to punish impenitent idlers by confinement in prison on a bread and water diet. In the country each parish was allowed to set up a poor-relief office with similar functions and powers.[29]

Under the trading companies the country was defended by soldiers of fortune in the service of the companies and by the settlers themselves. During the first two years of the royal régime Canada's only soldiers continued to be troops of irregulars, but in 1665 the Carignan regiment was sent out to impose peace on the Iroquois. Between the departure of the Carignan regiment in 1668 and the cancellation of the West India Company's charter in 1674, the Company maintained garrisons whose members were recruited in France and in Canada. The King continued this mode of defence until 1683, when the country was faced with the threat of a war with the Iroquois. At that time he entrusted the defence of the country to companies of Marines, so called because they fell under the authority of the Ministry of Marine, and this system continued until the conquest. In 1688 there were thirty-five companies, each composed of fifty men, but the figures vary with conditions in the colony.[30] Among these troops the governors on occasion enrolled Canadians whom they found "incomparably more useful" than Europeans since they knew the country. Well-born young Canadians were commissioned at sixteen as ensigns or cadets, and provided an important quota of officers, many of whom were distinguished by their skill in Indian warfare.[31]

As military uniforms were not introduced until 1670, soldiers of the Carignan regiment wore civilian dress. The Marines' uniform consisted of a blue coat with a white linen collar, and blue stockings. They were paid six *sous* a day, and as they had no barracks, they were billeted on the townspeople. Officers received from forty to seventy *livres* a month, according to their rank. They had no uniform, but as the insignia of their authority, they wore a crescent-shaped gorget of gilded copper.[32]

To supplement its troops, the colony had a militia, instituted in 1669 by Courcelles on instructions from the King. It included all males between sixteen and sixty, and its members served without pay and provided a part of their own equipment. Each man had a rifle, either his own or one lent from the royal armouries for the duration of an expedition. Each parish had its militia company with its captain, lieutenant and ensign commissioned by the Governor. In the country districts, where no administrative organization existed, militia officers performed very useful service as agents of the governors and intendants whose orders they published and who delegated various public duties to them.[33] In recognition of their valuable services, they had the honour of walking immediately after churchwardens in religious processions and of receiving before the other parishioners the bread blessed by the priest and distributed during the solemn high mass.

The authorities in France would have liked to revive an idea mooted earlier by Champlain and the Company of New France: to augment the population by incorporating the natives into the colony. Colbert, who put forward the idea in 1666, thought it could be realized by educating the children and converting the adults, but all the efforts of the Jesuits, Sulpicians and Ursulines were unavailing. "It has been our experience," wrote Mother Marie de l'Incarnation in 1668, "that of all the Indian girls who have passed through our hands, we have hardly succeeded in civilizing a single one." De Meulles, too, remarked in 1682, speaking of Indians living in the colony, that "you seldom see them praying, and never speaking French."[35]

It was also hoped that the integration of the Indians might be accomplished by establishing native villages within the colony. In 1685 there were 1,538 Indians, Iroquois, Hurons and Algonquins, in the villages of Sault St. Louis, La Montagne in Montreal, Sillery, Lorette and Chaudière. In 1705 settlements of Abenakis at Bécancourt and St.-François-du-Lac brought the number of Indians within the colony to 2,500,[36] but the existence of these villages did not result in any appreciable degree of assimilation. French men and girls refused to intermarry with natives. Between 1663 and 1700 only nine French colonists took Indian wives and only one French girl married an Indian husband. In the West, the rare marriages and the free unions between *coureurs de bois* and squaws made "libertines and idlers" of the husbands, while the children were no better than their fathers. The result was that Vaudreuil and Raudot advised against Franco-Indian marriages.[37] Although they had settled in the colony, the Indians were too proud to perform the tasks of a settled life. Many of them refused to accept monogamy, which was foreign to their customs. They also opposed the application of French laws in their villages, and they claimed the right to trade with the English. In short, the effort to assimilate the Indians was a complete fiasco. The failure was, however, fortunate in that the Canadian race, free from any mixture of alien blood, remained pure and homogeneous.[38]

When the Treaty of Utrecht brought peace to the colony, the elements of social life already existed in its three small towns. Isolated as they were, Canadians seized every opportunity for public celebrations and social gatherings, and all Quebec turned out when Frontenac inaugurated his term of office and satisfied his own love of pomp with an imposing assembly of the three orders in the colony. Under La Barre, who was too much occupied by his own business interests, and the austere Denonville, there were few ceremonies and receptions, but when Frontenac returned in 1690, he immediately re-established his little court. After the defeat of Phipps, the weddings of Vaudreuil and Ramezay were great social events, and when the English attacked La Prairie, the Governor was attending a ball at Three Rivers. Frontenac also gave his patronage and encouragement to the amateur players who presented Corneille and Racine at the Château St. Louis, and in 1708 Raudot organized concerts and a masquerade so magnificent that it delighted everybody.[39]

Father Allart, the Superior of the Récollets, who later became Bishop of Vence, described this "polite" society. He knew "no province in the kingdom where one would find, generally and in proportion to numbers, more native intelligence, more penetrating judgment, more polished manners, even finer clothes." Canadians, continued Father Allart, were "quite ambitious, and liked to impress others," but they were also "generous men, dauntless in the face of danger and capable of great things." This was the age that produced men like Frontenac, Jolliet, La Salle and d'Iberville, and women like Madame de Vaudreuil, Madame de Ramezay and Madame de Repentigny. Louis XIV observed that the vigorous and vital society of New France was not without its "public scandals between army officers and local wives," but he made this comment after he had become the husband of the prudish Madame de Maintenon. In other circumstances, he would probably have accepted the habits of Courcelles, the adventures of d'Iberville and the gossip about Mlle de Thavenet and Mlle de Cournoyer as the inevitable ingredient of human frailty accompanying the virtues of a pioneer age: attachment to the land, boldness, initiative, valiance in the face of natural and human enemies.[40]

The majority of the population was now made up of second generation Canadians, who had grown up in the country and who were beginning to reveal distinctive national traits. Social classes continued to exist, but, although they maintained their traditions of precedence and deference, Canadians had simpler manners than their French cousins; they were more independent and outspoken. Moreover, direct and constant contact between classes resulted in a tendency towards egalitarianism. Since noblemen were not debarred from business, they formed partnerships with merchants, and families which were allied by business were also frequently allied by marriage. Le Moyne and La Chesnaye were among the merchants whose services were rewarded by patents of nobility and other commoners, Juchereau and Bécancourt, for example, were honoured in the same way. Even freeholders sometime rose into the ranks of the aristocracy by buying seignories. Out of 86 seigneurs listed in 1712, at least ten were former farmers.[41] Moreover, the captains of militia, representatives on occasion of the governor or the intendant, held rank in the administrative hierarchy. They took precedence in parish ceremonies, and were quite independent both of the seigneur and the *curé*. Another sign of the times was that a certain number of the tenant farmers (who as a class were not inclined to recognize their seigneur as their superior) were shareholders in the Company of the Colony.[42]

Father Charlevoix, who taught in the country from 1705 to 1709, and who wrote a history of New France, points out a few special characteristics of this young people. Quebec, he writes, is "a select little world endowed with everything anyone could wish for in a society. Canadians breathe from birth an air of liberty which makes them very pleasant to associate with, and nowhere else is a purer French spoken." There are no great fortunes in the country, but farmers are generally better off than seigneurs. Vanity is one of the petty foibles of Canadians, and while they like to live well, they would not hesitate to "cut down on their table in order to be well dressed." "Everyone here is well built" concludes the enthusiastic Father. "You couldn't find finer types of either sex anywhere. Even the people in the most remote rural districts have alert minds and gentle, polite manners."[43]

CHAPTER TWENTY-ONE

REVIEW: POLITICAL ORGANIZATION
1663-1713

Instruments of administration. Functions of the governor and the intendant. Local governments. Municipal organization. The Sovereign Council. Finance: receipts and expenditures. Permanent deficit. Proposed taxes. Import duties. Participation of citizens in government: official consultation, meeting, petitions. Protest demonstrations.

The administrative structure of New France under the royal régime, introduced in 1663, received its final form in 1665 with the appointment of an intendant.

The governor, as personal representative of the King, occupied the highest place in the administration. His first duty was to maintain French sovereignty in the country, and he had exclusive and sovereign jurisdiction in all military matters. He directed the policy of Canada in its intercourse with other colonies, with which he was empowered to contract agreements and treaties, and he was also responsible for Indian affairs including decisions concerning war and peace. In the judicial field, the governor's function was that of an auxiliary to the intendant, but in case of a crisis involving "the service of the King and the public good," his decision was supreme. Financial matters were the responsibility of the intendant, but the annual budget was drawn up in consultation with the governor, who also decided questions relating to military expenses. Moreover, when confronted with an urgent necessity the governor could authorize an extraordinary expenditure, in which case he was required to report at once to the Minister the reasons for his action. In the domain of religion, the governor and the intendant shared responsibility for providing the colonists with facilities for the practice of their religion and for supplying the needs of priests engaged in the work of evangelization. In matters of internal policy, they collaborated to encourage the expansion of agriculture and industry.[1]

The "second person in the country," coming immediately after the governor in power and dignity, was the intendant of justice, police and finance. He was commissioned as the chief civil administrator, and in the domain of justice his authority was exclusive and supreme. Although the governor and the bishop took precedence over him in the Sovereign Council, as chairman he was in a position to give effective direction to its meetings. He had supervision over judges and courts, including cases related to the security of the state, the levying of taxes, and disputes between seigneurs and tenants. The administration of public finances constituted the second function of the intendant. He was directly and solely responsible for the disposal of funds, supplies and munitions, as well as for levying and collecting taxes and duties. He ordered and directed the manufacture of card money, Canada's own special form of currency. As controller of the public purse, the intendant supervised public works, paid the troops and provided for their food and lodging. In religious matters, he shared responsibility for direction and assistance with the governor. They also had joint jurisdiction in the field of general administration, but in practice the intendant acted alone in questions relating to public morals and security, as well as road-building and the encouragement of industry and commerce. Finally, since there was no municipal organization, the duty of administering the towns also fell to the intendant.[2]

As a result of their joint authority in several fields, differences of opinion between the two chief officials were almost inevitable, and such differences were still more likely to occur since the governor was generally a soldier and an aristocrat, whereas the intendant was more often a civilian and a commoner. Quarrels between governors and intendants continued almost without interruption throughout the period under review, from Courcelles and Talon, through Frontenac and Duchesneau, to Vaudreuil and Raudot. In such cases, if they did not reach agreement, the procedure required that they send a joint communication to the Minister, who in reply transmitted the King's decision to them. If the matter under dispute required immediate action, the governor had authority to make the decision.[3]

The commission of Canada's governors and intendants gave them jurisdiction over "Acadia, Newfoundland and other countries in North America,"[4] but in practice, they intervened in the

other colonies only in moments of crisis, when they sent men,
munitions and food, as required. The governors of Acadia and
Newfoundland reported occasionally to Quebec, but received
their instructions directly from Versailles.[5]

In Quebec, the governor and the intendant administered but
did not govern: they were agents whose duty it was to execute
orders and carry out instructions from Versailles. Except in cases
of crisis where immediate decisions had to be made, the field in
which they could exercise their discretion was necessarily limited.
The governor, acting on his own initiative, could appoint only
militia officers, the intendant only bailiffs. All other appointments, civil and military, were made by the King, although the
governor and the intendant could recommend candidates for
posts which fell under their respective jurisdictions.[6]

The two officials were expected to follow as closely as possible
the directives which they received from Versailles; they were
never to exceed the expenditures authorized by the Court, nor
embark on any project without first obtaining the Minister's consent. This consent had to be obtained, for instance, before they
could have essential repairs made in the Château St. Louis. When
Frontenac and Champigny, faced with the threat of an English
invasion, ventured to fortify Quebec "without orders and without
funds," Louis XIV expressed displeasure at their action. On other
occasions the royal disapproval was manifested in counter-orders,
or threats of recall or of withholding the amount of unauthorized
expenditures from the salary of the offending official. Supervision
by the Court covered every aspect of the life of the colony and was
exercised in the most minute details.[7]

In order to maintain this close direction and to communicate
these numerous instructions, the King and the Minister sent the
governor and the intendant interminable memoranda and dispatches, which were generally written between March and May and
which reached Quebec in the course of the summer. The answers of
the governor and the intendant were equally long and equally de-
tailed. They wrote separate letters covering matters in which one
official had exclusive jurisdiction, and joint letters concerning questions for which they shared responsibility. Their letters, dated
October or November, arrived in Versailles about the beginning of
the following year, and, since communication was cut off during
the winter, Quebec waited almost a year for answers to its requests, and Versailles for replies to its instructions. In such con-

ditions the wheels of administration turned with what must have been maddening slowness.

Under the governor-general, the country was divided into three districts. In Quebec, the governor-general also carried out the functions of a local governor, while Montreal and Three Rivers each had its own governor and its own civil and military administration. Except during the early régime of the syndics, none of the three governments had any representative institutions. In the towns, except for the brief period when there were *échevins* in Quebec (1673-1678), there was no municipal organization, properly so called. Urban administration depended on three authorities: the intendant, the Sovereign Council and the local royal judge. They provided a legal framework for community life, while the crown attorney ensured that orders were observed and carried out.[7a]

At the beginning of the royal régime, the Sovereign Council inherited the powers of the former Council of Quebec, and under the direction of the governor, exercised administrative functions: it regulated commerce and finance, issued police orders, and appointed officers of justice. In 1665 these powers were transferred to the intendant, who not only directed the finances of the country, but could also, if he so desired, act on his own authority in matters of police jurisdiction. At the same time the King reserved to the Crown the direction of commerce and the fur trade, as well as the appointment of officers of justice. Versailles did not maintain a consistent policy in regard to the Sovereign Council, at times according legislative powers to it, at others withdrawing them. The Council, in conjunction with the intendant, sometimes drew up orders. However, on at least one occasion when it ventured to adopt a police order, a royal edict (March 10, 1683) annulled the action and forbade the Council to take any such action on its own authority. By 1713 the Council had become in practice a court of appeal which might be called upon to participate in matters which the governor or the intendant chose to submit to it.[8]

In accordance with a royal declaration of 1664 and the terms of the intendants' commissions, the Sovereign Council, like all courts in the colony, was guided by the laws and ordinances of France, but the King also invested it with the essential right, or duty, of registering laws, and thus making them effective in the colony. In fact, however, practice and principle were frequently at

variance in this matter and French laws, whether registered in
Canada or not, were regularly followed without any objection
from Canadian courts. Finally, in 1703 the King changed the title
Sovereign Council to the more accurate and more modest design-
tion, Superior Council.[9]

In the field of fiinance, the colony's budget was drawn up under two headings: "Western Domain," and "Ministery of Marine."
The fiscal revenue of the colony itself constituted the receipts of
the "Domain," while royal subsidies were provided by the Ministry of Marine which was equally a ministry of colonies. In the
Domain's expenditure column were placed all the fixed charges
of administration: salaries of governors-general, local governors,
councillors and officers of justice, grants to the clergy and to
religious communities, honoraria and other such incidental out-
lays. This budget, which for 1665 was 54,000 *livres,* increased to
83,000 in 1697, and later ranged from 80,000 *livres* to 90,000. The
revenues of the Domain were derived from the tax of twenty-five
per cent on beaver and ten per cent on moose hides, and from the
profits of the Tadoussac fur trade. There were also small revenues
from domains and seigniories as well as the ten per cent import
duty on "dry merchandise" and alcohol, reserved until 1676 to pay
off the debt of the Community of Habitants. These various taxes
brought about 40,000 *livres* to the Royal Treasury, little more
than half the corresponding expenditures.[9a]

The budget of the Western Domain covered only the fixed
charges, the smallest part of the outlay of the colony. The important expenses figure in the budget of subsidies furnished by the
Ministry of Marine. The largest of these were: officers' salaries,
soldiers' pay, supplies in food and equipment, fortifications,
salaries of general officers, employees' wages, presents to the
Indians. The total sum increased in the course of the years, and
especially during the Anglo-Indian wars, from 250,000 *livres* to
560,000 *livres,* the figure for 1712.

The double budget of the colony was never balanced. No new
taxes were instituted during the period and revenues were drawn
from already established sources: taxes on furs, import and export
duties on goods, fees from seigniories and other domains, rent
from the Tadoussac fur farm and profits from the royal warehouses. The total ranged between 125,000 and 150,000 *livres,*
which meant that the King had to make up an annual deficit of
about 200,000 *livres.* However, the mother country received certain benefits which compensated for this expense: her workers

were employed to supply the goods which her merchants sold in the colony, while the fur trade in Europe and commerce with Canada were profitable investments for French capital.[9b]

The Canadian deficit had worried Pontchartrain for years. In 1713 he wrote that Canada was the "least useful and most costly" of all the King's colonies. Resurrecting an idea which had been proposed by Seignelay in 1684, and rejected by the notables of the country, he suggested that Canadians should contribute to the public expenditures by an assessment of ten per cent on the value of their property. Vaudreuil and Bégon replied that even if Canadians had not contributed money for the war, it must not be forgotten that they had contributed work and military service, and that they had suffered losses in lives and property. It would be most unwise to create disaffection by imposing a levy. On the contrary, every possible consideration should be given to the population since in time of war one is even more dependent "on the inhabitants than on soldiers." Faced with such determined opposition in Canada, Versailles did not press the point, and Canadians continued to pay only the taxes which had been accepted by the Community before the beginning of the royal régime. The so-called tax of ten per cent on merchandise, slightly altered, was now applied to imports and exports in the following manner: there were import duties of ten *livres* on a cask of wine and twenty-five on a cask of brandy, fifty *livres* a hundredweight on woven materials, twenty-five *livres* a hundredweight on hardware, fifty *sous* a hundredweight on groceries and five *sous* on a dozen pieces of china. Export duties were paid on furs, five *livres* a hundredweight on small skins and twenty *sous* a hundredweight on beaver, whether "dry" or "greasy." Imports from the West Indies, among which were rum and tobacco, were not subject to duty.[9c]

One naturally wonders whether, in this country administered by a civilian and military authority, the citizens enjoyed any political rights in the period between 1663 and 1713. In 1664 the three towns of the colony had syndics, elected representatives whose duty it was to watch over the interests of their respective communities and to intervene with the authorities if these interests were threatened. Thus in 1672 Quebec's syndic, LeMire, presented a petition to Frontenac asking for an investigation of the manner in which the ten per cent tax was collected. In 1673 Frontenac replaced the Quebec syndic with *échevins,* who in turn disappeared in 1678. The syndic of Three Rivers gave no sign of life after 1665 and the office was abolished in Montreal in 1674. In 1673 when Frontenac displayed his power by creating *échevins,* he also instituted town meetings which were to be called every six months in order to give the citizens an opportunity to discuss such matters as agriculture, commerce and industry, and to submit suggestions to the Governor. Royal disapproval, however, brought Frontenac's experiment to an untimely end, and after the disappearance of Quebec's *échevins* in 1678, there no longer existed any elected body or delegate to express the opinion of the population or to defend its rights.[10]

The King deviated rather surprisingly from this policy of non-participation when in 1675 he instructed Duchesneau to "consult the principal inhabitants and the Sovereign Council" so that he might judge what regulations would be of advantage to the country. Accordingly, the Council ordered that the lieutenant-general of police should hold semi-annual meetings at which the principal habitants of Quebec would consider means of developing the colony, and of which a report would be submitted for the Council's consideration. These meetings, which at first were held fairly regularly, gradually became less frequent until finally the intervals between them were as long as two or even three years. They were, of course, purely deliberative, but they constituted none the less a means by which the people participated in government at the municipal level.[11]

Acting on this same desire to sound out opinion and, as far as possible, to satisfy it, the King recommended that, as the occasion demanded, the authorities in New France should consult the most prominent members of the community, or call a meeting of citizens in order to explore their thoughts on matters of general interest.[12] The system served a double purpose: the government was made aware of the feeling of the people, although it was under no obligation to accept the opinion of a purely consultative gathering, while at the same time the meeting gave the people a means of expressing a consensus and a possibility of steering royal decisions in their favour.

It is interesting to note the most important of these consultations. In 1675 Duchesneau held a meeting to consider taxes on furs, and three years later, under the King's orders, twenty notable citizens were asked to discuss the sale of liquor to the Indians. In 1680 a group of seigneurs considered the question of the priests' salaries. The following year, a meeting was held to discuss the circulation of foreign money. In 1682 La Barre called the nobles into consultation on the question of war with the Iroquois, and in 1684 the Intendant asked an assembly to consider the possibility of levying a head-tax and of transferring the right to levy taxes to the people of Canada. In 1696 Frontenac consulted the principal habitants on the price of furs, while in 1702 and 1703 the subjects of deliberation were, respectively, the possibility of abolishing the tax on beaver and the imposition of new taxes.[13]

These public meetings became so deeply embedded in official habit that Louis XIV ordered Vaudreuil and Raudot to draw up a code of procedure to govern them in the future. They proposed that, when matters relating to trade were to be considered, the meetings should be limited to merchants from the three towns, but that "all the inhabitants of this Colony" should participate in meetings called to deliberate on questions of general interest. Subjects for discussion would be proposed by the authorities, and presented by the person under whose direction the meeting was held. The governor and the intendant would state their views, but only after the other speakers had expressed their opinions. Minutes of the meeting would be signed by the secretary, the governor, the intendant, and five of the citizens present, two from Quebec, two from Montreal and one from Three Rivers. After reading their proposals, the King asked Vaudreuil and Raudot to present them "in simple, legal form" so that they might serve as regulations "for meetings to be held every year." In spite of this royal declaration, the meetings were held, not annually, but only when a question of urgent importance arose.[13a] Even such rare meetings constituted a kind of referendum through which the people were allowed to participate in the administration of the colony.

Even though they had no representative body and were consulted irregularly and at the pleasure of the authorities, Canadians could make known their needs and expose their grievances in Quebec, and even in distant Versailles, by way of petitions, delegations, or unofficial public meetings. In the last case, as the right of assembly was not admitted by law, the citizens had to obtain official permission to hold a meeting. An unauthorized assembly constituted a serious crime, reserved for judgment as a "royal case." After permission was given, the meeting was held with a representative of the authorities present, but even these precautions were apparently considered insufficient for after one such assembly held in Montreal in 1675, Frontenac issued a ban on any meeting whatever. The citizens present at a gathering in Quebec in 1685 signed a petition which they presented to the Intendant, but their only answer was an order forbidding "such public assemblies" and condemning signatories of the petition to fines of twenty *livres*.[14]

Realizing the futility of attempting to express their wishes by means of meetings, the colonists more often had recourse to petitions and delegations which could be received either by the Sovereign Council or by individual officials. In 1667 representations concerning commerce and public roads were made to the Sovereign Council. In 1675 and 1676 the Intendant received petitions dealing with pedlars, and in 1684 the citizens' grievances in connection with the liquor trade were put before the Governor. When Montreal was deprived of its fur fair, the townspeople petitioned the King himself, with the result that the fair was re-established, and in 1700 delegates from the colony presented a humble remonstrance to the King's Minister, Pontchartrain, pointing out to him the pitiful situation of the fur trade.[15]

One must recognize then that, although there were no representative institutions, the people had various means of expressing their wishes and participating indirectly, and often effectively, in the public affairs of the country. However, these legal outlets for expression were ill-suited to moments of sudden crisis or distress. In a very small number of cases the people resorted to sedition and demonstrations. The Montreal riots of 1704-1705, provoked by the high cost of salt, were quickly put down, and their leaders fined.[16] The cause of an uprising which took place in Lorette and St. Augustin ten years later, in August 1714, was again the high price of merchandise. This time some of the rioters were armed with rifles and they threatened to invade the town, but when they heard that troops had been ordered to march against them, they dispersed and their leaders took refuge in the forest.[17]

From the fact that over a period of fifty years there were no more than three brief outbreaks of violence one would conclude that the Canadians, conditioned to the political discipline of the age, were not dissatisfied with their administrative régime, nor with the means at their disposal for making known their ideas and their reactions to evolving conditions.

CHAPTER TWENTY-TWO

REVIEW: CANADA'S ECONOMY
1663-1713

*Progress and decline. Granting of seigniories. Seignior-
ial abuses. Progress of farmers: agriculture and stock-
raising. Shipbuilding. Export of wood. Fisheries. Hemp.
Weaving. Tar. Tanneries. Mines. Building stone and
limestone. Brickyards. Export of cereals. Difficulties in
the fur trade. Lack of roads. Project of a canal at Lachine. Shortsightedness of Versailles. Lack of capital and
settlers.*

In the period between 1663 and 1713, the period of colonization
and organization, the pressure of events accelerated the country's
economic evolution. During the early years, Colbert's expansionist
policy and generous royal subsidies combined with the unwearying energy of Talon to stimulate economic growth and to direct
the colony towards the utilization of its natural resources. However, following Talon's departure, and with the discontinuance of
subsidies, the rate of growth became progressively slower under
Frontenac and Duchesneau during the period of the Iroquois
wars. De Meulles continued to urge that France send out the
workmen and establish the manufactures which would make it
possible to utilize the resources of the country, but his suggestions
fell on deaf ears. The colony itself, while rich in resources, was
very poor in capital. The seigneurs had royal assurance that they
might engage in business without loss of rank, but they were often
almost penniless, and the urban notables, who scarcely had "sheets
for their beds," were not much better off than the seigneurs.
Moreover, even if there had been money in the country, labour
was so scarce that a proposal was made to import negroes.[1]

Within the seigniorial framework, the land held pride of place
in the country's economy. In 1672 Talon completed the distribution of forty-five concessions between Ile Perrot and Kamou-

raska. To these seigniories Frontenac and Duchesneau added twenty-six between 1676 and 1679, while in 1688 and 1689, even in the midst of the Iroquois war, Denonville and Champigny added twenty-three more. Twenty-five seigniories were created during the War of the Spanish Succession, some by Callières and Champigny, and some by Vaudreuil and Raudot. For 1712, after eliminating undeveloped lands to which the title had been annulled, Catalogne counted a total of eighty seigniories between Chateauguay in the west and Ile-Verte in the east. A study of censuses reveals that greatest progress was made in the districts of Montreal, where the land was very fertile, and Quebec, which was more secure from Iroquois raids. Three Rivers, which included land without easy access to the St. Lawrence, developed more slowly. The most thickly settled and most prosperous seigniories belonged to merchants and religious communities. The former had the advantage of business experience, while the members of communities made up for any such lack by careful personal attention to the administration of their property. Six seigniories, Notre-Dame-des-Anges, Sillery, Beaupré, St. Lawrence county, Champlain and Batiscan, had the right to maintain seigniorial courts.[2]

Not all the concessions had been developed,[3] and in 1711, after denouncing this "unjustifiable negligence," the King decreed that any seigniory which at the end of a year still had no land cleared and no settlers would be forfeit to the crown. In 1714 he ruled that no new seigniorial courts would be established. Thus all cases would come before the royal courts, and it was hoped that the measure would encourage settlement in the seigniories.[4]

A certain number of seigneurs had called down upon themselves the displeasure of the Court. For a period of several years after the conclusion of peace with the Iroquois in 1701, production had increased, and several proprietors had tried to raise the rent and fees paid by the farmers. Raudot received a considerable number of complaints, some of which he dismissed as exaggerated. He also made sure, however, that no tenant was the victim of injustice. At the same time he informed Versailles of any illegal manœuvres attempted by the proprietors. The King recognized the tenant's need for protection, but he also demanded that the freeholder should fulfil his own obligations, and in 1711 he addressed orders not only to seigneurs, but to lessees, whose title would lapse if they had not established a homestead on their land within the year. Action was to be based on reports from *curés* and captains of militia. Unfortunately for the progress of the colony, some seigneurs had influence in the higher ranks of administration, and militia captains refused to denounce fellow tenants. Hence, these wise orders from the mother country were not put into effect. Three years later, the King dispatched a memorandum to Vaudreuil and Bégon, expressing pained surprise that they had not reported execution of his orders, and expressly recommending that action be taken in the matter.[5]

The great majority of landholders were actively engaged over this period of fifty years in a vigorous and victorious offensive against the tall Laurentian timber. In 1667 they had 11,448 *arpents* under cultivation and they owned 3,107 head of cattle; twenty years later these figures had more than doubled with 28,663 *arpents* and 7,719 head of cattle. Iroquois raids brought a regression, but in 1713 the rate of development was such that a population of 15,000 had 54,929 *arpents* of cultivated land with a yearly yield of 250,763 bushels of wheat and 92,657 bushels of peas, oats and small grain, as well as 36,123 pounds of flax and 7,272 pounds of hemp. The animal population, which had increased remarkably, now included 3,007 horses, 15,456 cattle, 5,852 sheep and 11,940 pigs, while above the wheat fields the white sails of sixty-nine mills turned in the wind.[6]

Wood was first exported from Canada in 1636, but it was Talon's policy which created Canada's lumbering and shipbuilding industries. In 1669 "three new ships made of local timber" were anchored off Quebec, and the following year two more were under construction. The Intendant also seemed to be glancing into the future when he proposed that Canada send to the West Indies prefabricated houses in the form of "prepared materials with the wood all cut; even the roof would be included."[7]

Shipbuilding continued under Duchesneau, and thirteen ships were built in six years, but it declined after 1681. One ship was launched in 1686 and one in 1706. Naval construction again became active between 1710 and 1716; a Quebec merchant, Prat, laid down a four-hundred-ton vessel, and Ignace Duchesnay built seven in two years. Most of these ships were sold to French shipowners for trade between France, Canada and the West Indies.[8]

After Talon's departure the lumber trade entered upon a period of stagnation, but in 1684 the Minister once more brought forward Colbert's idea of getting masts from the Canadian forests. The project was realized in 1686 by a merchant, François Hazeur, who was associated with Champigny in some of his business enterprises. In partnership with business men in La Rochelle, Hazeur exported masts, stave-wood and planks. His sawmill at La Malbaie was pillaged by the English during Phipps' expedition of 1690, but it was refitted, and three years later Hazeur was once more exporting masts, planks and building wood to France.[9] To maintain the supply of masts the Minister established a royal yard at Baie St.-Paul at an annual cost of 8,000 *livres*. This subsidy brought the price of Canadian masts up to that of French ones, and as the enterprise was a profitable one other Canadian business men, such as La Chesnaye and Ramezay, invested in it. Masts were sold to the Royal Navy, and the King's merchantmen continued to carry them to France between 1702 and 1714.[10]

After 1663, as before, the Canadians took great quantities of fish from the St. Lawrence: eels which came down from Lake Ontario, salmon and herring, cod, seals and porpoises which came up from the Gulf as far as La Malbaie. In 1671 the first permanent fishing station, for cod and seals, was established by François Bissot at Sept-Iles. In 1685 Riverin received a royal subsidy for a salmon and whale fishing station at Matane. It was "quite successful," and in 1693 he exported 450 quintals of fish to Bordeaux.[11] In 1701 a royal subsidy was granted to a seal fishery at Rivière-Ouelle, and the seals provided valuable oil as well as shoe leather.[12] In 1704 the Sieur Martel sent a seal and cod expedition to the Labrador coast.[13] Hazeur's establishment at Kamouraska produced a hundred barrels of porpoise oil in 1708, and since the oil fetched from 60 to 100 *livres* a barrel, about ten fishing stations sprang up below Baie St.-Paul. Even farmers ventured to band together at Rivière-Ouelle in 1707 and at La Bouteillerie in 1709 to fish porpoises off their own shores.[14]

Soon after the suspension of royal economic aid and after Talon had gone, some of his small industries began to falter. The production of hemp gradually diminished, and de Meulles' plea for a subsidy to stimulate it was refused by the Court. Just a few individual weavers in Beaupré were still manufacturing cloth. However, here and there women were working at the loom and making homespun coats and shirts. The depression in the fur market at the beginning of the century, which deprived habitants of the means to buy manufactured materials, also encouraged them to plant hemp and to weave their own, and so much hemp was harvested that the Intendant asked to have weavers sent out to utilize the surplus. The King, however, refused the request, explaining that it had never been the intention of the Court that "cloth should be woven in Canada so that Canadians could do without French materials." For the purpose of colonies is to be of service "to the mother country and not to compete with it."[15]

The war introduced another complication into this situation. When, in the summer of 1704, the English captured the *Seine* and its cargo, woven materials became scarcer than ever, and the habitants again brought out their spinning wheels and their looms. It was probably at this time that the people of the Island of Orleans began to make and to sell linen and drugget. An enterprising and energetic woman, Madame de Repentigny, set up a weavers' workshop. She obtained the services of nine English prisoners, weavers by trade, to train a number of Canadian apprentices, and her workshop produced not only homespun woollen cloth, but coarse material and blankets made of thistle fibre. In 1706 the King recognized the establishments as one of public utility by granting it an annual subsidy of 200 *livres*. Other families followed the example of Madame de Repentigny, and in Montreal alone one could count twenty looms producing 120 ells of cloth a day.[16]

Another of Talon's little industries, the manufacture of tar, had practically disappeared after a more or less profitable period. It was re-established by Raudot in 1706 with the support and help of Pontchartrain, who sent out four skilled workers to train Canadian apprentices. As it was not easy to find workers, Raudot engaged soldiers who received extra pay for this work. When tests had shown the tar to be satisfactory, the Minister of Marine bought the output of the plant which ran between 150 and 200 barrels a year. Unfortunately, a fire destroyed a large part of the Baie St.-Paul pine forest which provided most of the raw material, and regular production was once more interrupted.[17]

The tanning industry, another of Talon's creations, continued to thrive. Bissot's first tannery, founded at Pointe-Lévis in 1668, succeeded so well that several others were set up in Quebec and Montreal. They all flourished, and in 1671 they were supplying enough leather from the hides of wild and domestic animals to supply one third of the colony's needs in shoes.[18]

Talon did not neglect the possibility of discovering and exploiting mineral wealth. Father Allouez had brought back samples of copper ore from Lake Superior in 1667, and under the orders of Talon and Denonville, various travellers explored the region, but without discovering any workable mine. Pierre Lesueur found copper deposits in the upper Mississippi in 1693. In 1697 he was given permission to mine them, and in 1701 he brought back two hundred pounds of ore. The enterprise was abandoned, probably because of the distance of the mine from the colony and the great cost entailed in working it.[19]

Iron had been discovered in the neighbourhood of Three Rivers, and in 1670, at Talon's request, Colbert sent out an ironmaster who took samples of the ore back to France. However, the tests were probably unfavourable, since no further action was taken. Reports on the deposits were again presented in 1683, and de Meulles, after visiting the site, expressed the opinion that there was very little ore that could be worked. The idea of exploiting the mine reappeared, however, under Raudot, and again in 1714, when to Bégon's proposal that a foundry be built, Versailles answered that it was not necessary to bring new iron mines into production, since there was enough iron in France to meet the country's needs.[20]

From its earliest years the colony had been self-sufficient in building materials. It had an abundance of field stone, and its limestone was processed in two lime-kilns in Montreal and one in Pointe-Lévis. There was also excellent sand practically everywhere. The Canadians built their churches and public buildings of stone, but elsewhere they preferred wood, which was cheap and plentiful. Brick did not come into use until later. In 1689 the King sent out two master brickmakers, the first in the colony, and later brickyards were established in Quebec, Montreal and Three Rivers.[21]

In order to support and increase production, and also to bring money into the country, Canada needed export trade, and she had products to export: wheat, vegetables, fish and wood. Talon found excellent markets in the West Indies, although the volume of sales diminished under Duchesneau and de Meulles. However, in 1685, when the wheat harvest was especially abundant, 18,000 pecks were exported to the West Indies and La Rochelle, and the following year the surplus of a second excellent crop was disposed of. The Iroquois war brought a serious set-back to all farming operations, but after 1701 grain exports were resumed and in 1709 Canada sold 958,000 pounds of cereals in Placentia and the West Indies. At the same time trade expanded and became more varied. Exports included flour, lumber, oils, cod, eels, salmon, and even butter, cheese and eggs, while the ships brought back wine, cloth, hardware and groceries from France, and sugar and rum from Martinique and Santo Domingo.[22]

In this developing economy, furs from Tadoussac, Hudson

Bay, and the western regions continued to be the most important item both in volume and in profit. This was so in spite of the loss of furs and profit to the English colonies and Louisiana, for neither the suppression of *congés* in 1696 nor the amnesty of 1703 had put an end to the contraband trade. After the failure of the Canada Company, the "pitiable state" of the colony was aggravated by a decline in the value of beaver skins and a rise in the price of manufactured goods, but in July 1706 the beaver monopoly was sold to a private company headed by Aubert, Néret and Gayot,[23] and since Aubert paid cash for his pelts, the situation became "somewhat better." However, as French goods were expensive, many of the Indians still preferred to go to Albany where the English paid high prices for their furs and sold them cheap rum. Vaudreuil had perhaps a motive of personal interest when he proposed the revival of the system of *congés* as a means of curbing the illegal traffic, but the reasons which the King gave, in 1711 and again in 1714, for rejecting the proposal, were the war and potential abuses.[24]

Meanwhile threats of flogging or galley service did not deter the *coureurs de bois* or *voyageurs,* who continued to be attracted by a life of adventure and encouraged by the knowledge that they would be abetted in their defiance of the law. Colonists warned them of impending arrest, judges imposed light sentences or no sentence at all, and even the Superior Council was slow to prosecute offenders. Obviously, when lawbreakers could count on such complicity, their number was not likely to diminish. In 1712 twelve *voyageurs* "escaped" to the West and the following year eighty left the colony secretly to add their number to the two hundred *coureurs de bois* who lived and traded in the interior. As pelts sold for thirty *sous* in Quebec, compared with sixty in Albany, it was inevitable that large quantities of furs should find their way into the hands of the Indians to be sold in the English colonies, and that Canada's profits should be reduced as the quantity of furs to be sold on her market diminished.[25]

The only highway stretching through the colony (which was still, as Catalogne said, a great forest) was the river along whose shores the settlers had built their homesteads.[26] Robineau de Bécancourt had been appointed as surveyor and supervisor of public roads in 1667, but it was not until 1703, at the suggestion of Callières, that the authorities in France considered the desirability of building a road between Quebec and Montreal. Even then the question was forgotten in the difficulties of the moment, and a project for building a road from Montreal to Chambly, which was considered in 1704, was not realized. However, essential roads with fences and ditches were built in the seigniories between parishes. These roads were laid out by the road-surveyor acting in consultation with the seigneur and the captain of militia, and on instructions from the intendant. In winter the Canadians adopted the system, probably borrowed from their experience as mariners, of marking the sides of the road. Small trees were used for this purpose and failure to provide markers was punishable by a fine of ten *livres*.[27]

Unfortunately, communication by the great St. Lawrence waterway was interrupted just above Montreal by the boiling Lachine rapids. Canoes had to be hauled through the shallow water along the banks, or unloaded and portaged with their cargo to a place where they could be put into the water again. In order to obviate the difficulty of this part of the journey, which involved great fatigue, loss of time and money, and sometimes even loss of life, Dollier de Casson, a former officer and now Superior of the Sulpicians, decided to build a canal to link the little St. Peter's River with the calm waters of the St. Lawrence above the rapids. In 1700, under the direction of the engineer Gédéon de Catalogne, a start was made on the canal, which was to be three hundred fathoms long, twelve feet wide and nine feet deep, and which was to provide power for several mills. Unhappily, Dollier de Casson died with a third of the work still unfinished. The canal was being built at the Seminary's expense and, as it had cost 20,000 *livres*, five times as much as had been anticipated, work was suspended. In 1703 the new Superior, the Abbé Breslay, proposed that a part of the expense should be assumed by the Royal Treasury, since the canal would reduce considerably the price of transport above Montreal. In spite of urging by Quebec in 1706, Pontchartrain finally decided not to support this important project. The excuse which he offered for this very short-sighted policy was that the expense entailed was too heavy.[28]

As one glances over the situation of the country between 1663 and 1713, Canada's economy may seem restricted and primitive, but such an impression does not do justice to the colony, whose real progress must be judged in relation to several factors. The first of these is the policy of the mother country: royal aid which was cut off in 1672 was not restored even after the Treaty of Nymwegen had established France's position as the leading European power. Colbert's successors understood neither the present importance nor the future possibilities of Canada. Seignelay gave little help to the colony and Pontchartrain's directives were changeable and unreliable. To the uncertain and amorphous policy of Colbert's successors must be added two weaknesses noted by Vaudreuil as inherent in the country. "The small number of inhabitants," he wrote, and the "excessive price" of labour "cause every enterprise to fail." Restricted markets and the high price of labour paralyzed the initiative of business men in the country.[29]

Finally, one must remember the environment in which the people lived, and their resources. Canada was still "almost entirely a forest" along the edges of which a population of eighteen thousand was thinly spread out from Tadoussac to Ile Perrot, a distance of some three hundred miles. In such conditions it was difficult for industries to be built up, for manufactures to be created, or for agricultural markets to be developed. At that time colonies could not export to foreign countries, and France forbade the manufacture in the colonies of articles which she herself produced. One must remember, too, that the country possessed only very limited capital and that the merchant shipowners of France preferred the quick profits of the important West India trade to the meagre returns from the Canadian market. Lastly, thirty years of war inflicted heavy losses on New France at sea and on land. The astonishing thing is not that its economy made so little progress, but that it survived and grew stronger, and that on more than one occasion it displayed initiative, boldness and perseverance. In a normal period, the colony could provide for its own essential needs; it was even in a position to export certain products. In 1708 its merchants established the first Canadian stock exchange in Quebec, and in 1712, by assembling all their resources, they were able to lend 150,000 *livres* to the King for the Royal Treasury. All that Canada needed in order to achieve constant growth was substantial immigration from the mother country and a more far-sighted colonial policy in Versailles.

EPILOGUE
1663-1713

In the history of New France the heroic age of foundation under the trading companies was followed by a half-century (from 1663 to 1713) during which the colony took shape and became firmly rooted in the soil of Canada.

At the beginning of this period Colbert rescued the colony by placing it directly under royal authority and entrusting its administration to the Ministry of Marine. Then the Carignan regiment was dispatched by the King to free the country from the Iroquois war which threatened its very existence, and such was the success of their mission that twenty years of peace ensued.

At the same time selected immigrants were landing in successive waves in Quebec: farm workers, artisans, soldiers and "King's daughters." In seven years four thousand settlers came to join the two thousand pioneers already established. A remarkably high birth-rate helped to swell the numbers of the population, which gradually spread out along both shores of the St. Lawrence from Tadoussac to Lachine. In the course of the years, thanks to the expansion of the fur trade, official exploration and establishment of missions, this small colony's territory was increased ten-fold until it reached from Labrador on the Atlantic coast to the regions beyond Lake Superior, and south to the Gulf of Mexico.

Translating Colbert's programme into action, Talon transformed the struggling settlement into an active and vigorous colony. He divided the land along both shores of the river and granted seigniories in which farms were allotted to immigrants and soldiers. He established industries and found export outlets for surplus products of the soil. Under the wing of the mother country the colony had its own administrative structure, with a governor, an intendant and a Sovereign Council. It was self-sufficient in food and clothing, and it looked forward with confidence to a peaceful and promising future.

The military ambitions of Louis XIV were a calamity for Canada. Stimulated by his conquest of Flanders (1668) and urged on by Louvois, his War Minister, he neglected his colony, after 1672, in favour of the great armies required for the realization of his dream of European domination. As royal aid to immigration was withdrawn and royal subsidies ceased, the colony had to struggle along as best it could on its own resources. Its one great source of wealth was the western beaver trade, but here the Canadians found themselves in fierce competition with the English and their crafty and intelligent Iroquois allies. Moreover, for some time the colony had suffered from the desertion of numbers of its young men who were attracted to the life of the forest by the lure of high profits, adventures and freedom to indulge licentious appetites. Royal orders and penalties were powerless to stop the exodus of *coureurs de bois* and the contraband trade with New York, and both the land and the population suffered serious loss by the defection of so many able-bodied young men.

Even when the Treaty of Nymwegen confirmed the position of Louis XIV as the most powerful monarch in Europe, the King did not return to Colbert's policy for New France, and the situation in Canada became very grave when in 1682 the Iroquois broke the long peace and again took to the warpath. In 1689 England's declaration of war on France, coming at a time when Canada had no more than ten thousand inhabitants, further aggravated the situation. At the eastern extremity of the continent, the borders of the struggling colony of Acadia were repeatedly violated by English encroachments, and in 1690 Port Royal was captured by Phipps. However, Canada, which was stronger and less exposed than Acadia, drove Phipps and his fleet away from Quebec, and Canadian and Indian raiding parties carried the war into New England. On the other hand, the French villages were subjected to constant harassment by the Iroquois, whose most savage attack was the Lachine massacre, but French reprisals were so prompt and so severe that in 1701 the Indians were obliged to accept the general peace which finally put an end to twenty years of war.

For nine years, from 1689 to 1697, the country was under constant threat of English invasion. The Treaty of Ryswick (1697), re-establishing the *status quo,* proved to be only a truce, and with the War of the Spanish Succession (1702), hostilities again broke out in America. The Franco-Abenaki attacks and the wrecking of Walker's ships assured the safety of the colony for the time being, but with the fall of Port Royal in 1710, Acadia was definitively lost to France. The Treaty of Utrecht (1713) gave to England not only Acadia, but also Newfoundland and the Hudson Bay basin.

Even while New France was waging war with the English colonies, two internal crises shook the very foundations of its domestic economy: the failure of the Canada Company and the disastrous bankruptcy of the credit system based on card money.

To sum up, the movement of royal colonization, which had begun brilliantly and had brought new life and strength to Canada, was arrested after ten years of steady progress. Then, for a period of thirty years during which all its energies were consumed in wars with the Iroquois and the English, the colony marked time in its economic and social development. After the conclusion of peace with the Iroquois and the failure of the English offensive against Quebec the forward movement resumed, so that the end of the fifty-year period of colonization marked substantial growth in agriculture and in population, both of which had increased sevenfold. During this period, too, some of Canada's great historic figures had left their indelible mark on the country, among them Talon, Frontenac, Jolliet, La Salle and d'Iberville.

At the end of this active and troubled period, Canada emerged from the war with her essential territory from the Gulf to the Great Lakes intact, with a reformed economy and an optimistic and confident spirit. Strengthened by its glorious resistance and rejoicing in the restoration of peace, the country was ready to make a fresh step forward, and to enter upon a long and fruitful period of expansion.

ADMINISTRATIVE POWERS

A Commission as Governor and Lieutenant-General in Canada, Acadia and the Island of Newfoundland, and other countries in North America, for M. de Courcelles, March 23, 1665.

Louis, by the Grace of God, King of France and of Navarre, to all who see these present letters, greeting:

Having resolved to withdraw the Sieur de Mézy from the post of Governor and our Lieutenant-General in Canada, and to appoint in his place a person on whose competence and fidelity we can rely for the guidance of our peoples in the said country, for propagating Christianity, improving commerce and increasing the number of colonies, we have chosen to assume this charge our dear and well-beloved Sieur de Courcelles, our lieutenant in the government of Thionville, who has on several occasions given proof of his experience and valour, and whom we know to have all the qualities necessary to acquit himself worthily of the said charge.

For these reasons, and moved by other sound considerations, we have made, constituted, ordained and established, and by these presents signed by our hand we do now make, constitute, ordain and establish the said Sieur de Courcelles Governor and Lieutenant-General in Canada, Acadia and the Island of Newfoundland, and other countries in North America, to have command, instead, as has been said, of the said Sieur de Mézy, whom we are withdrawing from this post, over all governors and our lieutenants established in the said countries, as also over the officers of the Sovereign Council established there and over French vessels which may sail there, whether they be war vessels belonging to us or merchant vessels; and to readminister the oath of allegiance to the said governors and officers of the said council as well as to the three orders in the said countries.

We enjoin the said governors, officers of the said council and others to recognize the Sieur de Courcelles and to obey him in anything which he may command: to assemble the communities

229

when need arises, to have them take up arms; to take cognizance of, compose and reconcile any differences which might exist or may arise in the said countries, whether between the seigneurs and the chief officers in these countries, or between private individuals; to besiege and capture fortified places and castles, if the need arises, to have artillery transported there and brought into action; to establish garrisons where the importance of the place requires it; to command the peoples of the said countries as well as all our other subjects living there, ecclesiastics, nobles, troops and others, of whatever rank and condition they may be; to call the unconverted peoples by all possible gentle means to the knowledge of God and the light of faith and the Catholic, Apostolic and Roman religion, and to establish the exercise of that religion to the exclusion of all others; to defend the said places with all his power, to maintain and keep the said peoples untroubled, tranquil and at peace, and to command at sea as well as on land; to order and execute everything that he or those he commissions consider they should and can do to extend and keep the said places under our authority and obedient to us; and generally to do and order by his authority everything appertaining to the said charge of Governor and Lieutenant-General in the said countries, to hold and exercise that charge, to enjoy and use the honours, powers, authority, prerogatives, rights of precedence, liberties, rights, fruits, profits, revenues and emoluments appertaining to it, as well as the salary and wages which shall be assigned to him, all this, however, under the authority of the Sieur de Tracy, our Lieutenant-General, when he is present in the said country of Canada.

Further, we inform all governors and our lieutenants in the said countries, officers of the Sovereign Council and all other judges and officers each in his function, that they must recognize and obey the said Sieur de Courcelles, from whom we have received the customary oath required in such cases, and they must cause, suffer and allow him to enjoy and use the said position and charge. We wish that the said wages and salary be paid in cash each year by the keeper of our royal treasury or other appointed accounting officers on the customary terms and in the customary manner, according to the orders and statements which will be signed and dispatched by us, and which are to be added to these presents in duly collated copies thereof. The payment is to be made at one time and a proper receipt collected. We desire that the sum paid to him at that time be transferred and allocated to the accounts of those who have made the payment, by our beloved and faithful servants, the keepers of our accounts in Paris, whom we enjoin to do this without demur and to remove any obstacle to the accomplishment of this action.

We advise and order our dear and well-beloved uncle the Duke of Vendôme, peer, grand master, chief and superintendent-general of France's navigation and commerce, his lieutenants and others concerned, to give the said Sieur de Courcelles, or those who are commissioned by him or sent to the said country of Canada, all permits and passports which ships and vessels are obliged to have when going to sea to go and come, without let or hindrance, to the said countries with merchandise with which the ships will be loaded, and the men and women they will want to transport. We further order and enjoin all our other officers and subjects concerned, being in the said countries of Canada, to recognize the said Sieur de Courcelles in the said station of Governor and our Lieutenant-General in the said countries, and to obey him and give heed to him in matters concerning the said charge: for such is our pleasure.

We beg and request all Kings, potentates, princes, states and others our good friends, allies, associates, their ministers and officers, and all others not subject to us to give him and those who are commissioned or delegated by him every aid, favour and help which they may solicit for the execution of their duty, and we offer in like case to do the same for those who are recommended to us in their name. In witness of which, we have caused our seal to be set on these presents, given in Paris, the twenty-third day of the month of March, the year of grace one thousand, six hundred and sixty-five, and of our reign the twenty-second.

Signed: Louis

and on the fold,

By the King's order

Signed: De Lionne[1]

And sealed on a double ribbon with the great seal on yellow wax.

Read and published in the Sovereign Council assembled in the Château St. Louis in Quebec, the twenty-third of September, one thousand, six hundred and sixty-five; and registered in the records of the Council's registry, as required by the order of the date above-mentioned, and by the undersigned registrar and secretary of the said Council to serve any suitable purpose. This is the re-

[1]*Edits et Ord.*, III, pp. 31-3.

cord. The above-mentioned registration is not in its proper place, as it should have been on the front of the seventh sheet following. It is in this place only by inadvertance, as the following registrations had been overlooked because there was a blank page.

Signed: Peuvret,
Registrar

INTENDANT

A Commission as Intendant of Justice, Police and Finance in Canada, Acadia, Newfoundland and other countries in North America for M. Talon, dated March 23, 1665.

Louis, by the Grace of God, King of France and of Navarre, to our beloved and loyal Councillor in our Councils, the Sieur Talon, greeting:

Considering that, for the good of our peoples and the ordering of justice, police and finance in our countries of Canada, it is necessary to establish in the charge of the resident intendant a person capable of serving us there worthily, we have to this end cast our eyes upon you because of the special confidence we have in your experience, wise conduct and integrity, qualities of which you have given proof on every occasion which you have had to show your devotion to our service.

Moved by these and other reasons, we have commissioned, ordained and deputed you, and we do now, by these presents signed by our hand, commission, ordain, and depute you Intendant of Justice, Police and Finance in our countries of Canada, Acadia and Newfoundland, and other countries in North America, to be present in this function at councils of war which will be held by our Lieutenant-General in America, and by the Governor and our Lieutenant-General in the said countries of Canada: to hear the complaints which will be brought to you by our peoples in the said countries, by soldiers and all others, concerning abuses, wrongs or violence from which they have suffered; to dispense true and summary justice; to report on any enterprise, practice or intrigue directed against our service; to bring to justice those, of whatever rank or station they may be, who are guilty of any crime, to have them tried and to have sentence pronounced and executed, to call to serve with you the number of judges and graduates indicated in the ordinances, and generally to investigate all crime and offences, abuses and malversations which might be committed in our said countries whoever the culprits may be; to preside at the Sovereign Council in the absence of the Sieurs de Tracy, our Lieutenant-General in America, and de Courcelles, Governor and Lieutenant-General in our said countries of Canada; to be sole and sovereign judge in civil matters, and to order everything as you see it to be just and appropriate; and we validate from the present and for the future the judgments which will be pronounced by you, just as if they had emanated from our Sovereign Courts, and this notwithstanding objections, appeals, edicts, ordinances or anything else which might be opposed to this.

We desire also that you keep watch over the disposition, handling and distribution of our public monies destined for the maintenance of the troops, for provisions, munitions, fortifications, reparations, unforeseen expeditions, borrowings and levies which may have been made and which may be made to meet the expenses of these last, as well as other expenditures to be made for our service; we desire you to examine and confirm the statements and orders in connection with these expenses which will be dispatched to the payers concerned by our Lieutenant-General-in-Chief and, in his absence, by our other Lieutenants-General; to have presented to you copies of pay parade reports, accounts and registers, and in all the circumstances and situations noted above to do and order that which is necessary for the good and advantage of our service and which pertains to the function and exercise of the said charge of the Intendant of Justice, Police and Finance in our said countries. It is our intention that you enjoy the honours, powers, authority, prerogatives, and rights of precedence which belong to that office and the salary which we shall assign to you, and we give you power, authority, our commission and special order to do so.

We advise the Sieurs de Tracy and de Courcelles to cause you to implement the effect and content of these presents; we order officers of the Sovereign Council and all our other officers, judges and subjects, to recognize and heed you, and to obey you in the said office, to aid you and to provide force and prisons if need be for the execution of the said presents; for such is our pleasure.

Commissions of Governors and Intendants

Given in Paris, the twenty-third day of March, the year of grace one thousand, six hundred and sixty-five, and of our reign the twenty-second.

Signed: Louis

And below, by the King's order,

Signed: De Lionne

And sealed on a single ribbon with the great seal on yellow wax.

Read and published in the Sovereign Council assembled in the Château St. Louis in Quebec, the twenty-third day of September, one thousand, six hundred and sixty-five; and registered in the records of the Council's registry as required by the order of the date above-mentioned, by the registrar and secretary, undersigned, of the said Council to serve any suitable purpose. This is the record.

Signed: Peuvret[1]

[1]*Edits et Ord.*, III, pp. 33-5.

SOVEREIGN COUNCIL

Edict Creating the Superior Council of Quebec

Louis, by the Grace of God, King of France and of Navarre, to all those present and to come, greeting:

The property of the country of New France, which belonged to a company of our subjects which had been formed to establish colonies there in virtue of concessions accorded to it by the late King, our deeply honoured Lord and father of glorious memory, by the Treaty signed the twenty-third of April, one thousand, six hundred and twenty-eight, having been ceded to us by a voluntary contract, which the persons interested in the said Company made in our favour on February the twenty-fourth last: we considered at the same time that in order to bring prosperity to the said country and to allow those who dwell there to enjoy the same calm and felicity as our other subjects do, since it has pleased God to give us peace, it was necessary to provide for the establishment of justice as being the principle and an absolutely necessary prerequisite for a good administration of affairs and a stable government whose strength depends as much upon the maintenance of laws and the execution of our orders as upon the power of our arms. Being well informed that the distance of these places is too great for it to be possible to remedy all ills from here with necessary diligence, since the state of the said affairs is generally changed when our orders arrive on the spot, and since conditions and pressing ills need swifter remedies than those which we can apply from such a distance, we thought we could make no better decision than to establish a regular system of justice and a sovereign council in the said country, in order to cause the law to prosper there, to maintain and support the virtuous, to punish evil-doers and to keep all in the path of duty, preserving, as far as possible, the same form of justice as is exercised in our kingdom, and to compose the said Sovereign Council of a number of officers fitted to render justice. Moved by these and other considerations and with the advice of our Council at which there were present the Queen, our honoured Lady and mother, our dear and beloved only brother, the Duc d'Orléans, our beloved cousin, the Prince de Condé, and several other princes, noblemen and notable personages, members of the Council, and in our sure knowledge, full power and royal authority, we have created, erected and established a Sovereign Council in our said country of New France, ceded to us as aforementioned by the contract of cession of the Company to which the property belonged; to be the said Sovereign Council sitting in our town of Quebec. Reserving to ourselves, however, the option of transferring the said Sovereign Council to any other town or place in the said country, as may seem desirable to us according to events and circumstances: this Sovereign Council we desire to be composed of our dear and well-beloved Sieurs de Mézy, the Governor, representing our person, de Laval, Bishop of Petrea, or the senior ecclesiastic there, and five others whom they will choose jointly and in concert; and of our attorney in the Sovereign Council, and they will administer the oath of allegiance to them. These five persons chosen to act as councillors will be changed or continued in office each year according as is considered desirable by the said Governor and Bishop or senior ecclesiastic present; further, we have given and attributed, and we do now give and attribute to the said Sovereign Council, the power to investigate all civil and criminal cases and to give sovereign judgment without appeal, according to the laws and ordinances of our kingdom, and to proceed as far as possible, according to the forms and manner practised in the province of our *Parlement de Paris,* reserving to ourselves, however, the sovereign power to change, reform and amplify the said laws and ordinances, to set them aside, to abolish them, to create new laws or rulings, statutes or constitutions, according as we see them to be useful for our service and for the good of our subjects in the said countries. It is our wish, intention and pleasure that in the said Council the spending of public funds be authorized, and that regulations be formulated for the fur traffic with the Indians and for any trade the inhabitants may have with the merchants of this kingdom; also, that all the country's police affairs, whether

public or private, be settled there in the place and on the day and
hour designated for that purpose; we also give power to the said
Council to commission in Quebec, Montreal and Three Rivers,
and in any other place, as many persons as they think necessary to
judge in lower courts, without long and formal legal procedure,
different cases which may arise between private parties; to appoint
such clerks, notaries, constables and other officers of justice as they
consider appropriate, our desire being to reduce legal action to a
minimum in the said country of New France, in order that justice
may be rendered promptly and speedily.

Inasmuch as for the preservation of minutes of decisions, judgments and other acts or notices of the said Council a registrar or
secretary will be needed, we desire that a person who is considered
suitable by the said Governor and Bishop, or senior ecclesiastic, be
commissioned in the same way to fulfil the function of registrar
or secretary, and that he be changed or continued, according as it
is considered appropriate by the above-mentioned gentlemen. We
desire, moreover, that the five councillors chosen by the said
Governor and the Bishop, or senior ecclesiastic, be commissioned
to dispatch cases and affairs of minor importance, and to give their
attention to and see to the execution of affairs judged by the
Council, in order that the said commissioners may inform themselves more completely on affairs which will be brought before the
Council, at the same time reporting those with which they may
be charged by the colonists' syndics of the said country, inhabitants
of the country, foreigners, travellers and others to whom it is our
intention and wish that prompt justice be dispensed; and we desire
that those who have been appointed to the said offices enjoy the
honours, powers, authority, rights of precedence, privileges and
liberties appertaining to them as well as the wages which will
be assigned by the statement which we shall cause to be dispatched
to them with the provision that the officers of the Sovereign
Council may not, except with our permission, exercise any other
function, or receive wages, presents or pensions except those
ordered by us, from anyone whatsoever. Further, we command
the Sieurs de Mézy, Governor, and de Laval, Bishop of Petrea, or
senior priest present, to execute this present edict and cause it to
be executed by choosing the said councillors, our registrar and
attorney, and when they have been assembled, to have it published
and registered, point by point, according to its form and tenor, and
to cause its contents to be maintained and observed in spite of any
obstacle, opposition or appeal, and if there is any such inter-

vention, we have reserved its investigation to ourselves, and we shall send it back to the said Council in New France, and to this effect we have forbidden any of our other courts or judges to deal with it; and because the present edict could be required in several different places in the said country, we desire that copies collated by the registrar of the said council be honoured in the same way as the original; they must, however, be sealed with our arms, as must all official notices dispatched by the said Council. We also order all judges, officials, inhabitants of the said country, transients and others to obey and submit without demur to the rulings made by our Sovereign Council. For such is our pleasure; and in order that it may be firm and stable for all time, we have had our seal set on this present edict as a perpetual and irrevocable edict, reserving only our sovereign right in all other things and the sovereign rights of others in all things.

Given in Paris, in the month of April, the year of grace one thousand, six hundred and sixty-three, and of our reign, the twentieth.

Signed: Louis

And lower, by order of the King, De Lionne, and at the side visa Séguier, to serve for letters of establishment of a Sovereign Council in the province of Canada or New France. And below, read in the council, signed Colbert and sealed with green wax on a double knot of red and green silk, and countersealed with the same wax and knots.

Mézy,
François, Bishop of Petrea.[1]

[1]*Edits et Ord.*, I, pp. 37-9.

ECONOMIC TABLES

CANADA'S FIRST CENSUS [1]
1666

LOCALITIES	FAMILIES	POPULATION	MALE	FEMALE
Quebec	71	547	360	187
Beaupré	89	533	315	218
Beauport	29	185	117	68
Island of Orleans	96	452	291	161
Côte St. Jean Côte St. François Côte St. Michel	27	153	99	54
Sillery	23	140	93	47
Notre-Dame-des-Anges Rivière St. Charles Charlesbourg	24	112	67	45
Lauzon	3	13	9	4
Three Rivers and district	69	455	299	156
Montreal and district	107	625	384	241
TOTAL	538	3,215	2,034	1,181

[1]*Recensements du Canada,* 1665-1871, IV, pp. 2-4.

NOTE: This first census in Canada was made on Talon's instructions during the months of February and March 1666. This has been verified by a study of parish registers.

The King's troops, 1,000 to 1,200 men in twenty-four companies, are not included in this census. The names of thirty priests and nuns are missing, namely: four secular priests in Quebec and five in Montreal, ten nuns in Montreal, and eleven Jesuits employed in the Indian missions.

The clergy as a whole included a bishop, eighteen priests and ecclesiastics, thirty-one Jesuit priests and brothers. There were nineteen Ursuline sisters, twenty-three Hospital Sisters, and four Sisters of the Congregation. Members of the nobility and the clergy, public servants and farmers are not listed in the following census of professions and trades.

PROFESSIONS AND TRADES

Professions and Trades	Quebec	North Shore	Orleans and South Shore	Three Rivers	Montreal	Total
Armourers	2		2			4
Arquebusiers	2			2	3	7
Bailiffs	3	1				4
Bakers	1	3	4		3	11
Bourgeois	15	1				16
Brewers	1					1
Brick-makers		1				1
Butchers		3	2		2	7
Button-makers		1				1
Carpenters	3	21	4	1	7	36
Chandlers	1	2				3
Charcoal-burners		1				1
Coopers	4	1		1	2	8
Coppersmiths		2			1	3
Curriers		1	4		3	8
Cutlers		1				1
Drapers		1	3			4
Engagés	93	115	47	72	74	401
Furriers	1					1
Gardeners	2	1				3
Goldsmiths			1			1
Hatters		4	1		2	7
Ironfounders	1					1
Joiners	9	8	3	2	5	27
Locksmiths		1		1	1	3
Masons	7	12	5		8	32
Merchants	13	1		1	3	18
Millers		5	2	1	1	9
Nail-makers	3		1			4
Notaries	2	1				3
Pastry cooks	3	1			1	5
Printers			1			1
Roofers		1				1
Rope-makers	1	3	1		1	6
Sabot-makers		1				1
Saddlers		1	1		1	3
Sailors	4	9	6		3	22
Schoolmasters	2			1		3
Shoemakers	6	7	3		4	20
Skippers	1					1
Stone-cutters	1					1
Surgeons	2	2			1	5
Sword mounters	1					1
Tailors	8	9	4	2	7	30
Tinsmiths	1					1
Tool-makers	8	1	2	1	2	14
Turners					1	1
Upholsterers		2	1			3
Weavers	1	11	3		1	16
Wheelwrights		2				2
Totals	202	238	101	85	137	763

AGRICULTURAL CENSUS [1]
1667

	Arpents under cultivation	Horned livestock	Sheep	Totals
Quebec	345	180		
Beaupré	1,679	578		
Beauport	832	251		
Island of Orleans	1,182	327		
Côte Ste. Geneviève ⎫				1,635
Côte St. François ⎬	832	129		
Côte St. Michel ⎭				
Sillery	256	59		
Cap Rouge	619	91		
Côte St. Ignace	104	10		
Notre-Dame-des-Anges ⎫				
Rivière St. Charles ⎬	995	765	85	850
Charlesbourg ⎭				
Lauzon	236	56		
Three Rivers	1,032	142		
Cap-de-la-Madeleine ⎫				
La Touche ⎬	1,489	175		717
Champlain ⎭				
Montreal and district	1,849	344		
Totals	11,448	3,107	85	3,192

[1]*Recensements du Canada,* 1665-1871, IV, p. 7.

CENSUS OF THE COLONY OF CANADA[1]
1713
Summary

Territory covered: from Bic to Chateauguay.

Population : 18,119 inhabitants
Houses : 2,859
Firearms : 3,805
Mills ı 69

Clergy	Quebec	Three Rivers	Montreal	Parishes
Priests	10			50
Jesuits	10		5	
Sulpicians			10	
Récollets	11	5	5	
Ursulines	38	7		
Hospital Sisters	50		36	
Sisters of the Congregation	6		45	12
Churches	7	3	8	56

Agriculture

Arpents under cultivation	54,929	
Arpents in pasture	6,774	
Wheat (pecks)	250,763	
Corn	7,869	
Peas, oats, etc. (pecks)	92,657	
Flax (pounds)	36,123	
Hemp (pounds)	7,272	
Horses		3,007
Horned cattle		15,456
Sheep		5,852
Pigs		11,940
Total of animals	36,255	

[1] Colonial Archives (France), G[1], vol. 461. A few figures have been corrected.

COMPARATIVE PRICES OF BEAVER [1]

Differences in trade with the Indians between Montreal in Canada, and Orange in New England.

The Indians must give:	In Orange and Boston	In Montreal
For eight pounds of powder	one beaver	four
For a rifle	two beaver	five
For forty pounds of lead	one beaver	three
For one red cloth blanket	one beaver	two
For a white one	one beaver	two
For a heavy coat	one beaver	two
For four shirts	one beaver	two
For ten pairs of stockings	one beaver	two

[1]*Collection de manuscrits contenant lettres, mémoires et autres documents historiques relatifs à la Nouvelle-France,* I, p. 476.

BIBLIOGRAPHY

PRELIMINARY NOTE

Some archival collections have been reclassified since the author consulted them, and for this reason some references may not indicate the present titles and numbers of collections or the present order of items in them. The date, which is indicated in each case, will serve to identify the document in question.

No attempt has been made to present an exhaustive bibliography of the period under review. The lists which follow contain only the names of essential works and those which have been consulted by the author.

DOCUMENTARY SOURCES IN MANUSCRIPT

There are copies or photostats of most of the following series and collections in the National Archives in Ottawa.

FRENCH SOURCES

Archives nationales:

Série E.	Conseils du Roi. I. Conseil des Finances.
Série F2A.	Colonies.
Série F3.	Collection Moreau de Saint-Méry.
Série G7.	Contrôle général des Finances.
Série J.	Trésor des Chartres.
Série K.	Section historique.
Série V6.	Grande Chancellerie et Conseil.
Série Z.	Juridictions spéciales et ordinaires.

Archives des Colonies:

Série A.	Actes du Pouvoir souverain.
Série B.	Correspondance ministérielle et Ordres et Dépêches du Roi. Lettres envoyées aux colonies.
Série C11A.	Canada et Dépendances. (Lettres des gouverneurs, intendants, et officiers et autres.)
Série C11C.	Terre-Neuve, Iles de la Madeleine et Saint-Jean.
Série C11D.	Acadie.

Archives de la Marine:
Dépôt des cartes et plans de la Marine.

Ministère des Affaires étrangères:
Mémoires et Documents: Amérique.
Correspondance politique: Angleterre.

Bibliothèque Nationale:
Fonds français.
Nouvelles Acquisitions.
Collection Moreau.
Mélanges Colbert.

ENGLISH SOURCES
    Public Record Office:
       State papers: Foreign
       France. Vol. I.
       Treaty Papers.

CANADIAN SOURCES:

    National Archives:
       Official Correspondence, Series II.
       Maps Division.
       Montreal, Palais de Justice. Ordonnances.
       Montreal, Palais de Justice. Registres judiciaires.
       Three Rivers, Pièces judiciaires.

    Archives of the Province of Quebec:
       Various series.
       Historical collections.

    Private Collections:
       Archives of the Séminaire de Saint-Sulpice.
       Archives of the Congrégation de Notre-Dame.
       Letters of the Archevêché de Québec.
       Archives of the Hôtel-Dieu de Québec.
       Séminaire de Québec. Pièces historiques.

PRINTED DOCUMENTARY SOURCES

Augustin-Thierry, *Un Colonial du temps de Colbert, Mémoires de Robert Challes, écrivain du roi* (Paris: Plon, 1931).

Baugy, Louis Henry, *Journal d'une expédition contre les Iroquois en 1687* (Paris, 1885).

Beaudoin, Abbé, *Journal d'Iberville en Acadie et à Terre-Neuve, Lettres d'Iberville* in Gosselin, Abbé Auguste, *Les Normands au Canada* (Evreux, 1800). With an introduction and notes.

Belmont, François Vachon de, *Histoire du Canada* (Quebec: Société littéraire et historique de Québec, 1840).

Casson, Dollier de, *Histoire de Montréal* (Montreal: Mémoires de la Société historique de Montréal, 1868).

Carayon, Father, *Premières Missions des Jésuits au Canada. Lettres et Documents inédits* (Paris, 1864).

Catalogne, Gédéon de, "Mémoire sur les plans des seigneuries et habitations des gouvernements de Québec, les Trois-Rivières et Montréal," *Bulletin des Recherches historiques* (Lévis, 1915).

Cavelier, Jean, *Relation du voyage entrepris par feu M. Robert Cavelier, Sieur de La Salle* (Manate, 1861).

Collection de manuscrits contenant lettres, mémoires et autres documents historiques relatifs à la Nouvelle-France (Quebec, 1883-85).

Colonial Office, 217, Nova Scotia & Cape Breton, Original correspondence (1702-1867).

Diéréville, N. de, *Relation du voyage de Port-Royal de l'Acadie ou de la Nouvelle-France* (Rouen, 1708).

Documents relatifs à la monnaie, au change et aux finances du Canada sous le régime français, ed. by Adam Shortt (Ottawa, 1925) 2 vols.

Documents relating to the Seigniorial Tenure in Canada, 1598-1854, ed. by W. B. Munro (Toronto, 1908).

Documents relating to the Colonial History of the State of New York, ed. by E. B. O'Callaghan (Albany, 1855-58).

Edits, ordonnances royaux, déclarations et arrêts du Conseil d'Etat du Roi, concernant le Canada (Quebec, 1854-56). 3 vols.

Extraits des Archives des Ministères de la Marine et de la Guerre à Paris, published under the direction of Abbé H. R. Casgrain, Canada. *Correspondance générale. MM. Duquesne et Vaudreuil, Gouverneurs-Généraux, 1755-60* (Quebec, 1860).

Franquet, Louis, *Voyages et Mémoires sur le Canada* (Quebec, 1889).

Hazard, Ebenezer, *Historical Collections consisting of State Papers and other Authentic Documents* (Philadelphia, 1792-94).

Hennepin, Louis, *Description de la Louisiane nouvellement découverte* (Paris, 1683).

Hennepin, Louis, *Nouvelle découverte d'un très grand pays situé dans l'Amérique* (Utrecht, 1697).

Hennepin, Louis, *Nouveau voyage d'un païs plus grand que l'Europe avec les réflections des entreprises de La Salle* (Utrecht, 1698). The first of these works is still useful. The others are padded with unreliable additions, notably the author's story of a voyage down the Mississippi which he claimed to have made before La Salle.

Histoire de l'Hôtel-Dieu de Québec (Montauban, 1751). The materials for this history were gathered by Mother Françoise Juchereau de St. Ignace and the text was written by Mother Marie Andrée Duplessis de Ste. Hélène. See also *Les Annales de l'Hôtel-Dieu*, edited by Dom Jamet (Quebec, 1939).

Historical Collections. Collection and researches by the Michigan Pioneer and Historical Society (Lansing, 1905) XXIV. This collection contains the papers of La Mothe-Cadillac (1682-1745).

Inventaire des insinuations du Conseil souverain de la Nouvelle-France ed. by P. G. Roy (Beauceville, 1921).

Inventaire des ordonnances des intendants de la Nouvelle-France conservées aux archives de la province de Québec, ed. by P. G. Roy (Beauceville, 1917). 3 vols.

Jesuit Relations and Allied Documents, the Travels and Explorations of the Jesuit Missionaries in New France, 1610-1791, ed. by R. G. Thwaites (Cleveland, 1896-1901). 73 vols.

Journal des Jésuites (Quebec, 1871).

Joutel, Henri, *Journal historique du dernier voyage que feu M. de La Salle fit dans le golfe du Mexique* (Paris, 1713).

Jugements et délibérations du Conseil souverain de la Nouvelle-France, published by order of the Quebec Legislature (Quebec, 1885). 6 vols.

Kalm, Peter, *Voyage de Kalm en Amérique*, French summary and translation from the original Swedish by L. W. Marchand (Montreal, 1880).

Kalm, Peter, *The America of 1750; Peter Kalm's Travels in North America* (New York: Benson, 1937).

La Hontan, Louis Armand d'Arce, baron de, *Nouveaux Voyages de M. le baron de Lahontan dans l'Amérique septentrionale* (The Hague, 1703). 2 vols. La Hontan spiced up his books with invented stories about the "King's daughters" and his discovery of the non-existent Rivière Longue.

La Potherie, Bacqueville de, *Histoire de l'Amérique septentrionale* (Paris, 1922). 4 vols.

La Tour, Abbé Bertrand de, *Mémoires sur la vie de Mgr de Laval* (Cologne, 1761).

Le Beau, C., *Aventures du Sr. C. Le Beau, ou, Voyage curieux et nouveau parmi les Sauvages de l'Amérique septentrionale* (Amsterdam, 1758).

Le Clerq, Chrétien, *Establissement de la foy dans la Nouvelle-France* (Paris, 1691).

Marie de l'Incarnation, *Lettres de la Révérende Mère* Marie de l'Incarnation, ed. by Richaudeau (Paris, 1873).

Massicotte, E. Z., *Arrêts, édits, ordonnances, mandements et règlements conservés dans les Archives du Palais du Justice de Montréal, 1653-1725* (Montreal, 1919).

Mémoires et documents pour servir à l'histoire des origines françaises des pays d'outre-mer, ed. by Pierre Margry (Paris, 1879-88). 6 vols. This work also includes the French discoveries and establishments in western and southern North America.

Morin, Sœur Marie, *Annales de l'Hôtel-Dieu, 1649-1657* (Montreal, 1921).

Nouvelle-France, documents historiques. Correspondance échangée entre les autorités françaises et les gouverneurs et intendants (Quebec, 1893). The only volume published. The documents are not well chosen and their sources are not indicated.

Nova Scotia Historical Society Collection, I, *Journal of Colonel Nicholson; Diary of John Thomas*; II, *Brown's Papers*; III & IV, *Colonel Winslow's Journal.*

Ordonnances, commissions, etc. des gouverneurs et intendants de la Nouvelle-France, 1639-1700, ed. by P. G. Roy (Beauceville, 1924). 2 vols.

Papiers Contrecœur et autres documents concernant le conflit anglo-français sur l'Ohio de 1745 à 1756, ed. by Bernard Grenier (Quebec, 1952).

Pièces et documents relatifs à la tenure seigneuriale (Quebec, 1852). 4 vols.

Rapports des Archives Publiques du Canada, 1882-1960. This collection contains a number of documents as well as tables of contents of its most important French and English collections.

Rapports de l'Archiviste de la Province de Québec, 1922-1960. This collection contains a great deal of historical material of prime importance.

Relations par lettres de l'Amérique septentrionale, ed. by Father de Rochemonteix (Paris, 1940). Attributed by the editor to R. P. Sylvy, this relation was drawn up by the intendant Antoine Raudot and is based on contemporary memoirs.

Rencensements du Canada (Ottawa, 1876) vol. IV. Contains statistics.

Saint-Vallier, Mgr de, *Etat présent de l'Eglise et de la colonie française dans la Nouvelle-France, par M. l'Evêque de Québec* (Quebec, 1856). Reprinted.

Steck, Francis Borgia, O.F.M., *Marquette Legends* (New York, 1960). Father Steck proves that Marquette was in no sense the discoverer of the Mississippi. Its one and only discoverer was Louis Jolliet. The narrative ascribed to Marquette is a fabrication of Father Claude Dablon, S.J.

Steck, Francis Borgia, O.F.M., *The Jolliet-Marquette Expedition, 1673* (Chicago, 1920).

Tonti, Henri de, *Dernières découvertes dans l'Amérique septentrionale de M. de la Salle* (Paris, 1697).

Les Ursulines de Québec depuis leur établissement jusqu'à nos jours (Quebec, 1863-66). 4 vols.

Les Ursulines de Trois-Rivières (1888-92). 2 vols.

Voyages of Pierre Esprit Radisson, ed. by Gideon D. Scull (Boston, 1885).

PRINCIPAL SECONDARY SOURCES

Beaumont, Gaston Duboscq de, *Les Derniers jours de l'Acadie* (Paris, 1899). Contains correspondence and memoirs; extracts from the papers of M. le Courtois de Surlaville.

Blet, Henri, *Histoire de la colonisation française* (Paris and Grenoble, 1646-50). 3 vols.

Bonnault, Claude de, *Histoire du Canada français, 1534-1763* (Paris, 1950).

Brebner, J. B., *New England's Outpost: Acadia before the Conquest of Canada* (New York, 1927).

Broadhead, John Romeyn, *History of the State of New York* (New York, 1859).

Bulletin des recherches historiques (Lévis, 1895-1961).

Caron, Abbé Ivanhoé, *La Colonisation du Canada sous la domination française* (Quebec, 1916).

Caron, Abbé Ivanhoé, *La Colonisation de la Province de Québec* (Quebec, 1923-27). 2 vols.

Casgrain, Abbé H. R., *Une paroisse canadienne au XVIIIᵉ siècle* (Quebec, 1880).

Chapais, Thomas, *Jean Talon: Intendant de la Nouvelle-France, 1665-1672* (Quebec, 1904).

Charlevoix, Father P.F.X. de, *Histoire et description générale de la Nouvelle-France* (Paris, 1744). 3 vols.

Colby, Charles William, *Canadian Types of the Old Régime* (New York, 1908).

Daviault, Pierre, *La Grande Aventure de Le Moyne d'Iberville* (Montreal, 1937).

Daviault, Pierre, *Le Baron de Saint-Castin, Chef Abénaquis* (Montreal, 1939).

Daviault, Pierre, "Mme de Freneuse et M. de Bonaventure," dans M.S.R.C. (1941).

Debien, G., "Liste des engagés pour le Canada au XVII siècle," *Revue d'histoire de l'Amérique française* (December, 1952).

Delanglez, Jean, S.J., *Life and Voyages of Louis Jolliet, 1645-1700* (Chicago, 1948).

Eccles, William John, *Jean Bochart de Champigny: Intendant of New France, 1686-1702.* Unpublished M.A. thesis, McGill University, 1952.

Faillon, Abbé E. M., *Histoire de la colonie française du Canada* (Montreal, 1865-66). 3 vols.

Fauteux, Noël, *Essai sur l'industrie au Canada sous le régime français* (Quebec, 1927). 2 vols.

Ferland, Abbé J. B., *Cours d'histoire du Canada* (Quebec, 1861-65). 2 vols.

Frégault, Guy, *La Civilisation de la Nouvelle-France* (Montreal, 1944).

Frégault, Guy, *Iberville, le conquérant* (Montreal, 1944).

Gagnon, Ernest, *Louis Jolliet: découvreur du Mississipi et du pays des Illinois* (Quebec, 1902).

Garneau, F. X., *Histoire du Canada* (Paris, 1920). 2 vols.

Garraghan, Gilbert J., S.J., *Marquette: Ardent Missioner, Daring Explorer* (New York, 1932).

Gaxotte, Pierre, *La France de Louis XIV* (Paris, 1946).

Gaxotte, Pierre, *Le Siècle de Louis XV* (Paris, 1958).

Gipson, H. L., *The British Empire Before the American Revolution*, vol. V, *Zones of International Friction; The Great Lakes Frontier, Canada, the West Indies, 1748-1754* (New York, 1942); vol. VI, *The Great War for the Empire; The Years of Defeat, 1754-1757* (New York, 1946).

Giraud, Marcel, *Histoire de la Louisiane française* (Paris, 1953-58). 2 vols.

Gosselin, Abbé Amédeé, *L'Instruction au Canada sous le régime français* (Quebec, 1911).

Gosselin, Abbé Auguste, *L'Eglise du Canada depuis Mgr de Laval jusqu'à la conquête* (Quebec, 1911-14). 3 vols.

Gosselin, Abbé Auguste, *Les Normands au Canada: Jean Bourdon* (Evreux, 1892).

Gosselin, Abbé Auguste, *Vie de Mgr de Laval* (Quebec, 1890). 2 vols.

Graham, Gerald, *The Walker Expedition, 1711* (Toronto, 1953).

Groulx, Abbé Lionel, *La Naissance d'une race* (Montreal, 1919).

Groulx, Canon Lionel, *Histoire du Canada* (Montreal, 1950-52). 4 vols.

Groulx, Canon Lionel, *Notre Belle Aventure* (Montreal, 1958).

Hamelin, Jean, *Economie et société en Nouvelle-France* (Quebec, 1960).

Hammang, F. H., *The Marquis de Vaudreuil* (Bruges, 1938).

Hardy, Georges, *Histoire sociale de la colonisation française* (Paris, 1953).

Harrisse, Henry, *Notes pour servir à l'histoire, à la bibliographie et à la cartographie de la Nouvelle-France et des pays adjacents, 1545-1700* (Paris, 1872).

Harvey, D. C., *The French in Prince Edward Island* (New Haven, 1926).

Histoire des colonies françaises et de l'expansion de la France dans le monde, ed. by Hanotaux and Martineau. Volume *L'Amérique* by Ch. de la Roncière, J. Tramond, E. Lauvrière and A. Martineau (Paris, 1929).

Hutchinson, T., *The History of the Colony of Massachusetts Bay* (London, 1765). Second edition.

Innis, H. A., *An Introduction to Canadian Economic History, Being the History of the Fur Trade in Canada* (New Haven, 1929).

Kingsford, William, *History of Canada* (Toronto, 1887-98). 10 vols.

Lacour-Gayet, G., *La Marine militaire de la France sous le règne de Louis XV* (Paris, 1902).

Lanctot, Gustave, *L'Administration de la Nouvelle-France* (Paris, 1929).

Lanctot, Gustave, *Filles de joie ou filles du Roi. Etude sur l'émigration féminine en Nouvelle-France* (Montreal, 1952).

La Roncière, Charles de, *Histoire de la Marine française* (Paris, 1910). 5 vols.

Laut, Agnes, *The Fur Trade of America* (New York, 1921).

Lauvrière, Emile, *La Tragédie d'un peuple: Histoire du peuple acadien de ses origines à nos jours* (Paris, 1922) 2 vols.

Le Blant, Robert, *Un Colonial sous Louis XIV: Philippe Pastour de Costebelle* (Dax, 1935).

Le Jeune, Father Louis-Marie, *Dictionnaire général de biographie, histoire, littérature, agriculture, industrie, commerce et des arts, sciences, mœurs, coutumes, institutions religieuses et politiques du Canada* (Ottawa, 1931). 2 vols.

Lunn, Jean, *Economic Development in New France, 1713-1760*. Unpublished Ph.D. thesis, McGill University, 1943.

Lorin, Henri, *Le Comte de Frontenac* (Paris, 1895).

Murdoch, Beamish, *History of Nova Scotia or Acadia* (Halifax, 1865-67). 3 vols.

Newton, A. P., "Newfoundland," *The Cambridge History of the British Empire* (London, 1930). Vol. VI, Chapter V.

Nute, Grace Lee, *Caesars of the Wilderness: Médard Chouard, Sieur des Groseilliers, and Pierre Esprit Radisson* (New York, 1943).
Parkman, F. A., *Count Frontenac and New France under Louis XIV* (Boston, 1882).
Parkman, F. A., *A Half Century of Conflict* (Toronto, 1898). 2 vols.
Parkman, F. A., *Jesuits in North America* (Boston, 1867).
Parkman, F. A., *The Old Régime in Canada* (Boston, 1902).
Penhallow, S., *History of the Wars of New England with the Eastern Indians* (Boston, 1726). New edition, 1859.
Prowse, Daniel Woodley, *A History of Newfoundland* (London, 1895).
Rameau de Saint-Père, *Une Colonie féodale en Amérique: L'Acadie, 1604-1881* (Paris, 1889).
Rameau de Saint-Père, *La France aux colonies* (Paris, 1859).
Rich, E. E., *The History of the Hudson's Bay Company* (London, 1958-1960). 3 vols.
Richard, Edouard, *Acadie*, ed. by Henri d'Arles (Quebec, 1916-1921). 3 vols.
Renaud, Paul-Emile, *Les Origines économiques du Canada* (Mamers, 1928).
Rochemonteix, Rev. Camille de, *Les Jésuites et la Nouvelle-France au XVIIe siècle* (Paris 1895-97). 3 vols.
Rochemonteix, Rev. Emile de, *Les Jésuites et la Nouvelle-France au XVIIIe siècle* (Paris, 1906) 2 vols.
Rogers, J. D., "Newfoundland," *Historical Geography of the British Colonies* (Oxford, 1911). Vol. V.
Roquebrune, Robert la Roque de, *La Guerre et l'amour au Canada d'autrefois: Les Cahiers reflets* (Beauceville, 1945).
Roquebrune, Robert la Roque de, *Les Canadiens d'autrefois* (Montreal, 1962).
Roquebrune, Robert la Roque de, "Uniformes et drapeaux des régiments au Canada sous Louis XIV et Louis XV," *Revue de l'Université d'Ottawa* (juillet & septembre, 1950).
Roy, Antoine, *Les Lettres, les sciences et les arts au Canada sous le régime français* (Paris, 1930).
Roy, Pierre Georges, *La Famille Rouer de Villeray* (Lévis, 1920).
Roy, Pierre Georges, *Les Petites choses de notre histoire* (Lévis, 1919-1925). 5 vols.
Roy, Régis, and Malchelosse, Gérard, *Le Régiment de Carignan* (Montreal, 1925).
Salone, Emile, *La Colonisation de la Nouvelle-France* (Paris, 1906).
Sulte, Benjamin, *Histoire des Canadiens-Français* (Montreal, 1925).
Surlaville, Le Sourtois de. See Beaumont.
Tessier, Abbé Albert, *Les Trois-Rivières: Quatre siècles d'histoire, 1535-1955.* (Trois-Rivières, 1954).
Tramond, Joannès, *Manuel d'histoire maritime* (Paris, 1915).
Trudel, Marcel, *L'Esclavage au Canada* (Quebec, 1960).
Villiers, Marc de, *L'Epédition de Cavelier de La Salle dans le golfe du Mexique, 1684-1687* (Paris, 1931).
Wrong, G. M., *The Rise and Fall of New France* (London, 1928). 2 vols.

MAP SOURCES

An Historical Atlas (Toronto, 1927). Edited with an introduction, notes and chronological tables, by L. J. Burpee.
Canada: Atlas déscriptif (Ottawa, 1951).
Catalogue of Maps, Plans and Charts in the Map Room of the Dominion Archives (Ottawa, 1912).
Dumas, Paul E., *Cartes géographiques du XVIIe siècle relatives au Canada.* (Map Division, Public Archives, Ottawa).
Fite, E. D., and Freeman, A., *A Book of Old Maps Delineating American History from the Earliest Days* (Cambridge, 1926).
Kerr, D. G. G., *An Historical Atlas of Canada* (Toronto, 1961).
Marcel, Gabriel, *Cartographie de la Nouvelle-France* (Paris, 1885).
Sixteenth Century Maps Relating to Canada: A Check-list and Bibliography, with introduction by T. E. Laing, (Ottawa, Public Archives of Canada, 1956).
Trudel, Marcel, *Atlas historique du Canada français, des origines à 1867* (Quebec, 1961).

NOTES

ABBREVIATIONS USED

Arch. Can.	Public Archives of Canada
Arch. Col.	Colonial Archives (France)
Arch. Nat.	National Archives (France)
Biblio. Nat.	Bibliothèque Nationale (Paris)
B. R. H.	Bulletin des recherches historiques
Col. Mss.	Collection des manuscrits contenant lettres, mémoires, et autres documents historiques relatifs à la Nouvelle-France
Corr. Pol.	Political Correspondence, Public Archives of Canada
Docts. N. Y.	Documents Relating to the Colonial History of the State of New York
Edits et Ord.	Edits et ordonnances royaux
Journal	Journal des Jésuites
Jug. et Dél.	Jugements et délibérations du Conseil
M. S. R. C.	Mémoires de la Société Royale du Canada
Marie de l'Incarnation	Lettres de la Révérende Mère Marie de l'Incarnation
Ordonnances	Ordonnances, commissions, etc. des gouverneurs et intendants de la Nouvelle-France
R. A. Q.	Rapport de l'archiviste de la province de Québec
R. A. C.	Report of the Canadian Archives
Relations	Jesuit Relations (The figure which follows indicates the date of the *Relation* to which the note refers.)

CHAPTER I

1 Charles Verlinden, *Précédents médiévaux de la colonisation en Amérique* (Mexico, 1954) p. 21.

1a *Edits et ordonnances royaux*, I, "Acceptation du roi, mars 1663," pp. 32-3.

2 *Lettres de la Révérende Mère Marie de l'Incarnation* (Paris, 1873) II, p. 267. A letter from Mgr. de Laval, October 26, 1663, in Camille de Rochemonteix, *Les Jésuites et la Nouvelle-France au XVIIe siècle* (Paris, 1906) II, p. 325.

3 *Rapport de l'archiviste de la province de Québec*, 1930-31, p. 6. *Histoire de l'Hôtel-Dieu* (Montauban, 1751) pp. 148-9. *Marie de l'Incarnation*, II, p. 267. F³, *Feb. 28, 1664*, p. 297. *Union Libérale* (Québec, 2 novembre 1889).

4 *Edits et Ord.*, III, "Commission du 1er mai 1663," pp. 21-2.

5 F³, 1, *Commission pour le Sieur Robert, 21 mars 1663*, fol. 278.

6*Edits et Ord.*, III, "Commissions du 7 mai 1663," pp. 22-3; "Instructions au Sieur Gaudais, 7 mai 1663," pp. 23-7.

7 *Edits et Ord.*, I, "Acte pour l'establissement de la Compagnie des Cents Associés, 29 avril 1627," p. 8.

8 Biblio. Nat. F. fr. 5581, *Edits de créations d'un Conseil souverain en la Nouvelle-France;* cf. Gustave Lanctot, *L'Administration de la Nouvelle-France* (Paris, 1929) pp. 85-6.

9 Edits et Ord., I, "Edit de création d'un Conseil souverain, avril 1663," pp. 37-8.

10 *Ibid.*

11 *Jugements et déliberations du Conseil souverain de Québec*, I, pp. 183 and 323.

12 *Ibid.*, p. 268.

[13] Lanctot, "Les Fonctions du Conseil," *op. cit.*, pp. 97-124.

[14] *Edits et Ord.*, I, pp. 38-9.

[15] *Ibid.*, "Révocation des concessions non défrichées, 21 mars 1663," p. 33.

[16] *Journal des Jésuites* (Quebec, 1871) p. 323.

[17] *Jug. et Dél.*, I, p. 1-2.

[18] *R.A.Q.*, 1930-31, "Mémoire du roi, 27 mars 1665," p. 5.   C11A,2, *Mémoire du Sieur Gaudais*, p. 199.

[18a] C11A,2, *Estat des charges du pays (1665)*, pp. 228-30.

[19] *Ibid.*, *Mémoire du Sieur Gaudais*, pp. 99-100.

[19a] *Jug. et Dél.*, I, p. 8-9.

[20] *Ibid.*, pp. 170-71.

[21] Marie de l'Incarnation, II, pp. 267-68.

[22] *Jug. et Dél.*, I, pp. 15, 18, 37, 250, 278 and 291.

[23] *Ibid.*, I, pp. 9-12 and 40.

[24] *Ibid.*, pp. 92-3 and 193-94.

[25] *Ibid.*, pp. 183-84.   *Edits et Ord.*, I, "Requête de M. Le Barroys, 13 juillet 1665," p. 51.   C11A,2, *Estats des charges du pays (1665)*, p. 228-30.

[26] F3, *Arrêt du 10 mars 1662*, p. 271 *ff.*   *Edits et Ord.*, I, "Etablissement de la Compagnie des Indes occidentales, mai 1664," p. 40 *ff.*   G7, carton 1312, 76, *Mémoire pour les intéressés en la sous-ferme du Canada.*

[27] *Jug. et Dél.*, I, "August 27, 1664," p. 269.

[28] *Ibid.*, pp. 58, 95, 194, 206 and 222.

[28a] *Ibid., passim.*

[29] *Ibid.*, p. 228.

[30] *Ibid.*, "Lettres du Conseil souverain au roi et à Colbert, 18 juin 1664," pp. 201-06.

[31] C11A,2, *Pour le secours qu'il plaist au roy de donner au Canada en 1664*, pp. 106-11.   *Jug. et Dél.*, I, pp. 29 and 263.

[32] *Jug. et Dél.*, I, pp. 29, 190 and 203-04.

[33] *Ibid.*, I, "September 18, 1663," p. 8; "November 12, 1664," p. 297; cf. *Ordonnances, commissions, etc. des gouverneurs et intendants de la Nouvelle-France* (Beauceville, 1924) I, p. 51.   *Edits et Ord.*, I, "Déclaration du roi, 1678," p. 107; "Edit du roi, 12 mai 1677," p. 97 *ff.*

[34] *Jug et Dél.*, I, pp. 33-4.   *Edits et Ord.*, II, p. 25; III, pp. 84-5.

[35] Arch. Séminaire de Sain-Sulpice, *Acte du 13 janvier 1663*.   *Edits et Ord.*, I, "Contrat de donation du 9 mars 1663," pp. 93-7.   *Jug. et Dél.*, I, p. 38.   E. M. Faillon, *Histoire de la colonie française en Canada* (Montreal, 1865-66) III, pp. 77-80.   *Ordonnances*, I, pp. 44-7.   Dollier de Casson, *Histoire de Montréal* (Montreal, 1868) p. 173.

CHAPTER II

[1] *Edits et ordonnances royaux*, I, "Etablissement du séminaire de Québec, 26 mars 1663," p. 33; "Approbation du roi pour l'établissement du séminaire du Québec, avril 1663," pp. 35-7.   *Lettres de la Révérende Mère Marie de l'Incarnation*, II, pp. 267-68.

[2] *Mandements des Evêques de Québec*, I, "Déclaration du 10 novembre 1663"; "Déclaration du 1er février 1664."   *Jugements et déliberations du Conseil souverain*, I, p. 169.   *Ordonnances, commissions, etc. des gouverneurs et intendants de la Nouvelle-France*, I, p. 70 *ff.*   Auguste Gosselin, *Vie de Mgr de Laval* (Quebec, 1890) I, pp. 395-415.

[3] *Relations des Jésuites*, 1663 (Quebec, 1858) pp. 10-11.

[4] *Relations*, 1664, pp. 26, 29, 33 and 34.

[5] *Ibid.*, p. 34-5.   *Journal des Jésuites*, "2 novembre 1681," pp. 133 and 326.

[6] *Ibid.*, p. 35.

[7] C11A,2, *Mémoire de DuMesnil*, p. 129.   *Rapport de l'archiviste de la province de Québec*, 1926-27, "Frontenac à Colbert, 14 novembre 1674," p. 64; "2 novembre 1681," p. 133.   *R.A.Q.*, 1930-31, "Mémoire du roi, 27 mars 1665," p. 11.   P. G. Roy, *La Famille Rouer de Villeray* (Lévis, 1920). The author presents a defence of Villeray.

[8] C11A,2, *Mémoire des abus introduits par les gouverneurs du Canada*, pp. 23-

5.   *R.A.Q.*, 1930-31, "Mémoire du roi," p. 6.   *Jug. et Dél.*, I, pp. 55, 67, 78 and 183.   *Journal,* p. 221.

9 B. de La Tour, *Mémoires sur la vie de Mgr de Laval* (Cologne, 1761) pp. 56-7, 84, 120, 158 and *passim.*   *Jug. et Dél.*, I, pp. 9 and 18.

10 *R.A.Q.*, 1930-31, "Mémoire du roi," p. 6.   C11A,2, *Colbert à Tracy, 15 novembre 1664*, p. 123.

11 F3, 3, *Papiers envoyés par M. de Mésy, 5 décembre 1663*, p. 290.   *Ordonnances,* I, pp. 16-17 and 18-20.   *Jug. et Dél.*, I, p. 121.

12 *Ibid.*

13 *Jug. et Dél.*, I, pp. 182, 184, 255 and 271.

14 *Ibid.*, pp. 278-81.

15 *Journal,* pp. 328-29.

16 *Ibid.*, pp. 330-31.

17 *Jug. et Dél.*, I, p. 336.   C11A, 2, *Colbert à Tracy, 15 novembre 1664*, p. 123.

17a F2,A, carton 13, *Mémoire (du Duc de Longueville) 1663.*

18 *Jug. et Dél.*, I, p. 544.   *Journal,* pp. 331-32.   Dollier de Casson, *Histoire de Montréal* (Montreal, 1868).   *Relations,* 1665, pp. 3, 8 and 9.

CHAPTER III

1 *Edits et ordonnances royaux,* III, "Commission pour M. de Tracy, 9 novembre 1663," pp. 27-9.   *Relations des Jésuites,* 1665, pp. 4-5.   *Journal des Jésuites,* p. 343.

1a *Relations,* 1665, pp. 3-4.   *Journal,* p. 232.

2 *Relations,* 1665, pp. 4-5.   *Lettres de la Révérende Mère Marie de l'Incarnation,* II, pp. 289-90.   *Jugements et déliberations du Conseil souverain,* I, pp. 363-66.

3 *Edits et Ord.,* III, "Commissions de Talon et de Courcelles," pp. 31-5. *Journal,* p. 343.

4 F3, *Pouvoirs aux Sieurs de Tracy, Courcelles et Talon, 23 mars 1665,* p. 333 *ff.   Rapport de l'archiviste de la province de Québec,* 1930-31, "Mémoire au roi, 27 mars 1665," p. 6; "Lettre de Talon, 4 octobre 1665," p. 35; "Lettre de Colbert, 5 janvier 1666," p. 46.   *Ordonnances, commissions, etc. des gouverneurs et intendants de la Nouvelle-France,* "Requête des Jésuites, 8 mai 1666," pp. 28-31. Camille de Rochemonteix, *Les Jésuites et la Nouvelle-France au XVIIe siècle* (Paris, 1895-97) II, pp. 528-30.

5 "Permission à M. de Maisonneuve," in Dollier de Casson, *Histoire de Montréal* (Montreal, 1868). Appendice, pp. 239-40, (a document).   Sœur Morin, *Annales de l'Hôtel-Dieu de Montréal, 1649-57* (Montreal, 1921) p. 83.   Arch. Séminaire de Saint-Sulpice, *Lettre de M. Tronson à M. Rémy, 1680.*   Emile Faillon, *Histoire de la colonie française en Canada* (Montreal, 1865-66) III, pp. 110-16 and 184-85.

6 *Journal,* pp. 332-34.   Régis Roy and Gérard Malchelosse, *Le Régiment de Carignan* (Montreal, 1921) *passim.   Relations,* 1665, pp. 10 and 25. See also p. 12 for a plan of the first three forts.   *R.A.Q.*, 1930-31, "Lettre de Talon, 3 novembre 1666," p. 50.

6a *Journal,* pp. 339-40.   *Relations,* 1666, p. 7.

7 *Relations,* 1666, pp. 6-7.   *Journal,* pp. 340-43.

8 *Journal,* p. 344.   *Relations,* 1666, p. 7.   *Traités de paix conclus entre Sa Majesté, le Roy de France et les Indiens du Canada* (Paris, 1667).

9 *Relations,* 1666, pp. 7-8.   *Journal,* pp. 346-49.

10 Jacques Boulanger, *Le Grand Siècle* (Paris, 1911) p. 231.   *Dictionary of American Biography* (London, 1932) XIII, pp. 515-16.   J. B. Ferland, *Cours d'histoire du Canada* (Quebec, 1861-65) II, pp. 45-51 and 57.

11 *R.A.Q.*, 1930-31, "1er septembre 1666," pp. 46-50.   *Journal,* p. 349.

12 *Journal,* p. 350.   *Relations,* 1666, pp. 8-9.   *Marie de l'Incarnation,* II, pp. 328-33.   Dollier de Casson, *op. cit.,* pp. 180-81.

13 *Relations,* 1666, p. 9.   *Marie de l'Incarnation,* II, pp. 333-35.   Bacqueville de La Potherie, *Histoire de l'Amérique Septentrionale* (Paris, 1922) p. 84 *ff.*

14 *Marie de l'Incarnation,* II, pp. 334-35.   *Relations,* 1666, p. 9.   La Potherie, *op. cit.,* II, p. 85.   *Traités de paix, etc.,* pp. 6-12.

15 *Journal*, pp. 353 and 355.   *Relations*, 1667, p. 28.   *Marie de l'Incarnation*, II, pp. 349-51.

16 *Edits et Ord.*, I, pp. 40-51.

16a *Ibid.*

17 *Ibid.   Jug. et Dél.*, I, pp. 364-65.

18 *Jug. et Dél.*, I, p. 366.

19 *Edits et Ord.*, I, "Requête de M. Le Barroys," pp. 53, 55 and 56.

20 *R.A.Q.*, 1930-31, "Talon, 4 octobre 1665," p. 34.   *Edits et Ord.*, I, "Arrêt du Conseil," pp. 60-1.

21 *R.A.Q.*, "Colbert à Talon, 5 avril 1667," p. 70.

CHAPTER IV

1 Louis-Marie Le Jeune, *Dictionnaire général* (Ottawa, 1931) II, p. 690.

2 *Edits et ordonnances royaux*, III, "Commission du 23 mars 1665," pp. 33-5.

3 *Rapport de l'archiviste de la province de Québec*, 1930-31, "Mémoire du roi, 27 mars 1665," pp. 11-20.

4 *Ibid.*, "Talon à Colbert, 4 octobre 1665," pp. 32-5.

5 *Ibid.*, "Colbert à Talon, 5 janvier 1666," p. 41; "20 février 1668," p. 96.

6 *Ibid.*, "Observations faites par Talon, 1669," p. 103.

7 Stanislas Lortie, "De l'origine des Canadiens francais," *Bulletin du Parler français* (Quebec, 1904) p. 18.

8 *R.A.Q.*, 1930-31, "Colbert à Talon, 5 janvier 1666," p. 45; "Talon à Colbert, 28 octobre 1667," p. 87.

9 *Ibid.*, "Colbert à Talon, 5 janvier 1666," p. 45; "Talon à Colbert, 29 octobre 1667," p. 87; "Mémoire de Talon, 10 novembre 1670," p. 125; "Colbert à Talon, 11 février 1671," p. 145.   *Lettres de la Révérende Mère Marie de l'Incarnation*, II, p. 435; cf. Gustave Lanctot, *Filles de joie ou filles du roi. Etude sur l'émigration féminine en Nouvelle-France* (Montreal, 1952) pp. 211-16 and 225-26.

10 *R.A.Q.*, 1930-31, "Colbert à Talon, 5 janvier 1666," p. 45; "Talon à Colbert, 27 octobre 1667," pp. 77-8; "Talon à Louvois, 19 décembre 1669," p. 90.   *Marie de l'Incarnation*, II, p. 435.

11 *R.A.Q.*, 1930-31, "Observations faites par Talon, 1666," p. 108; "Colbert à Talon, 11 février 1671," p. 145; "Mémoires de Talon, 10 novembre 1670," p. 125.

B, 1, *Instructions à Bouteroue, 5 avril 1668*, fol. 89.   *Ordonnances, commissions, etc. des gouverneurs et intendants de la Nouvelle-France*, "Ordonnance de Talon, 20 octobre 1671," pp. 104-05.   *Edits et Ord.*, I, "Arrêt du Conseil d'Etat, 12 avril 1670," pp. 67-8.

12 *R.A.Q.*, 1930-31, "Colbert à Talon, 5 avril 1667," p. 72; "Talon à Colbert, 27 octobre 1667," p. 84; "Colbert à Talon, 11 février 1671," p. 147.   *Marie de l'Incarnation*, II, pp. 393-94.

13 *Relations*, 1667, p. 4; 1661, p. 3.   *Ordonnances*, "Projet de règlements, 24 février 1667," pp. 59-62.   B, 5, *Estat de la dépense, mars 1669*, fol. 110½.   *Relations*, 1667, pp. 3-4.

14 *R.A.Q.*, 1930-31, "Colbert à Talon, 5 janvier 1666," p. 43; "Talon à Colbert, 13 novembre 1666," p. 56; "Talon à Colbert, 27 octobre 1667," p. 79; "Colbert à Talon, 27 février 1668," p. 93.

15 *Ibid.*, "Observations faites par Talon, 1669," pp. 103-06; "Mémoire succinct des principaux points, 18 mai 1669," p. 112; "Mémoire de Talon, 3 novembre 1671," p. 161.   *Recensements du Canada*, IV, p. 10.   *Marie de l'Incarnation*, II, p. 352.

16 *Relations*, 1667, pp. 3-4.   *Marie de l'Incarnation*, II, p. 446.   *R.A.Q.*, 1930-31, "Talon à Colbert, 27 octobre 1667," p. 80; "Mémoire de Talon, 2 novembre 1671," p. 160; "Colbert à Talon, 4 juin 1672," p. 168.

17 *R.A.Q.*, 1930-31, "Colbert à Talon, 8 avril 1667," p. 71; "Talon à Colbert, 27 octobre 1667," p. 84; "Mémoire de Talon, 10 novembre 1670," p. 126; "Mémoire de Talon, 2 novembre 1671," p. 160.   *Marie de l'Incarnation*, II, p. 446.

18 *R.A.Q.*, 1930-31, "Talon à Colbert, 13 novembre 1666," p. 57; "Colbert à Talon, 5 avril 1667," p. 70; "Talon à Colbert, 27 octobre 1667," p. 80; "Mémoire succinct, 18 mai 1669," p. 113.

19 *Ibid.*, "Mémoire de Talon, 10 novembre 1670," p. 122; "2 novembre 1671,"

pp. 159-60; "Mémoire succinct, 18 mai 1669," p. 112; "Mémoire de Talon, 12 novembre 1671," pp. 159-60.

20 *Relations*, 1667, p. 3.   *R.A.Q.*, 1930-31, "Talon à Colbert, 27 octobre 1667," p. 82.

21 *R.A.Q.*, 1930-31, "Talon à Colbert, 27 octobre 1667," p. 82; "Mémoire succinct, 1669," p. 112.

22 *Ibid.*, "Talon à Colbert, 15 novembre 1666"; "25 août 1667," p. 75; "25 octobre 1667," p. 77.

23 *Ibid.*, "Mémoire de Talon, 2 novembre 1671," p. 157; "Talon à Colbert, 11 novembre 1671," p. 165; "Mémoire de Talon, 1673," pp. 179-80.

24 *Ibid.*, "Colbert à Talon, 5 janvier 1666," p. 42; "Addition au présent mémoire (novembre 1670)," p. 133.   *Jugements et délibérations du Conseil souverain*, I, p. 254.   C11A,2, *Arrêt du 13 avril 1669*, fol. 390.

25 *Jug. et Dél.*, I, pp. 474-76.

26 *Ibid.*, p. 534.

27 *Ibid.* "26 juin 1669," pp. 558-59.   *Ordonnances*, I, "12 juillet 1670," pp. 95-6; "5 juin 1672," pp. 107-09.

28 *R.A.Q.*, 1930-31, "Le Roi à Talon, 15 mai 1669," p. 108; "Talon à Colbert, 13 novembre 1666," p. 61; "Lettre du roi à Talon, 9 avril 1667," p. 73; "Talon à Colbert, 26 août 1667," p. 76.

29 *Histoire de l'Hôtel-Dieu de Québec* (Montauban, 1751) *passim*.   *R.A.Q.*, 1930-31, "Mémoire de Talon, 10 novembre 1670," p. 129.   Le Jeune, *op. cit.*, I, pp. 236-37.

30 C11A,3, *Le Roi à Courcelles, 3 avril 1669*, pp. 3-5.   *R.A.Q.*, 1930-31, "Mémoire de Talon, 10 novembre 1670," p. 129.   *Marie de l'Incarnation*, II, pp. 437-40.

CHAPTER V

1 *Rapport de l'archiviste de la province de Québec*, 1930-31, "Le Roi à Talon, 15 mai 1669," p. 102.   *Relations*, 1670, p. 2.

2 *R.A.Q.*, 1930-31, "Talon à Colbert, 4 juillet 1669," p. 115; "15 juillet 1669," p. 115; "Colbert à Talon, 4 juin 1672," p. 169.   Emile Salone, *La Colonisation de la Nouvelle-France* (Paris, 1906) pp. 168-69.

3 *Edits et ordonnances royaux*, I, "Arrêt du 12 avril 1670," p. 67.   *Ordonnances, commissions, etc. des gouverneurs et intendants de la Nouvelle-France*, I, "20 octobre 1671," p. 104.

4 *Relations des Jésuites*, 1670, pp. 3-7.

5 *R.A.Q.*, 1930-31, "Addition au mémoire (10 novembre 1670)," pp. 133-34. Dollier de Casson, *Histoire de Montréal* (Montreal, 1868) pp. 202-03.   *Lettres de la Révérende Mère Marie de l'Incarnation*, II, pp. 529-30.   *Documents Relating to the Colonial History of the State of New York*, "Colbert à Courcelles, 15 mai 1669," E. B. O'Callaghan, ed. (Albany, 1855-58) IX, p. 62.   *Relations*, 1671, p. 3.

6 *R.A.Q.*, 1930-31, "Mémoire du roi, 27 mars 1665," p. 11; "Mémoire de Talon, 1667," p. 64; "Talon à Colbert, 26 août 1667," pp. 76 and 79; "Mémoire succinct, 18 mai 1669," p. 110; "Mémoire de Talon, 10 novembre 1670," p. 127. *Relations*, 1670, p. 2.

7 *R.A.Q.*, 1930-31, "Mémoire de Talon, 10 octobre 1670," p. 120; "10 novembre 1670," p. 129; "9 mars 1673," p. 172; "Addition au mémoire, 1670," p. 132; "Mémoire de Talon, 1673," pp. 175-77.

7a *Ibid.*

8 *Ibid.*, "Mémoire de Talon, 10 novembre 1670," p. 123; "Mémoire de Talon, 2 novembre 1671," p. 159; "Talon à Colbert, 11 novembre 1671," pp. 166-67. C11A, 2, p. 297.   J. E. Roy, *Histoire de la seigneurie de Lauzon* (Lévis, 1897) *passim*.

8a *R.A.Q.*, 1930-31, "Addition au mémoire, 1670," pp. 136-37; cf. Jean Delanglez, *Some La Salle Journeys* (Chicago, 1938).

9 *R.A.Q.*, 1930-31, "Colbert à Talon, 11 février 1671," p. 146; "Addition au mémoire, 1670," p. 136; "Mémoire de Talon, 2 novembre 1671," p. 157; cf. Delanglez, *op. cit.*   Jonathan Pearson, *Early Records of the City and County of*

Albany (Albany, 1869).

10 *R.A.Q.*, 1930-31, "Mémoire de Talon, 2 novembre 1671," pp. 157-58. *Relations*, 1671, pp. 26-8.

11 *R.A.Q.*, 1930-31, "Mémoire de Talon, 2 novembre 1671," p. 158. *Relations*, 1672, pp. 42-57.

12 *Journal des Jésuites*, pp. 286-87. *Collection de manuscrits contenant lettres, mémoires et autres documents historiques relatifs à la Nouvelle-France* (Quebec, 1883-85) I, pp. 254 and 261. Pierre Radisson, *Voyages of Peter Esprit Radisson*, Gideon Scull, ed. (Boston, 1885) pp. 229-32, 235-36 and 240-43; cf. Edwin Ernest Rich, *The History of the Hudson's Bay Company* (London, 1958-60). Grace Lee Nute, *Caesars of the Wilderness: Médard Chouart, Sieur des Groseilliers, and Pierre Esprit Radisson* (New York, 1943) pp. 68, 75 and 81-3.

13 Pierre Radisson, *op. cit.*, pp. 243-45. *Journal*, p. 308. Nute, *op. cit.*, pp. 94-6.

14 C11, A, 6, *Père Nouvel à Frontenac, 5 avril 1673*, pp. 95-6. *Relations*, 1672, p. 50. Nute, *op. cit.*, pp. 113, 117-18, 128-29 and 134-35. Letter of William Young, 20 December 1692, p. 332.

14a Nute, *op. cit.*, p. 114. Letter of William Young, p. 332. *Inventaire des insinuations du Conseil souverain de la Nouvelle-France*, P. G. Roy, ed. (Beauceville, 1921) p. 51. *Reports of the Canadian Archives*, "Dudouyt à Laval (1677)," p. XCIX *ff*.

15 *R.A.Q.*, 1926-27, "Frontenac à Colbert, 13 novembre 1673," p. 50. *Inventaire du Conseil souverain*, p. 51. *R.A.C.*, 1895, "Relations des voyages de Pierre Esprit Radisson," pp. 7-23. *Col. Mss.*, I, pp. 296-97. F3,4, *Ordonnance de M. de La Barre, octobre 1683*, fol. 50. F3, *Ordonnance du Roi, 10 avril 1684*, fol. 105. Nute, *op. cit.*, pp. 144, 153, 186, 200, 213, 216, 219 and 229. Letter of William Young, p. 333.

16 *R.A.Q.*, 1930-31, "Mémoire de Talon, 10 novembre 1670," p. 124. *R.A.Q.*, 1926-27, "Frontenac à Colbert, 14 novembre 1674," pp. 76-7.

17 *Edits et Ord.*, I, "Révocation des concessions non défrichées," p. 33; "Arrêt du 4 juin 1672," pp. 70-1. *Ordonnances*, "Lettres desterrier, 25 mai 1667," p. 81; "Ordonnance du 27 septembre 1673," pp. 117-18. Arch. Col., *Fois et hommages*, I and II; cf. Salone, *op. cit.*, pp. 184-87.

18 *Documents relatifs à la tenure seigneuriale* (Quebec, 1852) *passim;* cf. W. B. Munro, *The Seignorial System in Canada* (New York, 1907) and Marcel Trudel, *Le Régime Seigneurial* (Ottawa, 1956).

18a *Ibid.*

19 *Ibid.*

20 *R.A.Q.*, 1930-31, "Talon à Colbert, 26 août 1667," p. 76; "27 octobre 1667," pp. 80-1; "Le Roi à Talon, 15 mai 1669," p. 101; "Mémoire succinct, 18 mai 1669," p. 116; "Mémoire de Talon, 10 novembre 1670," p. 128; "Talon à Colbert, 2 novembre 1671," p. 155. *Relations*, 1672, p. 1. *R.A.Q.*, 1926-27, p. 57.

21 *R.A.Q.*, 1930-31, "Talon à Colbert, 4 octobre 1665," p. 37; "Colbert à Talon, 5 janvier 1666," p. 46; "Talon à Colbert, 10 novembre 1666," p. 57; "Colbert à Talon, 5 avril 1667," p. 70; "Mémoire de Talon, 10 octobre 1670," p. 120; "10 novembre 1670," p. 126. *Col. Mss.*, I, "Mémoire de La Chesnaye," p. 254.

22 *Recensements du Canada*, IV, p. XVI, gives a population of 6,705 for the following year, 1673.

23 The following sources contributed to this picture of the colony: *R.A.Q.*, 1930-31, "Etat du Canada en 1669," pp. 108-09; *Recensements du Canada*, IV, pp. 10 and 11; cf. also Rochemonteix, *Les Jésuites et la Nouvelle-France au XVIIe siècle* (Paris, 1895-97) II, pp. 395-401.

24 *Relations*, 1672, pp. 2-37. Rochemonteix, *op. cit.*, II, pp. 414-15.

25 B,5, *Estat de la dépense, 11 février 1671*, fol. 18. *R.A.Q.*, 1930-31, "Observations faites par Talon, 1669," pp. 103-08; "Colbert à Talon, 20 février 1668," pp. 91-2; "4 juin 1673," p. 169.

25a F3,2, *Arrêt du Conseil souverain, 20 octobre 1670*, fol. 8.

26 *R.A.Q.*, 1930-31, "Observations faites par Talon, 1669," pp. 103-08. Army pay is not included in this statement.

27 Thomas Chapais, *Jean Talon, Intendant de la Nouvelle-France* (Quebec, 1904) *passim*.

CHAPTER VI

[1] "Remarques sur l'oraison funèbre de feu M. de Frontenac," *Bulletin des recherches historiques*, I, pp. 99-100; cf. W. J. Eccles, *Frontenac the Courtier Governor* (Toronto, 1959).   *Jugements et délibérations du Conseil souverain*, I, p. 689.

[2] *Rapport de l'archiviste de la province de Québec*, 1926-27, "Frontenac au ministre, 2 novembre 1672," pp. 11-12; "Mémoire du roi, 7 avril 1672," pp. 3-10.

[3] *Ibid.*, "Frontenac au ministre, 2 novembre 1672," p. 21; "Colbert à Frontenac, 13 juin 1673," p. 25.

[3a] *Ibid.*, "Frontenac à Colbert, 2 novembre 1672," p. 16.

[4] *Ordonnances, commissions, etc. des gouverneurs et intendants de la Nouvelle-France*, I, "Règlements de police, 23 mars 1673," pp. 130-43.   *R.A.Q.*, 1926-27, "Colbert à Frontenac, 17 mai 1674," p. 56-7.   *Jug. et Dél.*, I, p. 147.   F3,3, *26 octobre 1678*, fol. 75.

[5] *R.A.Q.*, 1927-28, "Colbert à Frontenac, 13 juin 1673," p. 24.

[6] *Jug. et Dél.*, I, pp. 856-57 and 859.

[7] *R.A.Q.*, 1926-27, "Frontenac à Colbert, 2 novembre 1672," pp. 12-16; "13 novembre 1673," pp. 42-3 and 46.

[8] *Ibid.*, "Frontenac à Colbert, 2 novembre 1673," pp. 31-5; "Le Roi à Frontenac, 22 avril 1675," p. 82.   A memorandum of the Abbé d'Urfé, quoted in E. M. Faillon, *Histoire de la Colonie française* (Montreal, 1865-66) III, p. 404.

[9] C11A,4, *Le Père Nouvel à Frontenac, 19 mai 1673*, pp. 3-55.

[10] *R.A.Q.*, 1926-27, "Frontenac à Colbert, 14 novembre 1674," p. 68.

[11] *Ibid.*, "Frontenac à Colbert, 13 novembre 1673," pp. 36-41.

[12] B,4, *Le Roi à Frontenac, 12 juin 1672*, fol. 65½.   *Ordonnances*, I, "Ordonnance, 27 septembre 1672," pp. 73-4.   *Edits et Ordonnances royaux*, I, pp. 73-4.

[13] *R.A.Q.*, 1926-27, "Frontenac à Colbert, 2 novembre 1672," pp. 67-70; 16 février 1674," p. 53; "14 novembre 1674," pp. 68-9.

[14] *Ibid.*, "Frontenac à Colbert, 14 novembre 1674," pp. 67-70.   *Jug. et Dél.*, I, "30 janvier 1674," p. 790 and *passim* to p. 878.

[15] *Jug. et Dél.*, I, "21 août 1674," pp. 817-21 and *passim* to p. 877.   *R.A.Q.*, 1926-27, "Frontenac à Colbert, 14 novembre 1674," pp. 70-3.

[16] *Jug. et Dél.*, I, pp. 837-38 and 870.   *R.A.Q.*, 1926-27, "Frontenac à Colbert, 1673," p. 73; "Le Roi à Frontenac, 22 avril 1675," pp. 81-2; "Colbert à Frontenac, 13 mai 1675," pp. 83-4.   On the proceedings against Perrot and the Abbé Fénelon, see Faillon, *op cit.*, pp. 474-539.

[17] *R.A.Q.*, 1926-27, "Frontenac au ministre, 2 novembre 1672," p. 18; "14 novembre 1674," pp. 76-7.   *Relations inédites*, I, p. 193 *ff;* cf. Jean Delanglez, *Life and Voyages of Louis Jolliet* (Chicago, 1948).   F. B. Steck, *The Jolliet-Marquette Expedition* (Washington, 1927).

[18] *Edits et Ord.*, "Edit de révocation," pp. 74-6; "Articles présentés au roi, 15 avril 1676," pp. 87-9.   Arch. Nat., G7, carton 1312, 76.

[19] *Edits et Ord.*, III, pp. 42-3.

[20] *Ibid.*, "Déclaration du roi, 5 juin 1675," pp. 83-4.   *R.A.Q.*, 1926-27, Frontenac à Colbert, 14 novembre 1674," p. 64.   *Edits et Ord.*, I, "Déclaration du roi, 16 juin 1675," p. 300.

[21] Auguste Gosselin, *Vie de Mgr de Laval* (Quebec, 1890) *passim.*

[22] *Jug. et Dél.*, I, pp. 814-15.   *R.A.Q.*, 1926-27, "Frontenac à Colbert, 12 novembre 1674," p. 68.   Louis-Marie Le Jeune, *Dictionnaire général* (Ottawa, 1931) II, p. 431.

[23] *Jug. et Dél.*, I, pp. 923-24.

CHAPTER VII

[1] *Ordonnances, commissions, etc. des gouverneurs et intendants de la Nouvelle-France*, I, "5 novembre 1674," pp. 171-72.   C11A, 4, *Congé de Frontenac, 29 octobre 1674*, p. 210.   *Edits et ordonnances royaux*, I, "Ordonnance, 15 avril 1676," p. 86; "12 mai 1678," p. 105.   *Rapport de l'archiviste de la province de Québec*, 1926-27, "Colbert à Frontenac, 30 mai 1675," p. 85.

[2] *Ordonnances*, I, "21 juillet 1675," pp. 174-75.

[3] *R.A.Q.*, 1926-27, "Colbert à Frontenac, 18 mai 1677," p. 92.   B,7, *Colbert*

à Duchesneau, 1er mai 1676, fol. 6 ff.   Camille de Rochemonteix, Les Jésuites et la Nouvelle-France au XVIIe siècle (Paris, 1895-97) III, pp. 137-38.   Mandements des Evêques de Québec, I, p. 94.

4 F3,3, Procès-verbal de l'assemblée, 26 octobre 1678, fol. 75 ff.

5 Rochemonteix, op. cit., III, p. 144.   Edits et Ord., I, "Ordonnance, 24 mai 1679," pp. 235-36.   B, 10, Colbert à Mgr de Laval 3 août 1683, fol. 8.   R.A.Q., 1926-27, "Colbert à Frontenac, 26 mai 1679," p. 101.

6 R.A.Q., 1926-27, "Frontenac à Colbert, 14 novembre 1674," p. 68; "9 octobre 1679," p. 103; "Frontenac au roi, 2 novembre 1681," p. 126.   C11A,5, Duchesneau à Colbert, 10 novembre 1679, passim.   Collection de manuscrits contenant lettres, mémoires et autres documents historiques relatifs à la Nouvelle-France, I, "Différence des traites (1689)," p. 476.

7 C11A,5, Duchesneau à Colbert, 10 novembre 1679, pp. 40-64 passim; "13 novembre 1680," pp. 144-79.   R.A.Q., 1926-27, "Mémoire, 1681," pp. 120-24; "Frontenac à Seignelay, 2 novembre 1681," pp. 134-35; "Frontenac à Bellefonds, 14 novembre 1680," pp. 122-23; "Colbert à Frontenac, 20 avril 1680," pp. 112-13. C11A,5, Le Roi à Frontenac, 30 avril 1681," p. 348 ff.

8 Jugements et délibérations du Conseil souverain, II, pp. 441-45, 547-48, 564-79 and 597.

9 Edits et Ord., I, "Amnistie, mai 1681," pp. 248-49.   F3,4, Ordonnance, 2 mai 1681, fol. 10.

10 Louis Armand d'Arce, baron de La Hontan, Nouveaux voyages de M. le baron de Lahontan dans l'Amérique Septentrionale (The Hague, 1703) pp. 71-4 and 79-80.

11 C11A,5, Duchesneau à Colbert, 1680, fol. 161; Mémoire à Colbert, fol. 329. Ordonnances, I, "Ordonnance de Frontenac, 6 septembre 1681," pp. 296-98; "Ordonnance de Duchesneau, 8 mai 1682," pp. 312-13; "Ordonnance de La Barre, 1er octobre 1682," pp. 323-24.   F3,6, Arrêt du Conseil d'Etat, 19 mai 1703, fol. 334; Déclaration du roi, juin 1703, fol. 335.

12 R.A.Q., 1926-27, "Colbert à Frontenac, 18 mai 1677," p. 92.   B,8, Colbert à Duchesneau, 8 mai 1679, fol. 13½.

13 Edits et Ord., I, "Déclaration du roi, 5 juin 1675," p. 84.   Jug. et Dél., II, pp. 277, 310 and 319.   R.A.Q., 1926-27, "Le Roi à Frontenac, 29 avril 1680," pp. 114-16.   F3, 3, Arrêt du Conseil d'Etat, 28 mai 1680, fol. 354.

14 R.A.Q., 1926-27, "Frontenac à Colbert, 9 octobre 1679," p. 102.   Mémoires et documents pour servir à l'histoire des origines françaises des pays d'Outre-Mer, Pierre Margry, ed. (Paris, 1879-88) I, pp. 585 and 592.   C11A, 5, Frontenac au roi, 2 novembre 1681, p. 377 ff; Mémoire de Duchesneau, 13 novembre 1681, p. 301 ff.   R.A.Q., 1926-27, "Frontenac au roi, 2 novembre 1681," p. 131; "Mémoire de Frontenac, 12 septembre 1682," pp. 141-43.

15 C11A, 6, Extrait des avis donnés à la conférence tenue chez les RR. PP. Jésuites, 23 mars 1682, pp. 52-66; Harangue des Outaouais, 13 avril 1682, pp. 4-25; Paroles de Teganisorens, 11 septembre 1683, pp. 26-32; Réponses de Frontenac, 12 septembre 1682, pp. 33-43.

16 Recensements du Canada, IV, p. XVII (Census taken early in 1683).

17 Pièces et documents relatifs à la tenure seigneuriale, passim.   Emil Salone, La Colonisation de la Nouvelle-France (Paris, 1906) pp. 233-37.

18 C11A, 6, De Meulles à Colbert, 4 novembre 1683, fol. 181 ff.   La Hontan, op. cit., I, pp. 9-10.   Recensements, IV, pp. 13-14.

19 C11A, 6, De Meulles au ministre, 12 novembre 1682, p. 139 ff.

20 R.A.Q., 1926-27, "Le Roi à Frontenac, 9 mai 1682," p. 141.   B,9, Le Roi à Duchesneau, 9 mai 1682, fol. 30 v.

21 C11A, 6, La Barre au ministre, 1682, p. 75; La Barre au roi, 1682, p. 97.

22 R.A.Q., 1926-27, "Frontenac à Colbert, 14 novembre 1674," p. 78.   Mémoires et Documents, I, pp. 280, 291-98, 382, 435 and 575.   F3,3, Arrêt du 13 mai 1675, fol. 396.

23 F3,3, 12 mai 1678, fol. 41.   Biblio. Nat., Mémoire de Tonty.   Mémoires et Documents, pp. 287, 449, 562 and 579 ff.

24 Mémoires et Documents, I, "Relation de Nicolas de La Salle," p. 562 ff.

25 Ibid., I, p. 444; II, pp. 336-37; III, p. 92 ff.   C11A, 6, Mémoire à Seignelay, 1684, pp. 400-08.   B,11, Seignelay à La Barre, 14 avril 1684.

26 Mémoires et Documents, I, p. 562 ff; III, p. 92 ff.

CHAPTER VIII

1 *Edits et ordonnances royaux*, III, "Provisions du gouverneur pour le Sieur de La Barre, 1er mai 1682," pp. 44-5.   Louis-Marie Le Jeune, *Dictionnaire général* (Ottawa, 1931) II, p. 690.

2 Le Jeune, *op. cit.*, II, p. 269.   B,9, *Instruction du roi à M. de Meulles, 10 mai 1682*, fol. 15.   C11A, 6, *De Meulles au ministre, 6 octobre 1682*, p. 107 *ff*.

3 C11A,6, *Procès-verbal de l'assemblée, 10 octobre 1682*, pp. 101-05.

4 *Ibid.*, *Extrait des résumés des lettres de M. de La Barre, 4 octobre et 12 novembre 1682*, pp. 111-13; *La Barre au roi, 30 mai 1683*.   B, 10, *Le Roi à La Barre, 2 août 1683*, fol. 1 *ff*.

5 C11A,6, *La Barre au ministre, passim; 4 novembre 1683*, pp. 222-53; *De Meulles au ministre, 4 novembre 1683*, pp. 273-81; *Mémoire de Messieurs les Intéressés, 1683*, p. 351-56.   Arch. Can. Corr. Off., *Mémoire de La Salle, 1684*, pp. 400-08.   *Mémoires et documents pour servir à histoire des origines françaises des pays d'Outre-Mer*, Pierre Margry, ed. (Paris, 1879-88) II, pp. 336-37; "Relation de Tonty," p. 614.

6 Bacqueville de La Potherie, *Histoire de l'Amérique Septentrionale* (Paris, 1922) II, pp. 147 *ff* and 166 *ff*; cf. Nicolas Perrot, *Mémoires*, Ch. XXII.   C11A, 6, *La Barre au ministre, 4 novembre 1683*, pp. 222-53; *Du Luth à La Barre, 12 avril 1684*, p. 372 *ff*.

7 C11A, 6, *La Barre au Ministre, 4 novembre 1683*, p. 54 *ff*.   François Vachon de Belmont, *Histoire du Canada* (Quebec, 1840) pp. 15-16.

8 *Mémoires et Documents*, "Relation d'un voyage, 8 mai 1684," pp. 342-43. C11A,6, *La Barre à Seignelay, 5 juin 1684*, p. 445 *ff*.

9 C11A, 6, *La Barre à Seignelay, 5 juin 1684*, p. 445 *ff*; *De Meulles à Seignelay, 12 juillet 1684*, pp. 99-112; *R. P. Lamberville au gouverneur, 10 février 1684*, pp. 327-28; *R. P. Lamberville au gouverneur, 17 août 1684*, pp. 336-68; *La Barre au Colonel Dongan, 15 juin 1684*, p. 434; *La Barre au roi, 9 juillet 1684*, p. 460; *Dongan à La Barre, 25 juin 1684*, p. 436.

10 C11A,6, (2), *Mémoire de La Barre, 1er octobre 1684*, pp. 9-22.

11 C11A,6, (2), *R. P. Lamberville à La Barre, 28 août 1684*, pp. 369-73; *Mémoire de La Barre, 1er octobre 1684*, pp. 9-22; *De Meulles à Seignelay, 10 octobre 1684*, pp. 116-30.   Louis Armand d'Arce, baron de La Hontan, *Nouveaux voyages de M. le baron de Lahontan dans l'Amérique Septentrionale* (The Hague, 1703) pp. 46-63.

12 C11A,6, (2), *De Meulles à Seignelay, 10 octobre 1684*, pp. 116-30; *R. P. Lamberville à La Barre, 9 octobre 1684*, pp. 378-83.

13 B,11, *Seignelay à La Barre, 14 avril 1684*, fol. 37 v.

14 *Lettres, instructions et mémoires de Colbert*, Pierre Clément, ed. (Paris, 1861-73) III (2), "Colbert à Duchesneau, 15 mars 1678," p. 634.   C11A,5, *Duchesneau à Colbert, 13 novembre 1680*, fol. 161 *ff*; *Duchesneau à Colbert, 13 novembre 1681*, p. 290 *ff*.   *Edits et Ord.*, I, "Edit du roi, mai 1679," pp. 231-32. C11A,6, (2), *La Barre au roi, 15 novembre 1684*, p. 40 *ff*.   *Rapport de l'archiviste de la province de Québec*, 1926-27, "Frontenac à Colbert, 6 novembre 1679," p. 110.   B, 11, *Seignelay à Mgr de Laval, 18 avril 1684*, fol. 34; cf. Bertrand de la Tour, *Mémoires sur la vie de Mgr de Laval* (Cologne, 1761) and Auguste Gosselin, *Vie de Mgr de Laval* (Quebec, 1890).

15 B,11, *Le Roi à La Barre, 10 mars 1685*, fol. 6.   B, 10, *Ordre du roi pour interdire le Sieur Perrot, 6 août 1684*, fol. 4.

CHAPTER IX

1 *Edits et ordonnances royaux*, III, "Provisions de gouverneur, 1er janvier 1685," pp. 48-9.   Louis-Marie Le Jeune, *Dictionnaire général* (Ottawa, 1931) I, pp. 486-87.   C11A,10, *Mémoire instructif, 30 octobre 1688*, pp. 160-62.

2 B,11, *Instructions du roi, 10 mars 1685*, fol. 6½ *ff*.   C11A,7, *Denonville à Seignelay, 13 novembre 1685*, fol. 86 *ff*.

3 C11A,7, *Callières à Seignelay, 25 février 1685*, pp. 1-12.

4 *Edits et Ord.*, I, "Traité de neutralité, 16 novembre 1686," p. 257. *Documents Relating to the Colonial History of the State of New York*, IX, "Don-

gan à Denonville, 13 octobre 1685," p. 292.   C¹¹A,9, *Mémoire pour Seignelay,* *janvier 1687,* pp. 306-14.

    5 Arch. Col., B,8, *Mémoire du roi, 30 mars 1687,* p. 84½ *ff.*   C¹¹A,9, *Denonville à Seignelay, 12 juin 1686,* pp. 129-45; *Denonville à La Durantaye et à Du Luth et à La Forêt, 6 juin 1686,* pp. 114-28.

    6 C¹¹A,7, *Contrat de concessions, 1685,* p. 308; *Mémoire des Intéressés, 6 février 1685,* pp. 315-19.   C¹¹A,8, *Instruction pour de Troyes, 12 février 1686,* p. 7 *ff; Ordre de Denonville, 12 février 1686,* pp. 154-57; cf. Grace Lee Nute, *Caesars of the Wilderness: Médard Chouart, Sieur des Groseilliers, and Pierre Esprit Radisson* (New York, 1943) and P. Radisson, *Voyages of Radisson* (Boston, 1885).

    7 C¹¹A,9, *Nouvelles de ce qui a été fait par les Français dans la Baie d'Hudson,* pp. 69-98.   *Journal de l'expédition du Chevalier de Troyes à la Baie d'Hudson,* Ivanhoé Caron, ed. (Beauceville, 1918) *passim.* See also Guy Frégault, *Iberville, le conquérant* (Montreal, 1944), the best documented work on the subject.

    8 B,9, *Instruction du roi à M. de Meulles, 10 mars 1682,* fol. 15 *ff.   Edits et Ord.,* I, "Pouvoir à Frontenac et Duchesneau pour donner des concessions, 20 mai 1676," p. 89; "Arrêt portant confirmation des concessions, 17 septembre 1683," p. 251; "Arrêt défendant de saisir les bestiaux, 10 novembre 1683," p. 250.

    9 *Ordonnances, commissions, etc. des gouverneurs et intendants de la Nouvelle-France,* II, "Ordonnances de M. de Meulles au sujet du chanvre, 24 août 1685," pp. 121-22.

    10 C¹¹A,6, (2), *Mémoire de de Meulles à Seignelay, 12 novembre 1684,* p. 140 *ff.   Ordonnances,* II, "Ordonnance de de Meulles, 24 avril 1685," p. 96; "Ordonnances de de Meulles, 15 mai 1685," p. 104.

    11 C¹¹A,7, *Denonville à Seignelay, 13 novembre 1685,* p. 35 *ff.*

    12 C¹¹A,7, *De Meulles à Seignelay, 28 septembre 1685,* p. 131 *ff.*

    12a C¹¹A,7, *Castors venus du Canada,* p. 115.

    13 C¹¹A,6, *De Meulles au ministre, 12 novembre 1682,* fol. 81.   Emile Salone, *La Colonisation de la Nouvelle-France* (Paris, 1906) pp. 262-63.

    14 *Ordonnances,* II, "Ordonnance de M. de Meulles qui établit une monnaie de cartes, 8 juin 1685," pp. 112-14; "Ordonnance de M. de Meulles annonçant le remboursement en argent des billets de cartes, 6 septembre 1685," p. 125. C¹¹A,7, *De Meulles à Seignelay, 24 septembre 1685,* p. 116 *ff.*

    15 C¹¹A,8, *De Meulles au roi, 18 juillet 1685,* pp. 307-09; *De Meulles à Seignelay, 19 juillet 1685,* pp. 310-15.

    16 C¹¹A,7, *Denonville à Seignelay, 13 novembre 1685,* p. 88 *ff.* (Two letters). B,12, *Seignelay à de Meulles, 31 mai 1686,* fol. 22½.   Louis Armand d'Arce, baron de La Hontan, *Nouveaux voyages de M. le baron de Lahontan dans l'Amérique Septentrionale* (The Hague, 1703) I, pp. 82-3.

CHAPTER X

    1 Auguste Gosselin, *Vie de Mgr de Laval* (Quebec, 1850) II.   Bertrand de la Tour, *Mémoire sur la vie de Mgr de Laval* (Cologne, 1761).   Camille de Rochemonteix, *Les Jésuites et la Nouvelle-France au XVIIᵉ siècle* (Paris, 1895-97) III, pp. 306-08.

    2 C¹¹A,7, *Denonville à Seignelay, 13 novembre 1685,* p. 35 *ff; Champigny à Seignelay, 26 août 1687,* fol. 241-42.   *Ordonnances, commissions, etc. des gouverneurs et intendants de la Nouvelle-France,* II, "Ordonnance de La Barre pour réprimer l'abus des boissons, 28 septembre 1684," p. 77.   C¹¹A,7, *Mémoire de Denonville, 16 novembre 1685,* p. 42 *ff.*

    3 C¹¹A,9, *Denonville et Champigny à Seignelay, 6 novembre 1687,* p. 2 *ff.*

    4 *Mandements des Evêques de Québec,* "Mandement de Mgr de Laval, 26 février 1682," pp. 116-18; "Ordonnance de Mgr de Saint-Vallier, 31 octobre 1690," pp. 267-70.   Louis Armand d'Arce, baron de La Hontan, *Nouveaux Voyages de M. le baron de Lahontan dans l'Amérique Septentrionale* (The Hague, 1703) I, pp. 67-9.

    5 *Ordonnances,* II, "Arrêt du Conseil d'Etat, 15 avril 1684"; "Ordonnance de M. de Meulles, 6 octobre 1684," p. 83.

    6 Arch. Séminaire de Saint-Sulpice, Paris, *Documents pour servir à l'histoire*

de l'Eglise du Canada, I, 1674-1760.   *Mémoire dressé par un missionnaire de Saint-Sulpice établi à Montréal* (1684?).

[7] Eccles, W. J. *Jean Bochart de Champigny* (McGill University, 1952; unpublished thesis).

[8] C11A,9, *Denonville à Dongan, 22 août 1687,* pp. 61-3; *2 octobre 1687,* pp. 146-51.   C11A,8, *Denonville à Seignelay, 8 mai 1686,* p. 369 *ff; 16 novembre 1686,* p. 276 *ff.*   C11A,9, *Denonville à Seignelay, 8 juin 1687,* p. 31 *ff.*

[9] *Documents Relating to the Colonial History of the State of New York,* IX, "Commission of Major Gregory, December 4, 1686," pp. 318-19.   La Hontan, *op. cit.,* I, p. 115.   C11A,9, *Denonville à Seignelay, 8 juin 1687,* p. 31; *Dongan à Denonville, 9 septembre 1687,* pp. 126-38; *Prise de possession, 7 juin 1687,* pp. 267-68; *Champigny à Seignelay, 16 juillet 1687,* pp. 51-60.   François Vachon de Belmont, *Histoire du Canada* (Quebec, 1840) p. 19.   B,14, *Seignelay à Denonville, 23 juin 1687,* fol. 66½.

[10] C11A,9, *Denonville à Seignelay, 8 juin 1687,* pp. 51-60.   F3,4, *Mandement des grands vicaires, 24 avril 1687,* fol. 288; *Déclaration de Denonville, 3 mai 1687,* fol. 290.

[11] C11A,9, *Champigny à Seignelay, 16 juillet 1687,* pp. 51-60.

[12] *Ibid., Mémoire du voyage pour l'entreprise de M. de Denonville, octobre 1687,* p. 161.   *Collection de manuscrits contenant lettres, mémoires et autres documents historiques relatifs à la Nouvelle-France,* I, "Mémoire sur le Canada (1682-1712),*"* p. 559.   Belmont, *op. cit.,* p. 20.   La Hontan, *op. cit.,* pp. 110-12.   H. Lorin, *Le Comte de Frontenac* (Paris, 1895) pp. 331-32.   "Jean de Lamberville à un missionnaire, 23 juin 1695," in Rochemonteix, *Les Jésuites et la Nouvelle-France au XVIIe siècle,* III, p. 163 *ff.*

[13] B,11, *Le Roi à La Barre, 31 juillet 1684,* fol. 40½.   B,13, *Mémoire du roi, 30 mars 1687,* fol. 16¼.   B,15, *Seignelay à Denonville, 8 mars 1688,* pp. 33-9.   Belmont, *op. cit.,* p. 20.

[14] C11A,9, *Mémoire du voyage pour l'entreprise de M. de Denonville, octobre 1687,* pp. 161-98.   Le Chevalier de Baugy, *Journal d'une expédition contre les Iroquois en 1687* (Paris, 1883).

[15] C11A,9, *Mémoire,* pp. 161-98; *Denonville à Seignelay, 27 octobre 1687,* p. 199.   La Hontan, *op. cit.,* pp. 115-23.   Belmont, *op. cit.,* pp. 21-4.   Baugy, *op. cit.*

[16] *Ibid.*

[17] *Docts. N.Y.,* IX, "Prise de possession des terres des Tsounontouans, 19 juillet 1687," p. 354; "Prise de possession de Niagara, 31 juillet 1687," pp. 335-36.   C11A,9, *Mémoire de l'Etat présent des affaires du Canada, 27 octobre 1687,* p. 199 *ff.*   La Hontan, *op. cit.,* I, pp. 123-24.

[18] J. B. Ferland, *Cours d'histoire du Canada* (Quebec, 1861-65) II, p. 167.   Belmont, *op. cit.,* p. 25.

[19] C11A,9, *Mémoire,* p. 199 *ff.*   C11A, 10, *Relation des événements, 30 octobre 1688,* pp. 147-62.   Lamberville, "Récit d'un combat naval, 14 septembre 1687," in Rochemonteix, *op. cit.,* III, p. 621 *ff.*

[20] *Docts. N.Y.,* IX, "Callières à Seignelay, novembre 1687," p. 369.   *Ordonnances,* II, "Ordonnance, 15 juin 1687," pp. 163-64; "Ordonnance, 1er septembre 1687," pp. 166-68.

[21] C11A,10, *Relation des événements, 30 octobre 1688,* p. 142 *ff; Andros à Denonville, 21 août 1688,* pp. 128-29.   *Docts. N.Y.,* IX, "Callières à Seignelay," p. 402; "Projet du chevalier de Callières, janvier 1689," p. 404.   B,15, *Mémoire du roi, 1er mai 1689,* fol. 27 *ff.*

[22] Biblio. Nat. (Paris), Coll. Clairambault, 1016, *Callières à Seignelay, janvier 1689,* fol. 290.   C11A,10, *Relation, 30 octobre 1688,* pp. 147-62; *Propositions de paix des Iroquois, 15 juin 1688,* pp. 86-8.

[23] C11A,10, *Relation, 30 octobre 1688,* pp. 147-62; *Etat du fort du Niagara en 1688, 16 septembre 1688,* pp. 138-41.   La Hontan, *op. cit.,* I, pp. 170-71.

[24] C11A,10, *Champigny au ministre, 8 avril 1688,* p. 204.   *Mémoire de Denonville à Seignelay, 10 août 1688,* p. 105 *ff.*

[25] Belmont, *op. cit.,* p. 29.   La Hontan, *op. cit.,* I, pp. 169-70.

[26] La Hontan, *op. cit.,* I, pp. 165-71.   Belmont, *op. cit.,* p. 29.   C11A,10, *Mémoire de l'Etat présent des affaires de ce pays, 6 novembre 1688,* p. 174 *ff.*   Biblio. Nat., Coll. Clairambault, 1016, *Callières à Seignelay, janvier 1689,* fol. 290.

27 C11A,10, *Prise de possession par Nicolas Perrot, 8 mai 1689*, pp. 345-47; *Relation de ce qui s'est passé à la Baie du Nord, envoyée par le Sieur Patu, 14 novembre 1689*, p. 480 ff.

28 C11A,10, *Extrait des observations sur l'Etat présent des affaires, 1689*, p. 535 ff. La Hontan, *op. cit.*, I, p. 271. Belmont, *op. cit.*, pp. 29-30. Bacqueville de La Potherie, *Histoire de l'Amerique Septentrionale* (Paris, 1922) II, p. 228; III, p. 58. Biblio. Nat., Coll. Clairambault, 1016, *Lettre de Tonty, octobre 1689*, fol. 290 ff. C11A,10, *Frontenac à Seignelay, 15 novembre 1689*, p. 351 ff; *Champigny à Seignelay, 16 novembre 1689*, p. 389 ff.

29 F3,2, *Receuil de ce qui s'est passé au Canada au sujet de la guerre*, fol. 104-20. La Hontan, *op. cit.*, I, pp. 271-74. C11A,10, *Observations sur l'Etat des affaires du Canada, 1689*, p. 345.

29a *Ibid.*

30 Belmont, *op. cit.*, p. 31. C11A,10, *Denonville à Valrenne, 24 septembre 1689*, p. 326 ff.

31 C11A,9, *Mémoire de l'Etat présent des affaires du Canada, 27 octobre 1687*, fol. 143-44. B,15, *Mémoire du roi à Denonville et Champigny, 1er mai 1689*, fol. 47. Eccles, *op. cit.*, p. 199. B,15, *Le Roi à Denonville, 31 mai 1689*, fol. 75.

CHAPTER XI

1 *Edits et ordonnances royaux*, III, "Provisions de gouverneur, 15 mai 1689," pp. 52-3. *Rapport de l'archiviste de la province de Québec, 1927-28*, "Instructions pour le comte de Frontenac, 7 juin 1689," pp. 3-4, 6 and 9.

2 *R.A.Q.*, 1930-31, "Talon à Colbert, 27 octobre 1667," p. 77. *Collection de manuscrits contenant lettres, mémoires et autres documents historiques relatifs à la Nouvelle-France*, I, "Rapport de Duchesneau, 13 novembre 1681," p. 285.

2a C11A,10, *Projet du chevalier de Callières, janvier 1689*, p. 416-29. *R.A.Q.*, 1927-28, "Mémoire pour servir d'instruction à Monsieur le Comte de Frontenac, 7 juin 1689," pp. 12-16; "Frontenac à Seignelay, 15 novembre 1689," pp. 17-18. W. J. Eccles, *Frontenac, the Courtier Governor* (Toronto, 1959).

3 Louis Armand d'Arce, baron de La Hontan, *Nouveaux voyages de M. le baron de Lahontan dans l'Amérique Septentrionale* (The Hague, 1703) I, pp. 280-86.

4 *R.A.Q.*, 1927-28, "Frontenac au ministre, 15 novembre 1689," pp. 19-21. *Col. Mss.*, I, "Relation de ce qui s'est passé de plus remarquable au Canada par Monseignat, 1689-90," pp. 482-83.

5 *R.A.Q.*, 1927-28, "Frontenac à Seignelay, 17 novembre 1689," p. 24.

6 *Col. Mss.*, I, "Relation de Monseignat," pp. 488-92.

7 *Ibid.*, pp. 496-97.

8 *Ibid.*, pp. 497-500.

9 *Ibid.*, pp. 485-88 and 488-95. *R.A.Q.*, 1927-28, "Frontenac à Seignelay, 12 novembre 1690," pp. 44-5.

10 *Col. Mss.*, I, "Relation de Monseignat," pp. 501-02 and 507.

11 *Ibid.*, pp. 482-83. *R.A.Q.*, 1927-28, "Frontenac à Seignelay, 12 novembre 1690," p. 36.

12 *Ibid.*, "Frontenac à Seignelay, 30 avril 1690," pp. 29-30; "12 novembre 1690," pp. 190-93; "Remarques faites par l'intendant," pp. 194-96.

13 *Col. Mss.*, I, "Relation de Monseignat," pp. 495-96. *R.A.Q.*, 1927-28, "Frontenac à Seignelay, 12 novembre 1690," p. 36.

14 *Ibid. Col. Mss.*, I, "Relation de Monseignat," p. 508. Bacqueville de La Potherie, *Histoire de l'Amérique Septentrionale* (Paris, 1922) II, pp. 235-47.

15 *Col. Mss.*, "Relation de Monseignat," pp. 507-09. *R.A.Q.*, 1927-28, "Frontenac à Seignelay, 12 novembre 1690," pp. 38-9.

16 *Ibid.*

17 *Col. Mss.*, I, "Relation de Monseignat," pp. 512-15.

18 *R.A.Q.*, 1927-28, "Frontenac à Seignelay, 12 novembre 1690," p. 41. *Documents Relating to the Colonial History of the State of New York*, II, "Journal of Captain John Schuyler," p. 285; IV, "Major General Winthrop's Journal," pp. 195-96. *Report of the Canadian Archives*, 1912, Appendix G, "Letter from

Captain Nicholson, November 4, 1690," p. 77.

[19] *Col. Mss.,* I, "Relation de Monseignat," pp. 507 and 615-19; "Mémoire pour 1690," p. 577.   A letter from Father de Couvert in Ernest Myrand, *Sir William Phipps Before Quebec* (Quebec, 1893) p. 117.   *Annales de l'Hôtel-Dieu,* p. 252.   *Les Ursulines de Québec depuis leur établissement jusqu'à nos jours* (Quebec, 1863-66) I, p. 372.   *R.A.Q.,* 1927-28, "Frontenac au ministre, 12 novembre 1690," pp. 39-40.   La Hontan, *op. cit.,* I, pp. 296-98.

[20] *Col. Mss.,* I, "Relation de Monseignat," p. 519.   Louis-Marie Le Jeune, *Dictionnaire général* (Ottawa, 1931) II, pp. 439-40.

[21] Le Jeune, *op. cit.,* pp. 520-22.   La Hontan, *op. cit.,* I, pp. 299-302. *Les Annales de l'Hôtel-Dieu,* p. 250.

[22] *Col. Mss.,* I, "Relation de Monseignat," p. 552 *ff;* "Mémoire de ce qui s'est passé à la descente des Anglais devant Québec (Champigny) janvier 1691," fol. 343 *ff.*   Thomas Hutchinson, *The History of the Colony of Massachusetts Bay* (London, 1765) II, pp. 470-78.   Myrand, *op. cit.*   Eccles, *op. cit.,* pp. 234-41.

[23] *Ibid.*

[24] *Ibid.*

[25] *Col. Mss.,* I, "Relation de Monseignat," pp. 526-27.   *R.A.Q.,* 1927-28, "Frontenac à Seignelay, 12 novembre 1690," pp. 41-2.   *Docts. N.Y.,* III, "Governor Slaughter to Lord Nottingham, May 6, 1691," p. 761.   Letters of Father de Couvert in Myrand, *op. cit.,* p. 117.   Eccles, *op. cit.,* pp. 240-41.

[26] *Col. Mss.,* I, "Relation de Monseignat," p. 530.   *R.A.Q.,* 1927-28, "Frontenac à Seignelay, 12 novembre 1690," p. 43; "Mémoire du roi à Frontenac et à Champigny, 7 avril 1691," pp. 50 and 53.

[27] *R.A.Q.,* 1927-28, "Frontenac à Seignelay, 12 novembre 1690," p. 43. C11A,11, *Relation de ce qui s'est passé de plus considérable . . . depuis le 27 novembre 1690, etc.,* p. 344 *ff.*

[27a] *Ibid.*

CHAPTER XII

[1] C11A,11, *Relation de ce qui s'est passé de plus considérable au Canada depuis le départ de la Frégate Fleur-de-May, le 27 novembre 1690 jusqu'au départ de 1691,* p. 100 *ff.*   *Collection de manuscrits contenant lettres, mémoires et autres documents historiques relatifs à la Nouvelle-France,* I, "Mémoire sur le Canada (1682-1712)," p. 579.   W. J. Eccles, *Frontenac, the Courtier Governor* (Toronto, 1959) p. 252.

[2] C11A,11, *Relation de ce qui s'est passé de plus considérable . . . depuis le 27 novembre 1690, etc.,* p. 100 *ff.*   *Rapport de l'archiviste de la province de Québec,* 1927-28, "Frontenac à Seignelay, 12 novembre 1690," pp. 43-4 and 47.

[3] C11A,11, *Relation. . . .* p. 100 *ff.*

[4] *Ibid.,* pp. 100 *ff* and 442.

[5] *Col. Mss.,* I, "Mémoire sur le Canada," p. 580.

[6] *Ibid.,* pp. 580-86.   C11A,11, *Relation. . . .* p. 100 *ff;* Bénac, *Relation des actions . . . en cette campagne, 2 septembre 1691,* p. 552 *ff.*

[7] *Col. Mss.,* I, pp. 586-88.   *R.A.Q.,* 1927-28, "Frontenac à Seignelay, 20 octobre 1691," p. 70.

[8] C11A,11, Bénac, *Relation des actions . . . en cette campagne, 8 septembre 1691,* p. 552 *ff.*

[9] *Col. Mss.,* I, p. 569.   C11A,11, *Relation. . . .* p. 100 *ff.*   *R.A.Q.,* 1927-28, "Frontenac au ministre, 20 octobre 1691," pp. 72-4; "Le Ministre à Frontenac, avril 1692," p. 102.   C11A,11, *Champigny à Seignelay, 10 mai 1691.*

[10] C11A,12, Champigny, *Relation de ce qui s'est passé en Canada de novembre 1691 jusqu'au mois d'octobre 1692,* pp. 152-65.

[11] *Col. Mss.,* I, "Mémoire sur le Canada (1682-1712)," p. 591.   *R.A.Q.,* 1927-28, "Frontenac à Pontchartrain, 25 octobre 1693," p. 155; "Pontchartrain à Frontenac, 23 juillet 1692," pp. 103-04.

[12] *R.A.Q.,* 1927-28, "Mémoire du Gouverneur de Frontenac, 17 février 1692," p. 118.

[13] C11A,12, (1), *Relation de ce qui s'est passé au Canada depuis le mois de septembre 1692 jusqu'au départ des vaisseaux en 1693,* p. 358 *ff.*   *Documents*

Relating to the Colonial History of the State of New York, III, "Answer of the Five Nations, June 6, 1692," pp. 842-44.

14 F3, 5, *Relations des faits héroiques de Mademoiselle Madeleine de Verchères contre les Iroquois en l'année 1692,* fol. 427.

15 *R.A.Q.,* 1927-28, "Frontenac à Pontchartrain, 15 septembre 1692," pp. 115-16.   C11A,12, (1), *Relation de ce qui s'est passé au Canada, 1692-1693,* p. 358 *ff.*

16 *Ibid.   R.A.Q.,* 1927-28, "Frontenac à Pontchartrain, 25 octobre 1693," p. 159.   *Docts. N.Y.,* IV, "Schuyler's report, February 1692," pp. 16-19.

17 C11A,12, (1), *Relation de ce qui s'est passé au Canada, 1692-1693,* pp. 358-420.   *R.A.Q.,* 1927-28, "Frontenac et Champigny à Pontchartrain, 4 novembre 1693," pp. 167-68.

18 *Ibid.,* pp. 171-72.

19 *Ibid.,* "Frontenac à Pontchartrain, 25 octobre 1693," p. 159.   C11A,12, (1), *Relation de ce qui s'est passé au Canada, 1692-1693,* pp. 358-420.

20 *Ibid.*

21 C11A,13, *Callières au ministre, 19 octobre 1694,* pp. 118-35.   *Col. Mss.,* I, "Mémoire sur le Canada (1682-1712)," pp. 594-95.   C11A,13, *Députations et colliers des Iroquois pour la paix (Lamothe-Cadillac),* pp. 181-86; cf. *Docts. N.Y.,* IX, pp. 577-84.

22 C11A,13, *loc. cit.   Docts. N.Y.,* IV, "Fletcher's Address to the Five Nations, July 4, 1693," p. 40-3; "Answer to the Five Nations," p. 42.

23 C11A, 14, *Relation de ce qui s'est passé de plus remarquable en Canada depuis le mois de septembre 1694 jusqu'au départ de 1695,* p. 94 *ff.*   F3, 5, *Relation de Champigny de ce qui s'est passé en Canada au sujet de la guerre depuis le départ des vaisseaux en l'année 1694 jusqu'au mois de novembre 1695,* fol. 361.   C11A, 14, *Mémoire sur le Canada,* pp. 308-13.

24 *R.A.Q.,* 1927-28, "Pontchartrain à Frontenac, avril 1692," p. 100; "Frontenac à Lagny, 2 novembre 1695," pp. 371-92; "Mémoire de Champigny, 6 novembre 1695," p. 32 *ff;* "Callières au ministre, 27 octobre 1695," p. 449 *ff.*   W. J. Eccles, *Frontenac, the Courtier Governor* (Toronto, 1959) pp. 262-63.

25 C11A,14, *Relation de ce qui s'est passé . . . jusqu'au départ de 1695,* pp. 94-112; *Champigny à Pontchartrain, 18 août 1696,* pp. 279-85; cf. Eccles, *op. cit.,* p. 265.   B,17, *Articles et conditions que le roi accorde au Sieur d'Iberville, 1694,* fol. 35½; *Mémoire du roi à Frontenac et Champigny, 7 avril 1694,* fol. 28½.

26 C11A,14, *Relation par d'Iberville de l'expédition et prise du fort Nelson, 13 octobre 1695,* pp. 481-85; *Articles de la capitulation entre Guillaume Allen et le Sieur de la Forest, 31 août 1696,* pp. 27-8; cf. Guy Frégault, *Iberville, le conquérant* (Montreal, 1944).

27 *R.A.Q.,* 1928-29, "Frontenac et Champigny à Pontchartrain, 26 octobre 1695," p. 320.   C11A,14, *Relation de ce qui s'est passé de plus remarquable depuis le départ des vaisseaux de 1695 jusqu'au commencement de novembre 1696,* pp. 38-93; *Callières à Pontchartrain, 20 octobre 1698,* pp. 315-39.   *Col. Mss.,* I, "Mémoire sur le Canada (1682-1712)," pp. 598-600.

28 *Ibid.*

29 *Ibid.*

CHAPTER XIII

1 *Documents Relating to the Colonial History of the State of New York,* IV, "Fletcher to Council, August 7, 1696," pp. 175-76; "Meeting of the Sachems of the Five Nations, September 29 and October 1, 1696," p. 235 *ff.*   W. J. Eccles, *Frontenac, the Courtier Governor* (Toronto, 1959) p. 268.

2 *Rapport de l'archiviste de la province de Québec,* 1928-29, "Frontenac à Pontchartrain, 15 octobre 1697," pp. 340-41.   C11A,15, *Champigny à Pontchartrain, 26 août 1697,* fol. 107.   F3,6, *Relation de ce qui s'est passé de plus remarquable depuis le départ des vaisseaux en 1696 jusqu'au 15 octobre 1697,* p. 1 *ff.*

3 C11A,15, *Champigny à Pontchartrain, 26 août 1697,* fol. 107.

4 F3, 6, *Relation de ce qui s'est passé . . . 1696 . . . 1697,* p. 1 *ff.*

5 B,19, *Instruction à M. de Nesmond, 21 avril 1697,* fol. 201½; *Pontchartrain à M. de Nesmond, 15 juin 1697,* fol. 267½.   *R.A.Q.,* 1928-29, "Le Roi à Frontenac, 21 avril 1697," p. 327; "Frontenac à Pontchartrain, 15 octobre 1697," p. 339.

6 B,19, *Instruction pour le Sieur d'Iberville, 9 mars 1697,* fol. 102.

[7] Arch. Québec, *Manuscrits de la Nouvelle-France*, vol. 8, "Iberville à Pontchartrain, 8 novembre 1697." Bacqueville de La Potherie, *Histoire de l'Amérique Septentrionale* (Paris, 1922) III, pp. 92-6. Guy Frégault, *Iberville, le conquérant* (Montreal, 1944) pp. 247-49. *Report of the Canadian Archives, 1934*, pp. 6-7.

[8] C11A,13, *Articles et conditions que le roi à accordés au Sieur d'Iberville, 16 avril 1697*, pp. 486-89.

[9] B,21, *Offre au roi par d'Iberville pour le commerce de la Baie d'Hudson, 19 avril 1698*, fol. 45½; *Acceptation des offres d'Iberville, 30 avril 1698*, fol. 47.

[10] B,21, *Mémoire pour servir d'instruction au Sieur d'Iberville, 23 juillet 1698*, fol. 11½; *Pontchartrain à d'Iberville, 15 juin 1699*, fol. 244; cf Frégault, *op. cit.*

[11] C11A, 11, *Champigny à Pontchartrain, 10 mai 1696*, fol. 203. C11A,12, *Champigny à Pontchartrain, 4 novembre 1693*, fol. 287. See the end of the letter. B,18, *Pontchartrain à Champigny, 4 juin 1695*, fol. 163.

[12] *R.A.Q.*, 1927-28, "Le Roi à Frontenac et à Champigny, 7 avril 1692," pp. 79-80; "Pontchartrain à Frontenac, 4 juin 1605," p. 251; "Mémoire du roi à Frontenac et Champigny, 14 juin 1695," p. 262.

[13] Auguste Gosselin, *Vie de Mgr de Laval* (Quebec, 1890) II, p. 449. Camille de Rochemonteix, *Les Jésuites et la Nouvelle-France au XVIIᵉ siècle* (Paris, 1895-97) III, pp. 313-18. *Jugements et Déliberations*, I, pp. 747-48 and 752-54. Arch. Séminaire de Saint-Sulpice, *Cahiers de l'abbé Faillon;* cf. Arch. Archêveché de Québec.

[14] C11A,13, *Champigny à Pontchartrain, 27 octobre 1694*, p. 101 *ff; Mémoire de M. de Lamothe-Cadillac, 28 septembre 1694*, p. 230 *ff; D'auteuil à Pontchartrain, 26 octobre 1694*, pp. 144-50. Bertrand de la Tour, *Mémoires sur la vie de Mgr de Laval* (Cologne, 1761) *passim. Mandements des Evêques de Québec*, I, "16 janvier 1694," pp. 300-01.

[14a] *Ibid.*

[15] *Ordonnances, commissions, etc. des gouverneurs et intendants de la Nouvelle-France*, II, "Ordonnances de Champigny sur la requête de Mareuil, 19 janvier et 23 janvier 1694," pp. 232-38. *Jug. et Dél.*, I, pp. 747-48 and 752-54. *R.A.Q.*, 1928-29, "Frontenac à Pontchartrain, 4 novembre 1694," p. 193; "Pontchartrain à Frontenac, 4 juin 1695," p. 251.

[16] C11A, 13, *Mémoire pour l'évêque de Québec concernant l'interdit contre les Récollets de Ville-Marie*, pp. 268-95. C11A,13, *Champigny à Pontchartrain, 27 octobre 1694*, pp. 101-09; *Callières à Pontchartrain, 19 octobre 1694*, pp. 118-35.

[17] "Lettre de Mgr de Saint-Vallier aux RR.PP. Récollets, 13 mai 1694"; "Protestations des RR. PP. Récollets contre M. de Québec, 6 juillet 1694"; "Requête des Récollets à Monseigneur l'évêque de Québec," in Rochemonteix, *op. cit.*, III, pp. 631-80. B,17, *Pontchartrain à Mgr de Saint-Vallier, 8 mai 1694*, fol. 73½.

[18] *R.A.Q.*, 1928-29, "Pontchartrain à Frontenac, 4 juin 1695," pp. 251-52. B,18, *Pontchartrain à Champigny, 4 juin 1695*, fol. 103; *Pontchartrain à Champigny, 8 juin 1695*, fol. 115. Gosselin, *op. cit.*, pp. 460-61.

[19] C11A,12, *Suite des mémoires des PP. Jésuites à Pontchartrain, 1692*, fol. 125.

[20] *Ibid.* B,16, *Pontchartrain à Mgr de Saint-Vallier, 7 avril 1691*, fol. 38 *ff. Ordonnances*, I, "Ordonnance de Champigny, 11 septembre 1693," pp. 227-29; "Ordonnance de Frontenac, 12 septembre 1693," pp. 229-32.

[21] C11A,28, *Vaudreuil et Raudot à Pontchartrain, 14 novembre 1708*, fol. 54. C11A,29, *D'Aigremont à Pontchartrain, 14 novembre 1708*, fol. A letter from Carheil to Pontchartrain in Rochemonteix, *op. cit.*, III, pp. 499-501. C11A,14, *Champigny à Pontchartrain, 25 octobre 1696*, p. 286.

[22] *R.A.Q.*, 1927-28, "Le Roi à Frontenac et à Champigny, 7 avril 1692," p. 81; "Mémoire du roi à Frontenac et à Champigny (1693)," p. 94.

[23] *Ordonnances*, I, "Ordonnance de Frontenac, 12 septembre 1693," pp. 229-32. *R.A.Q.*, 1927-28, "Mémoire du roi à Frontenac et à Champigny (1693)," p. 95; "Mémoire du roi à Frontenac et à Champigny," p. 147; "Pontchartrain à Frontenac, 13 mars 1694," p. 180.

[23a] *R.A.Q.*, 1927-28, "Frontenac à Pontchartrain, 4 novembre 1694," p. 187; "Frontenac et Champigny à Pontchartrain, 4 novembre 1696," pp. 177-78.

[24] B,17, *Arrêt du Conseil du roi pour réception et le prix des castors, 30 mai 1695*, p. 67. C11A,19, *Ordonnance au sujet de l'achat des castors, 27 septembre 1695*, pp. 305-07.

25 C11A,14, *Congés et permissions pour la traite, 4 juin (1695)*, pp. 491-95.
Commerce du Canada, 1696, p. 372 *ff*.   F3, 5, *Déclaration du roi, 21 mai
1696*, fol. 387.   *R.A.Q.*, 1928-29, "Frontenac à Pontchartrain, 25 octobre 1696,"
p. 311.
26 *R.A.Q.*, 1928-29, "Frontenac à Pontchartrain, 25 octobre 1696," pp. 312-13.
27 C11A,14, *Champigny au ministre, 25 octobre 1696*, p. 286 *ff*.
28 *R.A.Q.*, 1928-29, "Mémoire du roi à Frontenac et à Champigny, 27 avril
1697," p. 331.
29 *Ibid.*, "Mémoire du roi à Frontenac et à Champigny, 21 mai 1698," p. 356;
"Pontchartrain à Frontenac, 21 mai 1698," pp. 361-62.
30 *Ordonnances*, II, "Ordonnance de Champigny, 15 juin 1698," pp. 274-76.
31 *R.A.Q.*, 1928-29, "Frontenac et Champigny à Pontchartrain, 15 octobre
1698," pp. 372-73; "25 octobre 1698," p. 381.   C11A,17, *Callières et Champigny
à Pontchartrain, 20 octobre 1699*, p. 1 *ff*.   C11A,18, *Callières à Pontchartrain, 16
octobre 1700*, p. 33 *ff*.
32 *R.A.Q.*, 1928-29, "Le Roi à Frontenac, 25 mars 1699," p. 383.
33 *Ibid.*, "Frontenac à Pontchartrain, 10 octobre 1698," p. 365; "15 octobre
1698," pp. 370-71.
34 F3,6, *Relation de ce qui s'est passé de plus remarquable en Canada depuis
le départ des vaisseaux de 1697 jusqu'au 20 octobre 1698*, fol. 46 *ff*.
35 *Ibid.*
36 *Ibid.*
37 *Ibid.*   C11A,16, *Bellomont à Frontenac, 13 et 17 août 1698; Frontenac
à Bellomont, 4 septembre 1698*, pp. 63-72; *Frontenac et Champigny à Pontchartrain, 15 octobre 1698*, p. 371.
38 C11A,16, *Champigny à Pontchartrain, 22 décembre 1698*, pp. 155-57.

CHAPTER XIV

1 *Collection de manuscrits contenant lettres, mémoires et autres documents
historiques relatifs à la Nouvelle-France*, I, pp. 601-02.   *Edits et ordonnances
royaux*, III, "Provisions de gouverneur pour le chevalier de Callières, 20 avril
1699," pp. 54-5.   C11A,17, *Vaudreuil et La Potherie au ministre, 2 juin 1699*,
pp. 157-61.
2 B,21, *Le Roi à Callières, 27 avril 1699*, fol. 170.
3 F3, 8, *Paroles de trois chefs iroquois, 8 mars 1699*, fol. 143; *Paroles des
délégués iroquois et réponses de Callières, 20 septembre 1699*, fol. 140½ *ff*.
F3, 18, *Mémoire de Callières, 21 juin 1700*, p. 42.
4 C11A,18, *Discours des délégués iroquois et réponse de Callières, 17 et 18
juillet 1700*, p. 45-51.
5 C11A,18, *Callières à Pontchartrain, 16 octobre 1700*, p. 32 *ff*.
6 F3,8, *Paroles des Iroquois, 3 septembre 1700*, fol. 186.   C11A,18, *Callières
et Champigny au ministre, 18 octobre 1700*, p. 2 *ff*.
7 C11A,18, *Callières à Pontchartrain, 16 octobre 1700*, p. 32 *ff*.
8 C11A,19, *Callières à Pontchartrain, 4 octobre 1701*, p. 91 *ff*.   F3,6, *Pour-
parlers entre M. de Callières, les Iroquois et les nations d'en haut, 29 juillet, 6
et 7 août 1701*, fol. 262, 270 and 278.   Bacqueville de La Potherie, *Histoire de
l'Amérique Septentrionale* (Paris, 1922) IV, pp. 200-06.   F3,8, *Paroles des Ag-
niers et réponse de Callières, 4 juillet 1702*, fol. 308.
9 *Ibid.*   C11A,19, *Callières au ministre, 6 août 1701*, pp. 87-90; *31 octobre
1701*, pp. 116-21.
10 *Extrait des informations du Conseil souverain, contre les sieurs Louvigny
et La Pérotière; Mémoires de Louvigny et de La Pérotière; arrêt du Conseil souverain, 27 octobre 1700*, pp. 142-54.
11 C11A,17, *Champigny à Pontchartrain, 26 mai 1699*, p. 81 *ff*.   B,22, *Le
Ministre à Champigny, 31 mai 1701*, fol. 245.
12 B,22, *Pontchartrain à Champigny, 4 juin 1701*, fol. 265½.
13 *Ordonnances, commissions, etc. des gouverneurs et intendants de la Nouvelle-France*, II, "Ordonnance du 1er mai 1700," pp. 284-86.   C11A,18, *Callières
au ministre, 16 octobre 1700*, p. 32 *ff*.
14 B,22, *Mémoire du roi à Callières, 3 mai 1701*, fol. 41 *ff*; *Pontchartrain à*

Callières, 31 mai 1701, fol. 207½.   *Ordonnances,* II, "Ordonnance de Beauharnois, 20 juin 1703," pp. 315-16.   F³,8, *Ordonnance du roi décrétant la peine de mort, 6 mai 1702,* fol. 294; *Ordonnance du roi contre la vente des boissons, 6 mai 1702,* fol. 296; *Déclaration du roi, juin 1703,* fol. 335.

¹⁵ *Mémoires et documents pour servir à l'histoire des origines françaises des pays d'Outre-Mer,* "Lettre de Lamothe-Cadillac, 18 octobre 1700," V, p. 166 *ff.*

¹⁶ B,22, *Mémoire du roi à Callières et à Champigny, 5 mai 1700,* fol. 85. C¹¹A,19, *Callières au ministre, 4 octobre 1700,* p. 91 *ff.*   Camille de Rochemonteix, *Les Jésuites et la Nouvelle-France au XVIIᵉ siècle* (Paris, 1906) III, p. 514.

¹⁷ C¹¹A,20, *Callières au ministre, 4 novembre 1702,* pp. 68 and 95.   *Rapport de l'archiviste de la province de Québec,* 1938-39, "Mémoire du roi à Vaudreuil et Beauharnois, 14 juin 1704," p. 38; "Vaudreuil et Beauharnois à Pontchartrain, 19 novembre 1704," pp. 52-3; "Vaudreuil et Raudot à Pontchartrain, 18 octobre 1705," p. 83; "Vaudreuil à Pontchartrain 19 octobre 1705," p. 92; "avril-novembre 1706," p. 112.

¹⁸ *Ordonnances,* II, "Règlement de Callières, 25 septembre 1702," p. 310. B,29, *Pontchartrain à Vaudreuil, 6 juin 1708,* fol. 10; *Pontchartrain à Cadillac, 6 juin 1708,* fol. 44½.   *R.A.Q.,* 1939-40, "Vaudreuil et Raudot à Pontchartrain, 14 novembre 1708," pp. 450-51.

¹⁹ F³,8, *Procès-verbal par Champigny, 23 septembre 1699,* fol. 116.

²⁰ *Ibid.,* *Arrêt du Conseil d'Etat, 9 février 1700,* fol. 149; *Procès-verbal d'assemblée, 15 octobre 1700,* fol. 149; *Délibérations des habitants de la Nouvelle-France, 15 octobre 1700,* fol. 200.   C¹¹A,18, *Champigny à Pontchartrain, 17 octobre 1700,* p. 77 *ff;* Raudot, *Liste générale des intéressés en la Compagnie du Canada, 1706,* pp. 531-64.

²¹ F³,8, *Arrêt du Conseil d'Etat établissant de nouveaux droits au lieu du quart des castors, 18 avril 1703,* fol. 323; *Arrêt du Conseil d'Etat, 29 juin 1706,* fol. 21; *Arrêt du Conseil d'Etat, 24 juin 1706,* fol. 26.   *Edits et Ord.,* I, "Arrêt du Conseil d'Etat au sujet des castors, 25 juin 1707," pp. 32-3.

²² B,37, *Pontchartrain à Ramezay et Bégon, 30 avril 1715,* fol. 102.   C¹¹A, 22, Riverin, *Mémoire historique, 12 janvier 1705,* fol. 351-77, (for *La Compagnie du Canada.*)   *R.A.Q.,* 1938-39, p. 139; *ibid.,* 1942-43, p. 44; cf. Guy Frégault, "La Compagnie de la Colonie," *Revue de l'Université d'Ottawa,* (janvier-mars, avril-juin, 1960).

²³ C¹¹A,18, *Callières à Pontchartrain, 16 octobre 1700,* pp. 32-41.   F³,8, (old classification) *Assemblée de M. de Callières avec les chefs iroquois, 7 août 1701,* fol. 278; *Paroles des Iroquois, 23 août 1702,* fol. 515.

²⁴ C¹¹A,20, *Callières à Pontchartrain, 4 novembre 1702,* p. 68 *ff;* cf. *Callières à Pontchartrain, 6 novembre 1703.*

²⁴ᵃ C¹¹A,19, *Projets contre la Nouvelle-Angleterre, (1701)* pp. 142-57; *Mémoire de d'Iberville sur Boston,* pp. 158-83.

²⁵ B,23, *Mémoire du roi pour servir d'instruction à M. de Beauharnois, 6 mai 1702,* fol. 62½.

²⁶ C¹¹A,20, *Callières à Pontchartrain, 4 novembre 1702,* p. 63.   C¹¹A,21, *Vaudreuil et Beauharnois à Pontchartrain, 15 novembre 1703,* p. 1.   Arch. Séminaire de Québec, *Lettres: Abbé Tremblay au chanoine Glandelet, 4 mars 1694.*

²⁷ *Les Annales de l'Hôtel-Dieu de Québec,* Dom Jamet, ed. (Quebec, 1939) pp. 307-08.   Arch. Can., *Lettres Canadiennes,* I.

CHAPTER XV

¹ After his appointment as governor, Vaudreuil assumed the courtesy title of Marquis. See F. H. Hammang, *The Marquis de Vaudreuil* (Bruges, 1938) p. 47, note.   *Edits et ordonnances royaux,* III, "Commission, 1ᵉʳ août 1703," pp. 58-9.   *Rapport de l'archiviste de la province de Québec,* 1938-39, "Pontchartrain à Vaudreuil, 14 juin 1704," p. 26; "9 juin 1706," p. 119.

² Georges Langlois, *Histoire de la population canadienne française* (Montreal, 1934) p. 121.   *R.A.Q.,* 1938-39, "Vaudreuil et Beauharnois à Pontchartrain, 15 novembre 1703," pp. 12 and 16; "Mémoire du roi à Vaudreuil et Beauharnois, 14 juin 1704," pp. 39-40.   C¹¹A,23, *Mémoire de Riverin, 7 janvier 1703,* fol. 5 and 6.

2a Charles de La Roncière, *Histoire de la Marine française* (Paris, 1910) IV, pp. 491-92.   *R.A.Q.*, 1947-48, "Madame de Vaudreuil à Pontchartrain, 16 octobre 1706," p. 74.   *R.A.Q.*, 1939-40, "Mgr de Laval au P. de la Chaise, août 1687," p. 277; "Mgr de Laval aux directeurs du Séminaire, 9 juin 1687," p. 278.   Louis-Marie Le Jeune, *Dictionnaire général* (Ottawa, 1931) II, p. 607.

2b B,23, *Pontchartrain à Callières, 20 juin 1703*, fol. 194.   B,25, *Pontchartrain à Vaudreuil et à Beauharnois, 14 juin 1705*, fol. 101½.   Arch. Séminaire de Québec, *Lettres: Abbé Tremblay à Mgr de Laval, 19 juin 1705*.   *Documents relatifs à la monnaie, au change et aux finances du Canada sous le régime français*, Adam Shortt, ed. (Ottawa, 1925) I, p. 117, note.

2c Arch. Can., Beauharnois Collection, *Raimbault à Beauharnois, 25 novembre 1704*, p. 390 *ff*.   *Ordonnances, commissions, etc. des gouverneurs et intendants de la Nouvelle-France*, II, "Ordonnance de Vaudreuil, 12 octobre 1704," pp. 320-27.

2d *Inventaire des ordonnances des intendants de la Nouvelle-France*, P. G. Roy, ed. (Beauceville, 1917) I, pp. 4-8.   *R.A.Q.*, 1938-39, "Vaudreuil et Raudot à Pontchartrain, 30 avril 1706," pp. 112-13.

2e *Documents relatifs à la monnaie, au change et aux finances du Canada sous le régime français*, "Mémoire du roi à Vaudreuil et Beauharnois, 14 juin 1704," p. 126.   B,27, *Pontchartrain à Beauharnois, 15 avril 1705*, fol. 4; *17 juin 1705*, fol. 51½.

3 *R.A.Q.*, 1938-39, "Vaudreuil et Beauharnois à Pontchartrain, 15 novembre 1703," pp. 12 and 19; "Vaudreuil à Pontchartrain, 3 avril 1704," p. 24.

4 *Ibid.*, "Vaudreuil et Beauharnois à Pontchartrain, 15 novembre 1703," p. 16.   Rev. Samuel Niles, *History of the Indian and French Wars* (Boston, 1837); cf. Pierre Daviault, *Le Baron de Saint-Castin* (Montreal, 1939) p. 152.

5 *Documents Relating to the Colonial History of the State of New York*, IX, "Abstract of certain parts of dispatch," p. 755. The notes are not by the Minister but by Champigny.   *R.A.Q.*, 1938-39, "Pontchartrain à Vaudreuil, 14 juin 1704," p. 26; "Mémoire du roi à Vaudreuil et à Beauharnois, 14 juin 1703," pp. 29-30. Hammang, *op. cit.*, pp. 123-24.

6 *R.A.Q.*, 1938-39, "Vaudreuil à Pontchartrain, 3 avril 1704," pp. 24-5; "Vaudreuil et Beauharnois à Pontchartrain, 17 novembre," p. 54.   J. B. Ferland, *Cours d'histoire du Canada* (Quebec, 1861-65) II, pp. 349-50.   C^{11}A,22, *Ramezay à Pontchartrain, 14 novembre 1704*.

7 *Collection de manuscrits contenant lettres, mémoires et autres documents historiques relatifs à la Nouvelle-France*, II, "Invasion des Anglais de Boston par M. de Labat, 1er juillet 1704," pp. 416-24; "Lettres: Dudley à Vaudreuil, 20 décembre 1704," p. 427; "Vaudreuil à Dudley, 26 mars 1705," pp. 428-30; "Instructions à Courtemanche, 1705," pp. 432-33.

8 *R.A.Q.*, 1938-39, "Vaudreuil à Pontchartrain, 19 novembre 1705," pp. 96-7.   *Col. Mss.*, II, "Ramezay à Vaudreuil, 12 octobre 1705," p. 448; "Notes du ministre sur la lettre de Vaudreuil," pp. 449-51.   *R.A.Q.*, 1938-39, "Pontchartrain à Vaudreuil," pp. 120-21.

9 *Col. Mss.*, II, "Dudley à Vaudreuil, 4 juillet 1705," p. 438; "Projets des articles de trêve à conclure entre les gouverneurs de la Nouvelle-France et de la Nouvelle-Angleterre, 6 octobre 1705," pp. 440-47.   *R.A.Q.*, 1938-39, "Vaudreuil à Pontchartrain, 19 octobre 1705," p. 96.

10 *R.A.Q.*, 1938-39, "Vaudreuil et Raudot à Pontchartrain, 30 avril 1706," p. 113; "3 novembre 1706," pp. 145-46.   *Col. Mss.*, II, "Subercase à Pontchartrain, 25 octobre 1706," p. 452.   *R.A.Q.*, 1939-40, "Le Roi à Vaudreuil et Raudot, 30 juin 1707," p. 375.

11 *Col. Mss.*, II, "Réponse de Vaudreuil aux Abénaquis, 1706," pp. 458-59. *Docts. N.Y.*, IX, "Schuyler to Vaudreuil, 26 September 1708," pp. 818-19.

12 *R.A.Q.*, 1938-39, "Vaudreuil à Pontchartrain, 16 novembre 1704," p. 47; "4 novembre 1706," pp. 169-70.   *R.A.Q.*, 1939-40, "Pontchartrain à Vaudreuil, 30 juin 1707," p. 374.   *R.A.Q.*, 1938-39, "Vaudreuil et Raudot à Pontchartrain, 3 novembre 1706," p. 157.   *Edits et Ord.*, I, "Edit du roi portant défenses de faire le commerce et le transport du castor chez les étrangers, 6 juillet 1709," p. 320.   *R.A.Q.*, 1939-40, "Vaudreuil à Pontchartrain, 5 novembre 1708," p. 433.

13 *R.A.Q.*, 1938-39, "Vaudreuil et Beauharnois à Pontchartrain, 15 novembre 1703," p. 12.   *R.A.Q.*, 1939-40, "Vaudreuil à Pontchartrain, 28 juin 1708," pp. 423-24.   *R.A.Q.*, 1938-39, "Vaudreuil et Beauharnois à Pontchartrain, 17 no-

vembre 1704," pp. 55-7; "Vaudreuil à Pontchartrain, 19 octobre 1705," p. 91.
R.A.Q., 1939-40, "Vaudreuil à Pontchartrain, 12 novembre 1708," p. 442.
14 *R.A.Q.*, 1938-39, "Vaudreuil à Pontchartrain, 16 novembre 1704," pp. 44-5.
15 *Ibid.*, "Vaudreuil et Beauharnois à Pontchartrain, 17 novembre 1704," pp. 55, 56 and 59.
16 *Ibid.*, "Vaudreuil à Pontchartrain, 19 octobre 1705," pp. 93-4; "20 avril 1706," pp. 100-01.   *R.A.Q.*, 1939-40, "Vaudreuil à Pontchartrain, 5 novembre 1708," p. 428.
17 *R.A.Q.*, 1939-40, "Vaudreuil à Pontchartrain, 1er et 4 novembre 1706," pp. 106-07; "Vaudreuil et Raudot à Pontchartrain, 3 novembre 1706," pp. 141-42; "4 novembre 1706," pp. 160-61, 164-66 and 173; "Vaudreuil et Raudot à Pontchartrain, 16 juillet 1707," p. 378.   P. F. X. Charlevoix, *Histoire et description générale de la Nouvelle-France* (Paris, 1744) book 20.
18 *R.A.Q.*, 1939-40, "Pontchartrain à Vaudreuil, 6 juin 1708," p. 418.
19 *Ibid.*, "Vaudreuil à Pontchartrain, 5 novembre 1708," pp. 430-33; "Vaudreuil et Raudot à Pontchartrain, 14 octobre 1708," pp. 457-58.
19a *R.A.Q.*, 1942-43, "Vaudreuil à Pontchartrain, 27 avril 1709," p. 400; 1er octobre 1709," pp. 404-05.   Hammang, *op. cit.*, pp. 154-56.   *Docts. N.Y.*, IX, "Ramezay to Vaudreuil, 1st October 1709," pp. 838-39.
20 *R.A.Q.*, 1942-43, "Vaudreuil à Pontchartrain, 14 novembre 1709," pp. 425-39; cf. Ferland, *op. cit.*, II, pp. 372-74.
21 *R.A.Q.*, 1942-43, pp. 432 and 439-40; "Vaudreuil à Pontchartrain, 1er mai 1710," pp. 441-42.   Charlevoix, *op. cit.*, book 19.   Thomas Hutchinson, *The History of the Colony of Massachusetts Bay* (London, 1765) p. 161.
21a C11A,26, *Vaudreuil et Raudot à Pontchartrain*, pp. 2-5; *Mémoire de Riverin, 11 avril 1707*, p. 82 *ff; Ramezay à Pontchartrain, 12 novembre 1707*, p. 3 *ff*.
22 *R.A.Q.*, 1942-43, "Vaudreuil à Pontchartrain, 27 avril 1709," p. 441; "14 novembre 1709," pp. 434-35.   *R.A.Q.*, 1946-47, "Pontchartrain à Vaudreuil, 10 mai 1710," pp. 371-72; "7 juillet 1711," p. 417.
22a Raudot, *Deux intendants au Canada*, Annexe 1854.   *Histoire de l'Hôtel-Dieu* (ed. 1751) pp. 450-51.   C11A,26, *Raudot à Pontchartrain, 10 novembre 1707*, fol. 150; *17 novembre 1707*.   *Ordonnances de Raudot*, "22 juin 1706," fol. 17; "26 mai 1706," fol. 52; "12 novembre 1706," fol. 52; "12 novembre 1706," fol. 37; "19 juillet 1710," fol. 182; "29 janvier 1706," fol. 42.   C11G, *Mémoire de Raudot sur les droits et redevenances, 1708*, fol. 66.
22b C11G, *Mémoire sur l'établissement du Cap Breton, 16 juillet 1708*, fol. 2; 20 août 1707, fol. 30½; 29 février 1710, fol. 72.
23 *R.A.Q.*, 1942-43, "Vaudreuil à Pontchartrain, 1er mai 1710," p. 422; "Juin 1710," pp. 380-81; "25 avril 1711," pp. 4-12.   Sir Hovenden Walker, *Journal or Full Account of the Late Expedition* (London, 1720) pp. 107-09 and 190-91. *Col. Mss.*, II, "La Ronde de Saint-Denys à Pontchartrain," p. 549.   *R.A.Q.*, 1946-47, "Vaudreuil à Pontchartrain, 25 octobre 1711," p. 431; "8 novembre 1711," p. 452.   C11A,32, *Raudot à Pontchartrain, 1er novembre 1711*.
24 *R.A.Q.*, 1942-43, "Vaudreuil à Pontchartrain, 14 novembre 1709," p. 431. *R.A.Q.*, 1946-47, "Vaudreuil à Pontchartrain, 25 octobre 1711," pp. 431-35.
24a *Ibid.*
25 *Les Annales de l'Hôtel-Dieu*, Dom Jamet, ed. (Quebec, 1939) pp. 366-69. Hugolin (Le May), *Echo héroï-comiques du naufrage des Anglais sur l'île aux Oeufs en 1711*.
26 *Col. Mss.*, II, "De La Ronde Denys à Pontchartrain, 30 décembre 1711," p. 349.   Walker, *op. cit.*, p. 110.   Charlevoix, *op. cit.*, book 20.
27 Walker, *op. cit.*, pp. 25, 119, 124-28, 300-03 and *passim*.   *Histoire de l'Hôtel-Dieu*, pp. 490-91.   *Docts. N.Y.*, IV, "General Hill to Governor Hunter, August 25, 1711," p. 277.   *R.A.Q.*, 1947-48, "Vaudreuil à Pontchartrain, 23 juillet 1712," p. 158; "Pontchartrain à Vaudreuil, 9 août 1712," p. 159.   Gerald Graham, *The Walker Expedition* (Toronto, 1953) p. 334.
28 *R.A.Q.*, 1947-48, "Vaudreuil à Pontchartrain, 27 juin 1712," p. 150. *R.A.Q.*, 1946-47, "Vaudreuil à Pontchartrain, 8 novembre 1711," p. 453.
29 *R.A.Q.*, 1942-43, "Vaudreuil à Pontchartrain, 7 novembre 1711," p. 455. *R.A.Q.*, 1947-48, "Vaudreuil à Pontchartrain, 25 juillet 1712," p. 158; "15 octobre 1712," pp. 161-62; "6 novembre 1712," pp. 163-64.
30 *Ibid.*   C11A,33, *Lettre de Du Buisson, 15 juin 1712*, pp. 215-55.

[31] *R.A.Q.*, 1947-48, "Vaudreuil à Pontchartrain, 25 juillet 1712," p. 158; "15 octobre 1712," pp. 161-62; "6 novembre 1712," pp. 163-66; "18 avril 1713," p. 200. [32] *Ibid.*, "Vaudreuil à Pontchartrain, 15 mai 1713," p. 204; "16 septembre 1714," p. 270.

CHAPTER XVI

[1] B,2, *Commission de Grandfontaine, 2 février 1670* and *Instructions du roi, 6 mars 1670*, fol. 57.   *Recensements du Canada*, IV, "Acadie 1671," p. 10. *Rapport de l'archiviste de la province de Québec*, 1930-31, "Mémoire de Talon, 10 octobre 1670," p. 131.   *Collection de manuscrits contenant lettres, mémoires et autres documents historiques relatifs à la Nouvelle-France*, II, "Mémoire du roi à Brouillan, 23 mars 1706," p. 333.   Biblio. Nat. (Paris), *Mélanges sur l'Amérique, Ternaux Compans*, 29.

[2] Lounsbury, *The British Fishery*, pp. 191-92.   Ruth Fulton Grant, *The Canadian Atlantic Fishery* (Toronto, 1934) pp. 12-14. $C^{11}A,3$, *Mémoire sur la pêche sur les côtes de l'Acadie, 27 octobre 1699*, fol. 205 *ff.*   *R.A.Q.*, 1930-31, "Talon à Colbert, 11 novembre 1670," p. 165.   *Col. Mss.*, I, "Rapport de Duchesneau, 15 novembre 1681," p. 286.

[3] *Relations des Jésuites*, 1611, pp. 36-7; *ibid.*, 1640, p. 35; *ibid.*, 1652, p. 26. *Col. Mss.*, I, "Mémoire," p. 272; "Rapport de Menneval, 10 septembre 1688," p. 435; II, "Brouillan à Pontchartrain, 1er juin 1703," p. 403.   *Handbook of Indians of Canada* (Ottawa, 1931) pp. 1-2; cf. Maurault, *Histoire des Abénakis*, Trumbull, *History of the Indian Wars* and Hubbard, *The History of the Indian Wars*.

[4] B,3, *Colbert à Grandfontaine, 11 et 30 mars 1671*, fol. $41\frac{1}{2}$ and $54\frac{1}{2}$. *R.A.Q.*, 1930-31, "Talon à Colbert, 11 novembre 1671," p. 165; "Mémoire de Talon, 10 octobre 1670," pp. 131-32.

[5] *Ibid.*, "Mémoire des expéditions (1671)," p. 142; "Mémoire de Talon, 10 octobre 1670," pp. 131-32.   *R.A.Q.*, 1926-27, "Frontenac à Colbert, 13 novembre 1673," p. 43; "1er février 1674," p. 54.

[6] Louis-Marie Le Jeune, *Dictionnaire général* (Ottawa, 1931) I, p. 118. *R.A.Q.*, 1926-27, "Frontenac à Colbert, 13 novembre 1673," p. 43. $C^{11}D$, I, *Ordre du roi au Sieur de Chambly, 5 mai 1673*, fol. 141; *Commission au Sieur de Chambly, 1676*, fol. 143.

[7] *R.A.Q.*, 1926-27, "Frontenac à Colbert, 13 novembre 1673," p. 43; "14 novembre 1674," p. 74.

[8] *Col. Mss.*, I, "Mémoire de Frontenac, 14 novembre 1674," p. 74; "Frontenac à Leverett, 24 septembre 1674," p. 229; "Relation de l'entreprise par Duchesneau, 28 septembre 1674," p. 229.

[9] *R.A.Q.*, 1926-27, "Louis XIV à Frontenac, 12 mai 1678," p. 96; "Frontenac à Louis XIV, 6 novembre 1679," p. 111; "2 novembre 1681," p. 128. $C^{11}D,1$, *Commission de Frontenac à La Vallière, 1678*, fol. 240.   *Edits et ordonnances royaux*, I, "Arrêt qui confirme les concessions, 29 mai 1680," p. 240.   Le Jeune, *op. cit.*, II, p. 109.

[10] *R.A.Q.*, 1926-27, "Frontenac à Colbert, 14 novembre 1674," p. 74; "Louis XIV à Frontenac, 22 avril 1675," p. 83.   Pierre Daviault, *Le Baron de Saint-Castin* (Montreal, 1939) pp. 55-61 and 199, note.

[11] Biblio. Nat., Collection Clairambault, 874, fol. 383. Text in Daviault, *op. cit.*, p. 187.

[12] *Col. Mss.*, I, "Saint-Castin à Denonville, 2 juillet 1687," p. 400.

[13] A letter from Father Petit, October 22, 1685, in *Etat présent de l'Eglise et de la Colonie française dans la Nouvelle-France, par M. l'Evêque de Québec* (Quebec, 1856) pp. 39-40.   *Col. Mss.*, I, "Saint-Castin à Denonville, 2 juillet 1687," pp. 399-400; "Mémoire de Menneval sur l'Acadie, 1er décembre 1687," p. 410; "Rapport de Menneval, 10 septembre 1688," p. 435; "Denonville à Seignelay, 10 novembre 1686," p. 371.

[14] *Col. Mss.*, I, "Instructions de Louis XIV à Menneval, 1687," p. 396; "Dongan aux Français, 1683," pp. 308-09; "Rapport de Frontenac, 2 novembre 1681," p. 281; "Perrot à Dongan, 29 août 1686," p. 366.   *Documents Relating to the Colonial History of the State of New York*, III, "Randolph's Report to the Council of Trade (1680)," p. 941.

[15] *R.A.Q.*, 1930-31, "Talon à Colbert, 11 novembre 1671," p. 164. *R.A.Q.*, 1926-27, "Frontenac à Seignelay, 2 novembre 1681," p. 128. *Col. Mss.*, I, "Rapport de Duchesneau, 15 novembre 1681," p. 286; "Mémoire de de Meulles, 4 novembre 1683," p. 301; "Mémoire du Sieur Bergier, 1685," p. 340.

[16] *Col. Mss.*, I, "Rapport de Duchesneau, 15 novembre 1681," pp. 285-86; "Rapport de M. de Meulles, 6 octobre 1683," p. 300; "Mémoire sur l'Acadie, 1684," pp. 293-95.

[17] *Ibid.*, "Lettres patentes en faveur des intéressés en la pêche de l'Acadie (1683)," pp. 304-06.

[18] *Ibid.*, "Les Intéressés à la pêche sédentaire, 1682," p. 290; "Mémoire sur l'Acadie (1683)," pp. 292.

[19] *Col. Mss.*, I, "Mémoire sur l'Acadie (1683)," pp. 292-95; "Mémoire de l'Ambassadeur de France, 6 novembre 1684," pp. 329-30.

[20] *Ibid.*, "Rapport de de Meulles, 4 novembre 1683," pp. 298-99; "Mémoire sur l'Acadie (1683)," pp. 291-96. *R.A.Q.*, 1926-27, "Frontenac à Louis XIV, 6 novembre 1679," p. 111; "Frontenac à Seignelay, 2 novembre 1681," p. 137.

[21] *Ibid.*, "Provisions de gouverneur pour le Sieur Perrot, 10 avril 1684," pp. 321-22; "Provisions de lieutenant-général pour le Sieur Bergier, 10 avril 1684," p. 323.

[22] *Ibid.*, "Mémoire du Sieur Perrot, 1685," p. 348; "Instructions à Menneval, 1687," p. 398; "Seignelay à Perrot, 21 janvier 1688," p. 416; "Saint-Castin à Denonville, 2 juillet 1687," p. 400; "Rapport de Menneval, 1er décembre 1687," p. 410.

[23] B,18, *Louis XIV au Sieur Perrot, 30 mars 1687*, fol. 43. *Col. Mss.*, I, "Seignelay à Perrot, 21 janvier 1688," p. 416.

[24] *Col. Mss.*, I, "Instructions du roi au Sieur de Menneval (10 avril) 1687," pp. 396-98; "Denonville et Champigny à Seignelay, 16 novembre 1687," p. 406; "Mémoire sur l'Acadie, 1689," p. 473.

[25] B,15, *Instructions au Sieur de Beaugard, 10 avril 1688*, fol. 36½; *Instructions au Sieur Gouttins, 10 avril 1688*, fol. 39; *Instructions au Sieur Pasquine, 10 avril 1688*, fol. 37½.

[26] *Col. Mss.*, I, "Rapport de Menneval, 10 septembre 1688," pp. 435-36; "Louis XIV à la Compagnie de l'Acadie, 21 février 1688," p. 415. Louis-Marie Le Jeune, *Tableaux synoptiques de l'histoire du Canada* (Ottawa, 1918). Fascicule spéciale, pp. 38-41. *Recensements du Canada*, IV, p. 20.

[27] *Col. Mss.*, I, "Observation sur l'estat présent de l'Acadie (1689)," pp. 472-73; "Denonville à Seignelay, 30 octobre 1688," p. 422; "Mémoire sur l'Acadie par Pasquine, 14 décembre 1688," p. 445; "Mémoire touchant les prises des Anglais, 10 et 15 août 1688," pp. 429-31; "Frontenac au ministre, 15 novembre 1689," p. 466.

[28] *Ibid.*, "Le Roi à Denonvile, 1er mai 1689," p. 448. H. M. Sylvester, *Indian Wars of New England* (Boston, 1910) II, p. 389.

[29] *Col. Mss.*, I, "Résumé des rapports du Canada, 1689," pp. 472-75; "Relation du combat de Canibas par Monsieur Thury, 1689," pp. 477-81. Pierre Daviault, *Le Baron de Saint-Castin* (Montreal, 1939) pp. 73-5 and 78-82.

CHAPTER XVII

[1] *Collection de manuscrits contenant lettres, mémoires et autres documents historiques relatifs à la Nouvelle-France*, I, "Relation (par Monseignat) 1689-90," pp. 496-500. Beamish Murdoch, *A History of Nova Scotia* (Halifax, 1865) I, pp. 183 and 190-91.

[2] *Col. Mss.*, II, "Prise du Port-Royal, 29 mai 1690," pp. 6-8; "Lettre de Menneval à Seignelay, 29 mai 1690," pp. 10-11; "Rapport de Champigny, 1690," p. 29; "Menneval à Pontchartrain, 6 avril 1691," pp. 41-4. *Col. Mss.*, I, "Relation 1689-90," pp. 502-03.

[3] *Ibid.*

[4] *Rapport de l'archiviste de la province de Québec*, 1927-28, "Frontenac à Seignelay, 12 novembre 1690," p. 43. *Documents Relating to the Colonial History of the State of New York*, IX, "Narrative of the most remarkable occurrences in Canada, 1690-91," p. 526. Pierre Daviault, *Le Baron de Saint-Castin* (Montreal, 1939) p. 93. Perrot, the former governor, who was trading in the region

at the time, was captured by the pirates and suffered ill-treatment at their hands, but he was later liberated by French vessels.

5 *R.A.Q.*, 1927-28, "Mémoire du roi à Frontenac, 7 avril 1691," p. 55; "Frontenac à Pontchartrain, 20 octobre 1691," p. 69. *Col. Mss.*, II, "Instructions au Sieur de Villebon, 7 avril 1691," pp. 45-6; "Esdit en faveur des sieurs de Saint-Aubin et Petitpas, 9 novembre 1692," p. 92; "Mémoire sur l'Acadie et la Nouvelle-Angleterre par Monsieur de Lagny, 1692," pp. 98-9.

6 *R.A.Q.*, 1927-28, "Frontenac à Pontchartrain, 10 mai 1691," p. 61; "25 octobre 1693," p. 156. P. Daviault, *op. cit.*, pp. 97-8. *Col. Mss.*, II, "Champigny à Pontchartrain, 5 octobre 1682," pp. 89-90; "Nouvelles de l'Acadie, 1693," p. 127. Robert Le Blant, *Une figure légendaire de l'histoire acadienne, le baron de Saint-Castin* (Dax, s.d.) p. 132.

7 *R.A.Q.*, 1927-28, "Pontchartrain à Frontenac, 14 février 1693," p. 130; "Frontenac à Pontchartrain, 15 septembre 1692," p. 114; "25 octobre 1693," p. 155; cf. Guy Frégault, *Iberville, le conquérant* (Montreal, 1944) pp. 159-63 and P. Daviault, *op. cit.*, pp. 109-10. They consider that d'Iberville was justified in his decision although the reasons given in his letter of 1692 to the Minister are vague and unconvincing.

8 *Col. Mss.*, II, "Rapport de Champigny, 26 octobre 1694," p. 166; "Relation du voyage fait par le Sieur de Villieu, 1694," p. 139. Samuel Niles, *History of the Indian and French Wars*, p. 234.

9 *R.A.Q.*, 1927-28, "Frontenac à Pontchartrain, 14 février 1693," p. 130; "Mémoire du roi à Frontenac et à Champigny, 28 juin 1693," p. 143. *Col. Mss.*, II, "Instructions au Sieur de Villebon, 14 février," pp. 137 and 139.

10 *R.A.Q.*, 1927-28, "Mémoire du roi à Frontenac, 28 juin 1693," p. 143. *Col. Mss.*, II, "Instructions au Sieur de Villebon, 14 février 1693," p. 107; "Champigny à Pontchartrain, 10 novembre 1692," p. 93; "Mémoire de Chauffour, 1692," p. 96.

11 *R.A.Q.*, 1927-28, "Pontchartrain à Frontenac, 14 février 1693," p. 130; "Frontenac à Pontchartrain, 14 août 1693," p. 154. *Col. Mss.*, II, "Estat des présents, 1693," p. 111; "Estat des munitions, 1693," p. 129.

12 *Col. Mss.*, II, "Villebon à Pontchartrain, 15 novembre 1692," p. 96; "Champigny à Pontchartrain, 24 octobre 1694," p. 163; "Relation des combats entre le capitaine Baptiste et les Bostonnais, 1694-95," pp. 151-54. *R.A.Q.*, 1927-28, "Frontenac à Pontchartrain, 25 octobre 1693," p. 156; "novembre 1694," p. 191.

13 *Col. Mss.*, II, "Relation du voyage fait par le Sieur de Villieu, 1694," pp. 135-43; "Rapport de Champigny, 26 octobre 1694," p. 167. B. de La Potherie, *Histoire de l'Amérique Septentrionale* (Paris, 1922) III, p. 229.

14 *Col. Mss.*, II, "R. P. Thury à Frontenac, 11 septembre 1694," p. 161. *R.A.Q.*, 1928-29, "Frontenac à Lagny, 2 novembre 1695," p. 263; "Frontenac à Pontchartrain, 4 novembre 1695," p. 273.

15 *Col. Mss.*, II, "R. P. Thury à Frontenac, 11 septembre 1694," p. 161; "Frontenac à Pontchartrain, 4 novembre 1694," p. 188; "Pontchartrain à Villebon, 16 avril 1695," p. 177. C11D, 2, *Projet pour l'entreprise de Pemquit, 1694*, fol. 220. *R.A.Q.*, 1927-28, "Pontchartrain à Frontenac, 28 mars 1696," p. 296. B, 19, *Mémoire pour servir d'instruction à M. d'Iberville, 28 avril 1696*, fol. 20½.

15a "Journal" by Father Beaudoin in A. Gosselin, *Les Normands au Canada* (Evreux, 1892) pp. 34-38. A letter from Iberville to Pontchartrain (September, 1696) in Gosselin, *op. cit.*, pp. 75-6; cf. Frégault, *op. cit.*, and Daviault, *op. cit.*

15b *Col. Mss.*, II, "Relation du siège [par Villebon] 22 octobre 1696," pp. 241-46; "Rapport de Champigny, 16 octobre 1697," p. 288. T. Hutchinson, *The History of the Great Indian Wars, passim.* Murdoch, *op. cit.*, I, pp. 220-31.

16 *Col. Mss.*, II, "Tibierge à Frontenac, 20 août 1697," p. 286; "Champigny à Pontchartrain, 24 octobre 1697," p. 288; "Instructions à M. le marquis de Nesmond, 21 avril 1697," pp. 263-68; "Mémoire sur l'entreprise de Boston, 21 avril 1697," p. 268. *R.A.Q.*, 1928-29, "Frontenac à Pontchartrain, 4 novembre 1695," pp. 272-73.

17 *Col. Mss.*, II, "Stoughton à Villebon, 3 mars 1698," p. 289; "Pontchartrain à Villebon, 26 mars 1698," pp. 295-96; "Villebon au ministre, 1698," pp. 305-06; "Instructions à Bonaventure, 26 mars 1698," p. 299; "Villebon à Stoughton, 8 février 1698," pp. 311-12; "Pontchartrain à Villebon, 9 avril 1700," pp. 334-35.

18 *Ibid.*, II, "Frontenac à Pontchartrain, 17 octobre 1698," p. 310; "Présent des sauvages de l'Acadie, 1698," p. 291; "Pontchartrain à Villebon, 15 avril 1699," pp. 315-16; "Callières à Pontchartrain, 17 mars 1699," p. 312.

19 Daviault, *op. cit.*, p. 131.   *Col. Mss.*, II, "Mémoire du roi à Brouillan, 23 mars 1700," p. 333; "Lettre de Saint-Castin, 21 novembre 1701," p. 387.

20 *Col. Mss.*, II, "Pontchartrain à Champigny, 16 avril 1695," p. 174.   B, 22, *Mémoire du roi à M. de Brouillan, 23 mars 1701*, fol. 144½.   C11D, 2, *Commission, 1er février 1702*, fol. 148.   *Col. Mss.*, II, "Brouillan à Pontchartrain, 30 octobre 1701," p. 385.

21 Daviault, *op. cit.*, pp. 146-49.   *Col. Mss.*, II, "Brouillan à Pontchartrain, 30 octobre 1701," p. 386.   *Recensements du Canada*, IV, pp. 20 and 45.   N. de Diéréville, *Relation du voyage du Port-Royal de l'Acadie ou de la Nouvelle-France* (Rouen, 1708) *passim*.

CHAPTER XVIII

1 C11D, 4, *Mémoire de Brouillan*, 1701, fol. 55 *ff.   Collection de manuscrits contenant lettres, mémoires et autres documents historiques relatifs à la Nouvelle-France*, II, "Projects contre la Nouvelle-Angleterre," pp. 393-94; "Brouillan à Pontchartrain, 30 octobre 1704," pp. 392-94; "Beauharnois à Pontchartrain, 11 novembre 1704," p. 396.

1a Pierre Daviault, *Le Baron de Saint-Castin* (Montreal, 1939) pp. 151-52. *Rapport de l'archiviste de la province de Québec*, 1938-39, "Vaudreuil et Beauharnois au ministre, 15 novembre 1703," p. 16; "17 novembre 1703," p. 54. Jeremy Belknap, *The History of New Hampshire*, pp. 282-83.   Daviault, *op. cit.*, p. 152.

1b *Col. Mss.*, II, "Invasion des Anglais de Boston par Monsieur La Bat, 1er mai 1704," pp. 416-25.   Thomas Hutchinson, *The History of the Colony of Massachusetts Bay* (London, 1765) II, p. 143.   B. Murdoch, *A History of Nova Scotia* (Halifax, 1865) I, pp. 272-74.

1c Joseph Williamson, *The History of the State of Maine*, p. 49.   *Col. Mss.*, II, "Vaudreuil à Dudley, 2 juin 1706," p. 452; "Paroles des Abénaquis, 14 septembre 1706," p. 456; "Bonaventure à Pontchartrain, 24 décembre 1706," p. 464. *R.A.Q.*, 1938-39, "Vaudreuil à Pontchartrain, 4 novembre 1706," p. 110.

2 C11D, 4, *Brouillan à Pontchartrain, 25 novembre 1703*, fol. 272 *ff.   Lettre* [du curé Maudoux] fol. 247.   C11A, 5, *Des Gouttins à Pontchartrain, 8 décembre 1704*, fol. 31; *De Labat à Pontchartrain, 1704*, fol. 54; *Lopinot, délégué des Acadiens, 15 juillet 1705*, fol. 95 *ff; Lettre des Acadiens, 1705*, fol. 212.   C11A, 6, *Pontchartrain à Subercase, 20 juin 1707*, fol. 4. The documentation on these subjects is particularly abundant, and this list of references could be lengthened considerably.

2a C11D, 5, *Subercase à Pontchartrain, 25 décembre 1706*, fol. 259; *Lopinot, délégué des Acadiens, 15 juillet 1705*, fol. 95 *ff.   Col. Mss.*, II, "Pontchartrain à Bonaventure, 30 juin 1707," pp. 472-73.   Murdoch, *op. cit.*, I, p. 283.   B, 25, *Pontchartrain à Bonaventure, 4 juin 1704*, fol. 64.   On Bonaventure's alleged liaison with Mme de Freneuse, see Pierre Daviault, "Madame de Freneuse et M. Bonaventure," *Proceedings of the Royal Society of Canada* (Ottawa, 1941).

3 *Col. Mss.*, II, "Entreprise des Anglais contre Port-Royal, 26 juin 1607," pp. 464-67; "Subercase à Pontchartrain, 26 juin 1707," pp. 467-70; "Entreprise des Bostonnais sur l'Acadie par Monsieur Labat, 6 juillet 1707," pp. 477-81.   Murdoch, *op. cit.*, I, pp. 289-94.

4 C11D, 5, *Subercase à Pontchartrain, 20 et 25 décembre 1707*, fol. 72; *Des Gouttins à Pontchartrain, 23 décembre 1707, passim*.   Hutchinson, *op. cit.*, I, pp. 289-94.

5 Emile Lauvrière, *La Tragédie d'un peuple; Histoire du peuple acadien de ses origines à nos jours* (Paris, 1922) I, p. 152.   *Col. Mss.*, II, "Nouvelles des Anglais prisonniers, 15 juillet 1709," p. 502; "Subercase à Pontchartrain, 19 octobre 1709," p. 507; "23 janvier 1710," p. 511.   C11D, 7, *Subercase à Pontchartrain, 1er octobre 1710*, fol. 90.

6 *Col. Mss.*, II, "Subercase à Pontchartrain, 26 octobre 1710," p. 528. Hutchinson, *op. cit.*, p. 181.   Murdoch, *op. cit.*, I, pp. 310-11.

7 *Col. Mss.*, II, "Subercase à Pontchartrain, 26 octobre 1710," pp. 528-29. Hutchinson, *op. cit.*, II, pp. 132 and 165.   Murdoch, *op. cit.*, I, pp. 310-15.

8 C11D, 7, *Articles de capitulation, 13 octobre 1710*, fol. 94.   *Col. Mss.*, II,

"Subercase à Pontchartrain, 26 octobre 1710," pp. 529-30.

9 Murdoch, *op. cit.*, I, p. 216. C11D, 7, *Lettres des habitants de Port-Royal, 13 novembre 1710*, fol. 98. *Col. Mss.*, II, "Des Gouttins à Pontchartrain, 17 novembre 1711," p. 547.

10 *R.A.Q.*, 1946-47, "Vaudreuil à Pontchartrain, 25 avril 1711," pp. 411-12. François de Gannes, "Observation sur les erreurs de la relation de siège de Port-Royal"; see P. F. X. Charlevoix, *History of New France*, J. Shea, ed. (New York, 1866-72) V, pp. 221, 227 and 231 (notes). Louis-Marie Le Jeune, *Dictionnaire général* (Ottawa, 1931) II, p. 673. B, 33, *Pontchartrain à Subercase, 3 juillet 1711*, fol. 59.

11 C11D, 7, *Pontchartrain à Beauharnois, 24 décembre 1710*, fol. 100. On projects for reconquest see fol. 103, 105, 125, 135, etc. *Col. Mss.*, II, "Mme de Vaudreuil à Pontchartrain, 1710," p. 512.

12 C11D, 7, *Nomination de Saint-Castin, 1er janvier 1711*, fol. 122; *Instructions de Vaudreuil à Saint-Castin, 18 janvier 1711*, fol. 129.

13 *R.A.Q.*, 1946-47, "Vaudreuil à Pontchartrain, 25 octobre 1711," pp. 430-31; "7 novembre 1711," p. 431. C11D, 7, *Le Sr. Gaulin, 5 septembre 1711*, fol. 177.

14 *Col. Mss.*, II, "Costebelle au gouvernement de Boston, 5 octobre 1712," p. 554.

15 *Recensements du Canada*, IV, p. 26 (incomplete). British Museum Manuscripts 13972. Calendar of State Papers, Colonial Series, 12 January 1677. R. D. Rogers, *Newfoundland* (Oxford, 1911) pp. 82-6.

16 *Recensements*, IV, p. XVII and 20. *Col. Mss.*, I, "Mémoire du Sieur Parat, 1686," p. 420.

17 Robert Le Blant, *Un Colonial sous Louis XIV: Philippe Pastour de Costebelle* (Paris, 1935). *Col. Mss.*, "Instructions pour le Sieur de Brouillan, 17 février 1691," p. 37. Rogers, *op. cit.*, pp. 90-1. B, 15, *Provisions de gouverneur pour le Sieur de Brouillan, 1er janvier 1690*, fol. 1; *Lettre pour rappeler le Sieur Parat, 23 juin 1690*, fol. 1½. Louis Armand d'Arce, baron de La Hontan, *Les Nouveaux voyages de M. le baron de Lahontan dans l'Amérique Septentrionale* (The Hague, 1703) pp. 340-44. C11A, 12, *Mémoire touchant le commerce de M. de Brouillan, 9 février 1692*, fol. 163.

18 *R.A.Q.*, 1928-29, "Pontchartrain à Frontenac, 21 mars 1696," p. 297; "Frontenac et Champigny à Pontchartrain, 26 octobre 1696," p. 323. B, 19, *Mémoire pour servir d'instruction au Sieur d'Iberville, 31 mars 1696*, fol. 38; *Mémoire pour servir d'instruction à Monsieur de Brouillan, avril 1696*, fol. 38; cf. Guy Frégault, *Iberville, le conquérant* (Montreal, 1944) pp. 214-35.

19 C11D, 3, *Journal de Baudoin*, pp. 38, 40 and 64. Biblio. Nat., Collection Clairambault 881, fol. 181. Iberville, a letter of October 29, 1696. Frégault, *op. cit.*, p. 230.

20 *R.A.Q.*, 1928-29, "Frontenac et Champigny à Pontchartrain, 26 octobre 1696," p. 297. C11D, 3, *Journal de Baudoin*, pp. 40-8, 51 and 64. Bacqueville de La Potherie, *Histoire de l'Amérique Septentrionale* (Paris, 1922) I, pp. 31-7. Calendar of State Papers, Colonial Series, 14 January 1697.

21 C11D, 3, *Journal de Baudoin*, pp. 46-64.

22 *Ibid.*, pp. 64-8. C11D, 4, *Villebon à Pontchartrain, 26 octobre 1696*, p. 297, fol. 68 *ff.* Frégault, *op. cit.*, pp. 228-30.

23 C11D,3, *Journal de Baudoin*, pp. 66, 68-9 and 139-42.

24 *Recensements*, IV, p. 38. Rogers, *op. cit.*, pp. 94-5. *Col. Mss.*, I, "Instructions à M. de Nesmond, 21 avril 1697," p. 264.

25 Gilbert Burnet, *History of My Own Times* (London, 1724) pp. 157-58. Charles de La Roncière, *Histoire de la Marine française* (Paris, 1910) pp. 94-5. Rogers, *op. cit.*, pp. 98-9.

26 B, 24, *Provisions de gouverneur pour M. de Subercase, 1er avril 1702*, fol. 160. *R.A.Q.*, 1938-39, "Vaudreuil et Beauharnois à Pontchartrain, 17 novembre 1704," p. 59. *Col. Mss.*, I, "Relation, 1705," pp. 608-14. Rogers, *op. cit.*, pp. 99-100. *R.A.Q.*, 1922-23, "Mémoire du Sieur de Montigny, 1705," pp. 293-98.

27 Rogers, *op. cit.*, pp. 101-03. B, 27, *Pontchartrain à Costebelle, 22 mai 1706*, fol. 13½. B, 30, *Pontchartrain à Saint-Ovide, 27 mars 1709*, fol. 269½. C11C, 2, *Costebelle à Pontchartrain, 23 septembre 1709*. *Col. Mss.*, II, "Costebelle à Pontchartrain, 7 août 1710," pp. 518-19.

CHAPTER XIX

[1] Charles de La Roncière, *Histoire de la Marine française* (Paris, 1910) IV, p. 386. Robert de Challes, *Un Colonial au temps de Colbert. Mémoires de Robert Challes, écrivain du Roi* (Paris, 1931) *passim*.

[1a] Aff. Ext. Mem. et Doc., 35, *Mémoire concernant les colonies, 2 janvier 1712*, fol. 13 *ff*. *Mémoires des commissaires du roi et de ceux de sa Majesté Britannique* (Paris, 1755-57) II, pp. 126-27. *Rapport de l'archiviste de la province de Québec*, 1947-48, "Pontchartrain à Vaudreuil, 30 avril 1713," pp. 201-02. B. Murdoch, *A History of Nova Scotia* (Halifax, 1865) I, pp. 331-32. Emile Lauvrière, *La Tragédie d'un peuple; Histoire du peuple acadien de ses origines à nos jours* (Paris, 1922) pp. 156-57. *Recensements du Canada*, IV, pp. XVII, XXI, 20, 44, 45, 48 and 49. These censuses are not always complete, but they can be used to complement one another.

[2] *R.A.Q.*, 1930-31, "Talon à Colbert, 11 novembre 1671," p. 163. *Collection de manuscrits contenant lettres, mémoires et autres documents historiques relatifs à la Nouvelle-France*, I, "Instructions au Sieur de Menneval, 1687," p. 396.

[3] *Ibid.*, "Mémoire des intéressez en la pêche de l'Acadie, 1er mars 1687," p. 393; "Mémoire de la Compagnie de l'Acadie, 1688," p. 437. *Recensements*, IV, 1871, p. 10. G1, 461, *1671*.

[4] N. de Diéréville, *Relation du voyage de Port-Royal de l'Acadie ou de la Nouvelle-France* (Rouen, 1708) p. 46. *Col. Mss.*, I, "Mémoire de la Compagnie de l'Acadie, 1688," p. 437. *Col. Mss.*, II, "Invasion des Anglais de Boston, 1er juillet 1704," pp. 419 and 424.

[5] Diéréville, *op. cit.*, p. 46. Recensements, IV, pp. 20, 32, 38, 45 and 49. G1, 466. There is no indication of source. Lauvrière, *op. cit.*, I, p. 170.

[6] *Col. Mss.*, I, "Mémoire sur l'Acadie, 1683," p. 202. Diéréville. *op. cit.*, pp. 44-65. As an accompaniment to his very mediocre verses this author gives the most complete information on the Acadian economy. *Recensements*, IV, 1871, pp. 44-5.

[7] Diéréville, *op. cit.*, pp. 45-63. Mgr de Saint-Vallier, *Etat présent de l'Eglise et de la Colonie française dans la Nouvelle-France* (Quebec, 1956) p. 36. Lauvrière, *op. cit.*, I, p. 187. B, 32, *Pontchartrain à Subercase, 10 août 1710*, fol. 173.

[8] *R.A.Q.*, 1930-31, "Talon à Colbert,, 11 novembre 1671," p. 163. *Col. Mss.*, I, "Le Roi aux intéressés en la Compagnie de l'Acadie, 21 février 1688," p. 415. Lauvrière, *op. cit.*, I, p. 165. Pierre Daviault, *Le Baron de Saint-Castin* (Montreal, 1939) p. 138. B, 22, *Pontchartrain à Villebon, 1er avril 1700*, fol. 57½. B, 23, *Pontchartrain à Bégon, 15 février 1702*, fol. 8½. *Commissions, ordonnances, etc. des gouverneurs et intendants de la Nouvelle-France*, II, "Ordonnance de Duchesneau, 21 mai 1677."

[9] *Col. Mss.*, I, "Mémoire sur l'Acadie, 1683," pp. 292-93; "Mémoire sur l'Acadie de Tibierge, 1er octobre 1695," p. 186; "Pontchartrain à Villebon, 26 mars 1698," p. 295; "Brouillan à Pontchartrain, 30 octobre 1702," p. 395.

[10] *R.A.Q.*, 1928-29, "Frontenac et Champigny à Pontchartrain, 10 novembre 1695," p. 286. *Col. Mss.*, II, "Mémoire sur l'Acadie par M. Tibierge, 1er octobre 1695," pp. 185-86; "Mémoire [de la Tour]" p. 362; "Villebon à Pontchartrain, 1698," pp. 305-06; "Bonaventure à Pontchartrain, 1698," p. 307; "Pontchartrain à Bonaventure, 30 juin 1707," pp. 472-73. Daviault, *op. cit.*, p. 138. Lauvrière, *op. cit.*, I, p. 136.

[11] *Recensements*, IV, pp. 45, 49 and *passim*. Diéréville, *op. cit.*, p. 37. *Col. Mss.*, II, "Pontchartrain à Villebon, 26 mars 1698," p. 298. *Col. Mss.*, I, "Perrot à Pontchartrain, 9 août 1686," p. 365. Lauvrière, *op. cit.*, I, p. 162. B, 16, *Mémoire au Sieur Goutin, 10 avril 1688*, fol. 39. B, 22, *Pontchartrain à Bégon, 30 mars 1701*, fol. 160½. C11D, 5, *Le Roi à Subercase, mai 1706*, fol. 222.

[12] Lauvrière, *op. cit.*, p. 162. *Recensements*, IV, pp. 44-5.

[12a] *Ibid.*

[13] *R.A.Q.*, 1930-31, "Talon au roi, 2 novembre 1671," p. 156. See also on this subject the series: Acadie, C11D, 2, fol. 258; C11D, 4, fol. 188, 191 and 222; C11D, 5, fol. 31, 49 and 127; C11D, 6, fol. 72, 215 and 279.

[14] *Col. Mss.*, II, "Pontchartrain à Mgr de Saint-Vallier, 8 mai 1694," pp. 155-56; "Villebon à Pontchartrain, 1698," p. 306; "Pontchartrain à Villebon, 15 avril 1699," p. 315. B, 22, *Pontchartrain à Brouillan, 9 avril 1701*, fol. 173. B, 27, *Pont-*

chartrain à Bégon, 5 mai 1705, fol. 3½.   C¹¹D, 5, *Subercase à Pontchartrain, 1706,* fol. 259 ff.

¹⁵ *Col. Mss.,* II, "Pontchartrain à Thury, 15 avril 1699," p. 317; "Brouillan à Pontchartrain, 30 octobre 1701," pp. 385-86; "Mémoire de Brouillan, 22 octobre 1701," p. 392.   Murdoch, *op. cit.,* I., p. 278.

¹⁶ Saint-Vallier, *op. cit.,* pp. 36-9.   A letter from Subercase in Murdoch, *op. cit.,* I, p. 308.

¹⁷ *Col. Mss.,* II, "Brouillan à Pontchartrain, 30 octobre 1701," p. 385; "10 novembre 1686," p. 388; "Mémoire sur l'Acadie de M. Tibierge, 1ᵉʳ octobre 1695," p. 187.

¹⁷ᵃ *Col. Mss.,* II, "Champigny à Pontchartrain, 10 novembre 1692," p. 93; "Le Roi à Frontenac et à Pontchartrain, 14 juin 1695," p. 183; "Mémoire sur l'Acadie," p. 186.   Georges Langlois, *Histoire de la population canadienne française* (Montreal, 1935) p. 101.   F³, 4, *Ordonnance qui défend la traite en Acadie, 12 mars 1678,* fol. 43.

¹⁸ *R.A.Q.,* 1930-31, "Colbert à Talon, 4 juin 1672," p. 169.

¹⁹ Daviault, *op. cit.,* p. 136.   B, 29, *Pontchartrain à Bégon, 25 mai 1707,* fol. 2.   B, 32, *Pontchartrain à Subercase, 10 août 1710,* fol. 173; *Pontchartrain à De Goutin, 20 mai 1710,* fol. 90½

CHAPTER XX

¹ *Edits et ordonnances royaux,* I, "Acceptation du roi de la démission de la Compagnie de la Nouvelle-France, mars 1663," pp. 31-2.   *Rapport de l'archiviste de la province de Québec,* 1930-31, "Colbert à Talon, 4 juin 1672," p. 108.   B, 23, *Mémoire du roi à Beauharnois, 6 mai 1702,* fol. 62½.

² *Recensements du Canada,* IV, pp. XVII, XXI and 28.   G¹, *Recensements,* 1713.

²ᵃ Stanislas Lortie, "De l'origine des Canadiens Français," *Bulletin du Parler français* (Quebec, 1903-04) II, p. 18.   Gustave Lanctot, *Filles de joie ou filles du roi: Etude sur l'émigration féminine en Nouvelle-France* (Montreal, 1952) p. 126.   Emile Salone, *La Colonisation de la Nouvelle-France* (Paris, 1906) pp. 168-69 and *passim.*   Paul-Emile Renaud, *Les Origines économiques du Canada* (Mamers, 1928) pp. 284-86.

³ C¹¹A,6, *De Meulles à Colbert, 12 novembre 1699,* fol. 399.

⁴ *R.A.Q.,* 1946-47, "Vaudreuil et Raudot à Pontchartrain, 7 novembre 1711," p. 438.   F³,8, *Ordonnance en faveur des soldats, 21 mars 1696,* pp. 186-87. *R.A.Q.,* 1928-29, "Frontenac et Champigny à Pontchartrain, 15 octobre 1698," p. 372.   *R.A.Q.,* 1946-47, "Vaudreuil et Raudot à Pontchartrain, 2 novembre 1710," p. 388.   C¹¹A,18, *Callières et Champigny à Pontchartrain, 13 octobre 1700,* fol. 3.

⁵ *R.A.Q.,* 1939-40, "Champigny à Pontchartrain, 26 octobre 1699," p. 350; "Le Roi à Vaudreuil et Raudot, 30 juin 1701," p. 365.   *R.A.Q.,* 1946-47, "Mémoire du roi à Vaudreuil et Bégon, 15 juin 1712," p. 140.   *R.A.Q.,* 1947-48, "Vaudreuil et Raudot à Pontchartrain, 7 novembre 1711," pp. 448-49.

⁶ *R.A.Q.,* 1927-28, "Frontenac à Seignelay, 2 novembre 1672," p. 19.   François Vachon de Belmont, *Histoire du Canada* (Quebec, 1890).   H. R. Casgrain, *Histoire de l'Hôtel-Dieu* (Quebec, 1878).   *R.A.Q.,* 1930-31, "Talon à Colbert, 11 novembre 1671," pp. 164 and 169.   *Collection de manuscrits contenant lettres, mémoires et autres documents historiques relatifs à la Nouvelle-France, 1711,* p. 549.

⁶ᵃ *Recensements,* IV, p. 216.   G¹, 451, *Recensements,* 1713. The figures were compiled from several lists and are approximate.

⁷ F³,3, *Frontenac à Seignelay, 2 novembre 1672,* pp. 180-81.

⁸ *R.A.Q.,* 1930-31, "Mémoire du roi à Talon, 27 mars 1665," p. 5; "Mémoire de Talon, 1677," p. 64.   G¹,461, *1698.*   *R.A.Q.,* 1926-27, "Le Roi à Frontenac, 22 avril 1675," p. 22.   *R.A.Q.,* 1938-39, p. 11; "Le Roi à Vaudreuil et Beauharnois, 14 juin 1704," p. 36.   Arch. Séminaire de Saint-Sulpice, Paris, *Documents pour l'histoire de l'Eglise du Canada,* I, room 3; *Mémoire dressé par un missionnaire de Saint-Sulpice établi à Montréal,* pp. 1 and 2.

⁹ B,9, *Instructions du roi à La Barre, 10 mai 1682,* fol. 1 & ff.   B,13, *Mémoire du roi à Denonville et Champigny, 30 mars 1687.*   *R.A.Q.,* 1939-40, "Mgr de

Laval à Mgr de Saint-Vallier, Paris, 1696," pp. 331-32.   Arch. Séminaire de Saint-Sulpice, *Documents sur l'histoire de l'Eglise*, "Mgr de Laval à Brisacier, 20 mars 1690."

[10] Gédéon de Catalogne, "Mémoire sur les plans des Seigneuries, 1712," *Bulletin des recherches historiques* (Lévis, 1915).   B,8, *Estat de la dépense, 1681*, fol. 12½.   *R.A.Q.*, 1939-40, "Seignelay à Mgr de Saint-Vallier, 31 mai 1686," p. 272; "Callières et Champigny à Pontchartrain, 20 octobre 1699," p. 350; "Champigny à Pontchartrain, 20 octobre 1699," p. 349.   *Mandements des Evêques de Québec*, I, pp. 426-27.

[11] *Mandements*, I,, "Ordonnance de Mgr de Saint-Vallier, 22 octobre 1686." Arch. Nat., 1232, *Mémoire de la conduite des Jésuites*.   *Recensements*, IV, 1871, p. 48.   *R.A.Q.*, 1939-40, "De Meulles à Seignelay, 4 novembre 1683," pp. 251-52. *R.A.Q.*, 1926-27, "Frontenac à Colbert, 13 novembre 1673," pp. 31-2.   *Inventaire des ordonnances*, I, "17 juillet 1707," pp. 31, 38 and 41.

[12] Arch. Séminaire de Saint-Sulpice, *Mémoire dressé par un missionnaire de Saint-Sulpice*.   *R.A.Q.*, 1939-40, "Callières et Champigny à Pontchartrain, 20 octobre 1699," p. 351; "Le Roi à Vaudreuil et Raudot, 9 juin 1706," p. 134.

[13] Archevêché de Québec, Eglise du Canada, 6, *Mémoire d'un missionnaire, 1671*.   *R.A.Q.*, 1939-40, "Mgr. de Laval aux MM. du Séminaire de Québec, 1685," p. 264.

[14] *R.A.Q.*, 1939-40, "Vaudreuil à Pontchartrain, 12 novembre 1707," p. 386.

[15] *Ibid.*, "Vaudreuil et Bégon à Pontchartrain, 20 septembre 1714," p. 272. Archevêché de Québec, Eglise du Canada, 6, *Mémoire d'un missionnaire,, 1671*.

[16] *R.A.Q.*, 1930-31, "Mémoire de Talon, 1667," p. 65.   Salone, *op. cit.*, pp. 310-11.   B,13, *Mémoire du roi à Denonville et Champigny, 30 mars 1687*.

[17] Louis Armand d'Arce, baron de La Hontan, *Nouveaux voyages de M. le baron de Lahontan dans l'Amérique Septentrionale* (The Hague, 1703).   Catalogne, *op. cit.*, p. 334.

[18] F³,6, *Arrêt portant défense de prendre qualité d'écuyer, 10 avril 1684*, fol. 104.   Gustave Lanctot, *l'Administration de la Nouvelle-France* (Paris, 1929) pp. 135-36.   F³,5, *Arrêt du 12 mai 1678*, pp. 44-6.   C¹¹A,5, *Duchesneau à Colbert, 13 novembre 1680*, p. 171.

[19] Catalogne, *op. cit.*, *passim*.   B,8, *Estat de la dépense, 1682*, fol. 86. C¹¹A, 110, *Liste générale des intéressés en la Compagnie de la Colonie du Canada, 1708*, pp. 531-34.   *Edits et Ord.*, I, "Règlement fait au sujet des honneurs dans les Eglises, 27 avril 1716," p. 353.

[20] *Recensements*, IV, pp. 7 and 17.

[21] G¹, 461, *Recensement général du Gouvernement du Canada, 1688*.

[22] *Ibid.*, *Recensements de la Colonie du Canada, 1713*.

[23] C¹¹A,5, *Duchesneau à Colbert, 6 octobre 1679*, fol. 21.   C¹¹A,6, *De Meulles à Colbert, 4 novembre 1683*, fol. 181.

[24] La Hontan, *op. cit.*, pp. 9-10.   Catalogne, *op. cit.*, p. 335.   *R.A.Q.*, 1947-48, "Pontchartrain à Vaudreuil, 25 juin 1712," p. 146.   *R.A.Q.*, 1939-40, "Mémoire de Champigny, 12 mai 1691," p. 299.

[25] *R.A.Q.*, 1939-40, "Denonville à Seignelay, 10 août 1688," p. 286.   B,34, *Mémoire du roi à Vaudreuil et Bégon, 15 juin 1712; Champigny à Pontchartrain, 20 octobre 1699*, p. 350.   *R.A.Q.*, 1938-39, "Vaudreuil à Pontchartrain, 28 avril, 30 octobre et 4 novembre 1706," p. 109; "Vaudreuil et Raudot, 1706," pp. 112-13; "Vaudreuil à Pontchartrain, 4 novembre 1706," p. 163.

[26] *Journal des Jésuites*, pp. 335 and 345.   *Edits et Ord.*, II, "Règlement du Conseil souverain, 29 janvier 1674."   Auguste Gosselin, *Henri de Bernières* (Evreux, 1896) pp. 148-49.   *R.A.Q.*, 1939-40, "Champigny à Pontchartrain, 20 octobre 1699," p. 349.   *R.A.Q.*, 1947-48, "Vaudreuil et Bégon à Pontchartrain, 20 septembre 1714," p. 272.   Catalogne, *op. cit.*, *passim*.   G¹, 461, *Recensements*, 1698 and 1713.   Antoine Roy, *Les Lettres, les sciences et les arts au Canada sous le régime français* (Paris, 1930) p. 11 and *passim*.

[27] Mgr de Saint-Vallier, *Etat présent de l'Eglise et de la Colonie française dans la Nouvelle-France* (Quebec, 1856) p. 20.   *Inventaire des ordonnances*, I, "Ordonnance de Raudot, 13 juin 1710," p. 102.   *Edits et Ord.*, I, "Etablissement d'un hôpital, mai 1703," p. 288.

[28] *R.A.Q.*, 1947-48, "Vaudreuil et Bégon à Pontchartrain, 20 septembre 1714," p. 273.   Louis-Marie Le Jeune, *Dictionnaire général* (Ottawa, 1931) I, p. 272.

R.A.Q., 1939-40, "Callières et Champigny à Pontchartrain, 30 octobre 1699," p. 351.
²⁹ *Edits et Ord.*, II, "Arrêt du Conseil Supérieur, 8 avril 1688," p. 119.
³⁰ Gustave Lanctot, "Les Troupes de la Nouvelle-France," *Réalisations françaises, de Cartier à Montcalm* (Montreal, 1951) pp. 74-8.
³¹ *R.A.Q.*, 1928-29, "Frontenac et Champigny à Pontchartrain, 10 novembre 1695," p. 287. *R.A.Q.*, 1939-40, "Le Roi à Vaudreuil et Raudot, 30 juin 1707," p. 362. *Report of the Canadian Archives*, 1899, Supplement, pp. 23-9. Arch. Col., Series D, *Troupes coloniales.*
³² Robert de Roquebrune, "Uniformes et drapeaux des régiments au Canada sous Louis XIV et Louis XV," *Revue de l'Université d'Ottawa* (juillet-septembre, 1950) p. 330. Lanctot, *op. cit.*, pp. 84 and 97. B,11, *Règlement pour le paiement des officiers et soldats de marine, 10 avril 1684*, pp. 18-21. B,51, *Etat de l'habillement pour les troupes des colonies, 1729*, pp. 191-93. *R.A.Q.*, 1947-48, "Vaudreuil et Bégon à Pontchartrain, 20 septembre 1714," p. 277.
³³ Lanctot, *op. cit.*, pp. 70-4. *R.A.Q.*, 1927-28, "Frontenac à Colbert, 13 novembre 1673," p. 47. *R.A.Q.*, 1947-48, "Vaudreuil et Bégon à Pontchartrain, 12 novembre 1712," p. 183; "30 septembre 1714," p. 278. *R.A.Q.*, 1942-43, "Vaudreuil à Pontchartrain, 14 novembre 1707," pp. 431-32.
³⁴ *Edits et Ord.*, II, "Ordonnance au sujet des capitaines des côtes, 25 juin 1710," p. 275. *R.A.Q.*, 1947-48, "Pontchartrain à Vaudreuil, 25 juin 1712," pp. 146 and 242.
³⁵ *R.A.Q.*, 1930-31, "Colbert à Talon, 5 avril 1666," in Salone, *op. cit.*, p. 192. Archevêché de Québec, Eglise du Canada, 4, *Mémoire d'un missionnaire, 1671*. *R.A.Q.*, 1939-40, "De Meulles à Seignelay, 6 octobre 1682," p. 247. *Lettres de la Révérende Mère Marie de l'Incarnation*, II, p. 372.
³⁶ B,12, *Mémoire du roi à Denonville, 31 mai 1686*, fol. 25½. *Recensements*, IV, pp. 16, 28, 34 and 40. G¹, 46, *1688.*
³⁷ *R.A.Q.*, 1942-43, "Vaudreuil et Raudot à Pontchartrain, 14 novembre 1709," p. 420. *Ordonnances des Intendants*, I, "Ordonnance de Raudot, 27 août 1707," p. 44.
³⁸ *R.A.Q.*, 1947-48, "Mémoire du roi à Vaudreuil et Bégon, 19 mars 1714," p. 244. *Edits et Ord.*, II, "Arrêt du Conseil Supérieur, 21 avril 1664," p. 16. Le Jeune, *Dictionnaire Général*, I, p. 551. *R.A.Q.*, 1947-48, "Vaudreuil et Bégon à Pontchartrain, 12 novembre 1712," p. 183.
³⁹ *R.A.Q.*, 1942-43, "Vaudreuil à Pontchartrain, 14 novembre 1709," p. 431. *Histoire de l'Hôtel-Dieu de Québec* (Montauban, 1751) pp. 180-81.
⁴⁰ *Col. Mss.*, II, "Mémoire (1690)," p. 588. Chrétien Le Clerq, *Etablissement de la foy dans la Nouvelle-France* (Paris, 1691), quotation in J. B. Ferland, *Cours d'histoire de l'Amérique française* (Quebec, 1861-65) II, p. 13. *Col. Mss.*, II, "Instructions pour le Sieur de Callières, 25 mai 1699," p. 322. Robert de Roquebrune, "La Guerre et l'amour au Canada d'autrefois," *Les Cahiers Reflets* (Three Rivers, 1945) I, pp. 17-19.
⁴¹ *Lettres de noblesse, généalogies, etc.*, P. G. Roy, ed., *passim*. Catalogne, *op. cit., passim.*
⁴² *Edits et Ord.*, II, "Ordonnance de Raudot, 25 juin 1710," p. 275. *R.A.Q.*, 1947-48, "Pontchartrain à Vaudreuil, 25 juin 1712," p. 146.
⁴³ Charlevoix, *op. cit.*, III, pp. 79-80.

CHAPTER XXI

¹ Gustave Lanctot, *L'Administration de la Nouvelle-France* (Paris, 1929) pp. 25-30. Moreau de Saint-Méry, "Le Ministre à Gallifet, 14 décembre 1701," *Lois et Constitutions* (Paris, 1784) p. 680. *Edits et ordonnances royaux*, III, See Commissions of Governors de Mésy and Vaudreuil, pp. 21 and 59.
² *Edits et Ord.*, III, See Commissions of intendants, pp. 33-65. Lanctot, *op. cit.*, pp. 56-82. Lanctot, *Réalisations françaises, de Cartier à Montcalm* (Montreal, 1951) pp. 123-24.
³ *Rapport de l'archiviste de la province de Québec*, 1930-31, "Talon à Colbert, 11 novembre 1671," p. 166. *Report of the Canadian Archives*, 1899, Supplement, pp. 253, 255 and 257. *R.A.Q.*, 1946-47, pp. 373 and 415.
⁴ Lanctot, *L'Administration de la Nouvelle-France*, pp. 24 and 52.

5 *R.A.Q.*, 1928-29, "Mémoire du roi à Frontenac et à Champigny, 21 mai 1698,"
p. 359.
6 *R.A.Q.*, 1928-29, "Frontenac à Pontchartrain, 10 octobre 1698," pp. 367-68.
7 B,7, *Colbert à Duchesneau, 28 avril 1677*, fol. 1 *ff; mai 1679*, fol. 16.
B,8, *Colbert à Duchesneau, 2 juin 1680*, fol. 23½; *Colbert à Frontenac, 20 avril
1680*, fol. 16½. *R.A.Q.*, 1928-29, "Mémoire du roi à Frontenac et à Champigny,
21 mai 1698," pp. 355-56. *Edits et Ord.*, I, "Edit de création du Conseil souverain, avril 1663," pp. 37-9.
7a Lanctot, "Le Régime municipal de la Nouvelle-France," *L'Administration
de la Nouvelle-France*, p. 133. *Edits et Ord.*, II, "Règlement du Conseil Supérieur, 1er février 1706," p. 135.
8 *Insinuations du Conseil souverain*, II, "Arrêt du 10 mars 1685," p. 303.
Jugements et Délibérations, VI, "30 juillet 1714," pp. 804-05. Lanctot, *L'Administration de la Nouvelle-France*, pp. 106-110.
9 *Edits et Ord.*, I, "Etablissement de la Compagnie des Indes occidentales,
mai 1664," p. 46; "Commissions de l'intendant Duchesneau, 5 juin 1675," p. 42.
Lanctot, *L'Administration de la Nouvelle-France*, pp. 116-19. *Edits et Ord.*, I,
"Déclaration du roi, 16 juin 1703," p. 299.
9a *Edits et Ord.*, I, "Arrêt du Conseil d'Etat, 6 avril 1666," pp. 60-1; "Articles
présentés au roi par Oudiette, 15 avril 1676," pp. 187-89. F3, 4-1, *Requête du
syndic de Québec, 1672*, pp. 140-43. Emile Salone, *La Colonisation de la Nouvelle-France* (Paris, 1906) pp. 279-81. C11A,2, *Estat des charges du pays (1665)*
p. 228. C11A,5, *Estat de la dépense, 25 avril 1679*, p. 98. B,8, *Etat de la
dépense pour l'année 1682*, fol. 85-6. Guy Frégault, "Essai sur les finances
canadiennes," *Revue d'histoire de l'Amérique française* (décembre 1958) p. 315.
9b C11A,33, *Bégon à Pontchartrain, 12 novembre 1712*, pp. 192-200. *R.A.Q.*,
1947-48, "Pontchartrain à Vaudreuil et Bégon, 16 juin 1716," p. 310; cf. Frégault,
"Finances Canadiennes," *R.H.A.F.* (mars 1959) pp. 460-61. Paul-Emile Renaud,
Les Origines économiques du Canada (Mamers, 1928) pp. 459 and 464.
9c C11A,34, *Raudot à Pontchartrain, 2 novembre 1706*, p. 86. C11A,36,
Instructions pour le Gouverneur et l'Intendant du Canada, 1716, pp. 40-1.
F3,4, *Réponses des notables, 4 novembre 1684*, fol. 148. B,35, *Pontchartrain
à Bégon, 8 juillet 1713*, fol. 112½. *R.A.Q.*, 1947-48, "Vaudreuil et Bégon à
Pontchartrain, 20 septembre 1714," pp. 281-82. F3,8, *Arrêt du Conseil d'Etat,
18 avril 1703*, pp. 402-05. C11A,41, *Vaudreuil et Bégon au Conseil de Marine,
26 octobre 1720*, pp. 241 *ff*.
10 F3,4-1, *Requeste du Syndic, 1672*, pp. 140-42. *Jug. et Dél.*, I, "14 novembre 1663," p. 57. *R.A.Q.*, 1926-27, "Frontenac à Colbert, 13 novembre 1673,"
p. 47. F3,4-1, *Règlement de police de Frontenac, 23 mars 1673*, p. 201.
Lanctot, *L'Administration de la Nouvelle-France*, pp. 128-30. B,6, *Colbert à
Frontenac, 17 mai 1674*, fol. 22.
11 B,6, *Instructions pour le Sieur Duchesneau, 7 juin 1675*, p. 94. *Jug. et
Dél.*, II, "11 mai 1676," p. 73; "20 décembre 1677," pp. 175-77. *Jug. et Dél.*,
III, "18 janvier 1687," pp. 110-11; "24 janvier 1688," pp. 206-07; "31 mars 1695,"
pp. 369-71. *Jug. et Dél.*, IV, "3 février 1698," p. 253. *Jug. et Dél.*, V, 1er
décembre 1705," pp. 195-96. *Edits et Ord.*, II, "Règlement du Conseil Supérieur,
1er février 1706," pp. 137-38.
12 C11A,2, *Le Roi à Frontenac, 22 avril 1675*, fol. 10. *R.A.Q.*, 1928-29,
"Pontchartrain à Frontenac, 21 mai 1698," p. 363.
13 See Lanctot, *L'Administration de la Nouvelle-France*, pp. 135-36, for references to these meetings. *R.A.Q.*, 1928-29, "Frontenac et Champigny à Pontchartrain, 26 octobre 1696," p. 321.
13a *R.A.Q.*, 1938-39, "Vaudreuil et Raudot à Pontchartrain, 3 novembre 1706,"
p. 154. *R.A.Q.*, 1939-40, "Le Roi à Vaudreuil et Raudot, 30 juin 1707," p. 361.
14 *Anciennes lois françaises*, 16, "Ordonnance sur les plaintes des Etats, janvier
1629," p. 275. Claude de Ferrière, *Dictionnaire de droit et de pratique*, I, pp.
132-33. Arch. Can., Registres judiciaires de Montréal, *Acte d'assemblée, 20
octobre 1675*. *Ordonnance de M. le juge d'Ailleboust, 3 avril 1677*. *Ordonnances, commissions, etc. des gouverneurs et intendants de la Nouvelle-France*,
II, "Ordonnance de M. de Meulles, 8 juin 1685," pp. 110-11. *Edits et Ord.*, II,
"Arrêt du Conseil souverain, 7 octobre 1675," p. 64.
15 *Jug. et Dél.*, I, "6 janvier 1667," p. 369; "24 janvier 1667," p. 372; "6 juin

1667," p. 398.   *Jug. et Dél.*, II, "23 mars 1675," p. 56.   F[3], 6, *Plainte et requête au gouverneur, 16 août 1684*, p. 197.   C[11]A,7, *Extrait des réponses, 18 janvier 1685*, p. 236.   C[11]A,8, *Délibérations des habitants de la Colonie, 15 octobre 1700*, p. 133.
    [16] *R.A.Q.*, 1938-39, "Vaudreuil à Pontchartrain, 4 octobre 1706," p. 109; "Pontchartrain à Vaudreuil, 9 juin 1706," p. 118.   *Ordonnances*, II, "Ordonnance, 12 décembre 1704," pp. 326-27.   C[11]A,24, *30 avril 1706*, p. 68.
    [17] C[11]A, 34, *Vaudreuil et Bégon, 20 septembre 1714*, p. 298.   *Jug. et Dél.*, VI, pp. 834-35, 838-39, 842 and 997 *ff.*

CHAPTER XXII

    [1] C[11]A,5, *De Meulles à Colbert, 12 novembre 1682*, p. 81; *Duchesneau à Seignelay, 13 novembre 1681*, fol. 290.   C[11]A,13, *Frontenac et Champigny à Pontchartrain, 10 novembre 1695*, p. 342.   F[3],4, *Arrêt du 10 mars 1685*, fol. 214.   *Collection de manuscrits contenant lettres, mémoires et autres documents historiques relatifs à la Nouvelle-France*, I, "Résumé des rapports du Conseil, 1689," p. 479.
    [2] Émile Salone, *La Colonisation de la Nouvelle-France* (Paris, 1906) pp. 183-87. The author's commentary, pp. 318-23, is based on Catalogne.   *Edits et ordonnances royaux*, I, "Arrêt du roi, 29 mai 1680," pp. 240-41; "Arrêt 14 juillet 1690," pp. 262-63; "Ratifications, 6 juillet 1711," pp. 323-24.
    [3] *Edits et Ord.*, I, "Arrêt qui confirme les concessions de 1676 à 1679, 29 mai 1680," p. 240; "Arrêt de confirmation des concessions de 1682 et 1683, 15 avril 1684," p. 251; "Arrêt en confirmation des concessions de 1688 et 1689, 14 juillet 1690," p. 262; "Ratification de concessions entre 1672 et 1700, 6 juillet 1711," p. 233.   Arch. Col., Canada, *Fois et hommages, passim.*   G. Catalogne, "Mémoire sur les plans des Seigneuries," *Bulletin des recherches historiques* (Lévis, 1915) *passim.*
    [4] *Edits et Ord.*, I, "Arrêt du roi, 6 juillet 1711," pp. 324-25.   *R.A.Q.*, 1927-28, "Mémoire du roi à Vaudreuil et Bégon, 15 juin 1710," p. 302; "19 mars 1714," p. 243.
    [5] C[11]A,26, *Raudot à Pontchartrain, 10 novembre 1707*, pp. 12-17.   C[11]A, 28, *18 octobre 1708*, pp. 178-79.   *Edits et Ord.*, I, "Arrêt du roi, 5 juillet 1711," p. 326.   *R.A.Q.*, 1947-48, "Mémoire du roi à Vaudreuil et Bégon, 19 mars 1714," p. 243.
    [6] *Recensements du Canada*, IV, pp. 7 and 23.   G[1], 461, *Recensement général du gouvernement du Canada, année 1688; Recensements de la Colonie du Canada, année 1713.*
    [7] *Jesuit Relations*, 1636 (Thwaites, ed.) p. 170.   *R.A.Q.*, 1930-31, "Mémoire du roi à Talon, 27 mars 1665," p. 10; "Colbert à Talon, 5 avril 1665," p. 44; "Mémoire de Talon, 18 mai 1669," p. 112; "Talon à Colbert, 10 novembre 1670," p. 130.
    [8] C[11]A,5, *Duchesneau à Seignelay, 13 novembre 1681*, fol. 290.   B,13, *Le Roi à Denonville et Champigny, 16 mars 1687*, fol. 16½.   C[11]G,3, *Raudot à Pontchartrain, novembre 1707*, fol. 154-55; *13 novembre 1708*, fol. 183½.   B,34, *Pontchartrain à Prat, 28 juin 1712*, fol. 70½.   B,35, *Pontchartrain à Prat, 8 juillet 1713*, fol. 112.   *R.A.Q.*, 1947-48, "Vaudreuil et Bégon au Conseil de Marine, 14 octobre 1716," p. 325.   C[11]A,36, *Prat au Conseil de Marine, 15 novembre 1716*, p. 164.
    [9] B,13, *Mémoire du roi à Denonville et Champigny, 30 mars 1687*, fol. 35. *R.A.Q.*, 1927-28, "Le Roi à Frontenac et Champigny, 7 avril 1692," p. 87; 28 juin 1693," p. 147; "4 novembre 1693," p. 36.
    [10] B,23, *Pontchartrain à Champigny, 6 mai 1702*, fol. 60½.   *R.A.Q.*, 1938-39, "Mémoire du roi à Vaudreuil et Beauharnois, 14 juin 1704," p. 36.   F[3],8, *Ordonnance du roi au sujet des cargaisons, 8 juillet 1705*, fol. 274.   B,36, *Pontchartrain à Bégon, 22 mars 1714*, fol. 372.   *R.A.Q.*, 1947-48, "Vaudreuil et Bégon au Conseil, 14 octobre 1716"; cf. Noël Fauteux, *Essai sur l'industrie au Canada sous le régime français* (Quebec, 1927) I, pp. 178-93.
    [11] *Jesuit Relations* (Thwaites, ed.) vol. 40, p. 214; vol. 42, p. 252.   B,1, *Seignelay à Courcelles, 11 mars 1671*, fol. 36½.   *R.A.Q.*, 1930-31, "Mémoire de

Talon au roi, 2 novembre 1671," pp. 161-62.   Joseph Edmond Roy, *Histoire de la seigneurie de Lauzon* (Lévis, 1897-1904) I, p. 452.   *R.A.Q.*, 1927-28, "Instruction du roi à Frontenac, 7 juin 1689," p. 10; "Frontenac et Champigny à Pontchartrain, 4 novembre 1693," p. 177.

[12] *R.A.Q.*, 1938-39, "Vaudreuil et Beauharnois à Pontchartrain, 15 novembre 1703," p. 14; "Mémoire du roi à Vaudreuil, 17 juin 1705," p. 68.   *Inventaire des ordonnances*, I, "15 juillet 1707," p. 41; "18 mars 1713," p. 127.   *R.A.Q.*, 1947-48, "Vaudreuil et Bégon au Conseil de Marine, 14 octobre 1716," p. 323.

[13] *R.A.Q.*, 1938-39, "Mémoire du roi à Vaudreuil et Beauharnois, 14 juin 1704," p. 31; "Vaudreuil et Raudot à Pontchartrain, 3 novembre 1706," p. 149; "14 novembre 1708," p. 452.

[14] C11A,37, *Brevet de concession au Sieur de Courtemanche, 12 novembre 1708*, p. 453.   *Documents Relating to the Colonial History of New York State*, IX, "Recensements du Canada, 1712," pp. 907-08.   Fauteux, *op. cit.*, II, pp. 517-20.   *Edits et Ord.*, III, "Ordonnance, 13 juillet 1707," p. 419; "Ordonnance, 6 juin 1710," p. 428.

[15] B,7, *Colbert à Duchesneau, 28 avril 1677*, fol. 1.   C11A,7, *Denonville au ministre, 15 novembre 1685*, pp. 56-60.   *R.A.Q.*, 1938-39, "Vaudreuil et Beauharnois à Pontchartrain, 15 novembre 1703," p. 14; "Mémoire du roi à Vaudreuil et Beauharnois, 14 juin 1704."   B,25, fol. 101½.

[16] Catalogne, *op. cit.*, p. 326.   *R.A.Q.*, 1938-39, "Vaudreuil et Beauharnois à Pontchartrain, 19 octobre 1705," p. 83; "Vaudreuil, Beauharnois et Raudot à Pontchartrain, 19 octobre 1705," p. 83; "Le Roi à Vaudreuil et Raudot, 9 juin 1706," p. 129.   C11A,22, *Madame de Repentigny au ministre, 13 octobre 1705*, fol. 343.   Fauteux, *op. cit.*, II, pp. 465-69.   *R.A.Q.*, 1939-40, "Vaudreuil et Raudot à Pontchartrain, 14 novembre 1707," p. 453.

[17] B,30, *Pontchartrain à Raudot, 10 octobre 1708*, fol. 43.   *R.A.Q.*, 1947-48, "Vaudreuil et Bégon au Conseil de Marine, 14 octobre 1716," p. 324.   Catalogne, *op. cit.*, p. 326.   Fauteux, *op. cit.*, II, pp. 311-16.

[18] *R.A.Q.*, 1930-31, "Mémoire de Talon au roi, 2 novembre 1671," p. 100.

[19] *Ibid.*, "Talon à Colbert, 27 octobre 1667," p. 80; "Addition au mémoire de Talon, 1670," pp. 136-37.   *R.A.Q.*, 1928-29, "Mémoire du roi à Frontenac et Champigny, 27 avril 1697," pp. 335-36; "Frontenac et Champigny à Pontchartrain, 25 octobre 1698," p. 381.   Fauteux, *op. cit.*, I, pp. 4-9.

[20] *R.A.Q.*, 1930-31, "Mémoire de Talon à Colbert, 10 novembre 1670," pp. 123 and 130.   C11A,6, *De Meulles à Pontchartrain*, pp. 306-11.   B,39, *Mémoire du roi à Vaudreuil et Bégon, 26 juin 1689*, p. 10.   Catalogne, *op. cit.*, Fauteux, *op. cit.*, I, p. 40 ff.

[21] *Relation des Jésuites*, 1636, p. 47.   *Recensements*, IV, "Professions et métiers," p. 13.   *R.A.Q.*, 1927-28, "Instructions pour Frontenac, 7 juin 1689," p. 10.   Fauteux, *op. cit.*, I, pp. 129-32 and 153-58.

[22] C11A,5, *Duchesneau à Seignelay, 13 novembre 1681*, fol. 290.   B,11, *Seignelay à de Meulles, 10 avril 1684*, fol. 18.   C11A,7, *Denonville à Seignelay, 13 novembre 1683*, fol. 69.   C11A,17, *Champigny à Pontchartrain, 20 octobre 1699*, pp. 106-08.   C11G,3, *Raudot à Pontchartrain, 12 novembre 1708*, fol. 183½. "Monseignat à Pontchartrain, 8 novembre 1716," *Documents relatifs à la monnaie, au change et aux finances du Canada sous le régime français* (Ottawa, 1925) p. 202.   C11A,36, *Prat au Conseil de Marine, 15 novembre 1716*, p. 164; *Etat des vaisseaux à Québec, 1716*, p. 153.   C11G,4, *Raudot à Pontchartrain, 1er novembre 1709*, fol. 22 ff.

[23] *Edits et Ord.*, I, "Edit du roi défendant la traite dans les bois, mai 1681," pp. 248-49.   F3,5, *Déclaration du roi, 21 mai 1696*, fol. 387.   F3,6, *Déclaration du roi, juin 1703*, fol. 335.   F3,7, *Acceptation par les intéressés en la Compagnie du Canada, 12 octobre 1706*, fol. 30; *Arrêt du Conseil d'Etat, 24 juillet 1706*, fol. 26.

[24] *R.A.Q.*, 1939-40, "Vaudreuil et Raudot à Pontchartrain, 14 novembre 1708," p. 445.   *R.A.Q.*, 1946-47, "Mémoire du roi à Vaudreuil et Raudot, 7 juillet 1711," p. 419; "Vaudreuil à Pontchartrain, 8 novembre 1711," p. 455.

[25] *R.A.Q.*, 1947-48, "Mémoire du roi à Vaudreuil et Raudot, 25 juin 1713," p. 213; "Vaudreuil à Pontchartrain, 14 novembre 1713," p. 235; "Mémoire du roi à Vaudreuil et Bégon, 19 mars 1714," p. 241; "Vaudreuil et Bégon à Pontchartrain, 20 septembre 1714," pp. 273-75.

[26] Catalogne, *op. cit.*, p. 258.

27 *Edits et Ord.*, III, "Provisions de l'office de Grand Voyer, 24 mai 1689," pp. 91-2; "Ordonnance qui ordonne de baliser, 23 janvier 1706," p. 412; "Ordonnance au sujet des clôtures et fossés, 12 juillet 1713," p. 434; "Règlement de Conseil Supérieur concernant la police, 1er février 1706," p. 317. C11A, *Lettres de l'année 1703*, fol. 180. *R.A.Q.*, 1938-39, "Vaudreuil et Beauharnois, 14 juin 1704," p. 31.

28 Catalogne, *op. cit.*, pp. 267-68. *R.A.Q.*, 1938-39, "Vaudreuil et Beauharnois à Pontchartrain, 15 novembre 1703," p. 18. B,36, *Pontchartrain à Bégon, 22 mars 1714*, fol. 362.

29 *Report of the Canadian Archives*, 1899, Supplement, "Pontchartrain à Raudot, 10 juin 1705," p. 194. C11G,3, *Raudot à Pontchartrain, 15 novembre, 1708*, p. 468; *Pontchartrain à Raudot, 6 juillet 1709*, p. 53. *Col. Mss.*, III, "Vaudreuil et Bégon à Pontchartrain, 14 octobre 1716," p. 21. C11A,33, *Vaudreuil à Pontchartrain, 27 juin 1712*, pp. 67-8.

INDEX

(Note: For forts see *Fort* —. For treaties see *Treaties*.)

WESTMAR COLLEGE LIBRARY

Date Due